When Worlds Unite
Working with Those Who Have Crossed

Bob Hickman & Thomas Alan Berg

When Worlds Unite

Copyright © 2009 by Bob Hickman

All rights reserved. No parts of this book may be reproduced or transmitted by any means, electronic or mechanical, including photocopying, recording, or by any information storage or retrieval system without written permission from the authors or publisher, except for inclusion of brief excerpts in reviews and articles.

ISBN 978-0-578-03627-4

Printed and bound in the United States of America

Cover Design: Kevin Baird

Back Cover Photography: "Bob Hickman" photo by Bob Hickman © 2009

"Thomas Alan Berg" photo by Thomas Alan Berg©2009

The book everyone is talking about!

Get your copy of "When Worlds Unite" today and pick up one for a friend!

Now available through Amazon.com and all major book retailers.

ADVANCE PRAISE FOR "WHEN WORLDS UNITE"

"When Worlds Unite" Is a truly captivating read! It gives a fresh perspective on many of the world's ancient spiritual teachings for the benefit of the Earth and its people at this great time of change. Communicated directly from the Spirit World in a very common sense, loving, friendly and humorous way that everybody will be able to relate to and understand.

"When Worlds Unite" Is not one to be missed and a highly positive and encouraging sign of things to come. The time for waiting is over— NOW is the time that our WORLDS MUST UNITE!

Peter David Hamilton, London - Artist & Spiritual Teacher/aka WanderingMaster of YouTube

*****

"An amazing book that quite literally opened the door to the Spirit World for me. I highly recommend this book to anyone searching for a deeper understanding of spirituality."

The Most Rev. Grace Howell, Silver Spring, MD - Bishop of the Church of the Ascension

*****

One of the fundamental principles of physics is that "Energy can neither be created nor destroyed. It can only change its form."

When we apply this to the individual energetic life form we realize when an individual life form changes or vibrates into another dimensional realm (i.e. death) that although it is not normally seen, heard or felt by our three dimensional limited bodily senses it does not mean it no longer exists.

During these extraordinary times the veil between the dimensions is thinning and massive energy realignment on both planetary and physical levels are opening up our energetic capacities. These are exciting times!

"When Worlds Unite" is a communication from across the veil. Its purpose is to open our hearts and minds to view our times from a larger and loving perspective. Our guides Fletcher, Rose, Orion and Edgar Cayce are loving friends wanting to help us through this amazing era.

So find a comfortable place to sit and relax, open this book along with your mind and heart and let's get going on this adventure we are living called eternal life.

Barbara Hall, San Francisco, CA

*****

Night Walk

Walking under an open sky at night
The stars speak to my soul
The spring wind is cool and I am awake - listening

Bob Hickman
May 2009

Dedications

To those of you who stood with me in the dark times, believed in me when others scoffed, and supported me over the years when others turned me away. I love each and every one of you. There are more names than I can possibly list here, but you know who you are – and to all of you I dedicate this work.

Bob Hickman
Psychic-Medium
Channel for "When World Unite"

I would like to dedicate "When World's Unite" to all the good spirits from the "Heavenly Realms of God" who have continually protected and guided me in this life. These include spirit helpers (who have crossed over) like my mom Adelaida Berg, my dad Edward Berg, my aunts Elizabeth Berg and Aurea Kellogg and my two best friends, Charles Lemme and Greg Scott. Here in Hawaii we call these spirit helpers our "Utterly Trustworthy Aumakua" and we honor them with remembrance, gratitude and love. If it wasn't for the loyal support of these wonderful and powerful spirit friends, (which now include my beloved Fletcher, Rose, Edgar and Orion - the great Archangels Raphael, Michael and Gabriel - and of course - the Master Jesus Christ), I would never have found "the Heaven on Earth" which now grows more real in my life, each and every day!

Thomas Alan Berg
Transcriber and Editor of When Worlds Unite

WHEN WORLDS UNITE
"Working with Those Who Have Crossed"

Channeled
by
Bob Hickman

Transcribed and Edited
By
Thomas Alan Berg

FORWARD

By

Thomas Alan Berg

"WE ARE NOT ALONE!"

When I was a young boy growing up in the 1950's I went to see a science fiction movie entitled, "When Worlds Collide" which, like so many other dark films of that genre, filled me with some very negative ideas about the future of Planet Earth. The message that our world was (and is) careening towards some kind of inevitable disaster and/or destruction, was common cultural propaganda back then - and those dark prophecies have only seemed to grow stronger over the years. The best-selling book series, "Left Behind" which is about the "end of the world" as we know it, is proof that this phenomenon has grown extremely large over the years. Traditional Christians ponder the disturbing prophecies in the Book of Revelation and of course, New Agers have their own frightening predications about 2012.

Our economic, social and political systems seem to be weakening by the day. And our world leaders appear, even at their best, to be overwhelmed by the magnitude of the growing problems. Our large organized religions seem disconnected from Divine Power and even aloof, while our electronic media saturates us with extremely negative scenarios 24/7. People are really scared and depressed. The world seems totally "messed up" (as my public school students used to say) and the future feels uncertain and frightening. Many humans feel totally stuck in this old paradigm and are asking, "Why IS there so much suffering? What's the point of it all? Is there a way out? And - are we alone?"

The good news that fills this book is that - in spite of the dire circumstances facing our world - we are NOT alone. There is another way of looking at events. There is another more optimistic paradigm bubbling to the surface of human consciousness, a movement that is growing stronger by the moment. Something amazing is happening to our race and to our planet. A spiritual, metaphysical awakening is unfolding in every culture, and in every corner of the Earth. A quantum leap is fast approaching, a leap for the human race that will be greater than when we invented fire and language, planted our first seeds, gathered into tribes or built our first cities!

A totally new scenario is being offered to the human race about the future of Planet Earth! A new story is beginning to be told - a prophecy of an outcome where the human race discovers that it is NOT alone and where Planet Earth neither self destructs nor sinks into another dark age. A new revolutionary God age is fast approaching, when our human world and the Spirit World from which we came, will unite in order to co-create a whole new way of life on Earth. Actually, that time is arriving right now. For many of us this age is already here! The grand metamorphosis in consciousness that will transform our imprisoned world of darkness and suffering into a paradise of freedom, joy and Light is what this book is all about! A new age of unbounded happiness, multidimensional connectedness and spiritual enlightenment for the human race is on the verge of beginning!

Why and how - you may ask - is this great new age going to happen? The reason is simple and true, although hard to accept by ego bound brains. A new age is coming because of one very important fact of life, a truth of cosmic proportions. We are NOT alone! We have never been alone and we will never be alone! There is another world - a Spirit World, and that higher dimensional realm of reality is attempting to contact us right now. We are being sent transmissions from this "other world", even as we speak. Help and guidance are being offered, right now! And thank God there are courageous people like Bob Hickman with the amazing ability to open to - and receive - these important messages and "nonphysical news bulletins" as they are being so lovingly offered. This book and the revolutionary ideas within it could never have been brought into the Earth plane without Bob's extraordinary willingness to act as a kind of "cell phone" between worlds.

My life has proven to me, beyond a shadow of any doubt, that there really is an all loving God Force - and an invisible Spirit World which is inhabited by high spiritual beings. This "high nonphysical world" is intimately involved in our Earthly lives, and is most willing to help us understand exactly what is the next most beneficial step for us to take. I have learned from experience, that when and IF we remember to call out to the God Force and to His Spirit World for help, support and guidance, we WILL most definitely be answered, often in ways that literally "blow our minds". If we are open to asking, the Spirit World is always ready, willing and able to blast through our egoic stuckness in order to bring us clear guidance, unexpected opportunities, protect us from unnecessary suffering, amplify our happiness, join us with our soul family, and totally jump start our lives.

History is replete with accounts of people who knew intuitively that the Spirit World and the human world were not really separate and apart. Those enlightened sages discovered that the God Force and the Spirit World were close and easily accessible. And, because they knew this truth, they courageously called out to God and the Spirit World for assistance and guidance whenever necessary. They acted as mediums between the worlds, a.k.a. intermediaries between dimensions. The Bible and many other great scriptural writings from around the world are replete with stories that show - not only how the early prophets and spiritual masters conversed with God and the Spirit World - but also how often they were answered quite enthusiastically with voices, visions, lights, pillars of fire, metaphysical messages, geopolitical liberations and other miraculous manifestations.

Divine interventions by high super intelligent spiritual powers became almost common place for those wise masters who knew the Spirit World was real, alive, accessible and dependable. This age old tradition of calling for "help from on high" can be seen in the stories of all the great biblical prophets like Moses, Abraham, Elijah, Ezekiel, King David, Isaiah in the Old Testament, and then continues on with the messages of the Angel Gabriel to both Mary and Joseph in the New Testament.

Jesus himself claimed to be channeling the power of "Our Father in Heaven" when he taught his parables of forgiveness, healed the sick, talked of Heaven on Earth, fed the multitudes and raised the dead.

This tradition of ongoing conversational contact with the Spirit World can be found in most world religions, from Hinduism in the East, to Islam in the West. Mohammed claimed that the Koran was dictated to him by the Angel Gabriel, and St. John said that he wrote the Book of Revelation only after communing with great spiritual beings on the island of Patmos. St. Paul explained that he was completely taken over by the Christ, which impelled him to teach and write and do all his amazing work throughout the Middle East. Even in modern America we have the life stories of people like Joseph Smith, Ralph Waldo Emerson, Walt Whitman, Mary Baker Eddy and of course Edgar Cayce, that profess to reveal contact between the Spirit World and the human world. This list includes many of our Founding Fathers and our greatest president Abraham Lincoln, who was said to have believed very strongly in communication with the Spirit World.

My own introduction to this phenomenon of "contact between worlds" came early on in my life, when I was a little boy sitting under an apple tree in my father's garden. (Bob had a similar event happen to him as child, as well). A bright Light of great loving intensity suddenly appeared to suffuse everything in the garden. It surrounded and in-filled me with the most incredible feelings of kindness, compassion and vast wisdom. The Light spoke to me, comforted me, infused me with metaphysical ecstasy and showed me some incredibly prophetical images of my future destiny. It assured me that although my life's mission would seem quite difficult at times, Divine Love would always be with me, and success was assured.

Later on when I was a teen, and after a series of "out of body" experiences, and some other extraordinary miracles I chronicle in "Uncle Tom's Classroom", my dad gave me two books to try and help me understand my metaphysical experiences. One was "The Sleeping Prophet" about the life work of Edgar Cayce and the other was filled with the amazing predictions of Ruth Montgomery. They truly opened my eyes, as I began to understand that my contact with the realm of Spirit was not unique. Humans had been in touch with other dimensions for as long as human history has been keeping records, (and I'm sure before). I soon understood that my awareness that the human world was not separate from the Spirit World was supported by countless writings the world over.

Little did I realize, when I read those books about channeling, prophetical writings and mediumship back in the 1960's, that one day I would have the extraordinary pleasure of talking with the Spirit World directly, through some truly great mediums/channelers. But I have! And let me say, most unequivocally, that Mr. Bob Hickman is one of the most adroit and "tuned in" channelers in the world today, as you will discover as you read this book. Bob has graciously introduced me to a MOST friendly family of good "spirit people" as he calls them - four wonderful, loving spirit entities who have renewed my confidence, uplifted my hopes, helped fulfill my dreams and greatly improved the quality of my everyday life. I dare say, although Bob still calls himself a medium, the extraordinary information and knowledge that came through his "spirit people", the transcribed messages that you are about to read in this book, will reveal that Mr. Hickman has been upgraded to official "prophet" and "spiritual seer".

How my collaboration with Bob and his spirit guides was orchestrated from "on high" was totally surprising and unexpected. I'd just recently published my book, "Uncle Tom's Classroom – How One Public School Teacher Awakened His Students to the Cosmic Super Self Within" in 2007 and moved to Hawaii to await its successful rise up onto the New York Times Best Sellers list. But, it didn't quite turn out that way. Except for a wonderful radio interview with Shirley MacLaine, my book didn't garner the attention I knew it deserved. My message about liberating America's school children from the hyper-materialistic brainwashing of the "military industrial complex" seemed to fall on mostly deaf ears. Not being a natural promoter, I fell into a kind of malaise, even depression. I became disillusioned and disappointed by the culture's apparent lack of interest in my call for an educational revolution that would allow a metaphysical component back into the public school classroom. So, I did what I always do in such circumstances. I began to call out for help from "on high". I just "gave up" trying to make things happen through human action - and prayed!

It was at that low point in my book's life, in July of 2008, when Bob and his spirit people suddenly appeared, like superheroes coming to my rescue. My call for help had been received and responded to - in a totally delightful way - and this time it was obvious that the Spirit World wanted my attention and my help. My first meeting with Bob was orchestrated perfectly. Bob had serendipitously seen a video I'd recorded about Shirley's book "Out on a Limb" on YouTube and contacted me about perhaps doing a reading for me. He said he felt "compelled" and "guided" by his spirit friends. Since he offered to do the reading "gratis", I acceded to his idea and we set up an appointment for the following week. I liked Bob's energy immediately and trusted his good intentions. The rest, as they say, is history!

Early on in July of 2008 we connected on Skype and Bob began the first session. What came through was a vast wave of uplifting energy that was so filled with love and friendship that I was instantly convinced of the goodness of the communication. The first messages that Bob channeled nearly blew my mind, as they blasted the dust from my chakras and offered me a whole new perspective on life. Those early transmissions offered me fresh insight on my book's progress, and they filled me with renewed HOPE that not only was I on the right track, but NOW I was receiving signs of help from some extraordinary new friends from the Spirit World. Since I'd been fascinated (and greatly enlightened) by the earlier work of Jane Robert's channeling of Seth and Esther Hick's work with the Abraham "cluster", the idea of spirits helping me and teaching me - through a human channel - was familiar and comfortable for me. What was new however - was that these spirit people were to become my first REAL spirit friends!

From the very beginning of my contact with Bob, I could feel the friendly intent of the vibrations pouring through him and I knew right away that this relationship was going to be an important breakthrough in my spiritual initiation and the next logical step in my soul's evolution. Bob's wonderful spirit friends and guides were (and are), kind, compassionate, uplifting, loving, humble, insightful, funny, irreverent, optimistic, clever, forthright and extraordinarily real. Sometimes they just "tell it like they see it"; even if what they say sounds a bit critical of what we humans are doing to our planet and to ourselves! At other times they encourage us to "just relax", stop being so "down on ourselves". They assure us that the path to a good life is not as difficult as we've been told. All we have to do is consciously combine the three realms of body, mind AND spirit. Their transmissions are meant to be helpful, healing and liberating. They want us to wake up from our imagined "aloneness" in the universe and realize (once and for all) that the only way for Earth to "make it" is for the human world and the Spirit World to re-unite consciously and experientially.

Since I'd already met with some of the world's greatest channelers - mediums like Dr. Richard Ireland, Kevin Ryerson, Esther Hicks and Darryl Anka, I was in no way an inexperienced novice to communication between worlds. I've been a long time student of Jesus Christ's most recent teachings as scribed by Helen Shuckman in "A Course in Miracles". And, I've poured over, compared and synthesized channeled messages from Ramtha via J.Z. Knight - the star beings of "Starseed Transmissions" via Ken Carey - the extraterrestrial Bashar via Darryl Anka - the Pleiadians via Barbara Marciniak and many others like Ptah, Emmanuel, Elias and Bartholomew, so I was well equipped to "sense" the uniquely practical value of the messages that were coming through Bob. Needless to say, I was thrilled after our very first session together, for I realized that I was being given the very help I'd prayed for in a way that I never could have predicted. And I was being offered a new kind of friendship, a friendship with beings from another world – the Spirit World!

Think about this! The Spirit World loves to surprise and delight us, and I must say that I was totally and completely delighted by the surprising appearance of Bob and the new spirit friends. I'd always hoped that I could develop an ongoing relationship with some high spirit guides, through great channelers like Jane Roberts or Esther Hicks, but I'd never even thought to pray for such a relationship to actually happen. And yet, here it was falling into my lap, four spirit friends were coming into my life through Bob, offering me their love, wisdom, comfort, guidance and happy companionship. WOW!

Here is what I believe is so valuable and unique about the information that came through (and continues to come from) my new spirit friends as they continue to speak through Bob. With the exception of the spirit Orion, who is an extremely evolved being who never incarnated as a human, Bob's spirit guides are totally "down to Earth" teachers of practical strategies for "making the most of life on Earth". They are not against the pleasures of the flesh, even though they want us to realize that there is MUCH more to life than our acquisition of things and people on the physical plane. They want us to have great lives while we're incarnated on Earth, by showing us how to unite our human energies with the awesome powers of Spirit. They want us to learn our self worth, by accepting that we are both human AND Spirit.

Fletcher is our number one guide in this writing adventure. Fletcher was, or I should say, was a young Canadian soldier who died in France, during World War I. He spent much of his short life "chasing the skirts" and hanging out at pubs, as he says so brightly. He left the tight constraints of traditional religious organizations and became a pseudo-atheist at a very young age. I say "pseudo" because Fletcher remained a bright spirit even while saying he didn't believe in the image of God that the churches were "selling". He still has a bright sense of humor and Light wit and is quite adamant about the fact that enlightenment demands that we all develop the courage to transcend many of the old narrow minded dogmas and "ologies" taught by modern day western religions. He loves to have fun and is a great proponent of living life to the fullest, without guilt, shame or self-hatred!

Fletcher once worked as a spirit guide through the famous trance channeler Arthur Ford, but complains about that relationship being "flawed" and the information "tainted" due to Ford's heavy drinking and overinflated ego. Fletcher is much happier working through Bob and seems bound and determined to "wake up the atheists of the world" to the happy realities of Spirit. He has tantalized me with stories about his "sex life in Heaven", which I have no doubt he will extrapolate on in much greater detail in our next book. And he assures us that there is nothing wrong with being happy and enjoying the great pleasures of life - whether they come to us on Earth OR in

Heaven. He merely warns us, that since all forms are temporary we must not get too attached to any specific avenues for our pleasure and happiness. Fletcher is a good and kind spirit, who has committed his energy to helping both Bob and me fulfill our destinies and develop to our fullest potential. He also acts as a kind of guardian angel and gatekeeper. He has been placed in charge of guarding Bob's psychic door, so as to ensure that no uninvited lower energy spirits can try to come through.

All of my sessions with Bob, which lasted from July through December of 2008, have involved a total of four primary spirit friends – Fletcher, Rose, Edgar Cayce and Orion. Of the four, the only female spirit is the one who calls herself Rose. And I must say, I have fallen head-over-heels in love with her. Rose is like no other spirit I've ever met before or since. She is not some highly enlightened "spirit cluster" like Abraham, or a great super wise mind like Seth. She is simply Rose, a rich, ex-noble woman from London who died unexpectedly and very unceremoniously in the blitz. Rose is not her real name, (she says), for she is protecting the anonymity of her aristocratic family from any unnecessary "embarrassment". She says that she still loves and enjoys her diamonds, mansions and cocktails in Heaven, and explains in great detail how - in the Spirit World - such things are made out of thought and Light. Her lessons in how to manifest "the good things of life" while still on Earth (and also in Heaven) are included in the latter chapters of this book, and should not be missed! She has taught me that we are supposed to learn how to create, just like our Creator creates, and that we were "at one" with God in the very beginning, helping with the creation of this universe! She is also a proficient "matchmaker", and has not only helped me meet members of my "soul family", but she has really sparked my "love life" as well.

Rose is Fletcher's number one student and "side kick". She is going through a training program to be prepared to be a full-fledged spirit guide. Right now she says that her main aim is to help humans get free of the "dark" by waking up to the presence of what she calls "the hands of Light" that are constantly reaching out to us to help us rise out of ignorance. She actually reminds me of the sweet angel Clarence, in the movie "It's a Wonderful Life" for she is so humble and sincere in the way she talks about her old atheistic days of "vanity, pure vanity". She tells an absolutely fascinating tale about her own demise one night in London during a bombing raid over her neighborhood. She takes us right along with her as she finds herself out of her body and floating in a place of confusion and darkness that she calls Purgatory. She says that Bob Hickman and other Spiritualists helped her get free of the dark and move towards the "hands of Light", through the power of prayer. Hearing about her real life adventures after she "crossed over" has helped me understand the "Other Side" in a way that has truly enriched my present life experience here on Earth. Rose has become a good and loyal friend, my spiritual sister!

Of the four spirits who speak in this book, the one who will probably be the most controversial is, of course, the spirit of Edgar Cayce. We will let you, dear reader, judge for yourself whether or not you feel that this is the real spirit of Edgar Cayce. Bob and I are convinced that this spirit IS Edgar Cayce and so is Barbara Hall, (my good friend) and one of our early readers - who Edgar offered to help heal. Her personal testimony will be found later on in the book. Bob and I both feel that we are merely doing what Edgar's spirit has asked us to do - which is to allow him to speak through us and our book, so that he can continue his work in the world, a spiritual work that he says, he is still deeply committed to completing. We are neither insisting nor demanding than anyone believes us, as we offer you these Edgar Cayce transcripts. We are merely giving you his words to you as he gave them to us - with the intention that perhaps his messages will uplift you as much as they uplifted us. As Edgar says himself, "No-one can own a spirit" so it is not up to us to try and convince his A.R.E. organization that this is the real Edgar. You, dear reader, can decide for yourself after you assimilate his words. He has taught me many things in these transcripts - like how to dissipate clouds with my mind, and how to experience Bible parables as if there were living holograms. He suggested that we place a Yin/yang symbol on the cover of this book, to remind everyone that we are already experiencing the interactions of our two worlds.

The other spirit friend that you will meet in these pages is the highest vibrational being of them all, a nonhuman energy vortex who calls himself Orion. He lives in a highly evolved dimension that he says is close to where the legendary "Elohim" live and abide, a hyper-frequency level of pure Light and Thought that is near to the Archangels and God Himself. Orion is an enigma to me. The name Orion is mentioned four times in the Bible, which offers us some tantalizing clues as to why he calls himself a name that invokes the Light of great star constellations.

I once asked Orion if he was a star being or a galactic being and he explained that he was even higher and more evolved than the physical stars and constellations that were named after him. In the Book of Job we find some clues, "God is so wise and mighty. He has stretched the heavens out and made Orion, the Pleiades and the constellations. Can you restrain Orion? Can you hold back the stars?" And in the Book of Amos we have, "Seek Him who created the Seven Stars and the constellation Orion, the One who turns darkness into morning and day into night." Perhaps Orion uses that name because he IS a ray of God's Divine Light that has actually found a way to speak to us. All I can say is that Orion's powerful Light has certainly radiated Light into my mind, which has dissolved many of its darkest thought forms.

Sometimes Bob and I have been almost "blown away" by Orion's unrestrained energy when he enters into one of our sessions. It is often impossible to sleep after he speaks to us. His high vibration feels like huge tidal waves of wisdom, love and Light pouring through our entire bodies. In fact, Bob is often dazed by the powerful energy blast that is downloaded into him when Orion chooses to come through. Hopefully, as you read and digest Orion's words for the first time, you too will be able to allow Orion's Light to constellate a new God energy within your own soul. Orion has promised that those who read, study and speak his words aloud will feel his presence and benefit from his power quite viscerally!

And now, dear reader, we come full circle from the fearful paradigm of the 1950's which gave us the old movie, "When Worlds Collide" - to the publication of "When World's Unite". The terrifying events of our post 9/11 world of failing governments, unending wars, crazy weather, hyper competition and imploding economies have brought us to a turning point in human history where we can clearly see that it is absolutely essential we take our next quantum leap as a species. We need a new paradigm that includes the Spirit World in our reality. Our very survival may be at stake. The time for the human world to wake up from its materialistic ignorance and atheistic separation from the Spirit World - is NOW!

With the help of trailblazers like Mr. Bob Hickman and his spirit friends, the time is approaching when we must ALL learn how to become human cell phones to the "Other Side". In this book we are given the knowledge and guidance that will help us accomplish the inner awakening that will allow us to open up and contact and our own spirit friends. The era of spiritual segregation can come to an end. The human world and the Spirit World can indeed unite once again - in and through US. This spiritual integration can happen right now - as we merge and blend and interweave and mesh with who we really are in the grand cosmic scheme of things. There is a Divine Cosmic Super Self within us all!

Bob and I invite you now to relax in your most comfortable chair, or find a grassy place under your favorite tree and begin to allow the loving Light of the Spirit World to "ray" into your human experience. The more time you spend reading and pondering the messages in books such as "When World's Unite", you will be developing your relationship with the good spirits of the higher dimensions of reality, and the better your life will unfold. Your life will be transformed almost immediately, because you will no longer feel so alone or powerless. Our good spirit friends are here with us, right now, and they bring us power, Light, peace and opportunity. They are eager to prove their existence, their energy AND their love – in order to uplift, inspire, save, protect, heal, empower, liberate, illumine and enlighten us.

Just as Scrooge learned in "The Christmas Carol" – the Spirit World is real, and the spirits are more than willing to come into our lives and help us find the right path to follow. Bob and I feel that "When World's Unite" is not just a book. It is more like a vibrational passport into another world - of Spirit - a high frequency realm that is God governed and totally filled with truth, joy, Light, power and love. Dear reader, please know that - as you read this book - the good spirits are inviting you to embark on a new kind of "adventure in friendship", a metaphysical journey that will transform your life, awaken your soul, free your mind, uplift your hopes, help your body - and perhaps, if we are lucky - even save our beloved planet while there is still time!

Rose said it best when she suggested that we must get to a point where we are so fed up with the old ways of suffering that we are willing to simply let go of the past and, "Take a quantum leap of faith" into a whole new paradigm, "When Worlds Unite". Thank you Bob, for showing the way, and letting this happen! LET THE ADVENTURE BEGIN!

CHAPTER ONE
THE FIRST NIGHT OF THE SPIRIT VOICES

July 15th, 2008

BOB HICKMAN PREVIEW:

From all outward appearances, I look like your normal next door neighbor. And for all purposes I am. But some things about me are a bit different from most. I don't have a normal 9 to 5 job these days, as I tend to work mostly at night sometimes with small groups of people gathered around me, sometimes in large halls filled with many. It is during these night time hours I speak with those who come from the Other Side of the Veil—the Spirit World to bring their messages of hope to Earth. My name is Bob Hickman. I am a trance channel.

I am a trance channel/medium of the Spiritualist tradition. That means that I regularly enter into a trance state in which my own consciousness is set aside for a time while spirit entities take control of my mind and body to communicate with those who have gathered to hear them. Trance work is as amazing experience for me to behold as it is for those who come to sit with me.

A few days prior to this first night of sitting with Tom, he had called me and asked me if I would do a trance channeling for him. He said he wanted to experience my spirit guides "in person". I was more than happy to oblige. I remember well this first night. I was getting to know Tom as I had done a private reading for him recently. In that reading, I did "conscious channeling". Conscious channeling is when I am wide-awake and bring over information to you as it is conveyed to me by the guides I see and hear while fully alert. Tonight would be different, for I was doing "trance channeling" for Tom. I love to trance channel, for me it is another chance to more intimately connect with my guides and a chance for others to meet "in person" those who so regularly influence my daily life. I don't think at the time, either of us was aware as to what the guides had planned (i.e., this book)!

I am always a bit nervous when I channel as I always "hope" the guides will show up. It's funny because I can't make them appear; I can only settle down and invite them to come through me. I always live in fear that they might just be busy one night, and not show up! So far I've been fortunate, as this has never happened. For many years I had Spiritualist mediums tell me that one day I would be a trance channel. I never believed them. I was comfortable just relaying information to people, but the idea of a spirit guide actually entering my body/mind and speaking through me, was a totally different matter. Not an idea I was at all comfortable with. I think my own fear of letting go of control was behind my reluctance to be open to the phenomena of trance channeling. But here I was now 10 years later from my very first trance channeling. Though I have been doing mediumship for 25 years, it has only been in the last 10 years that I opened up to trance channeling. The first time I had trance channeled was for a small group of Wiccan's who wanted guidance for their lives. Since that time, I have travelled around the country doing channelings for many different groups and individuals and now, thanks to the Internet, my channeling is reaching into other countries. The world is truly becoming a smaller place.

As I don't know what happens during the channeling, I rely on film and tape recorders to capture the event. I am always astounded at the fascinating information that the guides seem to deliver through me. After ever session, I am always shaking my head in amazement and saying "Did they really say that?" The following is my first trance channeling session with Thomas Alan Berg.

(Note: This was the first time that Bob actually went into a full trance in my presence and allowed the spirits, Fletcher, Rose and Edgar Cayce to come through for this book material.)

Fletcher: Oh hello, this is Fletcher. It is so good to be here. Give us just a moment while we take control of the medium's vibration.

It's so nice to be talking to you in a more direct fashion. You know, I always talk to our medium and he tries to relay our messages. But, right now I prefer to talk to you directly myself.

As I come closer to you I am looking at your energy fields. There is a lot of healing Light around you, my friend. I keep seeing a lot of Light here. You are going to be getting an extra charge here; a lot of vitality will be coming into you. How has your energy been lately?

Tom: Well actually, I have been feeling lethargic, kind of stuck!

Fletcher: That's right. But, be watching here because in about three days you will feel like an electric current flowing right through the body. This charge of energy that you'll feel will be coming from us. We are working with your energy field.

The reason why we are raising your vibration – is that you have a special friend – who is going to be working with you even more. I believe you know him. His name is Edgar Cayce.

Mr. Cayce is going to be working closely with you. I will help bring him over to speak with you. So, in about three days time you will be feeling a bit overwhelmed and it might even make you nervous. But, don't worry about it, because what you will be feeling is our energy moving through your system. As more and more of our energy comes through you, don't be concerned, because we promise we won't hurt you.

Tom: Thank you Fletcher.

Fletcher: Oh, you're so welcome. You know, you've been tuning into the vibrations of our world for a long time. And, there are a lot of people over here who are surrounding you and supporting you.

It's strange to say, but sometimes you feel like you are standing on a cliff and you're about to fall into a precipice. But, you need not be worrying about that cliff because – even if you were to fall – know that there are many angels and spirit beings around you, to hold you up. Actually, you are NOT going to fall. But, even if you did feel like you were falling, where would you be falling, except into our world? And from there, you would only be helped.

What we want you to understand is that, what you are feeling right now is a kind of balancing act between your world and our world. We are teaching you this balancing act to help you to better understand and accept your own humanity. You are both physical and non-physical. You have your feet in both worlds, in the spiritual and in the material.

When I was a young man, living on the Earth, I had an auntie who was a Spiritualist. She used to say to me all the time, "Fletcher, why don't you come and sit with us? We're having a séance tonight." But, I used to think she was daft.

"I don't believe in that", "I would say, "Auntie, I just don't believe in the Spirit World."

"Life is very short," she would answer, "and you should be giving some thought to the Spirit World." Well, I'm here to tell you that I would hear none of it.

What did I know? I was only nineteen years old. If the truth were told I'd be rather having a pint and chasing a skirt, I would. You see, I was in World War I, in France. I was in the army back then, and I kind of liked it actually, because I had a beautiful uniform. I used to strut around in me uniform, showing off all my brass buttons, thinking myself quite important, I did.

But, you know, all of that strutting around didn't serve me much because in the end, I was killed. I was standing with my mates and I remember hearing a whistling sound. You know, when you are on the battle field you start to get used to that sound, as things fly by you. Every time the bullets would whistle by us we used to laugh and even joke about it. But, one day, the whistling sound got louder than ever before, and all I remember after that, was waking up in a place of darkness.

I thought, "Oh my God, I've been shot and I've lost my sight." I couldn't see a thing. Everything was so dark and silent and then I thought to myself, "Is this death?" I tried to shout for help, but I couldn't see a thing or hear a thing.

It was at that point that I began to see a little bit of Light above me. It began to get brighter and larger, and then I saw hands reaching down. I thought, "What is that?" And then I heard a voice which said, "Fletcher, let us pull you up." I thought I must have fallen into a hole or a cave, because I was feeling so very disoriented.

Give us just a moment while we adjust the medium's vibration. [A short pause ensues then we again hear Fletcher's voice] ...There we go, can you hear us?

Tom: Yes, I can. Quite well.

Fletcher: There we go.

So I reached up and a grabbed hold of a hand that was pulling me up. And, then suddenly, I found myself in the world of the spirits. Oh, I've got to tell you, that was a total surprise. The first thing I thought was, "Everything my auntie told me was true." Because, I quickly realized then that I was in a place – that my auntie always referred to - as the "Other Side".

If only I had listened to her when I was alive, and known back then what I know now about the Spirit World! Well, we can't really look back any more, we can only look forward. The truth is that I am having a very good time over here now, and I love being able to help and serve a lot of people.

There is another person here who wants to talk to you as well. Give us just moment.

Rose: Greetings, my name is Rose. Can you hear my dear?

Tom: Yes I can. Hello Rose.

Rose: Hello. It is such a pleasure to be here with you. I was listening in to your discussion with Fletcher. You know, this brings to mind some aspects of my own journey. When I was alive, I thought myself quite important, I did. I lived in the Mayfair District of London, and I was quite wealthy. But, you know – all my wealth and success only seduced me to move further and further away from the Light.

I was a member of the Church of England, and I used to make such a show of attending that church. I thought that I was so very grand on those Sundays when I would put on my finest, so everyone would admire me. The truth was that I was dressing for my vanity. I used to think, "I wonder if the vicar will be impressed with my hat? I wonder if the vicar will like this dress?" You see, the way I attended church was really just for my own glorification and vanity. At that point in my life, church had little to do with my relationship to God. Instead, I used it as a means to be noticed, and to show off my wealth.

But, then one day, death found me and I was lifted into the Spirit World. You know, in those days, World War II was just beginning, and London was being bombed by the Nazis. The night that I was killed we were having a blackout and a series of raids. We were supposed to keep the lights off – you know – and keep all the curtains drawn. But, as I frequently did – I said to myself, "I can't stand it. I just can't stand staying in the house." I was so self-centered, pompous and vain. So, instead of following orders, and staying inside my home, I went out walking that night, saying to myself, "I don't care what happens. Let the Germans bomb away."

So, there I was, going out for a stroll in the middle of a bombing raid. I turned down an alley way - and then – all I remember – was a great roaring sound. And like Fletcher, I suddenly found myself in a place of almost complete darkness. At first, I thought I must have fallen into some kind of pit or open place in the ground. I remember a falling feeling, but I don't remember hitting anything at the bottom. Then I found myself in a place of emptiness . . . (her voice trails off with a sigh).

I looked about and said to myself, "Where am I? What is this about?" I started walking but I could not find where I was. You might say that I had completely lost my way. I could not determine where I was at all. I couldn't even feel any ground beneath my feet. Then, I thought, "Perhaps I am shell shocked. That's why there is complete numbness around my feet." But, you see, what had happened was that I had been killed. I was already deceased at that point – and I didn't know it.

Do you know I wandered for sixty Earth years; sixty years as measured by your time, in that state of almost total darkness. And, it was only through Fletcher and the magnificent work of our medium here, that I was raised up and lifted into the Light. I have great devotion to this one here - our medium - for he had a spiritual circle in his home one night with the specific purpose of helping souls such as mine.

It is ironic that I didn't really grow up thinking much about the existence of a higher power. You know, I told you already that I went to the Church of England. I was brought up in the Church of England, but that didn't make me really religious. It was all for show. When I was young I also traveled to India where I was exposed to other spiritual teachings. But, those experiences didn't wake me up either. I met a swami in India, who said to me, "Rose, you must avail yourself of your spiritual energy and of your psychic abilities." He taught me about the existence of the chakra system. But, instead of being grateful for this knowledge, I mocked the swami, saying, "Oh, please, this is all just rubbish. I don't believe this."

When I passed by those opportunities to learn about spiritual matters, I gave up so much. Time and time again, those of the Spirit World gave me a chance to learn about them and to serve them, but I did not. But, you know, as Fletcher has said, we must not look back too much.

But, I am now in the Spirit World and I am serving and helping those of you on your side. I've not been serving but a few years. I am new to this spiritual guide work. But, Tom, if I might call you Tom, I should like the honor and privilege to serve you, and to come to you more regularly. I will come to speak to you more directly in dreams, and I will even come in your house if you will give me a chance. I am so honored to serve you.

Tom: I would love that. Thank you so much. It would me an honor for me to work with you, as well. Did our souls know each other in past lives? Is that why you are coming to me now and offering your help?

Rose: I don't know what I am allowed to tell you about that. Fletcher will have to talk to you about that. I am limited in what I am permitted to reveal. I will let him speak now. Give us just a moment. I shall be back shortly.

Fletcher: Oh, hello there, this is Fletcher. I want to tell you something important about your soul growth. It is true that you and Rose have another connection, but we haven't revealed it yet, even to her, because she is learning so much already. It's not often that she encounters a soul that she has known before. And, she is - what you could call – a guide in training. She doesn't have so many years experience as I do, but you don't have to worry because she is always under our guidance. She won't disappoint you – I promise.

Tom: I am so grateful that you have come into my life at this time and I am curious as to how I earned such a wonderful privilege.

Fletcher: Well, you know – over here – we've got a little bit of – well – you could call it a score board. We've got certain names listed on it. You know, the Spirit World is a big place and we are each assigned certain segments of the Earth that we watch over.

For example, my main work is guiding this medium here. You know, he's a lot easier to work with than the other mediums I've worked with in the past. The other mediums gave me such a difficult time because they wouldn't listen. The reason why we are coming to you at this time to work with you is because you are on our board, over here.

In the coming years there are going to be some great changes upon the Earth. Our voices right now – the voices coming from the Spirit World - are not often heard. There are so many people who go around talking with us, on a daily basis, but they simply don't acknowledge it. We are constantly whispering in their ears, saying things like, "Don't go there, you are in danger." Or we might say, "You'd better listen up here, because you are being told a lie."

We often try to save people from going through unnecessary trauma in this life. There are a lot of souls right now – who are choosing not to follow the themes that are on their life charts and on their life paths. We think it is our duty to help those who are can hear us and will listen.

So, we saw you down here on the Earth struggling. And. we knew that we were going to arrange the meeting between you and our medium here. This is because each of you has got a lot of growth coming in the next five years. Well, I suppose we could say four years, because of 2012. But, let us not be stopping at 2012, because life and change are going beyond that. We are planning on working with you for at least the next five years. So, that's why we are putting you and Bob together now.

Bob has got a lot of great things coming in his life, as do you – and we feel that you will each be a help to the other. And so, you've got to be open here to listening to us and hearing our voices. You know, even if you can't be sitting with our medium as much as you might like, we will still come to you personally, and speak to you ourselves. We are already very close to your vibration.

Tom: I can feel your vibration more each day, and you all feel absolutely wonderful. Your vibration is very empowering, sweet and filled with love.

Fletcher: Thank you. In the last week here, we've been monitoring your energy, and we have seen how it has been a bit on hold, kind of dipped down you might say. Well, remember what we told you. It will soon be popping back up. And as that energy begins to increase once again, it will feel so powerful that it may even scare you a bit. But, don't be worrying. You will be feeling a vibration that you haven't ever felt before. Don't' be scared. For, as we told you, this is only to move your vibration closer to the vibrations in our world.

You need not hold back on your inspiration to write. You keep thinking, if only I could start on another project. So, you start it and you fiddle with it, but then you put it aside. The only problem is that you are trying too hard. You don't have to try so hard. Just let Spirit do the work though you. All you've got to do is sit at the keyboard there. We will do the work! Your Spiritual Self is always with you. He is the part of you that can hear us, and can then translate what we offer, for you, as words!

When I was in the army we used typewriters. But, we know that you have different technology now. In fact, we have to be most careful with your electrical appliances, because our energy can easily interfere with them. This medium gets so upset with me when the Light bulbs explode. He says, "Fletcher, why are you blowing out another bulb?" We don't mean to, but sometimes it happens. We will try not to do that when we come into your house.

We would also like to say here, that we like where you live. You know, when I was on the Earth last - I never got to go to the west - or to Hawaii. I only went to France – which is where I was killed. So you might say, my first chance of traveling didn't turn out so well. But, it doesn't really matter, because right now, I am able to be anywhere I want to be. We have no such limits over here. We are not bound by either time or space. So, what else may we be answering for you, Lad?

Tom: I'd like to ask you more about my spirit guides. I want to understand. You and Rose are offering your help. And last week you told Bob that Edgar Cayce was also offering his help. Are they any others?

Fletcher: You've got many guides around you, many guides. You know that guide John? He works with you as well. You know, John is the spirit who comes through your friend Kevin Ryerson. He works with you as well. So, you don't need to be worrying. You know, it doesn't really matter what our names are or who we are. What's important is that you just listen for our voices. We are with you every day.

Tom: Here in Hawaii the Kahunas call spirit guides the Aumakua – or our "utterly trustworthy spirits". I do have a question about my new career. Can you tell me how it might unfold?

Fletcher: Well, you don't have to be worrying about breaking into a new career. You are breaking into it already, as you are shattering all your old limits. It's like you are breaking through a glass. You've got a crack in the glass that is growing now. That crack is growing and expanding into five cracks. And if you be watching here, the whole window will be shattered and you will be stepping through the glass into a whole new place. You are entering into a time of phenomenal growth.

You may want to work on your speech and your presentation, for you will be invited to speak before a group of educators. Give us just a moment. All right. Rose is here. She wants to say something.

Rose: Oh hello, this is Rose. Can you hear me? It's such a pleasure to be back here. I think that when it comes to your presentation, you are well prepared already. All I would suggest is that you might want to incorporate a bit more visual imagery, to explain your words. Sometimes people need imagery to understand the realm of Spirit.

None of us in my circle knew a thing about spirituality. Oh, some of my acquaintances in Mayfair knew and followed Swami Vivekananda. But to tell you the truth, I thought they were a bit daft. What I am trying to say is that you are going to be speaking to people of my caliber, people like me.

I don't wish to sound like the old days of our class system. But it IS accurate to say that you must tailor your speeches to people – such as those in my class – who were so very worldly – such as myself. Do you know – if a gentleman such as yourself had shown up at my salon and had said, "You must believe in the Spirit World" I would have laughed. I wouldn't go to any of the séances that I was invited to back then.

I do believe sir that you carry a wisdom about you, and if you will look within that wisdom, you will be able to speak to people who were like me when I was on the Earth. You must continue to refine your ability to speak in order that you might better reach the minds and hearts of those who of us who chose to look the other way. There are many people in our world that will help you.

Over here, I've even spoken to Sir Winston Churchill. Perhaps he can influence you and help you. I will ask him. For none could inspire nations such as he. I believe that we won the war because of him.

Tom: Wow, that's really a coincidence. When I visited London a few years ago, I visited Churchill's underground bunker and saw where he lived during the Blitz. I felt a really powerful connection with his spirit, and I felt like I could still feel his presence down there. I brought back a poster of him and put it up on my classroom wall for inspiration.

Rose: It is true. This is what we are trying to show you. You have access to speakers of his caliber, and I will work personally to bring him into your energy field. For this man could inspire the nation with his words. If you look at the technical realities – Germany could have crushed us. But, it was the British resolve and Churchill's power with words that allowed us to sustain. He shall inspire you as well for if you have him with you, you cannot fail.

Tom: Great. I need all the help I can get. Because, my dream is to help the youth of our country get free of the lies of the old paradigm that seek to control them and turn them into little subservient "Uncle Tom's". The educational system is teaching kids that capitalism and competition are the reason for our existence, which isn't true. So, I would very much like to end that materialistic brainwashing, by helping kids discover who they REALLY are in the grand cosmic scheme of things.

Rose: Your noble task is well noted on our side. In our world, we know those who are working for the Light. Make no mistake, your name is not forgotten here. In fact, it is spoken of over here with great regard. We know that there is a great need upon the Earth for truth and Light.

I often think to myself and I say, "Rose, with all of your wealth . . ." (She sighs.)

I must tell you honestly that when I was alive I was very rich. But, when I crossed over I realize that my wealth was worth absolutely nothing in the Spirit World. For, it was then that I saw how empty I really was and how much I had ignored that fact that I was also a spiritual being. If I could go back to that life upon the Earth once again, I would have used my successes much differently.

Let my time in Purgatory be a lesson to you my friend. You will not go there - nor to any place even remotely close to that darkness. The world around you is very much in the darkness, however, so you are being prepared to be the voice of reason and Light to heal and help so many.

Tom: Having taught all grades from kindergarten to high school, I saw clearly how the older generation was using education to unintentionally teach kids to focus on some very dark, materialistic belief systems and limited views of reality. I saw close up exactly how the young people of America were having their natural spiritual joy and spontaneity literally squished right out of them.

Rose: Your insight is most profound. Yes, it is disturbing, my dear.

Tom: I know that children are born from the Light and are filled with the Light. Any adult can easily see their natural spiritual Light in their joy and natural love of life. But, once children start their formal education, most of them have their minds taken over by the system. Rules and regulations make them think that they are compliant little capitalistic consumers, rather than Cosmic Super Selves. I bet that happened to you as well. There is so much social pressure to force kids to fit into the economic merry go round – and to think materialistically, rather than metaphysically.

Rose: Very much so - VERY much so. As I said, I was quite the materialist myself. I only went to church for image, in order to impress the vicar. It was all show for me. Now, I find out that even my vicar had to do some time in Purgatory after he died. (She laughs softly.) He wouldn't like people to know that, but it's true nevertheless. Even he was bowed by social pressure and materialistic thinking.

It is so important that you continue in your work. You do not need to worry or fear. We will be guiding you and helping along the way. In the coming months and years, you will see a great upsurge in your book's sales. We will promote it from our world. And we will see to it that it will arrive in the hands of some well chosen, open-minded people.

You will eventually receive invitations from universities. Educators who are working with teachers will invite you to come and speak to their student teachers. This is an important step for you. Do not bypass these opportunities when they unfold. You will help many of these young teachers become aware and enlightened.

Tom: What I want to teach is very simple, and yet very radical. Most teachers and most schools do not realize that they are actually teaching kids how to be subservient, non-thinking clones of society's most prominent belief systems. I want to teach kids how to be who they really are – how to think for themselves – and how to consciously connect to the multidimensional, all powerful Cosmic Super Being who lives within.

Rose: Yes, it is so important for everyone to understand this. We will therefore – do all we can – to draw to you those who are ready for your message. Some will scoff and call your ideas rubbish. They will say you are insane. Do not listen to them. Their words are untrue and irrelevant. Just a moment, Fletcher wants to say something.

Fletcher: We've got to be careful here with our medium's nervous system. When we come into the body of our medium we have to be ever so very careful, because the nervous system of his body is the electrical system. And if we messed it up we would create a lot of problems for him.

It is so important that you know, that we will do what we can to protect you from those who would oppose you. The more you reach for the Light and teach the Light, there will also be a tidal wave of darkness that rises up in opposition. It will come from the disbeliever types. Although, I must admit, that I was a disbeliever myself . . . so I can't criticize them too much for their ignorance. They don't know what they are doing, in their opposition to the Light.

I see those types of people coming – who will talk against you. Don't be surprised when you see your name appearing in the newspaper because they are going to be doing reviews of your book. And don't be overly concerned if they are saying negative things. You must hold onto the courage of your convictions, like our medium does. He has had to exhibit great courage to work as our medium in public.

Just laugh at the opposition that appears in the press, because very few people will read it or believe it. You don't have to worry, because you won't follow a negative direction when it comes to your publications. Do you understand what we are saying to you?

Tom: Yes, I was sometimes told to keep my mouth shut – when I was just beginning my spiritual experiments in the classroom. But, once I changed the vocabulary and began referring to the Divine Inner Self of my kids as the Super Self - I was able to get around much of the opposition. I was even able to reach my so-called atheistic children, because they didn't reject the idea of the Cosmic Super Self as having anything to do with God. It was so cool to watch them discover and develop their Divine Super Powers, without ever mentioning anything that sounded even spiritual.

All I want to do is bring some semblance of spiritual understanding back into the way we bring up our kids – both at home and in school. I dream of the day when kids are no longer being programmed by the major thought systems to become only materialists. I feel so strongly that children have a God given right to know who they are – why they are here – and where they are going. And, I saw that when they ARE allowed freedom of speech in the classroom, they soar academically and their lives blossom in unbelievable ways.

Fletcher: Oh, you are ever so right. And, you need not be fearing any more. Because, those people who were against you and your message – we will be holding them back. You know, I have to say that when you talk about young children being taught to become atheists – it makes me quite sad. Even I wasn't an atheist until I grew up and forgot the spiritual truths that I knew and felt, as a child.

Young children today ARE having the spirit crushed out of them; that is true. It's enough to make you cry – isn't it? It is hard to imagine – but children now – ARE being taught NOT to believe in God. And they are being shown how to mock sacred things.

Tom: Most public schools are teaching that ONLY hard work and money are the stepping stones on the path to the "good life". Kids are being taught to think only materialistically, to believe that money is the only way to create. They are NOT being told the truth about who they really are – or that they have a vast array of Divine Super Powers to access and express!

Fletcher: You are absolutely right, you are! We certainly have our work cut out for us over here on our side - for we will be working with you in this campaign. You need not be fearing anything anymore. Remember what Rose told you about expecting some phone calls and invitations to appear, because we are going to be speaking to a lot of people about you and your book.

When anyone shouts at you or criticizes you or your work, just stay silent. Don't get all defensive. We will be with you at all times. We want you to remember, that we have the power to take control of the vibration of your environment so that you will always be safe. This is what we do for our medium as well. Your refusal to argue or fight will make you always victorious, when and if anyone speaks against you. You won't be in any danger physically, although it might sometimes be a bit jarring.

You ARE being monitored. You are being protected, just as we have always protected our medium. Your book will find its way to the desks of some of the most influential people in world. But don't be worried, because they are watching our medium also, and we keep him safe always. His name is well known in the highest of circles. He himself doesn't know who they are. We don't tell him everything, lest he gets all nervous about it.

Those of you who are following the Light and who are working for us WILL be tried and tested a bit. Oh, but you've had MUCH worse happen on this planet. Remember what was done to Jesus Christ for teaching about the Light. They dragged Him through the streets, beat him and nailed him to a cross. That wasn't a very good scene, now was it? Not at all! But, He didn't really die and neither will you. His Light and His life are eternal. They are realities forever. He could never be destroyed, not could his Light be put out by the worldly opposition. In fact, His Light is stronger now, than ever before!

So, don't worry. You are not going to be having to suffer like that. Just think of your so-called opposition as little flies to be swatted away. Just swat them away like the negative thoughts they really represent. They won't stop you. They won't be able to put out the Light. They can't!

Ask yourself this question. Can a little fly put out the Light of a bright Light bulb? Not at all!

Tom: That's a really helpful visual. Thank you.

Fletcher: That is so true. Oh, give us just a moment. There is someone here who wants to talk to you.

Orion: Greetings. I am Orion and I have come to discuss with you – your karmic evolution. You have lived many lifetimes and – in each lifetime – you have always sought the Higher Power. It is because of your continual quest FOR an Ongoing CONSCIOUS connection with the Higher Power, that you are given much reward in this life. This reward will be come to you as a great unfoldment in understanding and enlightenment – and will add much to your spiritual development.

It is true that you and Rose have known each other before, and that you DO have a karmic link with her. At this time we will not discuss this link any further because it is not important to your growth. It is only important for you continually to develop psychically, spiritually as well as physically.

You and your other human friends are now at a point in your spiritual education, where you are being taught how to balance the three aspects of your Real Self - the body, mind and spirit. These three aspects create both your inner reality and your outer reality, as well.

You are evolving towards the Light via the path of physical incarnation. Humanity is at a point in its spiritual evolution where it is having an actual encounter with the Light within. The Light within can only be contained so long before it shines outwards.

In the coming years, there will be a perceptible radiance around those who are following the path of Spirit. You will literally see a glow about them, at times. In fact, if you were to research your history – you would find that there have already been many on Earth – who have manifested this Light - and this glowing appearance. You shall be one who shall carry the Light as well. And, when you are with others, they will begin to say to you, "We see a Light about you."

Do not be afraid, because the Light is not of yourself or of your own making. It is radiating from that Higher Power that you think you have been seeking, without fully realizing that It is the Higher Power that has been seeking you. Your evolution has brought you much closer to our world than most - and in so doing – you have been involved in receiving the Light.

You had lifetimes in Atlantis, in which you followed this path, as well. Yes, you are back again – in order that you continue that which you started. There are many here at this time who are reincarnations of that time. You will meet those whom you incarnated with during the time of Atlantis, as your travel on your journey.

This medium is one who has also lived in Atlantis. Many of your present friends are those who have revealed to you that they have some inner knowledge, and some experience of that time. And so, we appeal to you to find your Atlantean roots again – and in so doing – you will access extra wisdom that is within you. My name is Orion.

Tom: Thank you so much Orion. That was very, very interesting.

Fletcher: Oh, hello there – this is Fletcher. We've got to be a little careful when we bring in Orion – because his vibration is so high – that it is hard on our medium's body and nervous system. And so we don't let him stay too long. What else I might be answering for you tonight?

Tom: Who is Orion? A star being? An ascended master? Is he an extraterrestrial?

Fletcher: Orion is a spiritual being who has never been incarnate upon the Earth. He is not necessarily an extraterrestrial, although you might think of him that way, since has never lived upon the Earth. He is a being who inhabits our world. Over here, there are Great Beings who have always been. Orion is one of those, and we have great respect for him. He has wisdom that even we spirit guides cannot yet begin to understand. He will be coming to speak with you more often in the coming weeks.

Tom: That's wonderful. I am totally open. What else should I be doing to enhance my spiritual growth at this time?

Fletcher: We want you to be watching the skies, because there is a lot of activity in that area where you are. In fact, there was an alien ship right outside our medium's house the other night, after you two spoke together. The craft was right outside his window.

Tom: Oh really? What happened?

Fletcher: We will tell you about it. We are letting the alien crafts come close to our medium because those beings are going to be working with him more, as time goes on. He's not quite aware of it yet – and has not yet consciously accepted what's happening - because he thinks that he isn't quite ready. He feels they might be coming close – but he doesn't really want to know about it yet, consciously. So, we are slowly guiding him in that direction. By the year 2012, the alien presence will be a lot more known upon the Earth. He is becoming more and more aware of this – as are you.

So, go out and sit on your balcony every night and look for patterns up there in the sky. They seem to travel in groups and patterns - all at the same time. They are preparing all of you to see them – so that they can have greater communication with you. Don't be afraid of them. Just sit out there on your balcony and talk to them directly. They will be hearing you – because they communicate with telepathic energy. You don't even have to speak out loud.

Just speak to them in your mind and they will hear you. This will lead you to eventually write about your communications with them and will quite naturally evolve into another new project for you. They will be working with you on a deeper level – but we won't be allowing them to take your body at night so much anymore. It has been a bit distracting to you. Do you have another question?

Tom: I have heard Jesus say that we should not be judgmental of others and yet, I know that I still do get quite judgmental. I can hear my mind talk about how ignorant the human race is behaving at times – so –my question is how can I stop judging the entire human race for acting in ways that sometimes seem so primitive and violent?

Fletcher: This is a bit hard for you because you had a previous life when you were a judge. And so you are very used to analyzing and scrutinizing others, according what you believed was the law. But that's OK, because you don't mean to do it. The difference now is that you are catching yourself. The human soul is always growing. Just the fact that you are becoming conscious that you are judging already brings you to a place in consciousness a hundred times more advanced than the average person. Just a moment, Rose is here.

Rose: Hello, this if Rose. It's so good to be here again. I was listening in to your conversation and I must tell you, that I was one of great judgmental types, as well. I used to go to parties at people's houses in the Mayfair District where I lived, and I would say, "Oh look, their house is not as grand as my house. Oh look at that dress; it's not as lovely as mine." I now realize that by my own judgment, I set myself up to be judged.

Sometimes I even judged – or talked out loud - about the hostess to her friends - and it always came back to me. It always traveled backwards, back to me. You see, in the process of so doing, I got my own critique back upon me. I heard you quoting the words of Jesus, and I used to hear that as well, in church, all the time. But, I never believed those words, even then. Isn't that ironic?

And so, just be gentle with yourself. If you are gentle with yourself, you will stop judging. If you love yourself more, you will not judge, because all judgment involves some kind of self condemnation. This is showing up in your vibration, this tendency towards self condemnation.

Tom: You are so right. I do feel an ongoing vibration of self condemnation, sometimes very strongly. I learned to feel a lot of guilt and self hatred because of my very sexuality, early on in my life. The Catholic Church was really good at that. So, how can I let that go, once and for all?

Rose: The thing that I first realized when I crossed over was that I was so full of shame. I was so ashamed when I saw the Light of God. I felt ashamed because I suddenly became SO aware of all my mockery of sacred things. I used to insult those things that were sacred. I didn't even keep a Bible in my house. And when I was in church, I would mock everything about it.

Tom: So, how did you forgive yourself and not judge yourself?

Rose: I realized that, when I was still living upon the Earth, I was simply unaware of the presence of the Light. But, after I passed over and realized that I was completely encompassed by the Light, I felt the healing influence of that Light.

Tom: What does it feel like?

Rose: If feels like a healing influence. But, you don't have to wait until you cross over to feel its loving power pour through you. You can actually feel the healing power of that Light even while you are alive and still IN the body. You don't have to leave the body or die, or come over to our world to feel the power of the Light as real. Our world and your world are very close.

You can actually touch God from your world, merely by asking for His Light. The swamis of India told me that the Light of God existed within me and now I know how true that was although I did not realize it back then. You can ask for that Light to shine brighter and brighter within you, right now, and it will heal all the hatred that you feel towards others – as well as the guilt and hatred you project upon yourself. Asking for, and welcoming the help of the Light is the only way to overcome shame, you see.

I know this from experience, because when I passed over to the Light of the Other Side, I was so ashamed that I cried and cried. And I called out, "God forgive me. Please God – forgive me!" And, I heard God say, "There is nothing to forgive. You are my daughter and I love you." That dawning awareness – that I was loved – totally loved - even after a lifetime of mockery and hatred – was so great – that I cannot find the words to describe it. It even brings tears to my eyes now. (She sighs and pauses).

You know, it is most important for you to learn to love yourself, because God loves you. If you judge yourself, you are judging God's own creation, and it is as if you are saying, "God, you don't know how to make quality items and people". You know and I know that God is always perfect. That means that you and I are – in our essence - always perfect too, because we share in that Light of God.

You know your friend, what's her name? Shirley MacLaine, I believe. I am just learning about her work here in our world. You know, she herself discovered that she had God within her. Perhaps a conversation about that reality, about her discovery of the God within, would help you understand it better yourself. I can tell you that, from the perspective of our world, the Light of God is obvious!

The only reason I wandered in the place of darkness for many Earth years after I crossed over, was because the Light will not force itself upon anyone who is doesn't want it. God will never force Himself upon anyone who is not wanting or welcoming of His Divine Influence. God will not force a soul to be with Him who does not want to be. I went into darkness, therefore, not because of punishment, but because that's what I chose with my free will.

It is true that in both our worlds – like attracts like. Our medium often says this, and I totally agree. Since I chose to live without an awareness of the Light, it was as if there no Light in me. And therefore, when I left the body, I was drawn to the realm that was most close to my vibration. In my case, that was darkness. But, you are going into the Light. In fact, you have already been there, so do not fear. My name is Rose.

Tom: Thank you Rose, I so appreciate this.

Fletcher: Oh hello there, this is Fletcher. Well, we need to be careful with our medium's vibration and his energy. So, might we be answering one more question for you while we are still here?

Tom: With all I know, I still sometimes wake up in the morning feeling lonely and depressed. So many of the people I've known and loved in my life have died. I only have two or three people in my life right now who are really supporting me emotionally. So, what's up with that?

Fletcher: You know why you are waking up feeling depressed? It's not because your friends have left you and have come over to the Other Side. On a very deep level, it's because you remember and miss the Other Side. You are suffering from a kind of spiritual homesickness.

Tom: Wow, I never thought of it like that.

Fletcher: You remember the beautiful reality of our Spirit World and your spirit longs to be with us once again. The thing is, we are raising up your vibration, and moving your vibration closer into alignment with our world, even as we speak. Because of this, you are remembering our world more and more. So what appears to your mind, to be depression, is really a deep longing for our world of Light, a world you once knew so well, and still know to be your true home.

Underneath your feelings of depression and loneliness, you are beginning to become aware of the fact that you are longing for the world that you left in order to come to Earth. And so, what you are feeling is not really depression – but a bit of a tug of war between the worlds. Don't worry about this, because the tug of war will be settling out for you quite soon.

Know that those who have come over here, all your loved ones who have died, are STILL alive, and they are supporting you. They are no more farther away than your own breath. If you breathe out – and put your hand in front of your mouth – feel the air and know--THAT is how close we are to you. Just talk to us freely and we will be present for you. Rose will be giving you more of her messages. You will be hearing her voice when you sit down to write. She will be pushing more things through. Listen!

I will be working with you as well, and perhaps, I will get Winston Churchill to come through. Our medium's vibration is not ready for that yet, but perhaps in some future session. We will do what we can to prepare him for that, so that we might bring Churchill over to you. We have to test it a little bit, because we have an agreement with him – with our medium – that only a few of us can use him to come through him in trance. I could put Mr. Churchill through right now, but our medium might become upset with me, because he has not agreed yet for us to do this. I will be talking to him about it.

Hold on - Rose wants to say one more thing – to add a bit to our message to you.

Rose: I just wanted to say how pleased I am to be working with you. Please know that in the coming days, we will be having a grand time together. We are going to discover and learn so much about each other. I now that you are going to be a wonderful worker with us, and because of our interaction, the Light will increase in the world, little by little.

You know, when I first started working as a guide, I wanted the whole world to be illuminated – instantly. Fletcher told me, "Rose you are going to have to learn to be a bit more patient". So I am learning, but even I become overly eager at times. I will try not to overwhelm our medium or you, and I promise, I won't wake you up at all hours. I've already gotten into trouble for doing that with our medium. You humans do have to sleep some. But, please be assured that I will be coming to you again soon. My name is Rose!

Fletcher: We are so honored that you took the time to visit with us. And it is such a pleasure as well. There are many humans who don't want to listen to us. But, we want you to know that we will be coming to you again in the coming days, and we want you to be watching for our signs. We assure that we will be bringing you our messages. So, you do not have to worry about how this unfolds.

Tom: Thank you so much. I can't tell you how much I appreciate this.

Bob: (Sighing and gasping for breath) – Wow! I feel really dizzy. Did they come through OK?

Tom: Did they? It was amazing? They answered all my questions – even before I asked them. The information is really valuable!

Bob: That makes me happy. You know, sometimes people write me hate e-mails, and then I wonder if it's all worth it. So, I am really pleased that you have found this reading so valuable. I just want to help people reconnect to the Spirit World in this overly atheistic culture. Sometimes I get discouraged, but when people express their gratitude, and tell me that I am really helping, then it makes it all seem worthwhile.

Tom: This work that you are doing is extremely valuable Bob, and I know that someday you will be as well known as Sylvia Browne and Kevin Ryerson. The information that is coming through you is extraordinary - and far beyond what you may realize! You are truly channeling an infusion of Light onto this planet!

Bob: You really think so?

Tom: Yes, absolutely. Because, the messages that Fletcher, Rose and Orion are bringing through are just so applicable to everyday life. What they said today in this transmission is going to transform my life totally! They even said that they were going to bring in Winston Churchill, to give me some pointers about public speaking, when and if you are agreeable.

Bob: Great. I've told Fletcher – that he is never allowed to bring in any other spirit – unless he clears it with me first. He is the gatekeeper.

Do you know how Rose came to me? One night, I was conducting a séance, and we were doing prayers especially for souls who were trapped between worlds. What's funny is that, I was not planning on doing any trance work that night. I was just doing conscious delivery. But during that séance, I suddenly felt myself going into a trance and I thought, "Well OK, I guess Fletcher is doing something." So, I just let it happen.

What's interesting is that he brought Rose through that night without my permission, which is the first time that Fletcher and I got into it. I was really angry with him. It really upset me at the time, because it was such a surprise. But since that first night, I've come to love Rose. She is a wonderful spirit and I'm glad we helped her find the Light. And, Fletcher has kept his promise NOT to bring any more spirits through me, unless I agree first.

Tom: I loved meeting Rose. She reminds me of Clarence, the angel, in "It's A Wonderful Life', because she said that was just learning how to be a spirit guide. She totally won me over, especially when she explained how the Light can and will love us into a state of total self-forgiveness!

Bob: Oh. I love that. I am so happy to hear that the reading went so well. Tom, I am so honored to read for you. I feel guided to make this more regular. How about another session next week?

Tom: I'd love that. Thanks so much Bob! I'll be looking forward to it all week! And, I'll have the tape recorder ready!

BOB HICKMAN POSTSCRIPT:

This is a night I will never forget. It was my first time doing a trance channeling for someone as prominent as Tom. I must admit—I was rather nervous as I knew Tom was a nationally published author, TV show producer, and a friend of Shirley MacLaine, and had recently appeared on her radio talk show. The energy that night was electric—so electric that static several times interrupted our call and we almost didn't complete the channeling...yet despite the technical challenges, I knew that we were going to get on well and that the Spirit Guides approved of our endeavor. In fact, they even said they arranged for us to meet! I eventually settled down and went into a rather deep trance.

When I go into a deep trance, I am not aware of the information that comes through me, for all purposes it is as if I am asleep. I occasionally hear the odd word or have awareness of certain presences, but to return to consciousness and hear from Tom what had occurred, was simply mind blowing for me. "Did they really say that?" I kept asking as Tom shared some of the evening's words of wisdom as sent from the Spirit Word.

Even more shocking revelations came in the days following when he sent me the first transcripts of that night of channeling. What was especially fascinating for me to see was the complex level of detail that the guides brought through me in my very first sitting with Tom. I learned in great detail of their lives and journey on earth and in the Spirit World. I learnt just how much those from the Other Side were willing to help someone struggling on their path. I was fascinated as they answered Tom's every question, and he seemed to agree with their answers. I had channeled for others, but from what I had learnt previously, most people were simply interested in jobs and money. It seemed that with Tom, the guides were now giving a deeper-level reading that hinted at even more profound truths to come.

I must admit—to hear that Edgar Cayce would be channeling through me was shocking. Even more shocking to my mind was the discussion about my involvement with UFOs! And to hear the guides even discuss Shirley MacLaine was something that told me that I had now entered a whole new level of spiritual work. I wondered if I was ready. It was a mixture of emotions that night, elation, fear, anxiety, excitement, and a giddy energy that kept me up all night. It always seems that channeling does that to me, it creates a super-high energy charge in my body and it's like I am on some drug and have the energy to run a marathon after a channeling session. I now understand what the Mediums of yester-year were saying when they told young mediums in training to be careful lest they damage their bodies' nervous systems with excessive trance work.

I pondered the session for several days. Was it true that I had lived in Atlantis before? Were alien beings in contact with me? Would I really be as well-known as Kevin Ryerson and Sylvia Browne whom both I greatly admire? I have to admit—I had no doubt that Tom and I had our meeting arranged by the guides. It was just so easy to be around him, that my initial intimidation was soon replaced with a joyful camaraderie. So, I guess the Spirits had more planned for us. Just what I didn't know nor could I even begin to guess. But as time has shown, what was yet to come from the guides was even more shocking that anyone could have foreseen.

CHAPTER TWO
THE SLEEPING PROPHET AWAKENS

July 30th, 2008

BOB HICKMAN PREVIEW:

After reviewing the transcripts from the previous session, it became very clear to Tom and I that the guides were encouraging us to continue our sittings. They had much they wanted to teach us and those who would later see their words. They had hinted that "other" guides might come through to speak. Who would be coming I wondered? Fletcher at my request had always been hesitant to let any spirit through. I was thankful for his guidance and protection.

Despite my concerns about "other" guides channeling through me, I looked forward to sitting with Tom again. He was such a pleasant person to work with. As Tom was on a spiritual journey himself, he brought to the sessions a higher vibration that I think helped me to be a better channel. I was sure the guides had arranged our meeting…and to think that now a book was possibly coming…well—it was quite a thrill for both of us. I so remember that evening, as it was a typical hot, humid Washington DC night.

Tom wanted to learn more about my journey as a medium and the opening of our session was an interview where Tom asked me questions about my spiritual journey. Here is our conversation, and the trance channeling session that followed.

Would the spirit guides appear? It was question that even today I still obsess over….fortunately for me I didn't have to worry, as Fletcher was timely as always. Below is the transcript of the night as it unfolded.

Tom: I think it would be interesting for our readers if you spoke a bit about your early work as a psychic.

Bob: OK. I began at the age of fifteen, with haunted house investigations. Friends of my family lived in a house that was haunted – and it was extremely traumatic for them. In fact, the family had to leave the house because the drama was so intense. Their beds would flip up on end in the middle of the night – and throw them out. They were not religious, and they didn't know where to turn for help - so they called my parents.

They asked my parents if I could come out to their house - because there had been talk – as I grew up - that I "knew" a lot about this "stuff". So, my mom said to me, "Bob, do you want to go out there and spend a weekend – and observe the house?" I eagerly agreed - and so I did spend a weekend at that house.

Tom: What happened?

Bob: Well, I actually witnessed physical phenomena – like cabinet doors opening and closing, dishes rattling, footsteps sounding, doors opening and closing. I saw all of that. I saw a vase that was sitting on a table move right across the table, for no apparent reason. Everybody was like – screaming. But, I wasn't scared thought because I knew a spirit had pushed it. I knew what was going on right away.

I told them that there was a boy named George in the house - who was eleven years – and who died in the Civil War. Everyone gasped - because they hadn't told me yet that – the week before – a young boy HAD visibly appeared in the house. They saw him appear as a fully formed materialization. But, it was another spirit that was also in the house – a hostile one – a lower astral entity - that was causing the problems. If had to give it a name – I would call it demonic.

Tom: I totally get what you are talking about. I often think – when I see some of the more miserable looking homeless people wandering around town – that they seem possessed. Some are babbling to themselves- and others are so dirty that it just seems as if some kind of evil energy had taken them over.

Bob: Yes, I agree. Do you know what I did one time? There was a homeless guy on the bus – who was talking to himself – and I immediately felt the presence of an evil force. I went into meditation – as I prayed that the Light would go into him. Suddenly, he began yelling at me, "Stop it – I hate the Light". And he ran off the bus.

Tom: Yeah. I like the way Rose told me last week how your prayers actually helped her find the way to the Light. So, we DO need to pray for those people who are caught in the darkness. It's as if they are caught inside their own dark thought forms – and have become so completely separated from the Light – that they really DO need help. So, what happened at that haunted house?

Bob: In those days, I wasn't trained, so I didn't even know how to do a cleansing. But, once I tuned into the spirit of this kid George – I talked to him – and found that he wasn't evil at all. He just liked playing in the house – and was trying to play with the two real kids - who were living in the house at the time. So, I assured the family that George wasn't going to hurt them – and that he actually just wanted to be friends. He just wanted to hang out.

Tom: Why hadn't George been drawn to the Light? What was it about his destiny that made him stick to that house, anyway?

Bob: That is good question. You know – I hate to admit it – but - at that point – I was still so new at this – that I didn't even know that spirits could get stuck on this plane. I was only fifteen at the time of this experience – and all I knew was – that spirits DID exist and - that I could sense their presence. It wasn't until some years later – when I learned much more about the afterlife – that I began to pray for George to help him cross over into the Light – which he finally did - about two years ago.

Tom: So what happened with the haunting?

Bob: The problem for that family actually escalated after my initial visit, and events became more violent. It was the demonic entity that escalated the violence, not the boy. I've noticed that this often happens right after I visit a haunted house. If there is a demonic presence in the house – it will act up much more the week following my visit. But – with that first haunting – I didn't know what to do to help that family except to tell them about the spirits I sensed there. So, things went from bad to worse – and they eventually had to move out. Glasses would shatter – and doors would slam so hard during the night - that the doorframes would break. It all became so serious that they left.

So, it was around the age of fifteen – when I became clear that - I REALLY was dealing with other levels of reality, which were beyond the physical. When I was in high school, all I did was haunted house investigations. I didn't actually start doing readings until I was eighteen. And even then, I never thought it terms of having a career as a psychic. It was just a hobby and a way of helping people.

What happened was - that – during my haunted house work – sometimes people would begin asking me questions about their own lives. And, I found that the answers would just kind of "come" to me. It would happen so automatically and easily – that the news spread about my psychic abilities. That was how I began to be known as a psychic. You know, I feel like I've done this all before and so - I try to draw on my soul memory – on my inner spirit – on my ancient psychic self - for guidance.

Tom: Yeah – I know what you mean. My students used to ask me how I knew that there was an invisible Super Self within them. And I would tell them that I'd always felt another self – a more powerful self – deep within me – even when I was a baby. I had so many out of body experiences as a little kid – that I just KNEW that there was much more to me – than my physical selfhood. In fact, I had so many psychic experiences that my dad gave me the Edgar Cayce biography, "The Sleeping Prophet" to read, and my mom kept a journal of all my ESP episodes. I also read the writings of Ruth Montgomery. So, tell me more about how your psychic experiences – ended up as an actual career?

Bob: Well, as I said - I started doing psychic readings for people when I was still mostly just investigating hauntings. I wasn't even doing "cleansings" at that time – only a kind of identification of spirit presences. I would walk through the houses pinpointing the phenomena and the times that they would happen. I've even worked on some murder cases. After high school – and I began college – I put this on this whole psychic thing on the shelf for a while because I wanted to be normal and have some privacy and freedom. Later on, after college I joined the Spiritualist Church.

Now - I actually do two types of channeling—"conscious" and "trance". As I said before - Fletcher is my number one guide. He used to work with the famous medium, Arthur Ford. I first reached Fletcher by calling and calling out for help – until he finally responded. I have found that - calling out for help from the Spirit World - is a very important step in making contact. I love Fletcher very much and trust him completely. Rose is like his assistant or student.

This work as a medium is a very sacred experience for me – and I don't want to waste my energy channeling for people who don't respect what I am doing. So I like to meet with them and talk to them first. Some people want to speak directly to Fletcher (trance channeling), while others prefer that I relate the information to them – after receiving it myself. If that is what they prefer - I stay totally conscious during the entire process (conscious channeling). At other times however – I will go completely to sleep – and let Fletcher talk through me to my clients.

Tom: Last week Fletcher said that – if it was alright with you – that he may someday bring Winston Churchill through you. That made me wonder if perhaps you were being prepared to channel some other great entities from history – like Lincoln or JFK? What do you think?

Bob: Wow! That would be something! I am very careful about who I let into me. Fletcher and I have to agree on this. I tend to be very slow about who I chose to let speak through me. When Orion began working with us – I was a bit wary at first. But – when I realized that he was an exalted being I was OK with it. Now - I love Orion – but – even today – his vibration is hard on me physically. He usually doesn't stay long. I told Fletcher – as long as he monitors the energy – I will trust him to be the gatekeeper. I am very careful still – because of what this process does to me – physiologically.

I do have to tell you though – that Fletcher put Rose through before telling me first - which was a complete surprise. There is still a lot I am learning about this – and my relationship with Fletcher keeps growing and changing. We are all learning – just like in any friendship.

So Tom, did you want to do some channeling tonight? I am ready – if you'd like to . . .

Tom: Yes – I am totally excited about this. What an honor!

Bob: OK - let's do it. I'm going to go under now. Give me just a little while here and we'll see who comes through. (He breathes deeply with eyes closed.)

Fletcher: Oh, hello there – this is Fletcher. Can you hear me out there?

Tom: Wow – it's good to hear your voice. Hello. Yes – I can hear you!

Fletcher: It is so good to come here. You know, we've got our medium's vibration pretty stable here. We've been asking him to find some more balance – and we are happy that he is listening to us – which helps his vibration. So – it's going to be a little easier for our reception tonight.

First of all – might I be saying that your energy vibration is looking quite nice. You've got a lot of purple Light around you here. You've been thinking about our realm – and when you go to that higher place – well – it brings in a higher vibration – doesn't it?

Tom: Yes it does.

Fletcher: Just a moment. Someone else is here who wants to speak to you tonight.

Rose: Hello – my name is Rose. It's so good to be here with you. I must say – Fletcher and I have been listening in to your conversations with our medium – and we are so pleased that we have arranged your friendship here. You and Bob are going to work well together. And - we are most pleased to be involved in this project.

Fletcher has been inspiring each of you – to advance the truths of the Spirit World. Do you know – that over here we often look in upon the Earth – and we think to ourselves – we say – or I should say - I say to myself – "Hmm, if I could reincarnate and return to the Earth what type of person would I be?" And I often think that if I ever were to go back – I would be an Indian – and be born in India.

I feel that in that country – in India - there is the greatest amount of spirituality that exists upon the Earth. The Indian people are very poor in the material sense – but they are very VERY wealthy spiritually. Even though I was an atheist in my last life – and a mocker - I saw their advanced knowledge and wisdom. So – I should think – that if I were to go to the Earth again – I would most definitely return to India.

It's important that a soul thinks about its future lives, as well as its past lives. So many humans spend all their time reflecting backwards – but – what about forward looking? This is important – just as well – don't you think?

Tom: Yes, I totally agree. We must take the time- and make the internal effort - to look to where we are going – and not be so obsessive about where we have already been.

Rose: Within each human – there exists a lot of energies in the soul. I've learned this about my soul as well. Every day - the soul is either moving closer to the Light – or moving away from it. Each time we chose a life – an incarnation – we move a little more in our knowledge - through our experience.

Some humans – however - use their incarnations for vile behavior. What a shame that is! It is only when you leave the body that you come to understand the growth or lack thereof – of the soul. I so often stop and I say to myself, "Rose, remember how much you used and wasted your last life. You used up all your opportunities for purposes of selfishness." Each soul must eventually choose to go through this kind of self-reflection.

Do you know, I looked in yesterday on an advanced spirit over here. You know – there are different levels of our reality. Your progression is earned, not given. So, I went to visit with this advanced spirit who I had heard had returned from the Earth – with great advancement of the spiritual soul. And when I saw him – his Light was glowing so brightly – that even my eyes were taken aback by it. You see, our eyes look to the Light always – but each soul's Light is brighter or dimmer – depending on their level of growth.

It is true that over here one cannot hide one's true self – for it is apparent for all to see. My Light is not quite as bright as Fletcher's Light. But – then – I've only recently been here. There is no judgment in the Light. It's not like one soul sees another and says, "Oh, I'm superior and you're inferior". No –it's not like when we were on the Earth and created judgments. You see – in our world – judgment is only given in love. And - even the word judgment is not quite the word I wish to say. We are told to love and understand each other – and to talk to each other.

You know – when I was on the Earth – in my time - people were more helpful to each other. There was support of each other – a give and take - on any given day. But now - I don't find that so much anymore – when I visit the Earth - and look in on people's lives. It's different today. In this world today – I find many of you living more and more separate from each other.

In my day – it is true – that there was a class structure. But, we were taught - that even though we were privileged – we still had to have compassion on the poor. And I was taught that. It was one of the few lessons that I did get in that lifetime. And – I did give a lot of money to hospitals and to charities. Mind you - sometimes I wasn't very kind to my contemporaries – but – even so – I tried to remember to give to those in need.

I do wish that the people upon the Earth in these present days would go back to – at least to - the way we treated each other in our times. For the lessons that we learned stay with us. I was taught to have consideration and compassion for those who were not as privileged as my family was. I was told to be kind to them. And I suppose – now that I think of it – I was more kind to the poor and the lower classes that I was to those in my own class. I was not so kind towards people in the higher classes. What happened was that competition and vanity overtook me – my dear.

Do you know how much money I spent on my clothes and dresses? I tell you, I don't even think that most people could spend that much money today on clothes with the present prices. One year, I spent over a hundred thousand pounds on my wardrobe, on shoes and hats and coats and dresses. I don't even know how much that would be in today's money. But, a hundred thousand pounds in my time was quite a bit of money. Hold on – Fletcher is here and would like to say something. I shall return shortly, my dear.

Tom: Thank you Rose.

Fletcher: Oh hello there – give us just moment. There is a lot of electrical energy in the atmosphere today which is giving us a bit of trouble. It is affecting us with some static. The good thing though – is that we ARE getting in and out of our medium's body without too many problems. Our medium's vibration is holding steady. He'll be alright.

Anyways – I was listening in to Rose's conversation. You know, she raises a very important point. The future lives of humans must always be considered as well - because - you are on an eternal journey. Sometimes you are looking to the past - and sometimes you'll be looking only to the present – but occasionally - you will have a glimpse into the future. And you think, "Oh well, if I don't do so well in this life, maybe God will give me another chance." And the truth is – that He will.

Each life is allowed unlimited chances for growth and success. Over here, we want everybody to get a promotion. It's kind of like – you know – you've got to climb the ladder. We don't see this as a competition. No - we just see it as a climbing up the ladder of "self". We've ALL got to be looking within ourselves. Even those of us who are spirit guides must do an ongoing inventory - by looking within ourselves - to understand - where are we - in relation to the Light.

We must ask, "Where is our Light?" If a guide's Light is not right, and not bright, then how can he impart the Light of God to his charge? And so, you must always be asking yourself, "Who am I talking to on the Other Side?" You've got a lot of spirit people around you – and so – we want you to ask, "What is their Light? What am I receiving? Is my Light in tune with their Light?"

What I am saying is that each Light, hopefully, will be working together with other lights. I like to think of it this way. It's as if we each have a torch – you know – that we shine on each other. I illuminate you and you illuminate me. We illuminate each other – and by helping each other this way – we all grow brighter. It is so important that we each try and grow brighter, because, that is how we can help the other.

That is what we are doing as guides. We are trying to help you all to grow brighter each day – and in time – you will! You know, sometimes I think, "Perhaps I should take a vacation from all this work on Earth and return full time to the Spirit World." But, if I did that, my Light would grow dimmer and dimmer.

I tell you, when I worked with Arthur Ford, it was a bit difficult - because he was always hitting the bottle to excess, which gave me such a difficult time. I had such a trying time with him, as I worked to get him to understand that his drinking excesses lowered his vibration. Eventually though – at my urging – he did "get himself together". He did overcome a big chunk of his love of the bottle, and our communications improved.

We are so glad that, with our medium Bob, we don't have such problems. He keeps himself on the right path. Every day we say to him, "Oh, you've got to be watching your path." And he tries. And we try, right along with him.

Remember always, that, what we talking about, is a partnership between our world and your world. It's not a competition or a race. There are some people over here in the Spirit World that still DO think that this IS some kind of a race. They think, "Oh, if I can just get in five more incarnations, then I will be an advanced soul". And they keep petitioning the Council. "Can we go back – can we go back?" But, the Council often tells them that they can't go back until they have fully digested the lessons from their last lifetime.

Even here, in our world - I must tell you - there is still sometimes a little bit of what you would call – ambition. People here still sometimes get caught up in the belief that – more lives equal more growth and more advancement. But – it is the quality of a life and an incarnation that matters, not the number. There are people who have had hundreds of lives, but those lives were shallow lives.

One life well lived, would have been more valuable to them for their growth, than a hundred squandered. So, on those days when you are reflecting back and you think, "Oh, I can only recall that I've had five lives", don't be thinking that you are a young soul, or that you don't have enough experience. This is not true. Don't be so harsh on yourself, because it is the quality of the lives you live, NOT the number that counts. There is a lot of bantering about on the Earth today that says, "Oh they've had over six hundred lives, so they must be a very advanced, old soul." But, all that really matters is the quality of the lives lived.

You know, Rose – in her last incarnation – basically wasted her whole lifetime. And she had to pay a terrible price for all the damage that she did. Would it have been better for her to have forty lives like that one? Or, only one very good life? You see, she could have advance greatly, if she had used that life more wisely. She lived forty years in that lifetime and basically wasted all of them.

It breaks our hearts over here, when we look at the people on Earth and see humans wasting their lives, chasing after all these things that are nothing but vanities. Rose can tell you herself that all the prestige and financial wealth in the world don't count for anything. It's ONLY the kindness in your heart that matters.

Do you ever think about your students and wonder, "Did I make a difference?" Well, I can tell you, from our world, that we can still see some of your students. There are students you taught many years ago who have already crossed over and they are growing. Some of them have already begun coming back. You might reincarnate – yourself – with them again in future lifetimes – and continue the cycle.

Each day is a journey – and we need many, many players in this. So, don't think that it's just isolated you. It's you – AND your students and your family – and all of us – over here – working together to accomplish the growth that is necessary. Did you have some questions for us tonight?

Tom: First of all, I want to just thank Bob and you for finding me this summer. I've been calling out for spiritual guidance and you heard me. What a miracle this is!

Fletcher: Oh yes, we've been here. We are pushing you along.

Tom: The first time we talked, three weeks ago when you introduced yourself through Bob, you talked about a new book that I would be working on between now and December. Can you give me some clarity about this new book project?

Fletcher: Well, this book idea is coming from a lot of sources. It is true we DID encourage this thought process – but it's not just from us. Your own Higher Self has been talking to you. As you have been doing more of your own spiritual work, your own Higher Self has been bringing up the truth about your incarnation here. Part of that, as you already know, is that you are supposed to be writing and teaching the world about our world. And I must say— we are most pleased to be inspiring you in this.

We've been talking to our medium here and telling him that he needs to be a little more public in his work. It is time for him to push out a little bit more - to get "out there" more, and so, we DID arrange for the meeting between you two. This was in order that you might work together. We don't have an exact plan that says, "It has to be this way or that way." But, we feel that each of you will serve each other well.

You know, you will be doing our medium a great service with this book, for this project will help his name become more known. And he will be doing you a great service by allowing you to connect with us audibly, through these transmissions. And so, we feel that each side is benefitting here. And – this interaction is for the good of both of you. Your Higher Self has been prompting you to take this path, and we have been directing you to be aware of that Self, as well.

We have told Bob that he has our blessing to go forward with this book. We've been wanting him to be out there and published. I've got to say that - as a spirit guide - I DO like to see my messages in print. I helped my previous charge, Arthur Ford. I helped him write books and I'd like to help in that way again.

This is because, on my journey, as a spirit guide, I am supposed to communicate. And so, it is in our interest that we do this together. It is part of my journey as a guide, and it is part of our medium's journey as a Spiritualist, and it is part of your journey as a scribe and a writer and a teacher of spiritual truths. We are all benefitting and you have our blessing. We'll be with you as you are sitting and relaxing and just looking out your window.

Tom: I could feel your words talking to me all week.

Fletcher: See how advanced you are. You ARE already hearing us more and more clearly. I am so glad because we want this for you. We try to communicate our guidance to many people, but they don't get our messages because they let our words bounce right off them. We don't want to be too harsh on those who don't hear us however, because they are doing the best they can, given their level of awakening.

That is another reason why we want to teach and communicate through this book project. This is true. We have been trying to get our message out to a lot of people. Our medium has been quite good at being open to letting us come through. His crowds have been growing, so his work and our teaching efforts ARE getting out there. But we have been saying to him, "You need a bit more of push here." And so we have arranged this book project for both of you.

Tom: Well then, I will continue to record and transcribe these talks, as long as you want me to. I kind of feel like Robert Butts when he began transcribing the Seth books. This type of communication between dimensions is a real "dream come true" for me - and I am very excited. The Earth really needs your lessons of Light, right now.

Fletcher: And it IS our intention to bring the Light on through. Hold on. Just a moment here. Someone else is here to speak with you.

Rose: Hello, this is Rose.

Tom: It's good to hear you again Rose. Welcome!

Rose: I cannot stand by just listening because I am becoming more and more excited by the whole idea of this project, I must say. Do you know – for me – to have my words published – makes me wonder if I'm even worthy of that. But, I will accept the great blessing that you and our medium are offering me, as we move forward.

Tom: Your message last week, about fashion and clothes being so unimportant when based on vanity and self inflation, was really interesting to me, because our culture has become materialistic. So many of us really DO still think we are what we wear and how we look. Perhaps, we are even more caught up in this illusion of appearance, that even in your time.

Rose: It is SO true. And, it distresses me greatly because I see so many people following the very path that I myself took, a path of vanity and self importance.

Tom: Shirley MacLaine told me in our interview, that many of the young people she meets are only interested in whether or not she is wearing a labeled outfit. She says they are much more concerned about what she is wearing than the metaphysical world view she is trying to share.

Rose: Please convey this message to Ms. MacLaine. She must keep speaking her truth because those younger people about her - who seem to be blinded to her reality - will eventually begin to see. Next year there will be a breakthrough for her - in January. There is a wonderful young lady she worked with, her name is Cameron Diaz. Her journey of spirit will be greatly influenced by Ms. MacLaine. And so, please let her know that she has accomplished much more than she will ever know, just by her presence in people's lives.

The younger generation, as much as they wish to be in the façade of the material world, do need what she teaches. They need her truths, and whether she is aware of it or not, she has made a positive impact. Each of those people she has worked with, especially those who are still quite young, will receive her message at whatever level they are able. The seeds of her truth will sprout – I assure you.

Jennifer Anniston is one as well who is beginning a new phase of her spiritual journey. Yes. Ms. MacLaine has no idea of how much influence she has already had on that talented young lady. Watch, in the coming year, for you will see her making great progress in her spiritual journey. Please let Ms. MacLaine know that we will be helping her as well. There are about her many spirits and guides. And also those extraterrestrials are even now with her, helping her.

Please remind Ms. MacLaine that her words are not going into nothingness, but are being stored in the hearts of those with whom she is present. Her vibration is influencing those around her in a very positive way, even when words are NOT being used. She does not even need to speak as much as simply be present, for in her vibration are many of those from our world who work secretly and silently behind the scenes. Let her know that even when she goes and makes a public appearance, and even when she doesn't feel that it is appropriate to speak about our world of Spirit, we are present there. We are working and influencing the very people who she thinks have no awareness of - or faith in our world – silently. We are with her.

Tom: I will send these words to her in an email.

Rose: You are most kind. Do it however you wish. I'm not familiar with your new technology. I still like to write with a pen. Hold on - Fletcher is here and he wishes to add something.

Tom: Thank you Rose.

Fletcher: Oh hello there. This is Fletcher. I want to follow up here on what Rose was saying about Ms. MacLaine. She has been around all of us before, because has had many past lives where she herself was a medium. And so her vibration is more naturally attuned to Spirit. You could say that she is a medium even when she is not trying to be one. We were always around her when she was performing upon the stage. Not just me, but a lot guides from our world were with her when she was dancing. There was – in particular – the spirit of a ballerina from Russia - who was one of her principle guides while she danced.

If you were to ask her, "When you were moving in your dance, did it ever feel that you were moving in harmony with something invisible?" And - she would probably say, "Yes." Because, as she moved in her dance, the world of Spirit was moving with her. She became great, but NOT by chance or good luck, as she likes to think, but because of pure guidance and openness to Spirit. The more she allowed herself to be guided by Spirit, and the more she danced WITH Spirit, the more she danced with beauty and grace. And each time that she would act so brilliantly upon the stage, or in a movie, it was because she was so open to the vibration of the Spirit. She herself – in very many ways – is a channel. And I believe, on a deep level, she knows this.

If she can but keep working and acting as a conduit, she will impact even more people. For her, sometimes, she gets a bit frustrated because she feels that nobody is really hearing her. But, ears are being opened than she not is even aware of. There are people listening in to her, who would not have been introduced to the reality of the Spirit World otherwise. And so, please let her know that she is doing a great service to humanity.

Hold on, yes – alright. Did you have another question for us?

Tom: I can't think of one right now.

Fletcher: Good, then, I have a special guest here who wants to talk to you. Give us just a moment. We are going to try and bring him through for you. Rose, can you assist me? (Deep breathing and sighing.)

Edgar Cayce: Hello, can you hear me?

Tom: Yes, very well.

Edgar: Well, this is the first time I've ever come through our medium like this. I suppose I should introduce myself. It's not polite to just appear in a person's life without proper introductions. Perhaps you will recognize me. You've read my books. My name is Edgar Cayce.

Tom: Oh, hello Mr. Cayce. Wow, what a thrill this is for me! I have read books about you and your work.

Edgar: This medium is not used to my energy and so we must be very careful with him. I can tell you that from our world – what you are and our medium are doing right now - IS of the Light. When I was alive and on the Earth, I often questioned – and asked myself, "Does the Master Jesus want me to do this kind of spiritual work?" I had a lot of fear at first - because I was concerned – that it might be the influence of demonic forces. My own family even questioned it. We were devout Christians at that time, and we wanted to be assured that I wasn't being used by the so-called "forces of darkness".

The assurances we asked for, came as requested. I was taught over the years that the spirits that were coming to me were most definitely of the Light. The spirits would approach me and talk to me often - all through my life. And I must say here, that I knew intuitively, they were always GOOD spirits. They were always loving and helpful, ALWAYS! I could actually see some of them, when I was a boy, when I was out playing. I could not understand why my friends could not see them as well. I learned in time that I was a different from the rest of the boys. I suppose you could say that I was just a little bit "touched in the head". That's how they talked about it back. They would say, "Oh that Edgar, he's just a bit touched in the head, he is." But, I didn't mind.

I actually wanted to be a great preacher. I was inspired by Moody. He would travel and preach and I wanted be like that. I truly wanted to be a preacher, I did. I had no idea however, how big God really was, though. I always thought to myself that God was what I understood Him to be. I really did think that I understood God, the God that was described in the Bible.

I read the Bible often and I must say that it DOES have a lot of wisdom and truth. But, it's only since I've come over here that

I've understood how far truth goes beyond that book. Oh, the Bible is truly a blessed book, it is. But now that I am here in the Spirit World, I have had the great privilege to see Jesus Christ, my Master – face to face. I tell you, I could not believe, when I left the body . . . (he sighs). . .

Let me digress. I was warned early on in my last life, to take care of myself and to better prepare myself for the day when I would cross over. There were many Spiritualists going around in those times who talked to me about the Spirit World. I was not a Spiritualist however, and I did not go along with the Spiritualist teachings. I was a Christian. And yet, those Spiritualists would say to me, "Mr. Cayce, you need to be careful because you are overstraining the body." I didn't pay attention to them though.

I did readings every single day, day in and day out. Many times a day, I would do readings. And, I did not listen to the Spiritualists. I hate to say it but, I actually judged some of them as not being of God. I hate to admit it, but I did judge them – I did! But, the truth is, that they knew about the energy of the Spirit World in a way that I did not. Now I am able to share with you - from my present perspective – that there is IN you - the Light of Spirit - that is revealing more truth to you every day.

Back when I was alive, I didn't completely understand the voices that would come through me during my trance. So, in the very beginning I had to ask myself, "What is this that is coming through me? Is it a demon?" As a good Christian, I had to consider that possibility. But, I saw the teachings, and the value of the assistance being offered through me, and I could tell that people were being healed. I said to myself, "How is this happening, that people are being helped in this strange way? How and why IS this happening? How is this possible?"

My wife, she used to say, "Now Edgar, I don't understand what you do – or HOW you do what you do - but I know you are helping." In the early days, she herself wondered and questioned, as I did. But, then she came to believe fully in the value of my readings. Somehow – through it all - I knew that I was serving the higher Spirit World, and I eventually came to an understanding, that went far beyond the belief systems of my church.

Tom: I read "The Sleeping Prophet" when I was a teenager – so I can tell you that your life story certainly helped me understand the strange metaphysical experiences that I was having back then.

Edgar: We are so pleased to be here with you. I am also very pleased to be able to come through this medium – because his guide Fletcher is a good friend of mine. Over here, we live in a vast world with a wide variety of friendships. I don't believe, when I was upon the Earth, that I understood exactly what Heaven was. I still don't call this realm the Spirit World, as much as I like calling it Heaven. I grew up calling this realm Heaven, and that is what I still call it, even now.

We DO eventually outgrow old terms and old definitions, however, once we get over here. So, I must say, that Heaven is very different than what we imagined when we were still upon the Earth. But, you know, the things that I used to experience on the Earth - and the visions that I had while there - they all came to give me a broader understanding of this world. This is the truth. The first being I saw over here was Jesus Christ and He said to me, "Well well, you have been waiting to see Me all your life." It was a wonderful way to be welcomed here.

I am going to be coming to you and speaking to you a little more regularly, as much as I can. I just wanted to say hello to you today. I can't be staying in this medium's body too long because Fletcher is telling me to step out so he can rest. Our medium is not yet completely used to my vibration. I just wanted to briefly greet you – however – and express my heartfelt gratitude to Fletcher and our medium for having given us this wonderful opportunity to meet in this way. So, I just wanted to say, "Hello" today to you while I have this brief opportunity.

Tom: Thank you very much.

Edgar Cayce: It's been wonderful being here and I so enjoyed meeting you in this way. I look forward to further conversations. Keep eating those blueberries, for they will heal those floaters in your eye.

I received my healing techniques, not from my own mind but from the Spirit of God, the Higher Self and all those wonderful blessed souls who volunteered to come through me. There was a great council that would speak through me many times, and I am still in communication with them. I do believe that I will be permitted by this medium's guide to bring over much more information from them. And, perhaps some of the spirits that worked with me will come through and assist us in this project, as well. So, I would consider that a privilege and a pleasure and an opportunity to help.

Tom: Well, as you know, our civilization is going through tumultuous changes so we really do need help from spirit people like you.

Edgar Cayce: You know, I served the Master always. And I continue to do so. Fletcher wants to say something . . .

Fletcher: Oh hello there, this is Fletcher. Give us just a moment here. Edgar Cayce carries a new vibration for our medium's body to get used to – so we have to be extremely careful here with him. The power is diminishing now, so we aren't going to stay much longer. But – I believe that Rose has something she would like to add before we conclude.

Rose: Hello, this is Rose. Well, you know, it has been such a pleasure being here with you this evening. I myself truly enjoyed hearing Mr. Cayce, as well. I knew of him, when I was on the Earth and I only wish that I had listened to his teachings more when I was I alive. But, now that we are both over here in the Spirit World, I have had the extraordinary privilege of seeing him and meeting him – often. This has been a great treat for me. I have also - since arriving here - been able to meet many of the other greatest minds who once lived on the Earth.

I have met and talked with some of the greatest beings to ever incarnate on Earth, including some of those who lived in many different times and eras, not just when I was alive in the early Twentieth Century. Perhaps Fletcher will let more of them come through. I cannot say, because Fletcher is really the "gatekeeper" for our medium. And though it is his decision, I will encourage it, I must say.

Tom: Well, we here on Earth need all the help you can offer.

Rose: We are so pleased to be here. And I DO hope that you will bring my message to those who will receive it, so as to bring more souls into our world of Light. I don't wish for anybody to return to that place where I spent so many Earth years in darkness. But, you know, so many young people on the Earth, as well as many in the older generations, have lost their way. But, I see a time of great return TO the Light - and so it gives me great inspiration– to do my part to assist in this effort.

We are so very pleased that you are hearing our voices and that you are willing to try to rescue all those who are perishing. Perishing may seem to be a word that sounds strange to you, but if you could see it from our world – you would agree. It is as if people are walking into a great chasm – a chasm of darkness. Oh, we know that everyone has a little spark of the Light within them - which can't ever be completely extinguished. But, it can be greatly dimmed, almost to the point of seeming to perish. But, you are helping to illuminate souls and minds and spirits and we are SO pleased – that there are those on the Earth like you and our medium – who will do this work. We will bless you greatly. You are both – blessing us – in turn - by listening to us - and letting us speak to the people of the Earth through you.

Tom: I'll be listening to you all week Rose - out there - lying under those coconut palm trees on Waikiki Beach. I'll be listening to you whispering to me through the trade winds, and through the waves. I'll try and stay as open as possible . . .

Rose: And I promise that I will there be with you too. I shall come again often, my dear. My name is Rose.

Fletcher: Oh hello, this Fletcher here. We've been monitoring the body of our medium and the vibration is dropping a bit, so we will having to leave his body for now. We don't want to overtax our medium's nervous system. But, we so enjoy our conversation today, and we will be coming back again soon.

We must be very careful with our medium. In fact, we often make his sit down and put his feet up and rest. And he listens – because he's not fighting us like he did in the early days. We are pleased with him. When I started working with Bob, I thought, "Oh my, I've got another Arthur Ford on my hands, here." Arthur Ford was as a bit stubborn you know, and sometimes he would argue with me and do everything that he shouldn't be doing'.

In the beginning, we encountered a little of that with Bob, as well. We would tell him, "Don't go out of the house today, you need to stay in", but he would go out anyway and then he would become overtired the next day and put strain on his body. But, now he listens better and we are very pleased with him. We love working with him.

Anyways, our power is starting to become depleted here so we want to tell you how much we enjoyed talking with you and we look forward to coming back again. This is Fletcher.

Bob: (Sighing deeply, gasping for breath.) When I come back from channeling I feel so spaced out. I'm not exhausted though, just dizzy. Coming out of a trance is like getting off a roller coaster. How did it go?

Tom: It was amazing. Thanks, so much. All I can say is "wow".

Bob: I need to ground now. Sometimes after I channel I feel really hyper. Tonight, I'll probably be up half the night because I feel so charged up. But, that's ok. I don't mind.

Tom: Did you realize it when Edgar Cayce came through?

Bob: Yes, I DID feel his vibration. And I heard him say the word "Cayce". And I thought, "Oh my God, he's coming through."

Tom: The first part of this that I'll transcribe this week will be the message that Fletcher and Rose gave for Shirley MacLaine, about all the wonderful work she is doing with the young people in her life. I told them that I would email it to her.

Bob: Send it to me first, so I can see what they said. I didn't hear that part. But, I totally trust my guides, so I'm sure their message will be fine. I'll call you again you next Wednesday, same time, same station for the next session.

Tom: Fabulous. My body is vibrating so strongly now –after today's downloading - that I need to go to the beach to just calm down. Thank you. See you next week.

Bob: We'll meet you then. Bye.

BOB HICKMAN POSTSCRIPT:

Wow! Just when I think I can't be any more amazed—then a new spirit speaks through me—Edgar Cayce—known in his day as "The Sleeping Prophet". I find the irony of the situation typical of the Spirit World. When alive, Edgar Cayce would go into trance to speak spiritual messages. Now 65 years after his death, I go into trance in order that he can speak in an awakened state. What can I say except this was an amazing experience for me to behold. I think the guides are testing the limits and pushing me to grow in my channeling abilities. Up to this night, I had resisted letting anyone else through except for Fletcher, Rose, and Orion. But now—here was Edgar Cayce!

Hearing of Mr. Cayce's early struggles with accepting his psychic abilities was a blessing for me. I think anyone who seriously undertakes this profession often has doubts and fears and wonders if this is all really occurring, or if one has gone completely insane. I always say to those who sit with me in séances, "Just because a spirit says something, does not mean you are obligated to follow it, or even believe it, as death does not necessarily bring enlightenment, just a change from the physical body to the spiritual body...Now, that spiritual body has a greater chance to have access to the hidden mysteries and ascended guides and masters, but it is up to them to use that chance of access for their own growth." Fortunately, I have had the good fortune to only draw to myself the highest of spirit guides. As I study the transcripts I feel that I am beginning to know Fletcher and Rose more intimately, and I can clearly see that they are particularly interested in serving Tom as well. This makes me happy, for I know that Tom will greatly benefit from this connection, as I have over the last few years.

The evening was especially nice as I enjoyed having Tom interview me about my early days as a younger medium. It's funny because I don't think being a psychic-medium is included "Career Options" at most schools, yet somehow those of us called to this work find our way to it. Being a psychic-medium is not just a job—it is a calling. One that I take quite seriously and I even hold a ministerial license as a legally ordained minister in the Commonwealth of Virginia.

CHAPTER THREE
WISDOM OF THE AGED

August 20th, 2008

BOB HICKMAN PREVIEW:

Tom and I gathered this night after he returned from his trip to San Francisco where he lived and taught for many years. San Francisco is also where he was inspired to write his first book "Uncle Tom's Classroom" which is a profoundly moving book about Tom's transformative work in the inner city public school system.

It was a hot, muggy summer night in Washington, DC when we sat down together, but before I was even in trance, you could already feel the spirit energy buzzing around the room. As I dimmed the lights and got comfortable in my chair, I could tell the guides were eager to come through. I hoped they would be leading us on toward more amazing teachings and revelations. Here is what happened that night:

Bob: Welcome back from your vacation. Are you ready for today's session? I can feel that the spirits are eager to begin, and I am full of energy tonight.

Tom: I am more than ready. But, I just have to tell you Bob, that I am so excited about this whole adventure and so appreciative. What an honor this is for me to be transcribing the words of your spirit guides for the general public! So, if you and the spirits are ready for another session, so am I! I can't wait to hear what Fletcher and Rose have to say this week!

Bob: OK. Just give me a moment here. There's a lot of electrical static tonight, but I think we'll be able to keep our contact open. I'll see you after the session. (He sighs... breathing deeply).

Fletcher: Oh hello there, this is Fletcher. Can you hear me?

Tom: Yes I can. It is wonderful hearing your voice again.

Fletcher: It is good to be back with you. As our medium said, there is a lot of electrical energy in the air tonight, but we'll see if we can't tone down our vibration a bit – so as not to interrupt this contact. As we said before, our energy can sometimes blow out his electronics. We must always be careful – therefore – NOT to overtax either our medium OR his electronic machines.

And so, Mr. Berg, what would you like to be talking about tonight? We know you have a long list of things you want to discuss. We've seen you writing it . . . (laughing).

Tom: I just got back from my "holiday" in San Francisco (as you and Rose call it) and it made me realize - more than ever - how much I have missed the companionship of my old friends from the mainland.

Fletcher: Oh yes. Friendship is a gift from God, you know. Each human being, no matter how much they think they are self-sufficient, in the end, they are designed for companionship. So many people on the Earth today think that they are being self-sufficient, but really, what they are being, is stubborn. This is because they don't want to spend the time to develop a friendship. You know, a friendship takes work on both parts.

But, I think that you are in the right place now and that you are ready for more friendship. We kind of had to let you go through a period of isolation so you would appreciate what we are going to be bringing to you. During your trip to San Francisco, you had a little preview of what you've been missing (and what we will be bringing you soon.)

Tom: My friends were so wonderful to me in San Francisco, that I realized how much I've been missing friends here in the islands. I am so grateful that Bob has allowed you all to come to me in this way. I was quite lonely before I met you, but I have to admit – that I'm feeling much better. To have friends from the Spirit World is a real miracle – one that I never expected.

Fletcher: We are also most pleased. When I was growing up in Canada, I never got to visit either San Francisco, or Hawaii. I would have liked to have had a swim in your ocean.

But, that's alright, because over here in the Spirit World everything is so beautiful. We have natural beauty here – somewhat like yours – although ours is more pure, full of Light and immortal. The lakes are pristine. There is no pollution here at all. When people go fishing, the fish like to be caught, but they never die. Everybody puts them back. There is no death over here.

This leads me into an important lesson that I would like to impart to you - about the material world. We want you to understand the difference between the Eternal, versus the temporary. Those of you who are living in the material world, when you are looking about, you see that everything seems to end up being in a state of decay. If you were to look at your old bicycle, you'd be seeing that it is rusting a bit. If you look at an old car, you would also see a bit of rust around it. Even the finest cars will eventually fall into decay. The human body also seems to decay and break down. This is the way of the physical world.

You know, if you would be taking stock of your body, you would see that it is not as elastic as it used to be. The bones start to hurt a little and the skin sags a bit. This is what life is like for most people in your material world. It's one of aging and apparent decay.

Sometimes humans get bitter about this process known as aging. They say, "Oh, if only I were twenty years old again." But, we want you to understand that death is not the end of anything. It is instead - the ultimate door to eternal life. So, we see physical aging as one way we wean you humans off of your addiction to being in the physical body. What you call aging is how we move you closer to considering the eternal qualities of the Spirit World.

Tom: Wow, that's a brilliant way of looking at aging. We live in a culture right now, here in America that tells us in many ways, every day, that aging is wrong and even inappropriate. So, tell me more about how YOU see aging.

Fletcher: Well, you know. It has not always been this way on the Earth. Over here I get to study the Akashic Records and I've been doing some history studying. Do you know, that back in the early days of mankind, back in the Babylonian and Egyptian times, age was considered to be a sign of great nobility and power. If you were to have told an old man that you were going to dye his hair or offer him a face lift, he wouldn't have taken well to that, because he was proud of his age.

You see, each human being has a certain span of years on their charts, which make up each lifetime. And, so – what happens is that we are born into the body. The body grows and matures and then it goes on and starts to decay. This is the natural order of things. But, many people don't want to age and they resist it. As you look about, you see the younger generation judging anybody over a certain age. This illusion in your society is going to have destructive consequences down the road.

Now, we don't mind when you try to stay healthy and keep fit. There is nothing wrong with trying to look your best at whatever age you are. In fact, that is encouraged, because the body is your vehicle while you are on the Earth. The body should be honored, taken care of and preserved. But, what we are talking about is an attitude in your culture that says - you are MOST valuable when you are young and beautiful. This distraction is an illusion that will lead to much destruction.

There are a lot of young people who will have a difficult time aging, and will fall into despair, because they don't have the spiritual fortitude to make it through the body's many transitions. There are already some young girls who are determined to starve themselves because of their attitudes about what is beautiful. But what happens when their hair turns grey? They could dye it, that's true. But, eventually, no matter how much effort one puts into looking young, there will come a time for aging.

Those who have not developed an awareness of the Immortal Self, and the physical process known as growing old, will feel like aging is a most destructive time, and this perception will lead to anxieties . Each Soul, you see, must make itself aware of its life's journey. This will be more difficult for many young people today, because they are atheists. I am not faulting them here, because I myself was an atheist when I was a young man. Even when I died, I didn't believe, until I crossed over.

Many young people today are going to live a long time, which means that they are going to experience aging. It's not like in our day, when people died at a younger age. These young people of your day think that they are going to be youthful forever and that they are always going to be beautiful. Oh, this idea of the superiority of youth over other stages of life is just an illusion of the material world. (There is a slight pause as if Fletcher has stepped away.) Rose is here and wishes to say something.

Tom: That is brilliant Fletcher. Thank you so much.

Rose: Hello, this is Rose, can you hear me?

Tom: Yes, hello Rose. It's really good to hear you again.

Rose: You know, I couldn't help but listen in to this conversation and I have to say, even in my day, I was filled with vanity. So I do understand the younger generation. The difference is, that in my day, there was much more respect for the aged. Today it seems that the younger people are not having respect for the older generation, and do not understand them.

I remember one day, when I was on the bus in London. I saw an old woman get on the bus. Then, I noticed a young man and a young lady help the old woman find a seat. Offering assistance to older people was what we thought was proper behavior in our day. It was simply done as a common practice – and we didn't even think about it.

But, today, I see many older people struggling, and there is no such assistance offered to them. Many younger people actually look at the older ones with an attitude of disdain, as if to say, "Oh, what is the value of that ugly old person?" This is not acceptable. Even with all my vanity and the way I "gloried in my own self", I did have a better attitude towards the elderly.

Remember how I told you that I traveled to India? Well, often during my trips there, I saw how the younger people were filled with great veneration for the aged. Once, I saw an aged swami. There are so many, you know. You cannot walk about in India without stepping on a swami. Anyway, I met one swami of about ninety seven years of age, who was approached by a young boy of about twelve or thirteen. He went and prostrated himself before the swami. He bowed and crouched upon the ground and touched his head to the feet of the holy man. I asked the boy why and he said it was because the swami had great wisdom. I said, "Yes, I suppose that at ninety seven years old you would have wisdom." So you see, throughout the world, as in India, there is this awareness, this respect for age.

Tom: It's almost the complete opposite here in America. We have a kind of celebrity culture, where the young and beautiful are worshipped. Then, when the so-called "stars" reach the age of forty of fifty, they are often considered "over the hill" and are quickly replaced in the media, by younger ones. When Madonna turned forty, she commented on this phenomenon, when she said, "What am I supposed to do – put myself out to pasture just because I'm forty?"

Rose: Yet, there is a tendency now in the United States, and I would dare say also in my own England, for the culture - as a whole - to have a lack of interest and respect for the aged. This is because the older people are seen as unimportant and expendable.

My Dear Mr. Berg, you know that, the thoughts about age that were the most dangerous, I can assure you, were the teachings of Adolph Hitler. I became aware - in the late 1930's - that his pogroms started with the disposal of the elderly because they were not considered productive to the Reich. I had a girlfriend who went to Germany, way before Hitler's pogroms became public knowledge. She returned to me and said to me, "My goodness Rose, you wouldn't believe the programs that are being enacted in Germany. "

"What are you talking about?" I asked.

"The Nazis are exterminating the elderly!"

I couldn't believe it at first, so I said, "That's bogus. I can't accept that. It's all rubbish!" But, you know - times showed her words to be true. And, I've come to understand that not only were the elderly people disposed of, but the retarded children as well. They were not the Jewish children - they were the German children that were exterminated first.

So, you see, the younger people who look at the elderly with disdain are in many ways, beginning again the mind-set that destroyed many lives. I must tell you honestly – that I have great concern - that there could another rise of a being like Hitler. Do not think that history could not repeat itself, good Sir.

Tom: I wonder if this isn't already happening in America. It seems as if some people in positions of power and influence over the major institutions ARE teaching the youth to dislike older people and to hate the sacred things of Spirit. It's strange to say but there is a part of our culture that actually seems to hate the sacred. God is presented (by the media) as being either inept, nonexistent, or distant.

I don't think people would admit it – but I saw this disdain for God, clearly - in the school system. Kids were being taught to think ONLY materialistically, and were being brainwashed to ignore the presence and influence of any kind of spiritual influence in their lives. The dominant paradigm of the public curriculum was "get a job and make money". The world of Spirit was completely ignored, ridiculed and even censored.

Rose: I do believe that there is a mind-set against spiritual things that could be dangerous, if allowed to go unchecked. We must, therefore, be ever mindful and utterly on guard.

Do you know that in England we had the brown shirts – no – the black shirts? I even knew one of the leaders briefly. The way they tried to draw the British people into their hateful belief system, was just ghastly – ghastly. They were traitors to the United Kingdom. Please forgive me for bringing up old wounds. It's just so important, you see.

Each soul must be aware of its own thought systems – and account for itself. Each soul must become aware of its own attitudes, and take responsibility for what it chooses to believe is true. I myself was full of vanity and the desire for "self-glory". I even had a bit of disdain for anyone who was not beautiful. It's a shameful thing to say, but true.

As you were saying in regards to your public school system, it is true that many of the governments of the world have given themselves over to extreme materialism. This focus on extreme materialism could be the destruction of the civilizations of the Earth, I do believe. You can see it already happening now, can't you?

Tom: Yes, I can. In our culture today, the dominant paradigm is very materialistic. The sacred dimension of life is almost completely ignored by the media and the other political and economic institutions that govern the way our society thinks and behaves. Thank God there are people like Bob who are courageous enough to reveal the existence of the world of Spirit. We need many more people – like him – who are able to open up communication between the physical and nonphysical worlds.

Rose: Oh, I think you are so right – you are. Hold on, Fletcher is here. Give me just a moment.

Fletcher: Hello there, this is Fletcher. I can't stay silent on this issue. There is a lot more very important information to add here about the physical perspective being far too dominant in your culture.

Just look at all these tattoos that the younger people are putting on their physical bodies today. You see, they get all tattooed up because they are thinking that they are only physical and that their young bodies are going to be living forever. Oh, I don't mind people being creative, mind you, but – if you ask me – the tattoos are reflective of an attitude that worships only the physical, material side of life. Do you understand?

Tom: Fletcher, are you looking through my eyes? Since coming back to Hawaii, I have been noticing so many young people who have practically covered up their whole bodies with tattoos. Since many people wear only bathing suits here – even on the streets – you can see the tattoos. And, I have to admit – that I have been looking at them with some judgment, wondering how they could cover their bodies with so many purple and black tattoos. Some of the tattoos are of demons and serpents - which really make me wonder what they are thinking about and secretly worshipping.

Fletcher: I have been around you and with you , so I can't help but notice this too. Anyways, hold on – someone else is here and wants to talk to you. Give us just a moment. We have to adjust the medium's vibration.

Tom: Thank you very much Fletcher.

Fletcher: Oh, Mr. Tom, you are most welcome.

Edgar Cayce: Hello. Can you hear me out there?

Tom: Is this Edgar Cayce? Hello Edgar!

Edgar: Yes. It is so good to be back there with you. I have been listening in with great rapt attention. You know, when I was alive, people were much more conservative when it came to their bodies. I suppose that I myself was also conservative. People would never walk around with the kind of clothes that you see today. It was quite different back then. There was more modesty in the way we dressed.

Anyway, what I'd like talk to you about tonight, are the many great changes that are coming upon the Earth in the coming years. I want you all to be watching for them. When people have faulted my predictions and said that I was wrong, I want to answer them by saying, that I was mainly mistaken in my timing.

In our Spirit World I can see a lot clearer over here. When I was on the Earth, I was not always the clearest of channels. And, I suppose that every medium on the Earth has this struggle. I am trying therefore to amend my ways of error and bring truth forward to the Earth, where I can, this day. So, while I am present, I wish to bring over to you some more information to clarify and even correct some of my previous words.

Tom: Thank you Edgar. Bob and I are planning on disseminating this information to the world in a book – so please do tell us what we need to know. Thank you.

Edgar: It is so important. Thank you so much for allowing me to be here with you.

I would like to clarify some of my teachings about the world's ancient civilizations. The continent of Atlantis DOES exist, off of the eastern coast of the United States. It will be seen in the coming years. In the next six or seven years there will be some earthquakes and there will be an awareness of a release of energy from that area. Scientists will discover cities that once existed there.

I would also like to say that there is an important connection between the Egyptians and the Atlanteans. There is a submerged pyramid – it is true and it has been reported already by the press – that is off of the coast of Bermuda. This pyramid actually came before – and foreshadowed the pyramids of Egypt. This pyramid will come into great discussion in the coming years, as it is explored and evaluated more officially and formally.

There will be many people in positions of power - who will not want to acknowledge this - and will say that this is fraudulent. Therefore, at this time I should hope that my previous writings will be revealed and my readings quoted - because in them you will find the evidences of the Atlantean culture which I outlined before. I suggest that you be monitoring and researching this material – because my words will come to pass.

There are also some other events that are important to discuss. The Earth is going through a time of great changes. It's strange but even the seasons are shifting. They are going to continue to change, and they will, in the coming years – become truncated. Spring and summer will feel shorter and milder. Those seasons will become more similar until we will hardly be able to tell differences between them. So, when it is August, which should be a hot time, it will feel more like the end of September. And in September it will feel more like October. Do you follow what I am saying?

Tom: Is this because of the so-called "speeding up of time" leading to 2012?

Edgar: It is not so much the speeding of time as it is that major Earth changes are coming. The vibration of Planet Earth is changing.

There is evidence coming upon the Earth that will show that this theory of global warming is true. Humans have created much destruction upon the Earth and so - there will be a balancing act. As they say, Mother Nature will not be soiled. So remember to be watching for the signs.

You know, Jesus always said, "How can it be that one can tell the weather of the coming days, yet not see signs of the coming ages?" And so, those who are wise are watching for the signs of the coming changes on a much larger scale. Today, you may look out your window and believe that it is going to rain. It would be better that each person look within themselves and ask, "Where am I in relation to the harmony of the Earth?"

If you look upon the Earth, as Fletcher and Rose pointed out to this guide, there is great turmoil internally for many people, for they have forgotten the truths of Spirit. But, the important thing is that - each person must eventually come to know the true self that lies within. Humans must wake up to their nonphysical spiritual selves. This is where they can find the truth about who they really are. But, instead of looking within, they are looking outside of themselves for joy. They are looking for happiness in the buying and selling of things.

You know, in the Bible, Jesus said, "In the end times, it will be as in the days of Noah. People will be buying and selling. Just as in the times of Noah, destruction will come upon them." I don't wish to be a naysayer here or a prophet of doom but I am bringing over a reality that is already present. And yet, there is still time. Humanity can still change the course of the coming destruction if it would but change the focus of its consciousness. There needs to be a rebalancing of the physical and nonphysical aspects of life. Humanity must come to a new understanding of the Spirit that lives within. Give us just a moment. Fletcher wants to say something.

Fletcher: This is Fletcher here. Give me just a moment as I adjust the vibration of our medium. There is some interference in the atmosphere.

Edgar: Can you hear me?

Tom: Yes I can Mr. Cayce. I can hear you loud and clear. Thank you. Please go on.

Edgar: Well, thank you so much. As I was previously saying, I wanted you to understand that I am not implying that there will be absolute and total destruction coming upon the Earth. There will be however, changes of a magnitude that for many people on the Earth, will seem like the end of the times. However, if a human being will look within themselves, and will choose the spiritual way – the way of love, the way of forgiveness, the way of self giving, there could be great positive changes.

Remember - as you think, so you will reap. As you sow, you will reap. This is what the Good Book says. So you see, each human being is responsible for their thoughts, beliefs and actions. Your very minds and thoughts affect the clouds above you. You influence the weather on your planet with your attitudes and emotional vibrations.

I should like that one night, while you out upon your balcony, that you sit in your chair and just watch the sky. I want you to focus on one cloud, because, if you will think of the cloud dissipating, you will shortly see it dissipate. It is your own very consciousness that will manifest, and I promise you will be able to do this. I will be there whispering encouragement in your ear.

Tom: I will try it tonight. (Note – I did attempt to dissolve a cloud that very night, and was successful.)

Edgar: It would be a good practice for you to do this exercise. And I would encourage you to teach others this method as well. For, if the humans would raise their consciousness then they would have greater clarity in many areas. Then, some of the destructions that we see building could be greatly dissipated – just like you dissipated the clouds.

If humans were to wake up to their inner spiritual potential and power, I could see that helping some of the coastal areas of the United States that will be experiencing great upheavals. Between the effects of global warming, and the coming tsunamis, there WILL be great changes coming to the coasts of the United States, both east and west.

Tom: May I ask a specific question about that?

Edgar: Please, go ahead my friend.

Tom: Well, I live on the coast here in Waikiki, Honolulu, and I have an apartment here until next summer. Will the cataclysms be affecting this Waikiki area in Hawaii and will it be affecting San Francisco?

Edgar: This destruction, which I have prophesied will not come to pass for several more years. So, you do not need to worry at this time. But, the important point to make – is that - IF you can get the message out that people should raise their consciousness - then much destruction will be averted. All of the coastal areas of North America will be endangered if humans do not raise their consciousness.

Tom: Are you talking about moving to safe places before the year 2012? Do we have until 2012 or 2011?

Edgar: The greatest changes will be after that time. Around 2012, the climactic shift really comes upon the Earth. Some Earthquakes will occur. However, that will only be the beginning. It will not be the culmination at that time. The year 2012 will be the beginning, because, at that point there will be a great shift in the space/time continuum. For, as the ancients have predicted, the calendars of time are closing. One calendar will close and a new era will begin.

Now, this new beginning – this new epoch beyond time - can be one of great joy, prosperity and peace, or it can be one of sorrow, anxiety and fear. But it will be humanity's choice as to which one is created. This is why I urge you to explore your thoughts and the power of your mind by observing the clouds and dissipating them with your inner resolve. You can do it, and in so doing you will be aware of just how one's consciousness can affect change positively.

Tom: I wanted to talk to you a bit more about the power of thought as a manifesting tool. Can you teach us more about the power of our minds and our states of consciousness, in relation to how we create our own realities?

Edgar: Each human being has within themselves – what I would call, mind energy. We are not speaking of the physical brain, though that is important – for it is a motor in a sense. But, the human mind comes from the Spirit and that power is unlimited. This is because inside each human there is spark of Divinity. You can call it God. This is the Higher Power – the Creative Force - that infuses, in-fills and encompasses all life!

You know, when I was alive upon the Earth, this was an idea that was difficult for me to grasp because I was very devoted to my church's viewpoint. They did not teach anything about the dimension of the Inner Self, which is why it took me so many years to understand that I had the Spirit of God within me.

I believed in the idea of the Holy Spirit but – for many years – I still thought of myself as separate from God. This was mainly because of my loyalties to the more fundamentalist teachings of my church. I now understand that I was much more connected to God within my own self than I ever understood while I was alive. But, each person is growing and learning this – at whatever rate they are willing.

It is important that you understand your life charge, which can go in many directions. Your energy and your life charge can take you to the highest levels of heaven of to the very pits of - what you might call hell. How you choose to live this life charge affects how you will think and how you think will affect what your reality.

You see, many people allow themselves to be drawn to darkness. They are drawn towards negativity because that is all they know, being so enmeshed in the material world. Humans come into the Earth and enter into a body which they soon find is very limiting and even decaying. So, naturally, they become veiled in the illusion that they ARE the body. In so doing, they minds are pulled downwards towards a lower vibration.

You know, if we were to raise the vibration of this medium's body too high, we would dissolve him into nothingness and into pure Light. Each person has within them the power to be in the Light and to become consciously at one with the Light. So, your own very mind can raise you up in order that you yourself become that very being which inhabits you. This is your true being - a Spirit Being of Light. Do you understand what I am saying?

Tom: Yes I do. Can you tell us exactly how to think? I mean, what I am trying to say is – is a thought an image or words? How would you teach someone to think WITH God instead of with the race mind of mankind, which is so full of fear at this time? Jung said the collective unconscious was where all those ancient thoughts of fears and hatreds come from. So, what can you tell me about the many levels of thought that are available to choose from – and how to best learn how to think productively and spiritually?

Edgar: The most important thing to remember is that all people progress at different rates. Some people think and see within themselves images and that's alright. The main idea that I would like you to consider - is that you are free to think with love, rather than with fear, anger or hatred. That conscious awareness of freedom would be enough to help you switch your level of consciousness from the darker depths of the collective unconscious to the higher ideas of Spirit and Divine Light.

Tom: I have another question - about anger. I know that Jesus expressed anger at the money changers. So, what should we do when we feel that people are out of line – or even trying to control us? What is the best way to handle people who are unawake or behaving in ways that we would call - inappropriate?

Edgar: My wife used to say to me, "Now Edgar, just come home, sit down and have a good meal". She would try to get my mind off what was upsetting me. There is something to that. What she meant for me to do - was turn away from that which angered me. All during my life, my wife taught me that - when I was angry that I should step away and take time to go within – back to my Inner Spirit, which is still one with Divine Love and Light.

There is a very good reason for this time of retreat. You see, if you are surrounded continually by those people who are negative, self-serving and materialistic, you might start to fall into the darkness, just like them. When you encounter people who are negative and you become angry – remember – that it could be time to retreat. Everybody should have a place of retreat. If you can just go to your own spiritual sanctuary (even if it is in your home) that is where you can just be with God. And, you've got to make it a habit everyday to go to that spiritual inner sanctum.

Tom: To me, Hawaii is like a spiritual sanctuary. But, I get frustrated. Sometimes I get emails from people that are critical of me and do not support me in my almost obsessive desire to free our nation's youth from the public school system "religion of materialism". How do I handle people like that, who do not agree with me or support me, when I need to go over my emails every day? Sometimes, after I read negative (unsupportive) emails, it feels as if my resolve and self confidence become weaker and less focused.

Edgar: You must create a sanctuary within yourself. It is not a geographical place or outside of you. It is a private sanctum, within your Real Self. Sometimes, if you receive such negative communications, you will have to literally move away from the negative comments or unsupportive attitudes. Go within. Even though you may sometimes have to deal with people who sound negative or unsupportive, you must learn how to step away from them emotionally, and return to your place of quietude in order to find yourself (your Real Self) again. The only place where you will ever really find true Self Confidence – is within your real Spiritual Self.

As for what to do about anger - whenever somebody on the Earth would anger me - I would talk it over with God. I used to always ask, "Lord, why I am getting so angry? You told me to always love – to love my neighbor as myself. But, in this case, I just don't feel able to do it."

So, even though I always tried my best to follow the words of the Master, I found it greatly challenging, I must admit. I used to hear the Lord speak to me in my heart and He would impress upon me – He would say, "Edgar, it is not for you to judge your fellow man. It is only for you to love them and forgive them."

And then I would say to the Lord, "Lord I cannot love them. I am just too angry."

But, the Lord would answer me, saying, "Of course you cannot within your human self. That is why I am present." And so I came to understand that I had to ask for God's Love - to love and forgive them - FOR me – and THROUGH me. Because, of my own accord, it was simply not possible. I just could not love and forgive my so-called enemies from the perspective of my human personality – only from the higher, deeper levels of my true Spiritual Self.

Tom: If you were to see people that you know and love going down the dark, negative path, would you tell them or would you just pray for them? What should I do when I see people going towards the "dark side"?

Edgar: I did tell them so. I had to speak my truths. You know, they called me "The Sleeping Prophet", although I was never comfortable with that title. To tell you that truth, I never thought of myself as a prophet. I believed, back then, that a prophet was a grand and glorious being, and I would never put myself in that category. But, I was honored that people took the time to listen . . .

I don't claim credit for any of those readings and healings. I believe now that it was the work of the Spirit. Anyways, as for the people who seem to be going down the path of darkness, you simply have to let them go and turn them over to God. I would always speak my truth clearly – but at a certain point, I always knew that I did not have to support those types of people.

Here is an example of how I handled difficult people. I had a business partner one time, who approached me and said, "Mr. Cayce, I can make you a rich man if you will work with me." And I said, "Well, what would I have to do?" And he answered, "I want you get up on a stage and hide behind some mystic veiled curtains. We will have body guards all around you so you won't be so accessible and in touch with the people. We must make you seem illusive. Then, they will love you even more."

And I said, "But, this is pretentiousness, a bunch of 'show'. And he said, "Yes, we will make you out to be great showmen." And I said, "I am not about being a showman. I am about serving God, and therefore, you may keep your money."

Well, that didn't stop him. He simply would not let up and continued to bother me, offering me more and more money. I would have been a millionaire if I had followed him. But, here in the Spirit world money doesn't matter. If I had given in and worked for that man (and was still living on the Earth) I would have millions to this day. But, the truth is - that I would not and could not do as he asked - because it was not of God. And in so doing, I actually had to end my friendship and part ways, because my true calling was higher than some show. Hold on one minute, Fletcher wants to talk.

Tom: Thank you so much. That was fascinating advice.

Fletcher: Well, hello there. This is Fletcher here. It is so good to be back here. We have to be careful with our medium because he is still isn't fully adjusted to Mr. Cayce's vibration. So, we are trying to be a little gentle with him. Rose wants to say something to you.

Rose: Oh, hello – this is Rose. I have been listening to your conversation with Mr. Cayce. You know, when I was alive I also had a problem with people around me who had negative vibrations. I, of course also was of a lower vibration, but I was still strangely aware of the destructive power of negative people – and - of the negative consequences of allowing such forces to be around me.

Negativity is always destructive. And so, I encourage you to always be mindful of your own vibration in relation to those around you. When you have an encounter with those who are – shall we say 'difficult' – you must look within yourself and ask yourself if you have been affected?" And if you have been affected, then ask yourself, "How shall I return to the Light?

When I speak of the Light, what I mean is – for me the Light is so precious. The Light is so very dear to me, because I wandered in the darkness for so long. Now that I have crossed over into the fullness of that Light, I have great joy and I don't wish to have anybody have an experience where that Light is dimmed or taken away from them.

Guard your interior Self, my dear. Your Spiritual Self is more valuable than any diamonds or gold or prestige upon the Earth. Now that I am in touch with that Spiritual Light within me, I will never let it go. NEVER! So many young people today need to know about the Light. And I hope that you will help them.

Do you know that our medium has found great joy reading your book? And, I must say, I've looked over his shoulder while he has been reading, and I am most intrigued and fascinated with your ideas. It makes me think of when I was a young girl. If only I had had a teacher like you, who would have taught me about my Real Self and the Power of God within me – how different my life might have been!

Your work, Mr. Berg, with the younger people is not through, by any means. I have been shown over here, by your guides, that there are even higher beings around you – guides that you are not yet aware of. There is much more work coming for you that will affect an even larger number of people. Many of your students still remember your name – and in the next few months and years – you will be hearing from them. They will be sending you messages of great joy, for the impact of your lessons changed them. When you see this happen, remember that I have told you this. You are becoming aware of your Spiritual Power and influence.

Tom: You told me that this would begin to happen during my trip to San Francisco. Just last week, when I was in the City, I met one of my students from twelve years ago, who was diagnosed as mildly autistic. He was very shy and withdrawn when I met him, but after a year in Bergland he blossomed forth as the real Super Self I knew he truly was. I helped him get free mentally and emotionally - of all the labels the state of California had placed upon him. He is now earning his masters degree at a major university. He and his mother thanked me very profusely for my teaching, which changed his life. So, thank you.

Rose: You have absolutely no idea or understanding of how much you have served God through your work. But, I assure you there will be even more of your past students coming to thank you. You will become aware of this soon. And so, know that - you have the blessing of our world upon you.

Tom: Thank you so much Rose. I really appreciate your encouragement.

Rose: You are most welcome, my dear. Hold on Fletcher is here.

Fletcher: Oh hello there, this is Fletcher here. Well, you know, we keep seeing a lot of more work for you from over here. You will soon have another book under your belt, our book - but that is only a small part of it. There will be many more books coming here for you – so you'd better be keeping your writing skills going – because you are going to busy in the coming years. Do you have any more questions?

Tom: I was wondering - can you whisper in people's ears now – to help me get me more interviews like the one I had with Shirley MacLaine? So far, she is the only really well known person to support my book - and help me get my ideas into the public conversation.

Fletcher: Oh yes, you can be sure that we are going to be helping with you that. We will be contacting a lot of people who will want to talk to you about your ideas. But - you must get yourself back on YouTube so you can be seen more. In the Earth plane, sometimes action needs to be started to get spiritual energy moving. We are going to be bringing much more energy to you that will begin a shift – a new impulse of energy that is going to be pushing you forward.

The problem with you – if we might say it – and we don't mean to be critical – is that you are a little bit shy at times. You've got to be a more brazen, knocking on doors, showing yourself off and making yourself seen. The public doesn't know you yet –

they don't know your face – and they don't have any knowledge of your book yet. You are going to be much more successful once people start to see you!

When I was on the Earth I was quite brazen. I would put on my army uniform and prance about, showing off for the ladies. We want you to be prancing about – like I did with my uniform on. Use our work together and this quiet time in Hawaii as a staging ground for what is to come. Follow our advice. Complete these transcripts. You are going to have more business than you know what to do with. Our new book will help a great deal.

Give us just a moment here. We'll be following you as you go along, and will be monitoring your progress, so you don't need to be worrying. Do you understand what I am saying?

Tom: Yes, thank you.

Fletcher: What else can we do for you today?

Tom: I feel sometimes that my self confidence is being attacked – and my mission sidetracked - by the people around me who don't believe in me or my work. What should I do about that? Can people who don't see the value of my work actually hurt my progress, or is that just my own imagination? Or, am I blaming others for what I see as my own self doubt?

Fletcher: Don't give other people more power than they really have. They don't have that much influence over your overall life path. It is so important for you to understand that the people who don't see or support your life's calling, OR your value, are merely reflecting your own self-doubts, back to you. These self doubts are actually fears which are coming from your old lower self, fears which you will eventually have to deal with.

Tom: What kind of fears?

Fletcher: These fears are based on a lack of faith in yourself, and are coming directly from your ego. The realization that you must face is - your lower self still has a lot of fear about your progression and success. When you listen to people 'out there' who speak for your lower self or ego - and you believe them and give them power - it becomes an easy excuse to not moving forward. Be careful, therefore, of the negative people that you are drawing to yourself. They are merely speaking for (and as) your own lower self.

When you hear people say that you can't be doing your dream, I want you to rise up into the third eye chakra and the crown chakra so you can feel the power of Spirit coursing through you. Ask yourself, from that perspective, "Do I have a fear here? What or who is my true Self? What is my true path? What does the Light want of me?"

When you get back into the higher chakras, you will suddenly see that the illusions around you are only illusions. They are not the truth about you. Once you understand completely that you have only drawn the naysayers to yourself as an excuse to be holding yourself back – you can decide to stop listening to them. It is sometimes best to lessen or even end those types of relationships.

Depressing people could not come around you if you were not carrying a bit of that low vibration yourself. So, it would be best to speak the truth – and always come from your highest Source. Tell them – AND your own lower self – that it is necessary now for both of you to shift the vibration of your consciousness. You must get off that slippery ground of negativity and get onto some solid rocks. Don't hold yourself back with these false and negative thoughts any longer.

Tom: Is there anything else that you can share with me about the new people that you and Rose said were going to be coming into my life.

Fletcher: Don't be worrying about that because all of that is being aligned for you. When you meet these people – you will know them because of their good energy. We're not going to be taxing our medium's body much more today. We hope you won't mind if we leave soon.

Tom: Yes, Bob is really working hard these days. He tells me that he is putting in long, long days with his clients. Edgar Cayce talked about how important it is that a channel gets adequate rest, so I agree - we must be careful not to overtax Bob.

Fletcher: Yes it's so true. Hold on, someone else is here for you.

Rose: I just had to pop in here to assure that we will be present with you. We shall be assisting you in the coming months– organizing some new relationships. All society used to come to my house in London, because I was known as quite the matchmaker. I was good at bringing people together, and so – even now – I am able to assist in that area. Matching people up together brings me great joy and happiness.

And so, do not fear. Many good things are coming to you, many great blessings of friendship and love. And remember that God will always be with you, helping you.

Tom: Thank you so much Rose. I really appreciate what you and Bob are doing for me.

Fletcher: We so enjoyed being with you here tonight, but now we are going to be stepping out of our medium's body. He needs to rest. Be watching because we will be coming back to you soon. We are about you all the time – so keep talking to us. We are going to be helping you even more. Don't be worrying. You have our blessing always. I will be walking with each and every day of the way. Keep looking within yourself and find the Light and let God bless you, because He is with you every day.

Tom: Thank you Fletcher.

BOB HICKMAN POSTSCRIPT:

What an amazing evening we had. When I returned from trance, Tom had a big grin on his face. He said the guides were bringing over a lot of fascinating information. I remember that I glanced at the clock—over an hour of time had passed! "Where did the time go?" I wondered. The experience of missing time, when I do trance channeling, is something that still amazes me. It seemed like I had just sat down, closed my eyes, and then opened them but a moment later. Not only did I find that an hour had passed, but that so much information had come through without my awareness. Upon reviewing the transcripts a few days later—I was pleasantly surprised to see that Edgar Cayce had indeed again appeared at our sitting that night. I had sensed his presence while under trance. Like a light-sleeper, I do occasionally sense things while under trance conditions, and I had been somewhat aware of Cayce's vibration in my energy field. The good thing was that I felt safe and did not feel overwhelmed by this new spirit who chose to use me as a vessel through which to pour his words of wisdom. As I write this, I am still amazed when I look over the transcripts, and can clearly see how he was present and helping us that night.

I was also fascinated to see how Rose helped us to understand the dangers of the "youth-obsessed mentality" by showing us how this attitude had played out in her time under the evil auspices of Adolf Hitler. "Could we be headed in that direction again?" Perhaps I read too much into the messages, but I couldn't help but wonder if this was a sort of veiled prophecy that Rose was trying to impart.

It also gave me great joy to see that Tom was continuing to have such an easy rapport with the guides. I could sense they were not only working with me now, but were also present for Tom and activating things in his life that would help him expand spiritually, emotionally, and even professionally. I thought about how good our guides are. They see to our complete development and well-being. I knew then that Tom and I were destined to be friends and business partners, for our friendship was truly formed in Heaven and manifested on Earth. It was that reality that brought us together, and led us to this book's creation.

CHAPTER FOUR
MANY WORLDS UNITE

August 28th, 2008

BOB HICKMAN PREVIEW:

This night Tom wanted to start our session with an interview. I am usually nervous about interviews for I usually have some reporter who is just trying to be rude and insulting. Luckily, Tom had met and sat with other trance channelers, notably the world-famous Kevin Ryerson. I have to admit, I was still just a tiny bit nervous. Tom was so kind and truly interested in my trance channeling experience. As I spoke to Tom, I realized that it must seem really strange to the general public what we mediums do. I am not sure that most people realize that we are really ordinary people, who just happen to have this connection. I hoped this interview would allow people to see just how normal we channelers are.

After the interview, I dimmed the lights and settled down and went into a profoundly deep trance. Below is the transcript of our session.

Tom: Bob, could you tell our readers exactly what you experience when you are allowing these spirits to talk through you. Are you completely unconscious - are you in another dimension – or what?

Bob: This is the way I like to explain my experience. Have you ever been lying on a couch watching TV and you start to drift off to sleep? You may hear sounds in the room but you are so far gone that don't respond -because you're not really awake. You may still hear snippets of conversation in the room, but you're not really present. This is what I experience when I channel. I don't go into another dimension – rather – I enter into a deep state of sleep. I feel a shift or current of energy in my body. There is no pain. It just feels like pressure around my back. It feels like the spirits are pushing into me from behind. You know when you are in water and you feel the pressure of the water all around your? It's a little bit like that.

Tom: Do you feel more pressure now that Edgar Cayce is talking through you? This is a big deal that his spirit has decided to come through you to talk with us!

Bob: Yes, it is a little bit harder on my body when he comes in – because I am not used to his energy. But, I trust Fletcher. He serves as my gatekeeper and he wouldn't ask me to do anything that wasn't safe. It is so important to have a spirit guide that you can totally trust – so I feel– that if Fletcher lets Edgar in – then it's going to be OK. I always leave it up to Fletcher as to which spirits come through me.

Tom: I feel the hugeness of what is happening with Edgar Cayce's involvement in our sessions. It is a really, really big deal that Edgar Cayce has chosen to talk with us about these important issues. I've been reading his past work, and what he is doing, is following up on what he channeled many decades ago, especially in regards to many of his predictions about the coming days of change. It is just amazing that he wants to use our conversations as a way to talk to the world once again.

Bob: It shocks me too – frankly - to tell you the truth. I haven't gotten my mind wrapped around the idea yet. I just read your transcripts and say,"Oh my God!" I'm happy and pleased, but the reality of it all has not really sunken in yet. It's probably better this way. I love my spirit guides. They are amazing. What's fascinating is that I can actually feel the energy and the vibration of the guides when I am reading the transcripts. Even if you stripped the names off – you would still know which spirits were talking by their energies.

Tom: I agree. Actually, I sent last week's transcript to my friend Barbara in San Francisco, and she told me that she could feel the energy of Fletcher and Rose, as she read their words. It was as if Fletcher and Rose and Edgar were actually alive somehow IN the words. When I transcribe our conversations I have that same experience, as well. I feel that the spirits are totally present and alive as I listen to the tapes and capture their words for the book.

Bob: You know, as a channel, I've not had the privilege to study what comes through me. So, for me, this is a new and amazing experience.

Tom: It's as if you are the cell phone. That is your function, while I am the philosopher and the scribe. So when we come together - amazing things are bound to happen. Barbara also told me that she could feel the goodness and the love of Fletcher, Rose and Edgar, as she read their words.

Bob: Yes, I always have felt a kinship with my guides, as if they were my very best friends. In fact, whenever anyone asks to meet a spirit guide - that should be one of the main criteria. Your relationship with your guides should be developed in comfort and trust. I asked for my guides to also be my friends, and that is what I got! I sometimes miss Fletcher when I don't feel he is present. The other day I was doing a reading in Leesburg, Virginia, and when I went to contact Fletcher – he wasn't there. I asked, "Fletcher, where ARE you?" and he eventually came to me and told me that he was visiting other spirits, helping some Earth bound souls in Leesburg.

Tom: Wow - that is so cool. I guess we'd better get into the channeling session while we still have enough bandwidth. My internet connection in Hawaii has been sporadic lately.

Bob: OK. We can ask the spirits to help us keep the connection open. Give me a minute now while I go under. (Note - the internet connection did give us enough Skype signal for the entire two hour conversation with the spirits, exactly as Bob said they would – which was a delightful and totally surprising aberration from the previous week of sporadic, weak internet service. I watched as Bob dimmed the lights, closed his eyes and settled into a deep trance state.)

Fletcher: Oh, hello there, this is Fletcher. Can you hear me?

Tom: Yes, it's wonderful to hear you again Fletcher.

Fletcher: It is wonderful to back here with you again, Mr. Tom. Might I say, to begin with, that your vibration is looking especially bright today. As I tune into you even closer, it looks like you have been taking the advice of Edgar Cayce, because I see his energy all around you there.

Tom: Thank you. I have been reading the writings of Edgar Cayce all week. I have a book filled with his channeled messages about soul and spirit and mind power. And, I have been feeling very close to him and you and Rose all week. So, thank you so much for coming into my life. I love you all very much.

Fletcher: We are so glad to be with you as well. Do you know how many humans never even listen for us? So many times we'll be walking about talking to people but nobody is listening. They don't hear us. We might as well be talk'n to the rocks on the ground. But, you know, from our perspective – we see each human being as a Light. And, as Rose has often told you, the Light within you is what we follow. It is that Light that we are most interested in. You see, each human being, on their life's journey, is making that Light a little brighter or a little darker. Some human beings – they tend to – well - run away from the Light because they have forgotten who they really are. Each person has within themselves knowledge of who they are, where they come from, why they're here and where they're going.

The problem is that many human beings – I suppose you could say – actually try to forget who they are. If they remembered who they really were or are - and they remembered all their lives - they might be a little overwhelmed. That's why we put the veil of forgetfulness about them. Oh, there a lot of people on the Earth today who are running about and saying that there is no such thing as reincarnation, but we beg to differ. Past lives are not remembered – not because they didn't happen – but because each soul has to forget the past in order to move forward.

Many people on the Earth in this lifetime suffer from great tragedies, which color their souls and their states of consciousness. These souls who cover themselves with fear and anxiety are actually turning away from the Light, and are moving more and more into the darkness. Each time they turn away from the Light they gradually remove themselves from the healing power of the Light, and they remove a little bit of their consciousness from the Light. If they allowed their consciousness to be more regularly bathed in the eternal Light, they would not only be healed of their current life tragedies, but they would even be healed from those past-life tragedies (which they don't remember). And yet, so many souls don't always choose to let their past sufferings go. You know, after each person dies, they come over here and go through a process of cleansing and evaluation. You might say it is a kind of debriefing. This debriefing occurs for each soul, on different levels. Some souls are not ready to have a full debriefing – however – because they don't want to deal with the past. And we guides are sensitive to that. We never intrude or invade a soul's privacy because that soul's personal experience is between them and God.

If souls don't seek the therapy of the Light, they can't be healed. Some souls are actually a bit rash and they rush back into a new incarnation upon the Earth, and so they complicate their lives. They try to do a new work without having completely resolved the soul's older work. Each soul that comes into this world should come in with a clean slate. But so many souls are like that blackboard. You used to be a teacher and you had a blackboard, didn't you?

Tom: Yes, I did.

Fletcher: Well, you know when you've been writing on the blackboard for quite a while and it's covered with a lot of chalk marks? And remember how sometimes you only half erased the old chalk marks – so that the old words would still be showing up there on the board? Do you understand what I am talking about?

Tom: Yes, absolutely.

Fletcher: Remember those times when you even tried to wash your blackboard – but you found that the old chalk marks were scraped so deeply into the board that they stayed? It's kind of like that when we talk about the soul. Because, old memories become – shall we say – imprinted and impressed on the souls like old chalk marks. Even when a soul chooses new growth, it still carries old trauma into that growth. Here on our side, the soul has time to be cleansed, so it doesn't carry the imprint or the stain of the painful memories into the new incarnation.

But, if a soul doesn't allow itself to by absorbed in the Light, and healed by the Light, it continues to carry that old dark karma. And so, when the soul reincarnates without a thorough debriefing and cleansing, it will carry along with it – not only its most current drama and trauma, but also the older dark karma and faint memories of the other lifetimes. And sometimes, those too – end up being a lot for a soul to be taking on. That is why we encourage all souls who come over to our world, to spend time to relax and rest – to find the Real Self again once again, and to be healed - before entering into a new incarnation.

We also want you to understand that, even in your current life, you would do well to spend more time in meditation. The more time you spend in meditation, the closer you move to the Light.

Your meditations will help in your overall healing process, so that when you do get over to our side there is not so much to do. Now, just a moment, somebody else is here.

Tom: Thanks Fletcher. I've been practicing Transcendental Meditation for many years now, and I know that what you say is true.

Rose: Hello, my name is Rose. Can you hear me?

Tom: Yes I can Rose. I love hearing your voice once again.

Rose: We are so pleased to be here with you. Fletcher was just discussing the Light, which is one of my favorite subjects. Do you know - when I was a young lady, I had an aunt who gave me a giant diamond broach. You cannot imagine the size of the diamond. I would say it was – well – as large as a robin's egg. Try to imagine – if you will - a diamond the size of a robin's egg. I used to hold that diamond up and look at it and reflect on its spectacular image. Do you know – I think that many souls on Earth are drawn to diamonds and other gemstones because they remember the Light. Diamonds are the best example on the Earth of a gemstone that reflects the Light.

When you see the Other Side, when you see the Godhead – it is like a giant diamond with great rays coming of it. And, in that Light is only peace and joy. Fletcher was so true when he said that if a soul refuses to absorb that Light, it will not be healed. I don't know how long I stayed in that Light, but all I know is that once I crossed over into the Light, it sees you and it brings you such peace. This was a type of peace – that I suppose – is difficult describe in words. It is a peace that only one who has actually experienced it, can understand. But, I assure you that it is in that Light that a soul is healed. And so, I stand in agreement with Fletcher. Do you have some questions for us this evening?

Tom: Yes I do. Thank you Rose.

Rose: You are most welcome, my dear. Hold on one moment. Fletcher, may take them? Alright, go on.

Tom: My first question is about the idea that we all have a right to make specific contracts with the Spirit World. Bob and Fletcher have told me about this idea of contracts between the human and Spirit Worlds and I like it. So, this is my question. As I see it, Jesus, Moses, Edgar Cayce, Mary Baker Eddy – and even Bob Hickman have all garnered attention from people – and moved into the public eye - because of their powers, their divine powers that come from Spirit.

What divine super powers do I have in my contract to do the work that I can exhibit even more clearly and develop - so that – like with Jesus and Moses and even Bob - more people will pay attention to my book's message about freeing our children from old materialistic belief systems? How can I develop more of my divine super powers – and what specific powers are available to me – to exhibit – as I continue to attempt to get people to pay attention to my overall message?

Rose: Oh, that is such a splendid question. If all our pupils would ask that, we should be most pleased. Your power that I see around you is the power of love. Do not underestimate that – by saying – it is not as fascinating to people as mediumship. Love is common – some are tempted to say – but really – love is quite rare in the world today. As per our discussion of the other week, we see love growing less and less upon the Earth. And so, love is a great treasure to be given. It is also true that you do share in the psychic gifts yourself. You do have the gift of clairaudience.

That means that you can hear our voice and our spirit. Although, for now, you hear us dimly. That is what St. Paul used to say. I can still remember how the vicars in my church used to quote Paul, when he said, "We see through a glass dimly". I used to laugh to myself and chuckle. I used to think to myself that St. Paul was never in my house. Our cut crystal didn't have a bit of dimness to it at all.

But, you see – it is true that the human senses aren't yet fully tuned in to Spirit. But, yours are developing and have been doing so for many years. Your power of clairaudience is becoming crisper by the day. You are becoming more and more tuned into our consciousness. You do have a sense of us being present. You already are becoming more and more sensitive to our presence. You are becoming more comfortable with us. We see that sense increasing for you. It goes in conjunction with your overall development. As you further develop your power of clairaudience – you will hear us speaking to you in more and more ways.

At times it may take the form of dreams, for example. You may hear a voice as you are waking in the morning. You may even hear voices speaking audibly in your room, or loud crashes, like cymbals crashing. If you are to really listen, while asking - know that - we will be there. This may not be as instantaneous as you may want, but it will develop. Even I myself, still have much to develop. As you know, I spent many years in that place of darkness. So, when I finally came into the Light – as glorious as that Light was – I was not yet fully developed. For my Light was rather weak, might I say.

There are higher beings who can see us and guide us and bring us closer to the Light. They brought me closer to the Light – and guided me to a point in my own development - where I too can now help those upon the Earth. Just because one is a spirit guide, does not mean that one is superior to those we help. We are all servants, and we do not mind taking your orders. If you cannot hear me audibly, then you must tell me so. You must ask me in a gentle way – mind you – because I am sensitive. If you tell me that you are not hearing me clearly today – I won't be offended – I promise. I shall do my level best to make myself known to you. I will also help you in your clairsentience, so that you will sense my presence. You may actually feel my walking by you. You may smell my favorite perfume. Even over here, might I say, I am allowed to wear my favorite fragrances.

I want you to see that each of your senses is developing, even though – sometimes to humans – it seems as if the flesh is a strong opponent to the things of Spirit. But, we don't mind the struggle, for we know that it is all for the best. Actually, it is important that you be grounded in your world rather than becoming too etheric. For, those students who become too ungrounded – and are always up in the ethers – are not as effective. So, if it seems that your senses are acting like what St. Paul said, when he described seeing through a glass darkly, don't worry or fear.

Accept this stage as a part of the struggle of learning how to be in the body and in the flesh. God does not except you to have developed your senses beyond the stage – where you are right now. He only wants you to keep trying to reach out for more. Wait one moment, for Fletcher is here.

Fletcher: Oh hello, this is Fletcher. It is so good be here with you. I wanted to drop in here, because – as you know – I can't stay quiet. I get a bit jealous when I feel like I am put in the background. I've got to speak here, so you can understand more about your contract. Your contract was – well – part of it was to develop and to bring the words of the Light and to be a teacher. And, you've been doing that. So, in terms of contract, you are making great progress. So, don't be worried about it because – as we see your progress we know you are doing it right. In the coming months you will be having a lot more – well – more "knockabouts".

When we say "knockabouts" what we mean is that you will be hearing us moving about your household. You may feel tables vibrating, which is our way of getting your attention. We promise that we won't scare you too much. But, if we are going to showing you that we are close to you, we are going to be having to giving you signs. You may notice our vibration affecting the electronics in your house. Even now, Bob gets a bit upset with me every time a Light bulb goes out, and he tells me that I am standing too close to the lamp. So, we'll try not to be doing that with you. Hold on just a moment while we adjust the vibration. Mr. Cayce would like to come through and speak.

Edgar Cayce: Well, hello there. Can you hear me out there? I am trying to come through this medium. I do not know if I have a firm connection with him tonight.

Tom: You sound great Edgar. It's wonderful hearing from you once again. What an honor it is for Bob and me to be receiving you this way. Thank you.

Edgar: We are so pleased to be here with you. I might say that I am very fascinated by the concept of the soul contract. When I was on the Earth, I had some understanding of this contract, but not quite in the capacity and to the extent to which I have learned about it, since coming to this world. Do you know that each human being has a contract and on that contract are included many options? I want you see that it is not like there is just this one straight "down on the paper" sort of thing. There are various subcategories and sub-subcategories. And each soul gets to choose whether or not to develop the numerous options that are built in.

For example, you might have decided when you incarnated back onto the Earth, to include two options on your contract. You might have had an option, that around the year of 1977, you could have left teaching and gone to work in Africa. The other option was to continue teaching through the year 1977. I will expand in that area. There are always numerous chances to develop and your guides are both supportive and flexible with you in regards to your contract, in order that humans don't feel boxed in or limited by their choices. And so, know that all the people in your life also have multiple contract options.

So, always be willing to give them lots of leeway in their choices. Might we say that – as I've understood it – you are doing well on your contract. That is what Fletcher has been telling me. And - I myself – might I say - have had a little peek at it also.

Tom: Thank you so much. I would like to talk about the possibility of expanding the parameters of my contract , because in my book and in all my writings – I am teaching about the God powers that are in children – the Cosmic Super Powers, that the public school system still ignore. As the system now stands, children (and teachers alike) are actually being prohibited from discussing the multidimensional or metaphysical meaning of life.

The one point of view, that preaches ONLY the values of materialism, the idea of "hard work=money= the good life", and the idea that capitalism is our only "savior" - has become the secret religion of the school systems' twelve-year curriculum of conformity.

I have been thinking a lot about your lesson from last week about learning how to use my will power and my mind power to dissolve clouds. I have begun to think that I need to exhibit more of these God powers when I am in the public eye, in order to get people to listen to my message. Jesus exhibited God powers - even you and Bob exhibit the powers. That's why people believe you and follow your teachings.

People seem listen to you because they sense the power of Spirit flowing through what you did – especially through your amazing holistic healings. So, I've decided that I want to develop my super divine God powers, so people will be more willing to listen to my message. Waking children up to who they really are – as Cosmic Super Beings - is my divine duty and right, and it is part of my contractual agreement.

Edgar: Might I say that your ambition is a noble one. But, be careful what you ask for at this point in your development, because the world does not really take to these powers very agreeably.

I myself suffered greatly through my own demonstrations. I ask you therefore, to be careful in what you ask for, for – as you ask – you will receive. I would like to encourage you to understand that your power is already revealed clearly in your gift of words. Realize that your extraordinary ability to influence children with your words is one of your greatest gifts to the universe. And the universe has given to you the knowledge of seeing how you will have affected generations yet to come.

Do not discredit yourself, or think that you are less than you are, because you do not – as they used to say – levitate like a Hindu holy man.

Tom: The reason that I was thinking about working on learning how to demonstrate more of my super God powers, was because Jesus himself used his God powers to garner attention and support. He changed water into wine and healed so many people in spectacular ways.

Our medium, Bob Hickman, has garnered attention through demonstrating the use of his psychic abilities. And even you yourself garnered attention because you were able to offer those extraordinary holistic healings to your many followers. I know I have the power of words, but if I could just demonstrate more actual God power, wouldn't that help my message get out there – to a doubting public – quicker?

Edgar: Not necessarily so.

It is important that you follow your contract. You will – however – be given lessons on developing your creative mind power, as with my cloud assignment of last week. I knew that you had within you that power that you could manifest creating a disillusion of the clouds. And so, you have the beginnings of understanding.

Power comes slowly, over many years and lifetimes. And, you have worked many years to open your body, mind and spirit and so you are in a place here more power will be given.

But, even so, you must be careful and very patient. I do believe that I heard Rose and Fletcher say that you will be developing, more clearly your power of clairaudience. And I hope that in time – you will start to be able to hear my messages to you, by yourself – in a more direct way – as I speak to you - without the outside aid of a medium. Then we will know that you truly developing. We do see this coming for you and we ask for patience as we work with you to adjust your vibration.

Your ambition to help many people is truly a noble one. But, please remember and understand what Jesus himself said, "Do not throw your pearls before swine." There will therefore – be times - when it seems that you do NOT have access to your gifts – not because you are not talented or not worthy – but it is simply for your own protection.

Tom: Oh. OK. Is it because our civilization is so negative right now and not yet ready to grasp the importance of my message?

Edgar: Yes. You know, there were times when I was on the Earth, when I would not be able to successfully access my gifts either. Sometimes, people would come for a reading – and it was funny – because my wife would suddenly say, "Edgar, I don't think you should try to give a reading to that person, today."

But, I was sometimes quite deaf and blind to the guidance of higher forces. Sometimes people around me like my wife would try and tell me things for my own good that I - the great psychic - totally missed. So, even those of us, who you believe are ahead of you, sometimes didn't understand the messages that were coming to us.

There were times when I was not the clearest of channels and the messages got muddled. I do believe that some people were quite let down by my lack of total purity and clarity. But, each human being grows as they can. And, the angels are not to be worshipped, because they are servants of the Most High.

So humans must be careful to not elevate psychics, mediums, clairvoyants, fortune tellers or even angels, up to a level beyond which they really are. For they too are merely servants of God.

I must say, I am most pleased to have a medium like this (like Bob) who is open to receiving my vibration. For I have longed to speak again. But, I did not find anyone sufficiently open to receiving my messages. And so, to have this opportunity for me is quite a gift as well.

Tom: And it is a real honor for Bob and me to be able to talk to you and relate with you like this - a really huge honor. We have both said, in our discussions, that neither of us quite grasps yet the real significance of this great gift of communication that you are giving us. May I ask you another question?

Edgar: Yes of course, as long as Fletcher feels our medium is up to having me stay. Is it alright Fletcher – if I continue this communication? (There is a short Pause at this point in the conversation). Fletcher has given us his permission.

Tom: Thank you so much. As you know, when I was writing my book, I felt as if I was downloading – what I called – the voice of the universal Cosmic Super Self. Am I being prepared to allow this voice to speak through me – as I teach the young people that we each contain a spark of this one vast Cosmic Super Self? Am I being primed to speak for this Cosmic Super Self?

Edgar: As I have understood it – Fletcher has asked me to relay to you – that the answer is yes. This is part of your journey, part of your chart, part of your contract. As you develop your power of clairaudience, I do believe that you will begin to be able to hear messages verbally - as well - from that source. And, I ask you to be faithful to document it. This is most important.

When I started to receive my messages I knew right away that I needed a stenographer to write down what I was hearing – for I realized that the information would be lost if not recorded. Since I myself was in trance, I had no memory of the messages and could not do the transcribing myself. I was fortunate to have my dear wife and a secretary who helped me so much, in understanding what was coming through me. And you would do well to keep this effort and practice as part of your habit.

Tom: Yes. This transcription of Bob's channeling is great practice. I really am enjoying transcribing your words – and I know that they will be a great help to our unhappy, frightened civilization.

Edgar: We are most pleased to be of assistance in this project, and we thank you for your effort in being loyal – in capturing our words. I do believe, as Fletcher often says, that we make for a good team. Might I address another issue?

Tom: Yes. I am already teaching many of my friends everything that I am learning – but I have noticed that there are many people still who simply doubt the existence of a loving God, because of the holocaust and other such atrocities. How would you answer people who wonder how a loving God could have allowed World Wars One and Two, and the holocaust? Why would a loving God have permitted such terrible treatment of children like Anne Frank? Why didn't God intervene on their behalf?

Edgar: Your question Sir, is one that I myself have asked. As I have come to understand it, the Good Lord allows humanity the freedom and opportunity to make either heaven or hell upon the Earth. Some people may argue that this seems callous, because it seems that God does not care. He must never force his children to believe that he is present. He will never force his omnipresent power upon people who don't believe in it.

From the very beginning of time, we have had God imprinted in our souls, and yet we have forgotten this. Do you remember how the Good Lord Jesus said, "Ye are Gods"? It is so important that we understand that because we were all there in the beginning, when this was all laid down.

The Councils that were formed in that time said each human being would be given free will upon this planet, and upon all the planets of God's creation. And we agreed with our Creator, on our deepest level of soul – and consciousness - that God would not interfere in our creations. For it was through our own creations, that we were going to be learning how to manifest our own realities. Those realities could – therefore – be positive or destructive. And it was agreed, from the very beginning, that

God would allow our realities to be exactly as we chose them to be.

And so, there is no bitterness in our world. There is – however – regret about all the evil that has come upon time and history. For we see, that it was mankind's own choices and beliefs that brought about so much destruction. It is very hard for humans – while in the body – to see it from our perspective, for the viewpoint is limited.

But, I assure you, people who experience that terrible suffering (such as happened in the two world wars and in the holocaust), have deep within themselves the knowledge of being there – in the beginning – when the world was created. And because of that - they retain – even during periods of great destruction - an inner knowingness - within them – that humans have been given the freedom - and have been allowed by God – to create absolutely anything desired upon Planet Earth, for better or for worse.

Tom: Thank you. I would like to ask how we actually do that creating. Do we create through our imagination or through our wishing? And, where does prayer come in? And what about the idea of just asking God to do it all for us, and totally surrendering all attempts to control the process?

On the one hand we have some churches teaching us that we should just "let go and let God". And – on the other hand - then we have great visionaries like Walt Disney who have taught us to "wish upon a star". And now, more recently, especially in the New Age community we have many channeled entities telling us that we create through our beliefs, our thinking and our emotional vibrations.

So, I guess what I am asking is – how can we reconcile these teachings into one coherent understanding? Where exactly do the imagination and wishing and prayer come into the process of creating our realities here on Planet Earth?

Edgar: That is a very good question, Mr. Berg. Many human beings, particularly in America and in the western world say that imagination is not a reality, when it comes to creation. They have dismissed the very gift that God has given them for the own growth. Such a materialistic mind set overlooks the factor that everything that exists started in the mind.

For example, look at the computer at which you sit in order to transcribe these notes. Where did it start? A materialist would say that the computer was made in the factory. And that is correct. But, where did the people in the factory learn how to make the computer? The factory was given a plan. But, where did the plan come from that led to the creation of the computer? It came from a design. Where did the designer get the design from that became the plan for the computer? It came from his own mind, did it not?

Now we must ask - where did these thoughts – that generated the idea for that computer - come from originally? Where and how did those ideas originate in mind? Might it have been in the university where the designer studied mathematics, physics and computer development? Where did that knowledge come from originally? The knowledge was passed on to him by others. And so, the earliest beginnings of that computer upon which you work today - originated in the minds of many people. Thoughts and ideas were transferred from one mind to another – from teacher to student - until a plan was created that eventually manifested as the computer. Do you understand what I am saying?

Tom: Yes I do. Now I must ask you. Is there any truth to the stories I have heard, that many of the ideas that led to our rapid advance in computer technology actually came to us from the imaginations of extraterrestrials? I've heard that some of our technology has been a gift – or a trade - offered to humanity – by some alien races that are visiting Planet Earth- and have actually negotiated secret deals with world governments. Is that true – that some of our most advanced technology has come from higher sources?

Edgar: The human being – in his very structure and essence – carries altered DNA - which was altered by alien races and extraterrestrial life forms. They have been visiting Planet Earth since the beginning of time. Humanity truly is related to those whom we call aliens. They can – in truth – be called - our space brothers. Do not be fearful of that reality, for it too – was in the plan – from the very beginning.

In the beginning, all the spirits in the Council, said, "We will create many worlds and let life evolve and develop freely upon those worlds." And so, these various worlds have always been in a kind of communion. It is the fear of humanity that has made mankind forget that connection to the Other Side - and also forget - the connection that connects each of you to your very core. This connection knows that you have more in you than basic Earth energies. The spiritual and the material are interlinked with the extraterrestrials, just as your physical world is linked with our Spirit World.

Tom: Would you agree that many of the great technological advances that we have been made in the last fifty years have come because of a secret cooperation between humanity and other – extraterrestrial – and multidimensional beings?

Edgar: You have spoken the words of truth. Right now, upon Planet Earth there are various people who are already in touch with these life forms. There are those who are already beginning to open the doors to communication with these other beings. Those with whom you work – the Essessani , I believe they are called – as well as the Pleaidians and those from Zeta Reticuli are all visiting our planet and have been here for thousands upon thousands of years. And yes, their technology has been shared with humans.

If you look back and study the ancient Egyptian culture, you will come to understand that Egypt came out of Atlantis. Both the ancient Egyptians and the Atlanteans were very directly in contact with such beings. I remember when I was upon the Earth, that there were many people who discussed these issues. I remember thinking that a good God could and would – undoubtedly - create life forms on many planets throughout the universe. All I had to do was look up into the sky and I could see that the universe was large and vast.

Tom: Thank you. Why do you keep telling people to look to Atlantis? What is the message that you are trying to convey to the world, about the connection between our Atlantean roots and what is happening today? What is so important about

Atlantis, that you keep referring to it, first in so many of your own readings, and now - more recently - in these transmissions?

Edgar: In Atlantis, are the very origins of humanity and the very truths about who you really are and who you are becoming. I should say – who WE are becoming –because I too am part of that evolution. In Atlantis, great truths were uncovered and understood – truths - which have now been all but forgotten upon the Earth. The Atlanteans were in direct communication with those from the Pleiades, Zeta Reticuli and the Essessani. All of them have had interactions with the Atlanteans. There were ports, and they would visit to exchange ideas. These visits were not considered strange, but accepted as normal. When Atlantis was destroyed and perished into itself, that knowledge was forgotten. So much so, that new truths – I should say lies – began to circulate in place of the ancient truths. It is not the truth that alien forces destroyed Atlantis. Atlantis destroyed itself by its own selfishness, greed and negativity.

The aliens were actually trying to warn the Atlanteans – but humanity is slow to learn. And so those aliens came again to the Egyptian people and brought them knowledge. But, the Egyptian people too – forgot their connection. Humanity struggles with its connection to its past. It is true- that if you can't remember your past – you are often condemned to repeat it. And so, if you look at all the great civilizations – you will see clearly that they have ALL fallen into ruin – and perished because they have forgotten or not acknowledged the truth of who they really are.

Fletcher: Hello, this is Fletcher here. Give me just a moment. We have to adjust our medium's vibration. Mr. Cayce will be offering you more information in just a moment.

Tom: Thank you.

Edgar: As I was saying previously, humanity must remember who it is. The very truths that humanity most needs at this time - actually scare most people, which is why you have great cover-ups. The Catholic Church has secret archives, which - I can tell you - are where many of those very truths are being kept hidden. The Church does not want humanity to know.

Tom: What are some of those truths that they are hiding?

Edgar: It will one day be revealed that in those archives, the Vatican has knowledge of how the ancient cultures were involved with beings from other planets. Rome even had encounters with those of the extraterrestrial realms. At the time of Jesus, many of the early church had similar connections.

Many of the tales in the Bible, which told of encounters with angels, were actually recordings of visits with beings from other worlds. They've been covered up, changed and falsified. But, the truth is about to emerge. Within a few years, you will see the coming of truth – and the Vatican itself will open its archives and be forced to admit its errors in hiding this knowledge from humanity.

Tom: Thank you – so much!

Edgar: Hold on there, someone else wants to have a word with you. It has been my pleasure to tell you of these things.

Rose: Hello, this is Rose. History will show - in time - that those of us in the upper levels of society were made well aware of many things – which the common man had no knowledge of – like Hitler's advances. We knew what was coming, though – I suppose –many of us were in denial. We did not want to know. So, we thought that if we could only look the other way, it would not affect us. And, I think that this trend is a failing in humanity.

The truth that alien cultures once inhabited the Earth – and still inhabit the Earth – is a truth that absolutely terrifies many people. And they think – falsely – that it would simply be easier to look the other way. There are – however - many courageous government officials and other influential people - who are coming out now - and are bravely telling the truth. They have my support and approval – and I wish them to understand - that they need not be afraid - for God is on their side. For wherever truth is – there is God's Light. And, wherever there is Light, there is love. Many of the alien races are our friends – and they are here to assist humanity in love.

Many people have asked why the aliens don't just land in London or in Washington. As I have understood it, this kind of landing would create great fear – for humanity is not yet evolved enough. I suppose – that I too - watch with rapt attention to see of how things may evolve upon Planet Earth. I had a friend who told me that she saw a craft, right around the outbreak of the war. I said, "Oh, you are just seeing one of those experimental crafts or something". But, she explained to me quite emphatically that it was a glowing saucer shaped vehicle. I didn't believe her – and thought that she was daft, because I hadn't yet come to understand that there were alien life forms upon the Earth.

Over here now, we understand that there is a plurality of worlds. Infinite Intelligence – you know - this is a term for God that I like very much. And so it is – that Infinite Intelligence – or God – has created all the worlds on which all the various life forms evolve. There is much yet to be revealed. I have had the privilege of talking with Mr. Cayce has told me that Planet Earth will be receiving many more visitations. In the coming four years, each year will get more and more dramatic as the extraterrestrials make themselves known in much bolder ways than ever before in the past. Their efforts in sharing themselves will be so forward and bold, that the world will no longer be able to deny it.

The United States government – I believe – will be the last to admit it – but eventually even they will admit the truth – for they know far more than they've revealed to date.

Tom: Thank you so much.

Rose: You are most welcome. Might I answer another question while I am present?

Tom: OK. I don't know if this question is for you or for Edgar, but I have a friend named Barbara Hall who is having some problems with her internal uterus area and she asked me if she could get some healing advice from the spirits, as to what she needs to do to find healing.

Rose: Oh yes. I shall give it a go and then I shall ask Fletcher's assistance as well. He's a far more advanced guide that I am. But – let me begin by sharing with you what I see – around that area. Would you tell me her name again so I may more closely tune into her vibration?

Tom: She has red hair and her name is Barbara Hall. She is living in San Francisco, California. She has already gone through one operation previously, and is now worried about her uterus – which is hurting her. It seems to be growing too large.

Rose: First of all, let me say that what she is experiencing physically is due to a chemical imbalance in the body. We would like her to monitor her thyroid, because it is creating an excessive growth hormone that is affecting the organs of the body.

Tom: Is there something she can do about this metaphysically, rather than just medically?

Rose: Oh yes. Only, let me allow Fletcher to address that. Just a moment.

Fletcher: It is so important to realize that she is dealing with a physical imbalance. Part of the reason that the organ is growing so fast is because her spirit is trying to escape the body. Oh, we don't mean to be saying that she is planning on dying. That is not what we are saying. What is happening is that - she is – in a strange way – trying to get out of her own skin.

She would do well to love herself - then her body would settle down. She also needs to meditate and ask for God's Light to be in her. There is spark of Light within which is the spark of the Divine Self. This God spark is centered in the area of the chest. What is the term you use in your book – the Super Self?

Tom: Yes.

Fletcher: Yes, she must get in touch with her Super Self. If she would find that Super Self and focus on it – and let that spark of Light expand – so she can send the Light down to the area of the uterus, and also up the thyroid area - she will bring balance to the body. She is having a bit of an imbalance here because she is trying to grow spiritually – while forgetting how important it is to acknowledge and love her body.

She must realize how important her body is to herself. She has tried to deny who she is – and has tried to escape the body. In so doing she creates the imbalance and the growth. If she were to do this meditation - she will soon find that body starts to return to normal once again. Just a moment here - Mr. Cayce wants to say something about this.

Tom: Thank you Fletcher.

Edgar: Hello there, this is Edgar. It is so good to be here. We are still trying to adjust to our medium's vibration here. There is a bit of a problem because our power seems to stress his nervous system. It is correct – the way that Rose and Fletcher have diagnosed the problem. Your friend needs not only to begin these meditations– but also – to swallow a teaspoon of salt water each day – just one. Ask your friend is she will do this. Just mix up a little salt in water in a cup and then sip a teaspoon full of this salt water each day. This will begin to bring balance to the thyroid and bring the vibration of the salt crystals into her body. This will start to kick in a higher vibration.

She would also do well to surround herself with quartz crystal - which is pure white crystal – with the power to greatly enhance the vibration around her.

She wants to have the pure healing Light all around. She would do well – therefore - to place some amethyst around her - for – I believe – that the amethyst vibration would help her greatly. Amethyst is of the seventh ray – the powerful healing Light. That would go well for her. These various things – though they may sound rather simple – are actually quite profound and will generate great results for her, if she will but follow our advice – regularly. She must also meditate and then – watch – because – it looks like she will be having some healing. I feel that there is about a four to six week period – during which time her body will start balancing again. And I don't see a need for further operations.

Tom: Good. Barbara is trying to grow into a spiritual life but was brought up by atheists. And so I have a general question about that. What is a good way to break free from childhood beliefs and wounds? So many of us grew up in families, where we were not told about our spiritual power and our spiritual freedom. She, like so many of my friends – are trying to break into the Light and into the truth – but they are up against so many childhood lies.

Edgar: That is a very, very good question – one that is pertinent to many people upon the Earth, at this time. I myself grew up in a rather strict Christian home, and it took me many years to become comfortable with the reality that I found myself in. This is why I understand this struggle and this reluctance.

It is very difficult to live up to these higher truths when one has been told – either that these truths were nonexistent – or – as in my case – that they were evil. You know, many people in my family would often say, "Edgar you are trafficking with the devil, doing that spiritual stuff." I never believed that for a moment - because I knew that – when the spirits would come through me – that it always felt right- and in line with God. I must say, however, that I was sometimes confused by some of the pronouncements, upon reading the transcripts – and did have struggle, myself.

As for your friend, Barbara – she must stop rejecting herself. She must become much more aware – that every time she forgets or rejects the truth about God or the higher self, she rejects her own very self. For – the truth is - that self is God within her. Tell her to not be ashamed or afraid to consider that reality – the truth that says - the spark of God is within her – and IS, in fact, her real self. The other thing that is important for your friend to understand – is - she also needs to be finding a way to get away from those who would negate her truth. It is important that she spend time alone – at times – in deep meditation and prayer.

If she will but ask the Master Jesus to be present – he will be there. In fact, he is already there – she just hasn't fully realized it yet. It is fear - and programming - from the past - that did block her. But she can overcome that, because every time that she starts to have a negative thought she needs to say, "I cancel that thought and I bring in the Light of God." Then, she needs to look inside of herself and try to see the Light inside of her.

Tom: Thank you so much.

Edgar: What else might I address for you today?

Tom: We talked last week about the so-called inevitability of bodily decay in the material world - but looking at redwood trees and sequoia trees - and the bible stories about ancient prophets living to be many hundreds of years old – I was wondering if we have DNA with the power to allow us to live many centuries instead of decades? Or, is it appropriate to die within eighty or ninety years. I myself am aging very slowly and so I have a feeling that maybe one of my super powers is staying young a lot longer than my physical age would show. According to God's imagination and plan – what is the appropriate aging process for humans?

Edgar: You've got to understand – as I learned it- God never meant for humans to die the way they do, in suffering. It was humanity's own forgetfulness of who they are – that brought in that whole idea of decay - into the aging process here on Earth. Humanity – if it would awaken to the God Light within – would be able to extend itself. It is true – that you, yourself – do have the gift of youthfulness. You will live a long life – and age very slowly - because you are tuning more and more into the Light of God. I want you to see that – when you are tuned into the Light there is no time. And, those of us – you –I – this medium - and all those who follow spiritual paths – are closer to the God Light. That Light is timelessness.

You know, Mr. Einstein used to talk about time and space being variables that could be manipulated. And I do believe he was right. So, what he was saying – was that – you can change time by changing your consciousness. If you elevate your consciousness, to be closer to the Light – you are also closer to timelessness, a place of timelessness. I don't even know how to call it – because it is not really a place. It's more like a transcendent reality that you are connected to – that allows you to share in God energy and Light energy. And so -when you share in that energy, the manifestation in the body is closer to the energy of timelessness – and so - takes on that reality. Humanity can live longer by living closer to the Light.

If you look at humanity today, you can see that many people are actually dying off younger and younger. I know that if you look at the statistics, they say that the life span is increasing, but – if you look at it over all – the young people are dying of ailments such as heart attacks and malfunctioning arteries - because they are becoming more and more enmeshed in materialism. Even if they are not showing any signs of age outwardly – inwardly they are aging more rapidly. It is an internal aging. Between that and the pollution and the bad food upon the Earth, humanity is actually shortening its life span. But, that life span can be improved - as I said – through an awareness of the God power within – and by becoming closer to the Light and power, which results in an experience of timelessness.

Tom: That brings me to a question about the great healer and founder of Christian Science, Mary Baker Eddy. I am reading about her amazing healing, through the power of prayer, and I am fascinated by her story. How did Mary Baker Eddy heal through the power of prayer – and is this power of healing also one of my super powers? Do you know of her?

Edgar: I have had the good fortune of meeting her. But, you must understand – that we spirits are all on our own journeys and we live in a vast world. Sometimes we come together for a while and sometimes we don't. It is not that different than relationships of the Earth. Remember that old saying, "As above, so below –and as below – so it is above".

But, it is true, I have met Mary Baker Eddy here, and I find her story fascinating. Over here, she has discovered some flaws in her teaching. She's says – while on the Earth - that she was slow to recognize and appreciate the reality of the material body. She was so focused on Spirit – that some of her teachings were imbalanced. If she were back upon the Earth, she would have encouraged people to have a little more balance between body, mind and spirit.

The human being – as you know – is a combination of the body, the mind and the spirit. She has told me that she over emphasized the mind and the spirit while neglecting the importance of the body. This three part teaching is a universal teaching. She did a lot of good in raising consciousness – but she now feels – that she would have changed things a bit if she would have realized this while on Earth.

Tom: What was her secret of prayer – the power that she discovered – that allowed her to heal so many people?

Edgar: She discovered that very self within – that Super Self you teach about. If you have the Light of God realized in your heart – then you have access to all of God's power – don't you?

Tom: Absolutely. What humans don't understand is that - in the Bible – when Jesus was talking about the gift of the Holy Spirit – he was giving to the apostles - a very simple energy charge – that they would have that Light more vigorously within them. This power wasn't only for the apostles – though – because this healing energy of God was to be shared with all humanity. Unfortunately, however – the power structures that are now upon the Earth - changed the teaching. The power structures made it seem to the masses that only the elite could have the power of healing. Actually – all of us upon the Earth are supposed to be like the apostles - but we just have not been taught that truth.

Tom: Are you saying that we are all being asked to learn the power of healing, through the power of the truth?

Edgar: Yes, you expressed it correctly. That is correct. In prayer, one finds their connection. In prayer, one finds truth. And the two together are powerful. And yes, I might say, you do have the power of healing.

Tom: I saw many of my middle school children become quite healthy once I taught them that their Super Self had the power to keep them strong and healthy. I very much want to help all my friends who are going through physical problems. What is the best way that I can help them best?

Edgar: It is true that it has been asked that we should pray for those in need. But, those for whom we pray must be responsible for opening up enough to receive the benefits of our prayers, to receive the gift that is being offered. This is not taught in the world today. The thing is – if you pray for people – they need to be willing to accept that power given to them.

When you pray for others, you are giving a gift of yourself and of your energy. You are interceding - so to speak – acting like a wire - that will give them connection to a charge of God energy.

But, today, many people don't believe in the power of prayer – and if you told them that you were going to pray for them – they would laugh at you and discount it. The attitude that is most necessary for accepting the gift of healing is humility – and also acceptance. This is because we are not allowed to force ourselves on anybody or overwhelm them. Fletcher and Rose have shared this also. This is of the truth. Hold on, somebody else is here.

Tom: Thank you so much.

Orion: This is Orion. It is time to become aware of the power that is manifesting through humanity. It exists in the Light. This is true, as you have been told. The soul must also remember the karmic balance that is always in play, for there will be times when you will pray for others without any response. Understand that there are times and conditions in which the soul is not ready to receive healing – because the suffering that it experiences – is for its own growth.

Look at the example of Rose, who wondered in the place of darkness – in the lower realms - for many Earth years. Any of us could have lifted her into the Light, but she did not want the help that was being sent. There were many who came to her – but she rejected them. There are those about you who are experiencing physical problems. They have drawn these problems to them for their own growth. The soul sometimes chooses to suffer upon the Earth, rather than accept the gift of prayer as it is offered. This is why the prayer does not have the result that you may intend. Please understand – however – that every prayer is valuable, because energy is shared and changed. This can only be of help to those who suffer.

If those, for whom you pray, do not appear to receive healings, do not be discouraged. Encourage them to be open up to receiving the benefits of your healing prayer. Know that your prayer is not wasted, because the energy that is sent out is used in many, many ways. There are guides about you and about those for whom you pray – who distribute the energy as needed. My name is Orion.

Tom: Thank you very much Orion.

Fletcher: This is Fletcher here. We are going to be careful here- for our medium's vibration is now thinning. So, we are not going to be staying in the body any longer. We have been so pleased to have been here with you and we want you to know that we will be walking with you. We will be showing you a lot more here.

Mr. Cayce wants me to tell you - the very power you are learning to use to dissolve the clouds - you may also use to dissolve the clouds of illness in people you want to help. Beam that same energy to them – and you can eradicate all sorts of problems.

Tom: What is the best way to practice dissolving the clouds?

Fletcher: You've got to have focused attention, Mr. Cayce says. You've got to look at them while you imagine that there are beams of Light coming out of your eyes. Focus those beams of

Light on anything you want. Learn to imagine and use that Light internally – while you see someone with a problem in your mind's eye – like your friend with the uterus problem. As you think of her, imagine Light coming from your eyes – in beams – which you can then focus specifically upon her uterus. You can use this power of Light to burn away any illness.

Tom: Thank you Fletcher.

Fletcher: We are going to be stepping out of the body now. It has been such a pleasure to have been talking with you and we will be coming back soon.

Tom: All I can say is "thank you" and WOW – WOW – WOW and WOW!!!

BOB HICKMAN POSTSCRIPT:

I came out of trance this night—again amazed that so much time had elapsed. This night I felt a bit over-tired. Tom confirmed that Orion had channeled through during the session. I always know when he comes through for it is like a 10,000 volt battery is put on my body! Orion is a wise and profound soul and his teaching mystify me and I ponder them for days. And to see that Edgar Cayce was now giving healing advice was beyond words for me! I thought to myself "Well...looks like he is still working! So much for the idea of retiring in the Spirit World!" I have to admit that when I learnt all that Cayce taught this night about the Atlantean/alien connections—I was stunned to the point of silence. Sometimes the reality of what all of this means—and could mean to the people of the Earth causes me as much panic as it does jubilation. But – I myself have seen an UFO and can't deny the strong possibility that we really are being contacted by people from other worlds.

I used to attend a Spiritualist church called "Church of Two Worlds"...I think they should change the name to be the Church of Ten Thousand Worlds. What does this mean I thought...What is happening? Am I being used by the Spirits to help bring forward alien evidence also? Sometimes I wished for the simpler days when I didn't have to confront such profound questions. If what Edgar Cayce was saying was true (and I had no reason to doubt him) then this meant my channeling was taking on way more profound implications than just a "pleasant hello" from the Other Side. Maybe long-lost truths were coming through me...Maybe the Spirits knowledge would change the world as we knew it. It was almost a bit much for me to grasp—and at times I even wanted to run away from it. But I knew that the guides were with me—and I didn't need to fear, at least not fear them or our Space Brothers....but what about those black helicopters that always seemed to be hovering outside my window. Were there powers that knew what I was being shown? Did those powers want to stop this revelation? I told Tom about the black helicopters—and he could even hear them over the phone often when we would sit for channeling—so much for imagination.

Well, no matter what the ultimate truth about the aliens and the world governments' knowledge about them, I resolved this night to continue this work because I knew that something big was unfolding, and if for no other reason than personal curiosity, I would see it through!

CHAPTER FIVE
RELATIVES FROM THE STARS
September 3rd, 2008

BOB HICKMAN PREVIEW:

Tom and I met for our weekly séance. We were both still stunned over the recent communication that came from Edgar Cayce. Tom was curious about my past in channeling, and I waxed nostalgic as I reflected back to my earlier days when I first met Fletcher and Rose. It's funny because I don't think I ever set out to become a trance channel, but somehow, a higher plan was enacted, and I found myself working as a vehicle for the Spirit World. The more I studied the transcripts from the past few weeks, the more surprised I became. I could only guess as to what the spirits would have for us this night. I was most eager to speak with Tom this night, as I had been having an increasing feeling that I was somehow "connected" to the UFO phenomena. Well—what happened this night left no doubt in my mind. It appears that I really was being contacted. Not only did I have a connection—but everyone on earth has a connection. We all share alien DNA! Below is the transcript of this most fascinating channeling.

Bob: Hi. Are you ready for another session? I can tell the spirits are eager.

Tom: I sure am. I have really grown to love Fletcher and Rose, but this conversation with the spirit of Edgar Cayce is blowing my mind. I can hardly grasp the significance of what this could mean for us - and for the world.

Bob: I know. I have to admit I'm pretty surprised by Edgar Cayce's appearance, as well.

Tom: Do you realize what you have accomplished, Bob – in allowing his spirit to some through you? Edgar Cayce is America's most famous "Sleeping Prophet", and now, he has decided to come and speak through you, so he can continue update his messages for the world. What an honor this is for us both! So, I have to ask you Bob - was this your idea, or Fletcher's idea to invite Edgar Cayce into our conversation? Or, do you think it was Edgar's idea?

Bob: Well, what I think is that it was all arranged from over there. Sometimes Fletcher just takes charge and I don't know for sure what going to happen next. But, we have an agreement that he won't do that generally, unless he decides it's absolutely necessary. I'm certainly not comfortable just letting anybody come through. Fletcher keeps this very limited, so I know that when a spirit comes through me, that it is happening with Fletcher's approval and guidance.

Tom: On the very first transcript, when you were not in a full trance yet, you said, "Oh my God" when you saw that Edgar Cayce had entered the scene and wanted to speak to us. So, I have to ask you, were you as surprised as I was?

Bob: I was totally surprised, but not unprepared. I always know it when a spirit is coming through that is not Fletcher or Rose. So, I did notice that a new vibration was coming through and that something different was going to occur. I was being prepared, so I just allowed it to happen. Now, after all these years, I trust Fletcher completely. He will often tell me during the day that something new will be coming, in order to prepare me.

Although, I must say, that's not exactly what happened when I met Rose. She was a total surprise!

Tom: What happened?

Bob: One day I was doing a séance to help lost souls – you know – those souls that were stuck in the lower astral realms. Fletcher put my under as always and I was sitting at a séance table when Rose first came through me. I didn't know it until later, when I listened to the tapes. To tell you the truth, when I realized what had happened, I got pretty upset with Fletcher. I told him that I'd trusted him and that letting Rose come through hadn't been our agreement or plan.

It took quite a few years before I became completely comfortable with being a trance channel. It was much easier for me, as a psychic, to practice clairaudience, because I could remain totally conscious. When you channel in a trance you have to put yourself in what feels like a very vulnerable place. My big fear, for many years me - was, "How do I know when I go under, that some evil spirit isn't going to take control over me?" That's why trust is something you must establish with your guide, right at the beginning, so that you will feel totally safe and protected.

Tom: Yeah. Edgar said that when he began trance channeling people in his family and in his church accused him of letting the devil work with him. And, that he had to learn to just trust that – since the messages coming through felt good and helpful – that they were indeed coming from a Light source, he called, "The Council".

Bob: I was lucky because I didn't have a Christian background with that kind of pressure. My own pressure was the fear that I placed upon myself. I have to admit that I didn't even know what trance channeling meant when I became part of the Spiritualist Church.

I saw people channeling all around me, but didn't want to have it THAT close to me. But, the people in the church assured me that – when I was ready – it would happen. The first time that Fletcher actually came in, I was doing a séance. I began to feel like I was nodding off, like I was really "out of it". I started to feel sleepy - like I needed to rest, like I wanted to go to sleep. I was already in a darkened room because I was doing a séance to levitate a table, so it was easy to go under. It's always easier for me to do into a trance in a darkened room.

I am a physical medium also, which means that I have the ability to work with physical objects. In those early years, I would often demonstrate this by making tables levitate. I don't do that so much anymore, but it was while I was in that kind of séance, attempting to make a table levitate, that Fletcher came through me for the very first time.

Tom: Wow! That is really interesting.

Bob: Oh, I almost forgot to tell you. Something really strange happened after our session last Wednesday night. I hadn't gone to bed yet, when I noticed more of those black helicopters flying around my apartment building. I swear, 'Big Brother' is watching. And I am getting the feeling that something is going on that involves the aliens.

Tom: Yes. I am going to ask about that today. Because, last week Rose and Edgar predicted that very soon we are going to be seeing large numbers of UFO's in the sky. Actually, this seems to be happening already. Did you watch that YouTube video that showed hundreds and hundreds of sightings in Great Britain recently?

Bob: Yes I did. It's coming. I can feel it. You know, I have channeled a Pleiadian named Altar twice. So maybe we can ask for him to come through again. It's always up to Fletcher, however.

Tom: Hey, that's a great idea. I'm also going to ask about our book's theme today.

It seems to me that there are two threads or themes developing. Both are about contact. One, is that each of us has to learn to be our own channel and learn how to consciously contact Spirit, like you do. You are a great model for all of us in that regard, because you show us that we do have the power to contact the Spirit World. And I have to tell you, that ever since we began these sessions last month, my life has become so much more peaceful. To understand that we CAN contact our spirit friends for help, and receive that help, changes everything for the better almost immediately. It seems to me that asking for this spiritual contact and then accepting it when it comes IS the missing link, the key to learning how to "create our own reality".

Bob: Yeah. My entire career is about this kind of contact. I left the regular nine to five work-a-day world to dedicate all my energies to this line of research. The more we learn how to contact the Spirit World, the better our lives are going to be . . .

Tom: Yes, I totally agree. And, now I'm also beginning to sense that there is another contact theme developing as well. When I asked Edgar last week, why he keeps talking about Atlantis, he said the extraterrestrials were trying to help the Atlanteans take steps that could have avoided their destruction. And now, they are trying to do the same thing with us.

According to Edgar, the ETs are attempting to contact us in order to help us wake up enough to we can avoid our own destruction. So, I am beginning to wonder if our book might not be part of their attempt to prepare mankind for this breakthrough, for a whole new level of contact. Edgar implies that, if the human race could just accept the help of the friendly extraterrestrials and spirit guides, and stop being so afraid, the worst of the destruction might still be avoided.

Bob: I wouldn't be where I am today, if it wasn't for the help of my spirit guides. All the good that has happened in my life and all the successes that have come to me recently, are only because of the help I am receiving. So, I am very grateful for their help, and I recognize that it is ONLY because of their help that I've been able to get to where I am. I think it's time for me to go under. I can feel that they want to get in on this conversation.

Tom: I agree. I will see you when you come back. Hang loose!

Fletcher: Hello, this is Fletcher here. Good evening, how are you?

Tom: I'm fine. It's wonderful hearing your voice again, Fletcher. How are you?

Fletcher: Oh, we're doing most well, here. There are lot of intense vibrations in the air today – causing a little bit of an electrical imbalance. But, we'll be keeping an eye on things, as we go along. We must always monitor the vibrations in our medium's body, much like the electronics within a computer. You know, it's all the same thing, ultimately. Everything is made of electrons roaming about. And so - one transmission affects the other – don't you understand? We are all electronic.

We are so glad to be back with you. We've been keeping an eye on you this week – and we've seen how eager you've been – typing away on these notes. But, we want to say that you have a tendency to overtax yourself. Even though you may not think you are like our medium here – in many ways - you are now becoming a medium yourself. We are coming through you as you type our words. We are trying to help you see things and refine the transmission.

Be careful to follow this process more slowly - so you don't overdo yourself. Your own body's nervous system could easily become overwhelmed. You tend to be a bit high strung you are – and you sometimes work yourself up to a fever pitch, for no reason. That doesn't do you well. When you get yourself all nervous and stressed out, your energy goes all over the place. And, you can't be a clear channel for us to come through.

Tom: Well, I've really enjoyed transcribing these transmissions. I really love capturing your words – along with Rose's and Edgar's and Orion's. I just love it – because I ride the high spiritual energy that is in your words. But you are right – when I do these transcriptions longer than two or three hours at a time – I get strangely exhausted.

Fletcher: As I was saying, it is so important that you learn how to be a good, clear channel. You know, we always try to keep our medium's energy balanced and we encourage him to rest and have a good diet – so he doesn't over strain himself. We also want you to take care of yourself. We can't have our book coming out – if both sides of the coin aren't working well. You are no less of a channel than our medium is. You might say that what you are doing with these transcripts - is a kind of automatic writing.

Tom: I can feel you with me as I transcribe your words. I can feel you helping me with the words, as I put the sentences together. I love the energy.

Fletcher: All we are saying is that you might want to slow it down a bit. There won't be a problem. We are going to be coming to you all the time, working with you, from now on. We can see the book developing at a good rate, in spite of how much I like to talk. And – as you have already surmised - I do like to talk.

The vibration of the Spirit World is all around you now - and as you realize and unify with the power of the Spirit World - to this degree - things will be manifesting much more quickly. So, be always open to the power of your Inner Spirit – and just let it manifest as it will – through you. Don't be afraid or try to hold it back. When you are transcribing, if you come upon some words that just don't sound quite right – we will help you rewrite it a little bit, as we go along. You could call us your editors, or your ghost writers.

And so, relax and know that we will be stepping in from time to help you modify some of the words when necessary. So, be listening for us and don't be afraid to follow our lead. Give us just a moment here. We have to adjust the vibration. Rose would like to say something.

Rose: Hello, my name is Rose. It is such a pleasure to be here with you this evening. I was listening in as I like to do. Whenever Fletcher is in a discussion – I am I always just around the corner, so to speak.

I always know when Fletcher is coming through, and that pleases me greatly, because it means that I may get to come through as well. His words are true when he says that we will be assisting you in the editing. We have been watching you and we are most pleased with your work so far. I do believe that you have captured me and my words accurately. This is a great pleasure for me. I have come a long way since crossing over . . . (she sighs).

I'll never forget that experience in London, the day when I died. I suddenly found myself walking in a place of darkness. I looked about and saw that I had nobody to speak with. I felt absolutely and utterly alone. It is true that – at some point – beings of Light came to me – although I could neither hear nor see them. I was so dense in my vibration that they were barely perceptible. And when they would approach me – I used to say, "Ah - who are these strange people? Away with you!"

I've been taught, since coming to the Spirit World, that we spirits are never to force our presence upon anyone. We can only go to those who are truly open and able to receive us. At a certain point after my passing, the higher beings of Light came to me and I was eventually able to receive them. I will be forever indebted to our medium for the part his work played in this . . .

Although I did not know the passing of time, (after I died so suddenly), it took many Earth years to fully understand what the spirits were saying to me. I was lost, in a spiritual sense, and had to move towards the doorway of Light. I share this experience with you – so you may understand that there will be many – at first – who will not be able to receive these words. They are like me, when – for many years – I could not accept the words of higher level beings. And so, that was the main reason why I wandered in that place of darkness after I crossed.

Please understand that many of the people, who will be reading these words, shall be very much like I was. Therefore, we must not be dismayed or judgmental. We must have great courage to carry on, knowing that our words will someday penetrate their minds. And, so, it is for this cause that I come – because my goal is to rescue those who are lost – to rescue those who are living in that realm of ignorance and darkness. My goal is to help them wake up to their connection with our world – the Spirit World.

The realm of darkness is a realm of mental ignorance because there is no recognition of a connection to the Spirit World or to God. There will be many who will say to you, "I don't want to hear your teachings. They are rubbish. I don't believe them." I used to say the same things myself when I was alive upon the Earth. Actually, I never said I didn't believe in God, but the truth was, that I really didn't care much about the higher truths. Although there are many who behave and live as I did, you must not be afraid or back down from your truth.

The day will come, and IS coming, when our words will eventually penetrate to the very core of their being. On that great day, when they awaken within their own mental darkness, they will begin to remember the world of Spirit – and their journey towards the Light will be sped up greatly. So, understand that the words that we bring will bring the knowledge of the Spirit World, though for some it may not be received until well after their physical deaths. Our words can and will penetrate those who wander - those especially - who find themselves in what we call Purgatory.

I want to say Mr. Berg, that there are coming for you more wonderful surprises yet. You have not yet heard from all of your students, nor seen the ongoing effects of your previous teachings. For, they are still growing and their lives are echoing your teachings, all through the world. Many people, the young people you once taught, do still think of you often these days. And so, when you imagine that you have been forgotten and your ex-students have gone on with their lives, know that – in many of their darkest moments – they remember your words that once brought Light to them. And in those moments, they often think to themselves, "What would Mr. Berg do?" and they feel their courage and inner guidance return. I am pleased to share this with you.

Tom: I really appreciate that Rose. Thank you very much.

Rose: You are most welcome. It is the truth – and all I wish to bring to you today are the words of truth. Someone else is here who would like to say something.

Edgar Cayce: Hello. I think I am here. Can you hear me out there?

Tom: Hello Edgar, I can hear you loud and clear.

Edgar: You can hear me? It is so good to be back here with you. I have been watching – with great interest – your conversations here this evening with these other two. And, I must say, that I am most impressed with this Fletcher. You know, I someday hope to aspire to the level of service that he has given to the world. For many years, he worked with Arthur Ford, who I knew when I was alive. I remember first encountering Fletcher through a meeting I had with Arthur Ford. It was most fascinating.

Fletcher tells me that you have a whole list of questions for us tonight. Hopefully, I will be able to answer some of them for you. And if I can't, Fletcher will.

Tom: Thank you so much. My first question follows up on our wonderful talk last week, in which you told me and our readers that our human DNA has been altered by aliens. How does that balance in with our free will? Why would the human race allow manipulation of our DNA – if it would make us forget our true identity? Why would we do that to ourselves – as a race – if we really do have free will? Why would we have chosen that strange path of apparent manipulation? How did it all happen?

Was there a divine plan at work - and why did the plan unfold as it did – if there really is free will – and a "prime directive" of non-intervention? I thought that more evolved civilizations were forbidden to interfere with less advanced civilization. And, how does this relate with all the UFO's that are appearing in the skies today – including those that have been showing up - outside of Bob's apartment after our sessions?

Edgar: Yes. You are asking quite a profound series of questions. I would like to address your points, one by one, if I may. First, the most important thing to understand is that at the beginning of time, all the spirits were gathered in the great council with God.

And they all agreed that humanity would go out from the Spirit World and evolve and form the Earth.

Planet Earth was formed by our own spiritual power, which is connected to the Divine Source. But, once we spirits got to the Earth, we found that the human body had limitations, which we had to accept, in order that we would be united to the Earth realm. We discovered for example, that we couldn't walk through walls – like we can here in this world in spirit form.

Although the human race always had free will, this did not disallow their asking for and receiving help from other life forms from other worlds, when needed. Interaction was always allowed when needed. There is not a conflict therefore, between free will, and the allowing of so-called alien races to work with the evolution of DNA within humans.

From the earliest human civilizations upon the Earth, humanity's contact with aliens actually brought the gift of greatly enhanced DNA. This was not an intrusion. The DNA that was introduced into the human strands was something that was actually a hidden gift, given for use at a later time. The injection of this DNA into human bodies was, in a sense, a hidden gift of great power. The alien DNA was bonded with the human codes.

All humans now have some traces of this extraterrestrial DNA. There are those, through the use of their free will and natural selection, who have advanced further and quicker, because they have allowed the DNA strands to take a more prominent role. These are the beings, which have already chosen to open themselves to the higher truths and realities. The spirit guides have said that humanity is indeed rising towards the Light. The extraterrestrials have ensured that humanity continues to move forward in evolution. Therefore, it is not so much a problem of them controlling humanity. It is more a story of them offering the gift of their DNA, and the opportunity that DNA brings for new growth and evolution.

As in all human matters of free will, humans can choose, on a deep and spiritual level, whether or not to accept growth and utilize all the DNA that has been made available. All humans have the same DNA as the most advanced souls upon the Earth, but on a deep soul level, some have decided not to carry forth their growth. And so, they choose to remain in their old state. No person is forced to grow or evolve or wake up.

Now, we do understand that you have been told, and many believe, that human DNA has been controlled for negative purposes and that humans are somehow subject to those changes in their genetic makeup. This is not true, because DNA is only a pattern that has been set. It is ALWAYS the consciousness of the human being that influences whether those DNA strands release their powers or not.

Here is an example. Within some human DNA there was a strand that produced a negative mutation called multiple sclerosis. But, on a deep soul level, each person may choose whether or not to activate that particular strand. It is the same thing, with the so-called manipulation of DNA, that has been blamed on extraterrestrial involvement. The real truth is that the so-called REmanipulation of certain strands of DNA was a gift, and that it was "allowed to happen" for the purposes of eventual change and evolution.

From over here in the Spirit realm, we have noticed that there are an increasing number of human beings who have said within themselves, "We want to know more. We want to have more. We want to be more." It is for these people that ask, people who are seeking higher knowledge, that the higher knowledge is being given. Do you understand what I am saying?

Tom: Yes I do, very much so. But I am still wondering about some of the things I've read in other channeled books about aliens and their involvement with our DNA. So, I must ask, are we in the process of reconnecting strands of DNA that have been disconnected by aliens – or was it a lie that said that we've had our DNA disconnected so that we could be better manipulated? I've read that we supposedly were created with twelve strands of DNA, but that ten of them were disconnected. Is that story true?

Edgar: The truth, as I understand it, is that within your DNA structure, you are already complete. It is not so much that there is anything that is lacking. It is more true to say that, many of you have chosen – for whatever reasons – not to implement the DNA that you already do have. So, if you are talking about any restructuring of your DNA being a detriment, I cannot and will not agree with that interpretation of what happened. Your DNA is fine just as it is. If it were incomplete you would not be alive as you are today. You would not be able to understand and utilize my words. You would not continue to evolve as you right now. Therefore, as it exists, your DNA contains within it, all the latent seeds of growth, with all the powers necessary, for you to create great opportunities for evolution.

Think about a farmer. A farmer plants seeds in the field and the seeds have the potential to grow. Now – the farmer's consciousness is involved in releasing that seed to grow, which allows a plant to come forth. It is the same thing within the human body. You have already the complete structures and patterns within your DNA, but you are always totally free to choose which seeds you will release.

Tom: So, are you saying that we do not have strands of DNA that were purposefully disconnected to make us remain ignorant and pliable to manipulation?

Edgar: I am saying that the story you have heard is not my understanding of the situation. But, I must admit, I am not fully awake yet in God, and therefore, my understanding is still somewhat limited. What I personally have been shown, is that – it was high level beings – much higher than myself - that implemented the intricacies of your genetic realties. I do understand, as they have explained to me, that the DNA of humanity is complete in and of itself. It is the free will of the consciousness of the individual human being that activates whichever seeds within the DNA are deemed most necessary, for the next stage of growth.

Tom: This is great news because many New Age people have been told that dark reptilian ETs have disconnected their DNA, which made them feel disempowered and even enslaved. So, are you saying that individual consciousness is the key to free will and further evolution?

Edgar: Yes, this is the truth as I know it. Consciousness, and what you do with it, is the ultimate key. Consciousness is the most important element at work here, although, it is also true that there are extraterrestrial races that have indeed ALWAYS studied human DNA and are most interested in how it operates.

Extraterrestrial beings have visited the Earth for many MANY years – but they do not have ultimate control over the human population. It is extremely important that you come to understand that humanity is not powerless.

But, humanity must wake up and realize, that it has now and always - great spiritual power within its grasp. The Almighty, the Being I call the Good Father above, would not allow his precious human children on the Earth, to be controlled or destroyed by another set of his equally precious children. Therefore, you must understand that the "aliens" – as your culture has come to refer to them – are actually your brothers in space. They are your spiritual family, and are children of the Most High, just as you are! (At this point – a loud static sound came through – and my Skype connection with Bob was interrupted).

Bob: (After a break of about five minutes . . .) Hello Tom? What happened?

Tom: Our Skype signal just went out. The connection crashed.

Bob: Yes, I felt a lot of static in the air. They just brought me back and I felt really jolted. Did we get anything at all yet for the book? I don't know if I'll be able to go back under or not?

Tom: Are you kidding? The information that is coming through today is absolutely amazing.

Bob: Like what? What was so amazing? I didn't hear a thing.

Tom: Edgar Cayce said that it was our free will – the free will of the race – that always allowed its DNA be worked with by alien races. He said it was actually part of the overall plan – from the very beginning – that we would have our DNA worked with, rewired and even enhanced. Having free will - meant that - we always retained the ultimate power over our own realities, within our own consciousness. We always retained the basic will free to override or ACTIVATE any of the genetic codes in our DNA, whenever we wanted to.

Bob: And so – what does that mean? I haven't read up on any of this? I've been too busy doing my 15-hour days.

Tom: This information is important, because it means that conscious choice and free will CAN override all prior patterning within our DNA. We – as individualized states of God Consciousness - are more powerful than any code or strand inside our DNA. Edgar is saying that our level of consciousness is the key that makes us free, no matter what the aliens have done or not done with our DNA. We have the ability to activate or DE-activate as many strands of DNA as we choose to. No outside force can prevent our activation and utilization of our own DNA – because of our free will. So, I think that you and I must be activating more strands of DNA which is what is allowing us to have these multidimensional experiences with the Light.

Bob: Wow! That is thrilling! This is really good stuff. Let me see if I can go back under. Give me some time.

Fletcher: (Connection re-established with Bob and the spirit guides). Hello there. This is Fletcher. Give us just a moment here. We are trying to get into the body here. We are having some difficulty today because of the electromagnetic energies. Just a moment. There is a lot of static in the atmosphere.

Rose: Hello, this is Rose. It is such a pleasure to be with you today. Fletcher asked me to come through because he felt that my energy would be gentler and our medium could handle it a little better. Do you know, that I've been listening in to your conversations with Mr. Cayce, and I must say – that I am most inspired to understand more about these things. In terms of spiritual greatness, I am relatively new to this spiritual world. I do not have the experience of great beings, like Mr. Cayce. But, I have learned, since coming to the spiritual world – that there is a plurality of worlds.

When I was upon the Earth, I only thought of Earthly things. I never suspected that there was anything of interest beyond the Earth. When people would speak to me of flying saucers, I thought they were daft. But, you know, in my time, there were many sightings of alien craft. Many people in England – not I mind you – but many of my fellow Englishmen believed that the aliens were going to end World War II. There were many instances of sightings during the War, sometimes at the very height of battle. You may find these sightings recorded and documented if you were to research news reports from that time period. I have learned much about this since coming over here. The alien craft would fly over the great battlefields, as if observing. It is just fascinating. Have you not seen any UFO's yourself, Mr. Berg?

Tom: Actually, that brings me to my next question. Bob has recently felt that the extraterrestrials are attempting, and have attempted, to reveal themselves to him, in the skies outside of his balcony windows. Bob actually has experienced a series of strange events the last couple Wednesday nights, right after our transmissions. And I too, have had the feeling that something is going on "up there", but neither of us has actually been able to see any physical craft, in our fully awake state. Bob had his recent Wednesday night sightings in a semi-dream state. He saw, what he describes as a large mother ship and some black helicopters. Can you please shed some Light on this?

Rose: First of all, let me assure you that Fletcher always stands guard over our medium, monitoring his well being. And it is part of my work, as a guide, as well. So, he can rest assured that there is no danger from the alien craft that he has sensed outside his building.

It is true that our medium is having contact with other beings, the Pleiadians especially. He has drawn the Pleiadians to himself without realizing it. If you were to ask him, if he was drawing the Pleiadians to himself consciously, he would deny it. But, I assure you that on a soul level, this contact is part of his evolution. You yourself have also drawn to yourself both the Pleiadians and the Essessani.

Our medium can remember seeing crafts – vaguely – flying outside of his window, on those Wednesday nights, but he was in a kind of a trance state. We brought him to the window, in that trance state, in order that he would see the craft and so the sighting would be impressed upon his subconscious mind. We allowed this to happen in this way in order to offer him a gentle exposure to what is about to unfold.

Please be assured, as both Fletcher and Mr. Cayce have said, that the day is soon coming when you both WILL see them, while you are fully awake and fully conscious. We don't wish that the people of the Earth should be overwhelmed, which is why many of you are being gently introduced to this reality with glimpses. This is what is happening to both our medium and to you as well. Your senses, and your awareness on the deepest of levels, are not closed down to the reality of the extraterrestrials. So, when you believe, that you have had some kind of contact and you feel this in your mind, please know that, the reason you feel that way is because you have such contact.

These experiences with beings from other worlds are coming in order that you raise your vibration, so as be better able to share these high spiritual truths. This is necessary, because the Earth is still in danger. Fletcher has told me that very clearly, that the danger comes from humanity's selfish, greedy ways of dealing with each other. Those beings from other worlds, as I have come to understand it, wish to bring harmony back to Planet Earth.

I can tell you Mr. Berg, from having lived through World War II, however briefly, that the destruction that humanity is capable of inflicting upon this planet is absolutely frightening. It is horrible and ghastly for my own mind to even think of it. Therefore, my prayer for humanity is that those of the higher consciousness might intervene. We guides have worked for many years, hoping to open the minds and hearts of our charges. But, sometimes a more direct method is necessary. Fletcher has said that it is for this cause that the aliens are coming and have been coming to the Earth.

The extraterrestrials are going to cause a direct intervention that will force humanity to face itself. After having gone through my own personal experience in World War II, I must say, "I think it is about time." I should like to see this happen soon, because people must come to a point where they are willing to work on themselves, and on their consciousness, and on their behavior. Fletcher is here. Just a moment.

Tom: Thank you very much Rose. That was fascinating.

Fletcher: We have been having some problems with the medium's vibration tonight because of electromagnetic interferences and currents in the atmosphere. So, we don't think that Mr. Cayce will be able to come through again tonight. There are too many problems in the electrical field. Is there something else that I can help you with?

Tom: This has been utterly fascinating. My next question is more of a personal nature, if that's OK with you. I would like you to help me understand, what I see as a paradox, between the so-called spiritual life of contemplative solitude, and one's human/physical need for family and friends. I am asking this, not only for myself, but also for all those who are going through this same paradoxical dilemma.

Does our spiritual growth time of inner work and introspection have to exclude romantic and familial relationships? We are all experiencing the very same problem, in that, we don't seem to have people in our lives right now to hug us, and kiss us, or caress us physically. Are periods of physical and emotional solitude part of the overall plan, or are we just keeping people away because of our unconscious thoughts and fears? Don't all humans need some touching and caressing, just like cats and dogs need petting and caressing? Are we keeping this loving touch away from ourselves through reasons we don't yet understand? And, what can we do to bring this kind of intimacy closer to us, even as keep growing spiritually?

Fletcher: Oh well, you are raising a very good point here. It is a balancing act, here. There are times that we take you away from too much closeness with humanity, to free your mind to hear our words. You and your friends have been crossing through a period of spiritual growth where you do seem to require that some limitations be placed upon the physical body and the physical life. It is important that you understand, that while you are on the Earth plane, the flesh can be quite distracting to the hearing of our voices. It can sometimes distract you from recognizing the presence of Spirit.

As you know, there are churches, like the one I was raised in, where the priests take vows of celibacy. That is actually not the best way, to tell you the truth, because they force it on everybody. But, there are many people, at certain times in their lives, who need a period of separation from others, in order that they may turn inward to the higher things of Spirit.

You see, when a touch comes to the body, it is very easy to let it stop at the level of the body, which causes people to forget the spiritual energy behind it. Let us talk about the difference between love and lust. The word lust describes what happens when people only think about the pleasures of the body and totally forget the inner essence of the other person, or the spiritual energies involved in the exchange. Lust is a form of physical selfishness. But, to love is to merge the energies of body and the spirit, to a place where there is an exchange of pleasure and emotion that goes deeply into the essence of each participant. In love there is a giving and sharing of the spiritual self and that giving of the spiritual self brings one to a place of being able to receive real love from others as well.

Right now, it is true that you, your friends (and even our medium) have deprived yourselves of some bodily connectedness. This will only be for a little while longer though, in order that you might develop spiritually. Because each of you are moving so rapidly in your growth, you will soon come to a place where you will be able to balance it all out quite nicely.

Tom: Are you saying that we are going to be having more love relationships, now that we have grown spiritually?

Fletcher: Yes, that is what we are saying. That is why we let you be in a little place of isolation in order that you would have the growth that you need for your spirit, without the distraction that most assuredly could come from romantic relationships. Now that you are growing in Spirit, so rapidly, you are ready to integrate the physical side of love once again. This is because you are in position now where you will be able to find a good balance. The spiritual growth would not have been possible for each of you, if you had not gone through this period of isolationism.

Tom: Are you saying to just surrender and trust God's timing? Do you mean– that – more physical relationships - (which would include both love and sex) - will be brought to us at the right time and in the right way and in the right place? Is it all about just surrendering?

Fletcher: You see, human relationships cannot be controlled from the level of your human personality, because relationships are NOT material things. True relationships are gifts of the Spirit, and are helped along by the guides. You know Rose was a great matchmaker while she was on Earth. She used to arrange to put all kinds of people together. I bet you that if you asked her for some help, she would be more than glad to help you.

Rose has, in fact, already helped you meet some new people, so that you will be learning the value of working with us.

Tom: So, are you saying that when we feel isolated, that means that it's part of the overall plan for our development and growth? Sometimes I worry that we have actually become afraid of love or romance or even sex, because we have fallen into the cultural belief system that says sex is dangerous, or even "bad". So, my next question is about combining sex, love AND romance. How do you balance them? So many people out at the clubs and bars are just kind of lusty and hungry sexually, and don't seem to be interested in the give and take of real loving relationships.

Fletcher: That is the truth. That's where many of your past partners have gone astray, because they have focused ONLY on trying to increase the pleasures of the body. The thing to remember is that there really is nothing wrong with physical, bodily pleasure, because you wouldn't have a body if you weren't supposed to enjoy it. I have to tell you, even we spirits experience what would be similar to your physical pleasure, over here in the Spirit World.

The thing is, the problem that humans have, is that they keep forgetting that behind the bodily pleasure there has to ALSO be a real feeling of love. How many people hook up with others sexually, (that's the word you use), and then they find the very next day, that they don't have anything in common and nothing comes of it? Then, they become depressed and disappointed.

What they must understand is that, this disappointment is inevitable, because neither side remembered to allow the spiritual self to come through and be fully involved in the sexual exchange. It was because, only the pleasures of the physical self mattered, and the true essence that generates the physical, the spirit, was not allowed to be present. It was for this reason that the relating could not be sustained.

Tom: So, how can we bring more love into our sexual experiences, and into our lives, in general?

Fletcher: Well, this is where you have to remember to ask your guides to draw to you those who are of like mind and spirit. We will be glad to help you. All good relationships are gifts of Spirit and are orchestrated from the spiritual realms. You yourself get a little bit fixated on surface appearances. You need to go beyond judging people just by how good looking they are. You may be in a group of three people, all who are beautiful looking. But you've got to remember now to look beyond their bodies and say, "OK, now I have three potential lovers here, and they all look quite beautiful - but - which of the three is the most like me in mind and spirit?"

Actually, I don't mind that you like beauty, and I don't judge you for doing that – because when I was alive upon the Earth, I used to put on my uniform and strut about, looking at the beautiful ladies. I still do a bit that even here. You know Mr. Tom, over here we still like to have our fun too.

Tom: Are you able to make love over there?

Fletcher: Yes, we do have a form of sexuality here, but it is different than what you know on Earth. Here in the Spirit World, sex is more of an exchange of energy. Souls do merge together much like in human intercourse. And we do experience great orgasms when our spirits successfully merge together into a vibration of oneness. You have much to look forward to over here. (At this point the Skype connection ended abruptly – which also terminated the transmission for September 3rd.)

BOB HICKMAN POSTSCRIPT:

Love, sex, aliens....It taken me a few days for me to even begin to write this, as I needed some deep reflection time. When I reviewed the above transcripts, I couldn't help but feel a mixture of emotions. Happiness, awe, anxiety, fascination, all of these went through my mind and heart. More and more of the "Other Side" is revealed, and now even more of "Other Worlds" are revealed. The realization that I am actually being contacted by aliens is more than I think I wanted to know, yet somehow, it all makes absolute sense to me. There really is a shift of awareness coming to the earth and the truth is – we are NOT alone! I asked myself over and over again—"Did you really see a ship that night?" "Are you really in contact?"...No matter how much I try to deny all of it, the fact remains that I know deep within that I am somehow connected to an alien presence that is visiting our world. I think the "normal" human reaction should be fear—even terror at the discovery of this reality, yet I am not afraid—stunned—yes—but not afraid. I suppose because I am a medium, the idea of connecting with people from the Spirit World (which is technically another world) has helped me to cope with this. I wonder about other people on the earth. Are they having similar experiences and can't tell anyone? Am I helping them by revealing this, or am I hurting them by opening what may be for them trauma? Am I totally insane? I look over the past few weeks, and take comfort in the fact that Tom is here, sharing this experience with me. In him I find a wise friend, a counselor who has faced the very questions that hit me at my deepest level of being. I am glad to have a confidant who understands the very world that is now opening to me. I feel fortunate that Rose broke the news of my alien contact, as her presence is always gentle and supportive. Fletcher seems to even be able to discuss love, lust, and sex. I like his conversations with Tom about all of this, for it brings me back to earth, and well, makes me feel more grounded. It's a comforting thought to know that even those in the Spirit World are interested in what many consider mundane realities of Earth life. I like my guides, and I trust them. I know they seem to always give Tom good advice, and I take comfort in that. Whatever this path before us is, I can walk it, for I have Tom with me and the Spirit Guides, seem to be so interested, kind, and supportive. I think tonight I will go out and watch the sky; maybe I will be able to see the Pleiades. Who knows, maybe I will meet my long lost relatives from the stars.

CHAPTER SIX
THE TRUTH OF THE CHRIST LIGHT
September 17, 2008

(There was a great deal of static in the Skype connection during this brief exchange.)

Fletcher: Oh hello there – this is Fletcher – can you hear me there?

Tom: Yes. Hello Fletcher, welcome back.

Fletcher: Give us just a moment. There is a lot of electromagnetic energy in the atmosphere tonight. We don't want to over stimulate the electrical system. Sometimes our own power can short circuit the connection. Oh, but it is so good to be here with you again.

Well, we can see that you humans have been having a most interesting week. (Note - this was the week when Fannie Mae and Freddie Mac were taken over by the US government, and the stock market fell sharply).

So, often, we follow you humans around, watching you. We like to keep an eye on things, although we like to be in the background. We don't want to interfere too much, because it's our real job to kind of guide you, but always in a most gentle way.

This week, it is most important that you be listening to us because we will be bringing over important information to guide you. Just a moment - we are sensing a strong vibrational disturbance here. (Skype connection broke up at this point, so we rescheduled for the following week.)

BOB HICKMAN POSTSCRIPT

It seems the more Tom and I get closer to working with the Guides, the more electrical disturbance this is. To me this is fascinating, and another evidence of spirit presence. Years ago I did paranormal investigations and we always found high electrical activity was present at many of the "haunted" locations. I find it fascinating to see that our computer connections regularly collapse—but only once I enter a trance state and the Spirit Guides appear.

CHAPTER SEVEN
DIVINE MERCY

September 23rd, 2008

BOB HICKMAN PREVIEW

Tom and I met up again this night for another séance. We hoped that the guides would know how to handle the electrical problems we had been having. As a psychic-medium, I can't wear a watch, for my body's electrical system is in high gear because of the spirit communication work I do and tends to short out any electronic devices I use. It was interesting to note that again we had electrical problems and when I went back into trance again, Fletcher had Rose come through. It seems that Rose's power is somewhat less intense than that of Fletcher or the others. Despite the technical difficulties—it was well worth the hassle and wait. Entire new worlds of understanding were revealed this night. Here is the amazing transcript of our session.

Fletcher: Oh, hello there. This is Fletcher – can you hear me out there?

Tom: Yes I can, welcome hack.

Fletcher: It's so good to back here again with you. Just a moment while I adjust the vibration. We are trying to pull in our power just a bit so we don't overtax our medium.

Well, there is a lot of spirit activity all over the Earth tonight. You know – that veil is getting a bit thin here – between the worlds. I can tell you that over the next few weeks you'll be having an easier time with these transmissions here - as you work with our medium. We are feeling like it will be easier for us to come into his vibration because we are able to access the energy of the Earth a bit better at this time.

Tom: That's good news. Bob is very concerned about that. We both are.

Fletcher: Yes, we need to keep an eye on him. He tends to take on a little too much. Sometimes, I tell him that Rome wasn't built in a day, but he doesn't listen. He's quite eager because he feels - I suppose you could say - a compulsion to help people. But, I have to say that I don't blame him, because sometimes we here in the Spirit World get a little bit overly eager, as well. So, we try not to push him too much. Actually, he pushes himself. He has a real softness for Rose - and souls like hers - because he remembers the night Rose came to him. He has a great deal of concern for those suffering souls who are crossing over to the Spirit World. But we are keeping an eye on him and we are going to try to help him find a little more balance here.

Tom: He seems to be working awfully long hours, every day of the week. Do you think that he is working too hard?

Fletcher: Yes, well, I do think that this is a bit of problem. But, you know, we are going to be giving him a little extra energy so that he can push through it all. We are going to be withdrawing some people from him for a little while – so he will have a little more free time.

It is important for our medium – and for yourself as well – to allow yourself more fun time. This is because - when you get all wrapped up in your work – like he does and like you do – then you have a bit of a problem. This causes you to be overtaxing your entire nervous system, which makes it harder for us to come through you. Your energy gets depleted— and that's the VERY energy we use to come in on.

It's like a wave length we travel upon. You know, think of a radio with batteries inside. It's the batteries which provide the power to pick up the signal from the radio station. But, if the batteries aren't so good – and become weakened - then the radio signal can't be picked up. Right?

Tom: Right!

Fletcher: We are trying to recharge the batteries. So, we are going to be mak'n him have a little more fun in the coming weeks. And, you wouldn't do bad yourself to do the same thing as well.

Tom: What about making money? He says that he is working really hard just to pay the bills.

Fletcher: Actually, he is not running out of money OR clients to serve! He has a very strong need to serve the people - a compulsion. But, we keep telling him, "Ain't nobody leaving ya

Bob." But he doesn't hear that, and he says back to us, "Oh but Fletcher, just one more call. People are waiting."

Oh, we do so admire his service, but we . . . (Skype transmission disconnected here – so Bob had to come out of his trance – call me back – and return to his trance state).

Rose: Greetings, this is Rose – can you hear me?

Tom: Yes, hello. It's wonderful to hear from you Rose. Hi!

Rose: Fletcher has asked me to come through, because he thinks that my energy might be gentler on your system here. Oh, it's such a pleasure to be here with you once again.

You know - sometimes - we do believe - that it is the power of our own vibration that is interfering with your computers – so we are very sensitive of that energy. It is not impossible for our energy to inadvertently destroy such items.

Tom: For some reason - lately – we have been having more problems maintaining our Skype connection –between Washington and Hawaii. So - I'm wondering - if Bob shouldn't get one of those new Blue Tooth speaker phones like the one I just bought – as a backup – or alternative communication system.

Rose: I must say, I am most fascinated with the technology of the Earth today! In our day, even to have a telephone was an amazing thing. I always thought that the Americans were more advanced than we were, in these matters. So, I think that perhaps our medium could handle the latest technologies. It would not be at all against our operations. You know, we try to always be most careful when working with your tools – especially with your electronic systems. May I say – that there are many spirits in the atmosphere – as Fletcher mentioned - that are causing an effect on global communications everywhere.

Tom: Right. We are using the global internet, rather than a regular phone for these conversations. And that is what is causing me concern, because the connection keeps breaking down, right in the middle of Bob's trances. We can actually hear the electronic static get louder - and then – the interference interrupts the call, completely!

Rose: Well, this is all fascinating to me. Do not worry, however. You will have success with whatever technology you use - because we are going to be helping you finish this project. There are great numbers of souls over here who are waiting to bring across their messages. Wait just a moment, Fletcher wishes to add something.

Tom: Thank you Rose, I love you.

Rose: I love you too my dear. Bless you!

Fletcher: Oh hello there – this is Fletcher. Well, it looks like we're having some success in sustaining the connection here, so we are going to be putting somebody else through right now. Give us just a moment.

Edgar Cayce: Well, I do believe that I have made it across! (He speaks with a southern accent – which is easily recognizable).

Tom: Yes – hello Edgar – how wonderful to hear your voice again!

Edgar: Well good evening. Please forgive my rather abrupt entrance. We are having some difficulty with the vibration tonight – but we are present – I do believe. Can you hear us out there?

Tom: Yes, I can hear you all the way here in Hawaii. Where are you right now?

Edgar: I am in the Spirit World – if the truth were to be told. But you see, the way that we work is - we come into the medium's body. It may seem as if we are inside the body, but in actuality our spirits merely overshadow the consciousness of the medium's body. This is how we spirits take control. Have you ever seen a puppet master?

Tom: Yes I have. I played with puppets as a child.

Edgar: You know, in my day when I was growing up, they had a 'show and tell' with puppets on strings. The puppet metaphor is a good one to consider when thinking about our relationship with our medium. We are very much puppet masters with Mr. Hickman. We create actual invisible strings of consciousness and energy that are attached to him when we speak through him. So, even though it appears that we are IN the body while we speak – in actuality - we are in OUR dimension using these invisible strings to attach us to the medium. It is through these strings, and across these strings, that we bring the vibration that animates the medium. This is how we take control of the vocal chords.

Tom: That is just fascinating. It reminds me of the new super string theories that I've been reading about recently is science magazines. Some scientists are now theorizing that all things in the universe - and even beyond this 3D universe - are somehow connected or even created by - super strings of invisible energy. Is that anything like what you are talking about here?

Edgar: It is very much a similar process, though science has not yet fully discovered the overarching truth of this theory. They are only just now touching on the very beginnings of understanding these strings of energy, but we are most pleased, for they are helping bring knowledge to the Earth. So, yes, the string theory can be applied in understanding trance mediumship. It is all a very similar situation.

Tom: That's just fascinating. So, according to what you are saying about these strings - science is getting close to discovering a theory that could explain how sprits contact humans, just like you contact Bob.

Edgar: It is very true – the interconnectedness of all life. You know, the ancient teachings have often talked about karma and how - those who do certain good actions - will receive the benefit back in exchange for their actions. This process could also be applied to the many string theories that are popping up in the scientific community.

Do you remember when you were still a child and used to play "telephone" with a wire and two cans? We used to make telephones in that way – and talk through them – because the vibration of our voices would travel along the wires or strings. We had to hold the strings tightly so the energy of sound could travel along them. This game of "telephone" - so common among children - is actually based on a real truth – that invisible strings of conscious energy actually do connect everything. This old game of "telephone "was actually a foreshadowing of the reality of vibrational truth. All of us are connected vibrationally, through the invisible wires made of Spirit.

Tom: I am beginning to feel your vibration quite powerfully and even viscerally, as I transcribe Bob's channelings. I am hearing your editing suggestions more and more easily. Thank you for coming to me so clearly. I am hearing you all better and better the longer we work together on this book, and I just love the feeling. Your energy feels wonderful to be with and to have around!

Edgar: Thank you so much. We are working on coming even closer to your vibration. Fletcher has assured me that they have raised your vibration quite successfully now – so that you are much more in tune with the vibrations of the higher frequencies than ever before. We are very happy to work with you.

I must give all due credit however, to Mr. Fletcher, for he has truly been the one to adjust the vibration. In truth, he is the gatekeeper spirit of our medium, which means that – as gatekeeper – he regulates the energies of the medium. If it were not for Fletcher, I would not be able to be present, for he shields the medium. This is why our medium cannot have just any spirit in his body. All contacts must be harmless and harmonious and Fletcher must approve of them first. But, we have been around you and we are seeking to impart our knowledge to you. And we are most pleased to say that, because of Fletcher's help, you are now receiving our messages.

Tom: I am. Today I was studying the "Song of Songs" from the Bible, and as I read it. I felt great inrushings of insight and revelations coming into my mind, with amazing messages about the all loving nature of God.

Edgar: The Bible is one of my favorite literatures. You know, when I read the Bible here in the Spirit World, I don't just read it, I experience it. St. Paul said, "We see through a glass dimly". Are you familiar with verse?

Tom: Yes I am. My Bible translates that quote as "We see through a glass darkly".

Edgar: Well, what this verse is referring to is that the scriptures have not yet been fully understood or illuminated upon the Earth. When you return to the Spirit World, however, you will come so see quite clearly and understand the truth of the gospel and the truth of the words of the Master.

Tom: I wanted to talk to you today about that very subject. Many people in the world are really afraid these days, especially with the economic system tottering on the brink of implosion. And, I have begun to think that much of this fear comes from actually misunderstanding, even fearing this Invisible Being we call God. Our society – especially the educational system - doesn't really encourage us to believe in a God Source that is with us, IN us, eager to help us, and always dependable, no matter what.

So many of the great institutions and thought systems of our day have taught us that God is distant, aloof, disinterested, nonexistent – or even cruel. So, I was wondering if one of the purposes of our book is to help people understand that the Spirit World, which of course is God's world, is a realm of love, Light and overflowing kindness, not of fear, suffering or cruelty. The love and Light that I feel coming from you and Fletcher and Rose have shown me that spiritual love is as real and GOOD as I always thought it was!

Your words have also helped substantiate everything I wrote about in "Uncle Tom's Classroom" when I spoke about the dependability of ALL the Divine Interventions that have always helped me out – whenever I MOST needed assistance. You have really opened my eyes even further to the truth that God's Spirit World is actually loving, and is even offering us help, if we would just open up to it.

Edgar: My whole life was about serving the Divine Creator and His wonderful world of Spirit. I remember talking to the Lord at the very beginning, when I was just starting my medium work, because I did not like being called a medium at all. I wasn't' at all comfortable with the connotations of that word and what people thought it meant. I felt like a Christian, I prayed like a Christian, and wanted to be seen as a Christian. I pleaded with the Lord and said, "Please take this spirit of mediumship away from me. I am afraid of becoming subject to demonic forces."

I had great fear that being a medium meant that I was toying with the forces of evil. So I said to the Lord, "Oh, Lord, if You want me to serve in this way, then I ask that I always serve only the good." And do you know what? God DID reveal to me that great good DID result from my work with the Spirit World. I was shown clear evidence that many people I served WERE cured and healed and set free from their suffering - and they found inner peace. And that is the only reason I continued!

The world today, as you say, has forgotten the truth about the spiritual realm. There are many reasons that this is occurring. This forgetfulness has become quite widespread, especially since the time of the rise of materialism and atheism. You know, during the Russian revolution, there was great sorrow in Heaven, because all the spirits here saw the unnecessary sorrow that would come upon the Earth as millions of people were turned against the Lord.

Organized religion, I must say, has also done its part to hinder the growth of spiritual understanding and the truth of Spirit upon the Earth. You know, I myself was often times limited in my own understanding, for I so often felt constrained to restrict myself to a strict literal scriptural interpretation of the Good Book. I do, even today, believe that the truths of the Bible, although I now see them somewhat differently, can guide humanity towards a fuller apprehension of the spiritual world. The Bible is a guidebook of the spiritual world but because so much of the Bible has never ever been really seen, read or interpreted correctly, humanity has lost its way.

There is a God who is of the Light, a God who is totally and completely loving. Jesus Christ is the Son of God, the highest soul who has ever, or will ever, exist. The problem is that many humans misinterpret the teachings of Jesus. When Jesus says, "I am the way, I am the truth and I am the Light – and no man comes to the Father but through Me," what He means is "I will bring all souls to the Father – through the door – through the gateway that I have opened to the Father – through ME." Whether one believes directly in the Christ, or is following some specific church, one can still be led to the Father by the Christ. The Christ is not about belief or any certain interpretation. The Christ simply is! Are you understanding me?

Tom: Yes, I do. Thank you. That is quite beautiful and clear. May I ask another question?

Edgar: Please.

Tom: It seems to me that many people today think that the gateway to God is closed or even nonexistent. They think and act almost completely as if our world is cut off from God's world, wherever that may or may not be. They fantasize that God is undependable, distant, and perhaps – even angry. And, as you know, there are so many Bible stories – especially in the Old Testament – that have added to our fear of God. Our world today doesn't really know God as pure Love and Light and Kindness, because of the way the huge institutions have taught us that money is god, or that military power is god, or that society is god.

Many schools and churches, and much of the mass media today, portray a world gone insane. They hypnotize us with images of a planet in dire danger, a world that is NOT under any kind of dependable protection from an all powerful Being of Love, at all! In fact, we are told in many different ways, from various sources, that, if there is a Being called God - He must be cruel, undependable, frightening and uncaring, OR He would never have allowed all of this suffering on Earth. Even the Bible stories about hell, Adam and Eve getting kicked out of the Garden of Eden, "original sin", the account of Noah's Flood wiping out all mankind, the smiting of whole cities, and the bloody crucifixion of Jesus - have all added fuel to people's fear and uncertainty about God.

Personally, I just can't believe that there is a God who would enjoy wiping out his own children, as He supposedly did in the great flood, and in the days of Sodom and Gomorrah. And yet, that is what many fundamentalist churches, and even some New Agers are saying even today. There is a great fear among many that God is preparing to annihilate much of humanity once again. The "Left Behind" book series has sold millions of copies to millions of people who think this the "end of the world". How could that kind of violent behavior - which is predicted in Revelation - come from a God of real love and forgiveness? It just doesn't make sense to me at all!

Edgar: Let's start at the very beginning. Many of the old Bible stories have been grossly misinterpreted and misunderstood. The ancient stories of God's so-called cruelty came out of mankind's attempt to project onto its Creator its own fear of itself. The story of the great flood – as you read in Genesis – did occur as a reality upon the Earth, but it was not in the way that it was interpreted, as an action of retribution by God. It was a natural occurrence upon the Earth. It is true, however, that in the time of Noah, that the consciousness of mankind had become extremely negative, hostile and full of darkness, much like you see on the Earth today.

The human mind generated such negative thought energy that it created – by its very consciousness – the calamity that it experienced. God's will, as it says in the Good Book is always - that "none shall perish and that all shall be saved". The Lord did not destroy the people of the Earth in the days of Noah, nor did he destroy the people of Sodom and Gomorrah. All of this was and IS mankind's false and confusing misinterpretation.

Let this be known. Humankind brings upon itself ALL its own calamities. The Lord God, the Creator of Life, who is of the Light and Love, would only seek to bring healing and love to the Earth. Humanity uses free will to forget God and to turn AWAY from God, and therefore, it SEEMS as if God leaves the human self to its own undoing. If the human self should destroy its own self, please know - THAT it is NOT God's will OF his plan. It is man's own ignorance and lack of listening to the higher self, which is made of Spirit. Man's ignorance of the Spirit World, which is fostered in so many ways by your materialistic culture, CAN appear to be very self-destructive! Materialism IS an unconscious form of atheism, and it CAN do great damage to the human world, if left unhealed.

And so, humanity does have great fear. It is socially produced and socially induced. Your society teaches you to be afraid from the moment you take your first breath. And there is SO much greed still upon the Earth with your economic system of capitalism. It is very true. In my day, there were many who sought to make monetary profit from my work, but I would not accept that as my purpose or focus. As you know I was not a wealthy man. I did accept offerings for my work but most of that money went to my foundation that still exists today.

Tom: Thank you so much. Can I ask another question?

Edgar: I would be honored.

Tom: I would like to ask you about the way some religions have interpreted the story of the Garden of Eden. They told us the story in a way that has made us think that we have been cast out of the Garden by a very angry God, just for eating an apple. As a Catholic boy, I was taught to believe that God became so angry with the first two humans, for this so-called "original sin", that we ALL still need to be baptized or our souls will end up in limbo or hell. We kids were taught that we were "tainted" as soon as we went to church. And so, we were brainwashed with a real palpable fear of God, from our earliest years. It has taken me a long time to recover from that shame game. So, I was thinking - can we use this book to alleviate this fear of God, once and for all?

Edgar: It is our hope, as your guides from the Spirit World, that the truth WILL finally be revealed. And, we would encourage you to bring this very important message to the world, via this book. The sad fact is that humanity did come to believe that it had separated itself from the Light. Or worse yet, that God had somehow cast it out of Its Divine Love! Mankind did kind of fall into a dream world, which was made out of thoughts of guilt, shame, fear, anger and self-hatred! That was the REAL meaning of the "fall of man" – the Eden story was meant to represent the fall of mankind into the insane dream of separation, self-hatred and fear!

Humankind, at its very core and nature, is at one with God. It always has been and always will be. The Garden of Eden story of exile was therefore, only a symbolic story - although when I was on the Earth – I too believed it was literally true. Since coming to the Spirit World, I have come to understand the Garden of Eden story in a larger sense – AND the real truth that it portrays. The true meaning and message behind the story of Eden was misrepresented by the writer, by the very people whose limited fears were projected onto the Creator. And thus, they created a false reality that mankind still has to wake up from!

Tom: Can you tell us the truth about Eden?

Edgar: I will try as best as I may – to tell you the truth - about this Garden of Eden story. You know, these truths are great and even I am still learning. As I understand it – and have been told here – Adam is symbolic of mankind – of maleness and male energy. Eve is symbolic of womankind and female energy. It is also symbolic of the duality of God, for God is both Mother and Father. There are many cultures in the world that understand this

– and worship the goddess as the mother aspect of God. These cultures are true in their belief because they have come understand that God is as much a mother as a father.

The issue of man leaving the Garden of Eden is actually a story that represents man's choosing to forget his unity with God. When we hear the story about man leaving the Garden – it is actually a symbol for how mankind chose to leave the world of Spirit for the world of matter and the flesh. The reason why Adam and Eve became "aware of their nakedness" was symbolic of how man fell into duality – which turned into acquisitiveness and selfish motivation.

Mankind and womankind are pure reflections of the dual nature of God. God is both Mother and Father. Adam and Eve represent the duality of divinity. When mankind and womankind left the Garden of Eden – it was symbolic of leaving the world of Spirit for the world of matter. And when they entered the world of matter they forgot their oneness with God. So, the fall is symbolic of taking upon the spiritual being – the Earth condition. It represented when the spirit fell into the flesh and into the bodily form – and then began to believe that it was ONLY the flesh, blood and bone that it inhabited.

Tom: So, what about the traditional interpretation of this story? We've been told that God became extremely angry at all of humanity - for doing this. What is the truth about all this so-called anger and vengefulness that the old Bible stories attribute to God?

Edgar: Humankind, because of its own fear of itself, has fled in thought and belief, from its own Creator. When humanity came into the Earth plane, it chose to forget its loving Father Mother God – its Source. And, in that ignorance, humankind created a myth that said that the Lord God was angry. I want you to see that it was not that God ran away from humanity in anger, but that humanity ran away from God, in fear of its own self. God loves, now and forever because God IS loves!

Tom: Yes, I do believe that God IS loving - and yet - we are still so afraid. So, what are we SO afraid of that we have run away from our own Creator? It just doesn't make sense to me. How could we have been so ignorant as to create so much suffering for ourselves?

Edgar: Well, the truth is that humanity became afraid of its own true self; because we forgot that our true self is divine within. Down deep, we KNOW that we are divine in our core. But humanity - when it came into the appearance of flesh and took on the Earth condition, began to forget the permanent nature of our divinity. This forgetfulness occurred when we started seeing things and forms and bodies actually dissolving and passing away before our very own eyes – when we saw what we called "death".

Because the things of the material world were constantly dissolving and passing away from view, a great fear arose, a belief system that said that every human would also lose its own consciousness and die. And so, humanity, in forgetting its true permanent eternal nature, began to think that this passing and dissolving was a form of punishment, perpetrated upon it, by an angry and unfair God. Humanity totally forgot that it chose to come here to the material realm – only for a very short time.

Tom: So, humanity is blaming God for our so-called physical impermanence?

Edgar: Yes. Mankind is blaming our Lord God for its own forgetfulness. In truth, we are all eternal beings and death is an illusion.

Tom: That leads me to another question about another Bible story that has really turned a lot of people off to God. Many parts of organized religion – especially some of the most fundamentalist sects of Christianity – have told the story about God, the Father, demanding that Jesus make a blood sacrifice of himself, on the cross, to somehow pay off God for OUR sins. We've been taught that God asked for the suffering of his own Son, on the cross, to cleanse us of our guilt and of our sins. Can you please tell us the truth about this event, once and for all, so we can get over our insane belief in a blood thirsty God who wants us to suffer? Can you reinterpret the crucifixion for us so we don't believe that it was an act of an angry God against "His Only Begotten Son"?

Edgar: What Father would take his child and torture him mercilessly? What possible good could come from such an act? Jesus Christ came to the Earth to bring humanity back into God's fold – to bring man back into alignment with the Lord.

The Master even told us, "Ye are Gods". And he asked us to have faith only the size of a mustard seed.

Is it so hard to have faith the size of a mustard seed? Such a little bit of faith would bring us into total alignment with the Lord. In truth, the real self, the divinity that we are in our core, is never ever really misaligned from God. We only accept beliefs that teach us to think that we are misaligned. We are not – in truth – ever really disconnected or cut off from God.

If you do not believe that you are loved by God – and become lost and bewildered inside your own mind's beliefs – then you will deny the divine love of Spirit that constantly surrounds you. Jesus Christ's crucifixion was a symbolic representation of how mankind became afraid of the truth - and even attempted to destroy any awareness of the presence and power of God, on Earth.

Wherever the true Light of Spirit shines, it reminds people of their true self – the real Divine Self of which they were afraid. So they had to kill the Christ - so they would not be aroused from their human dream – the mental story, that they were the same as their bodies of flesh. The crucifixion was acted out to show the denial of the Christ - on the part of humanity – not as an act of revenge by God, the Father.

Tom: And so, am I correct in my understanding that the resurrection became the proof of the presence, power and the love of a God Creator – who has the power to raise his beloved Son out of all human suffering – even crucifixion? Am I correct in assuming that the resurrection represents the power of Spirit , which can never be extinguished or killed, no matter how strongly the world's belief systems tell us that we are only physical, and subject to the limitations of the matrix of materiality?

Edgar: Yes. Jesus Christ wished for humanity to understand the eternal nature of the real self! And He acted out the crucifixion and resurrection in order to show that divine love and life has the power to overcome every earthly limitation – even death. Jesus rose to remind people that the material world is only a temporary illusion, while the realm of Spirit is real and eternal. Do you remember that passage in the Bible, when Jesus said to

Mary Magdalene, "Do not touch me for I have not yet ascended to the Father"?

Tom: Yes, I do. I remember reading that Mary Magdalene encountered Jesus on the morning of the resurrection, somewhere near the tomb.

Edgar: Many people wonder why she could not touch Jesus, but we must understand that what Mary was seeing was the ectoplasmic form of Jesus. When the body of Jesus was crucified and then resurrected – it was resurrected by spiritual power. That power took on an ectoplasmic form. This is the reason why Jesus Christ - who was so full of Light and Spirit, could not be touched physically, at that time - for the spiritual body had not yet fully solidified. There are many mediums who bring spirits into séances and, and though the spirits materialize, they cannot be touched because their forms had not yet been set or solidified. They are symbols of the existence of eternal life – and are in many ways – like Jesus Christ.

Tom: So, why are we afraid of our real spiritual selfhood, if by realizing that this spiritual selfhood is our true identity, we would be set free from the delusion of materialism and fear?

Edgar: It is because humanity, when clothed in flesh, takes upon its very consciousness the vibrational energy of the flesh, which is attached to the material, earthly realm. And, it is because of the earthly things that humanity clings to, and believes are real, that actually cause the mental delusion. Mankind has come to think, falsely, that the world of matter is the one and only true reality, but this is a delusion. Humanity has become deluded by material forms!

Tom: It reminds of me of Neo in that movie called "The Matrix". It's as if people are asleep to what is really going on – and they are asleep to who and what they really are – aren't they?

Edgar: Yes, millions, perhaps billions of humans are asleep. Those in the Spirit World are often cautioned before coming to the Earth. They are told, "Beware, for when you go down into the Earth realm, and enter the lower vibrations of physicality, you may forget who you are, and lose your way."

And, that is why there are many spiritual guides around every human being to this day. Because, even the most enlightened of souls tend to forget who they are, once they find themselves in the world of the flesh. And so, we are ever ready to help guide those erring souls back to their own truth, the reality of Spirit, so that, in the end, they may come home again.

Tom: So, how do we stop hating or blaming the world of the flesh for our troubles? Many religions actually taught us to hate our material bodies and our fleshy nature. So, is there any way to bring God's love and Light back into the flesh, so as to merge the flesh and spirit back together?

Edgar: Well, you must understand that this was all in the plan with the Father. In the beginning we were all together, and we agreed to form the Earth. You know, you yourself, Mr. Berg, also helped create the Earth in the very beginning. You were with God!

We created these bodily systems for the evolution of spirit. We knew, that if we took on a more challenging condition, that we would surely grow from it. The body was never meant to be hated, only seen for what it REALLY is. But, that reality, the way the body was supposed to be seen and utilized and understood, has been totally twisted.

Humanity, has taken what God created for blessing, and has turned it into an object of fear. If humankind hates the very body that God gave it, as a blessing and for growth, it will not be looking back to God or trusting God. This is another reason mankind became afraid of God.

Tom: Wow, that's really good. So, how do we bring our sexual nature into alignment with God?

Edgar: Well, let me explain to you in this way. The Lord God created you with all of your energies and with all of your potentialities. Your sexuality, whether you are male or female, heterosexual or homosexual, this is all part of your life chart – and is meant for your learning. By being true to your nature and your sexuality, you remain in alignment with the Lord's overarching will.

The only thing that God has asked is that mankind not abuse sexuality, while in the body. Because, when one has a sexual experience – it is an energy exchange that is far beyond a mere act of the flesh. Sex is meant to be commended to the spirit.

When people become united – or are joined in marriage – the sexual act is considered sacred. Even if a male joins with another male, there is no difference, as long as you remember to reverence the sexual act. You offer reverence to your sexual experience by remembering that sex is also a spiritual act – a movement that merges you closely, soul to soul.

This is why people should not waste their sexual energy without bringing a loving vibration into the equation. Sexuality was created for beauty and to express love in the soul. Sex is destined to become beautiful and loving on your planet. But, if you forget this, and use sexuality only for self-gratification, then you short change yourself from the blessing that God has given you. Sexuality is never an evil act, in and of itself. It is not that we humans are not supposed to have sexual desire. We were created in this form, with these desires in us. But we must learn how to use our sexuality in the highest and most loving of ways.

Tom: I want to. I REALLY do. And, I have prayed and prayed to bring my sexuality into alignment with my spiritual self, by including love in the equation, but I am still looking for that special partner who wants to merge love with sex. Am I doing something wrong? Am I somehow unconsciously blocking myself, or is it just not the right time yet?

Edgar: The timing has not been presented. Hold on, Fletcher wishes to address this issue.

Tom: Thank you so much. This is fascinating information – really helpful!

Edgar: It is my pleasure. Hold on while I step back from the medium's vibration.

Fletcher: Oh, hello there, this is Fletcher here. You know, I am functioning as a guide to you now, so I think that it is better that I address this issue for you. It's not that Mr. Cayce is not wise; it's just that this is an area where I am personally going to be working with you.

Tom: Well, I really need your help. Because, I really DO want to bring my sexual nature and my loving nature together, so I don't just experience sex in haphazard, unfulfilling ways. So, any help you can offer will be really, really welcomed.

Fletcher: Well you see, the thing here is, that we will be bringing you a person of a higher vibration, and that person has not yet entered your energy field. But, don't be worrying about it – because this WILL eventually manifest for you. And, in the meantime, we don't want you to be scrutinizing yourself so harshly because, what you are doing unconsciously, is going back to your Catholic programming, which is all about guilt and self-condemnation.

Tom: Ah. So, I am feeling guilty. Are you saying that I should just give up my guilt?

Fletcher: Yes, you have a little bit of that going on. And so, you have to learn how to allow yourself to be more free in that area. When you are naturally drawn to somebody sexually, you will know and FEEL that it is alright to pursue it. We want you to know, that as you keep growing in your spirit, you are going to draw to you the very type of person that you are truly seeking. You don't want just lust.

Tom: You're right. I'm tired of having sex without some form of ongoing love. I yearn for love, but, as you have said so clearly before, that REAL love is a gift of Spirit. Loving relationships are ALWAYS gifts that come from the realm of Spirit. So, now I know that I can't make a loving relationship happen all by myself. I can't force it! I can't make love happen, no matter what I do on a physical level, now can I?

Fletcher: You are right. You can't do it all by yourself. But, remember that you are in partnership with us – and with the Godhead. And, with these forces united, with all our forces united, this area of your life will be eventually balanced out for you quite beautifully.

Tom: So, why do you keep changing the time-frame around this meeting with my next partner? It seems as if we keep passing the dates that you say will be the time I will meet my next partner – and nothing happens. What's up with that?

Fletcher: It is true, that the dates HAVE been pushed back a little bit, because you are working on other projects – very important things like this book. There is a lot that you are now accomplishing and we don't want to you to be distracted by falling in love, not just yet. We want you to get your work done here.

Tom: I am willing to do what you say, because I know that this book is extremely important. I do have another question though. As you probably have heard – the world is going through a huge financial crisis right now, and my friends are asking me to ask you how to navigate through these economic earthquakes? There is so much fear in the air these days!

Fletcher: Well, you know, the whole thing is about greed. The entire situation was caused by human greed. When people stop being so greedy, there won't be any lack of money. There is no problem with there being a lack of money in the world. The truth is that there is plenty of money. The problem is, it's humankind's greed that's blocking it.

Tom: What can I tell my friends about how to handle all the fear that we are being bombarded with - on an almost daily basis? Every time the stock market falls, the TV news media blasts us with more reasons to panic and fear.

Fletcher: Well, my advice to everyone is - just sit tight. Hold on, Rose wants to talk to you.

Rose: Oh hello, this is Rose. Can you hear me?

Tom: Hello Rose, it's wonderful hearing your voice again. Do you have something to say about all this financial mess we're in?

Rose: Well, I simply cannot stay silent on this issue. I lived during the great stock market crash of 1929. I was 29 at the time. I was extremely fortunate, because my family was wealthy and had a great divestment of money, so we did not suffer at all. We maintained our wealth. But you see, many were not so fortunate, especially those of newer wealth.

What I remember seeing many people running to their banks, and pulling their money away. You know, I don't really think that you will have a depression again because I think that most Americans are quite simply leaving their money in their banks. And, as long as the Americans leave it be, and keep their money in the banks, there will not be a further problem.

Tom: That's good to hear. But, I have three really good friends - Sarah, Charlie and Barbara, who are all living basically - month to month. They face serious financial concerns every single month, just trying to pay their monthly rent and other expenses. So, what can we tell them, and other people who are "just getting by" so to speak, that might help assuage their fears at this time?

Rose: Well, you see. Their fear comes from being a bit too attached to the Earthly realm and to some old beliefs about struggle and hardship. If they were to just ask for our spiritual help and support, we would be glad to provide it. You know, even our medium sometimes gets nervous about his finances. And yet, we always provide him with all the money he needs, when he needs it. He is never in want of anything. Spirit will always provide! God's love will always answer those who ask!

Those who ask for, follow, and listen for our guidance, are always provided for. And, even you yourself, Mr. Berg, might I say, will not have any loss, nor need you fear during this time. All of your needs are being met. It was our assistance that brought you to your beautiful new home. You were being guided by Spirit before you even met us - through our medium. And now, we are only helping facilitate, and speeding up, that which you had already begun in your own journey.

Tom: I try to see you and feel you more and more Rose. Is there anything that I can do to bring you closer, so I can hear you better, or even see you?

Rose: I should like you to simply listen to me - just listen for my voice. I am going to try and bring you messages, especially when you are talking with your friends. I mean no offense against any of your friends – for they are lovely people – but they are not yet vibrating sufficiently – to be at the high level - where they can hear us directly.

We would also like for you and our medium to spend some together sometime, as well. I just love bringing people together. I was known as quite the matchmaker in my time. Just call me, and I will be with you, by your side, whenever you feel the least bit lonely. We spirits can be with our medium AND with you simultaneously, because for us - there is no time and space. We are so fortunate to not be restricted by time and space as humans are.

Tom: Thank you very much. May I ask one more question?

Rose: Yes, my dear. Please.

Tom: What would you tell the people of Earth to get them to stop being so upset and disappointed with God? As I was discussing with Mr. Cayce, I am beginning to think that if our book could just help people stop being so angry or upset with God, and feel how much God really loves them, we would be doing a great service to humanity.

So, what would you like to tell the human race, to help them through this crisis of confidence? So many people still don't really trust God or even believe in God. They don't have much faith in the power of spiritual assistance – probably because the western religions depicted God as an undependable, very judgmental patriarch in the sky. And of course, our great institutions and governments don't exactly promote an optimistic view of things either. There are lots of people worrying about, and even predicting the end of our civilization, as we know it.

Rose: Oh my dear, I do understand this. The frightening stories I heard about God were what turned me partially away from the church, as well. You know, as I told you, I acted like an upstanding member of the Church of England when I was alive. But, in truth I was actually much more interested in how I was seen, and how my membership in the church affected my social prestige, than I was in the teachings. In fact, I thought that the most of the teachings were full of bunk. I used to say, "I don't believe in these teachings, and I don't even believe in much of what they are telling us about God." All I really cared about was the prestige of being associated with that church.

You know, there are many churches today which still are locked into the old stories about God. And so - we would like to encourage you, your loved ones and your friends to stop looking only to the churches for your answers. You must understand that it is time to look instead, for answers about God, within your own hearts.

Do you remember when I told you about my trips to India, when I met the swami's? Well, those swamis kept telling me, "Rose, within you is God's Light". But, I didn't believe them. In fact, I looked at them mockingly, and said, "You are just like my parish priests, and what you are telling me is a bunch of bunk". I was not wise enough to hear the truth of their message. Their message was quite clear. They said, "Rose – look within, for God is within you." Had I perceived that reality, I do believe that my life would have turned out quite differently."

Tom: What have you learned about God since crossing over to the Other Side that you can share with us today?

Rose: You know – when I crossed over into the Light and saw the loving Father . . . (emotional pause)

First of all – there are no words that I might say - to accurately describe God. Even the term "Loving Father" is totally inadequate. God is love, absolute and total unconditional, all encompassing love. You know, it is not that God HAS love. God IS love! We so often say that humans have love, we have love - we give love, but God IS love! God is the Source of all love, no matter what the form. Humanity has forgotten . . .

Ask your friends to think about when they have experienced love in their lives. All of us, at some point, have experienced the reality of love, even if it was only the love of a simple little animal – an animal that looked at us with totally loving eyes. If you can remember a little puppy dog looking at you with that kind of pure love, then THAT is the same as remembering the love of God. God IS that love! God IS the love in the puppy dogs eyes!!! God is the love in the eyes of anyone and everyone who has ever looked at you with love!

You need not fear God, therefore, once you understand God AS love. God is NEVER judgmental. There is no judgment on the Other Side. Do you know, that idea of judgment AFTER death is what I feared the most? But, when I finally DID cross over into the Light, my first thought was, "My heavens, now I will have to answer for all my sins." But, that attitude was soon replaced with an overwhelming awareness of love. I could actually feel the loving presence of God's loving support all around me. I was bathed, literally bathed, in God's Light and Love. I do not have the words to convey to you, how completely that Divine Light healed my soul. It brought me up to levels (said with great feeling) that I cannot even begin to express to you in words. It healed me on all levels. It made me whole again! (She sounds almost as if she is going to cry).

Tom: That is just beautiful. May I ask, have you seen Jesus Christ personally?

Rose: Oh, how sweet that you would think of me as that advanced and evolved. Yes, I have seen Him, but only at a distance. It's not that I'm not good enough, but He is very busy, and occupied with His great works, you see. Edgar Cayce knows Jesus Christ better than I do, because he has spent much of his life in conversations with Him. I know of Him and I have seen Him from a distance, although I am not in His inner circle – I should say (laughing).

Jesus Christ is IN the Light with the Father. When we talk about the Throne of God, it's not really a throne; it's that place of meeting, where the Christ is. It's the place where the Christ is AT ONE with the Father. So, it is true, when the scriptures say that "Jesus sits at the right hand of the Father". It is actually true, that He is present there – (and we can meet Him there) - because he is of the Divine Light – in such a way, that He shares in the Godhood. They are ONE! And only Love comes from their Throne!

Tom: So, how do I deal with the religious teaching that say that God doesn't love gay people enough to allow them to get married, just like everybody else? That seems so unfair!

Rose: It's not God who is unfair. The people who say that God doesn't want gay people to marry are the ones who are unfair. And - please remember they are NOT speaking for God, nor do they represent the love that God IS! Just look at the history of the church's teachings, and you will see, that they are have been filled with terrible errors. From the very beginning, up to now - so many people have been tortured and murdered at the hands of the church. Even the Anglican Church spat at the Catholics and tortured many Catholics, as well. I would say that there are few churches in the world today that are truly IN the Light. Each person must find the God who lives within. Jesus Himself always taught that.

Tom: I agree completely. I have been feeling the love of God within me, more every day. I really appreciate your help in helping me get to this point. I can feel God's love so powerfully –pouring through these beautiful islands - and especially – through this gorgeous new home that you have given me. I now realize how intimately involved - you all have been - in providing me with this wonderful new life here in Hawaii - and I am so very grateful to you. You helped make my dream come true!

Rose: It is our pleasure to come to you and help you my dear. We are honored when humans listen to our voices, and receive our help. We would wish that more of the Earth would have mediums. If more people of the Earth were to raise their vibrations, we wouldn't even need mediums, because they could hear us, and contact Spirit, themselves. Were our vibrations more powerful, we would no longer need our mediums to assist us in contacting the people of the Earth. But, the vibrations of many humans right now, are so low and dense, that we still must utilize mediums as go-betweens. So many humans continue to feel disconnected from us, and our Spirit World - even though we are always with you!

We encourage you to listen for us, for we will do our best to make our messages clear. Even we have problems in getting through to our charges. The problem with the Earth realm is that there are so many energies and vibrations that must be manipulated before we can come through to you. Communication can be difficult sometimes, so I am fortunate, in that I have Fletcher to help me.

Tom: My friends and I feel so fortunate that you have come to us through Bob. And we are so grateful to Fletcher for his help, as well. Is there anything else you would like to teach us – for the book tonight?

Rose: Yes, I would like to say, that each person on the Earth must take responsibility for their spiritual lives. The grave error that many of the churches perpetrated – and my church did it to me as well – was teach us that humanity's spirituality was "in the hands" of the priests and ministers. This made people think that they didn't have to do anything except - go to church on Sundays. They were taught to believe that the priests and ministers would do it all for them. This is not how it was supposed to be.

The early Christian church of the first century A.D. was an active church, as I now understand it. Each and every person was expected to actively participate in their own spiritual growth. Today however, the so-called modern church has become a "spoon feeding" church – where you go and they take a spoon

- and load it with theology and shove it your mouth. They literally force you to swallow it, like a baby being spoon fed by a parent.

This is not what the Lord would wish – as I understand it. Many of you who come here to our world – especially those who have just crossed over – find it very hard to grasp the reality of the Spirit World. Many come here with great fear and baggage upon their soul, because each soul is allowed to have its own beliefs.

There was a gentleman who came here recently, who was a Baptist minister on Earth. When he came over – God was present to him – and said, "I am God, your Father. I love you and I forgive you for all your wrong doings. You are in my love." And, do you know what this minister said to the Father?

Tom: What?

Rose: He spoke back to the Father and said, "I am sinful. And so, you cannot be God, because God is not as kind as this! The real God would be holding me to account for my sins, so you must be the devil." He actually started an argument with God.

That was when I was called in, to help bring him closer to the Light. And yet - still he resisted. He was a Baptist minister. He said, "This is all a trick of the devil. It must be Satan, because the real Lord God would never be so accepting. I have not been righteous enough. I am a sinner."

Though God's very presence was welcoming him and absorbing him into the Divine Light – the minister resisted the Light, and treated it as if it didn't even exist! We did not force this gentleman into accepting the Light. We simply escorted him away from God's throne. We put him in a little rest area, where he was able to sit with himself and meditate on his beliefs. In fact, he is still there. And it may be a while yet before we can bring him into the fullness of the Light, because he refuses to face up to the truth. In fact, he now believes that he must be in hell. This is the amusing part for us, because we placed him in the most glorious park in all of Heaven.

We will often let those who cross over – sit for a while in the most beautiful of sceneries – in order to acclimatize, you see. When you come across, you will understand this better. So, we put him in a beautiful place to rest because he is not ready to accept God. He is not ready - because the God that he believes in- in his mind and in his rigid belief system - is not the God that he has encountered.

And so - God does not force Himself on this soul - nor does He force Himself on any other soul. The amusing part – I must say with laughter – is that he still believes he is in hell. He is thinking even now, "I must be in hell because I am not with the God that I was taught. So, I must have been separated from God." He doesn't realize that there are many spirit guides around him who are trying to get him to listen to the truth.

We are saying to him, "Please listen. What happened to you - was only - that you were blinded by your own teachings, and by misunderstandings that were given to you." But he will not hear.

Tom: Wow - that is just fascinating. What will happen to him next?

Rose: In time he shall begin to hear us - because he had great love in his heart - and did many wonderful things while on Earth. So, his loving vibration will eventually help him open up to the Light. He will not have to go into the darkness – as I did. His vibration is such that he has already been able to come into the Light – even though he hasn't recognized it yet. The park he sits in - is made entirely of Light.

It is interesting to me – speaking as one who did dwell in darkness for a time - because I rejected and feared the Light – that it all should be this way. So many churches on the Earth are teaching people in ways – that even when converted by God Himself – they still deny the reality of the Creator. Fletcher says that the power is growing weak, and that we must withdraw soon. So, I am going to let him speak now.

Tom: Thank you Rose. I am going to be trying to hear you this week.

Rose: I shall be coming to you. I promise!

Fletcher: Well, we hope you have given you some insight here tonight. Mr. Cayce is asking me to bring his greetings again to you, although we don't feel the power is sufficient to put him back into the medium's vibration. We are going to be withdrawing here and we must be careful with our medium.

Tom: This has been amazing tonight. Thank you so much. I am beginning to think that you are practically writing a new book for the Bible. You are reinterpreting many of those old Bible stories in a way that really does help reveal that God is pure love!

Fletcher: Well, we don't like to think of ourselves so greatly - mind you. We just like telling you the truth as we see it here and hopefully some more souls will be coming to the Light. Don't be getting angry with us, but we need to tell you that - you yourself are still stubbornly refusing to see your own Light. It is a form of self hatred. Until you see the Divine Light within yourself, you are not going to be seeing yourself clearly at all.

Tom: How does one see their inner Light when they still have guilt, and years of self judgment to get over?

Fletcher: You have not been spending enough time in your meditations. You need to work on remembering that the Divine Light IS within you. You know the meditation that our medium taught you – about seeing the Light filling you? Well, when you do that more often - you will be connecting with our world more closely.

It is good that you will be trying to listen for our messages - but we also want to remind you - that it is even better for you – if you were to be listening to and connecting to God directly. You CAN do it. You HAVE done it. Sometimes you just forget, and that is why we must just tell you the truth bluntly, because we want so much to wake you up.

Tom: I bet if I could just give up this life-long pattern of getting down on myself – and criticizing myself so much – that I could rise into the vibration of Light more quickly. It's all about giving up our guilt trips – isn't it?

Fletcher: Do you not know that God loves you? You are child of the Creator. How many people on the Earth spend their whole lives – and don't even think once – about whether or not God cares about their options? The very thought that you even give a darn about God – means that you are so far advanced. We are so happy to be bringing you more messages – so keep on listening for our voices. The power is growing weak now in our medium's vibration so we must leaving. (Voice fades away – transmission ends).

BOB HICKMAN POSTSCRIPT

Over the last few weeks, Tom and I noticed that the Spirit Guides were becoming more and more profound in their revelations. It seemed that we were now moving into much deeper levels of teaching, and I was so excited to see this. As I look over the transcripts of the channeling now, I shake my head in disbelief. It's like the power is rising. I remember this night coming back from trance and again being shocked that so much time had elapsed. Not only were my guides bringing forth AMAZING information, but they seemed to be also pushing my psychic batteries to a new level. I seemed to be in trance longer and longer, and this did not deplete me as it would have before. I wonder about the "string theory" and now have a bit more insight to what happens when I go into a trance and channel. It is still a mystery to me, but I feel happy to know that the guides' teachings seem to be in unison with natural law.

Tom seemed to have developed quite a great friendship with the Spirit Guides, and I can see in this transcript how wonderfully he is interacting with Fletcher, Rose, and Edgar Cayce. I am so thankful that the Guides are not only imparting "universal wisdom" but also willing and able to help individuals with the "here and now" problems of life, love, money, sex, happiness, etc. Hearing from Tom of the Guides personal help makes me feel so reassured. I know that they will help us even with the small stuff of our lives, as they want to help us be successful on our journey here.

I was amazed also to see that Cayce had returned. I am still surprised that he comes through me, for I would have expected it to be a rare occasion to have such a spirit present. But, it seems that the Guides are truly intent on employing whoever they can to impart their messages. I wonder if Cayce is going to stay with me now as a guide, and what this will mean to my future channeling work. Looking at Edgar Cayce's teachings from this night, I am truly fascinated and relieved. Like many Americans, I grew up with a more "literal" interpretation of the

Judeo-Christian teachings as found in the "Bible." To see Edgar Cayce's teachings on the Scriptures is not only enlivening, but freeing to my spirit. I don't think anyone raised in the western world is not in some way affected by the fearful teachings about the Creator. Cayce seems to have an enlightened view on life, death, salvation, and the hereafter. It seems that Cayce moved beyond his more fundamentalist views since crossing to the Other Side. I wonder if even the great souls like Edgar Cayce struggled at the death moment and hesitated moving towards the Light of God because of fear in their hearts. I like the teachings he is revealing and but am still shocked that he speaks through me. It is a comfort to my spirit to know that we need not fear judgment, but can and will be received by a loving Father of Light. I also can't help but laugh when I read Rose's account of the Baptist minister who wanted to argue with God! How sad—for there are so many today still carrying this fear and negativity in their hearts. Even worse is the thought that those in positions of spiritual authority in this world are actively teaching these negative ideas to their followers. It can't help but think of the phrase I saw recently on a t-shirt at the local shopping mall that said, "What Would Jesus Do?" I think in many ways, that phrase brings me back to the heart of what is real and true in the spiritual life. I think of Edgar Cayce and wonder what his thoughts about this phrase would be...

CHAPTER EIGHT
THE STRUGGLE

October 2nd, 2008

BOB HICKMAN PREVIEW:

Whenever Tom and I got together for a channeling session we were always so excited – just waiting to learn more. I think that if you follow the teachings of the Spirit Guides, you can't help but get excited. As you will see in the transcript below—neither of us could sleep after our sessions. Below is a fascinating transcript of the experience.

Fletcher: Hello there, this is Fletcher. Give us just a moment. We have to adjust the vibration a little bit.

Tom: Hello Fletcher, welcome back. It's wonderful to hear from you again.

Fletcher: Thank you. Alright – there we go. I think we are settled in here. It's good to be back here with you.

Tom: It's always a thrill to receive your messages. What would you like to tell us today, Fletcher?

Fletcher: Well, Bob has been a bit nervous about this book. So, I've been walking around with him, saying, "You know we are going to be bringing the book along just fine." He was having a little bit of anxiety. He kept asking me, over and over, if the book was coming along alright. And I said, "You've just got to settle down and have faith that the book will be finished all in its right time."

You know, we are VERY interested in this project over here, and we are making sure, with great effort, that everything unfolds with just the right timing. And might I say in advance - you both will be VERY impressed and quite pleased when you see how the book turns out. We aren't going to tell you exactly how it's all going to unfold in the end, but you and Bob will be extremely gratified with what we'll accomplish together. We are so impressed just to be here with you. Rose is here. Just a moment, she wishes to speak with you.

Tom: Thank you so much Fletcher.

Rose: Greetings. My name is Rose.

Tom: It's wonderful hearing from you again Rose. I love you. Welcome back!

Rose: You know, I must echo Fletcher's words when he speaks about the issue of timing. When I was upon the Earth I used to always discuss this with my father. I used to say, "Timing is everything, isn't it Father?" And he would say, "Rose, you are so right, especially in business."

Timing is so important on the Earth because it effects everything, although we here in the Spirit World, have no time. Although we are not bound to time, we do still retain a sense of time primarily because of our dealings with the people of the Earth. We know that humans tend to think in a linear fashion, as if they are moving through space time, from one space and time to the next. We do understand this.

Over here, we talk about a total progression of the soul. The soul grows through a series of unfolding cycles. So, although it is outside of time, there is a progress of the soul which is evolutionary. And I myself, I might say, am growing even stronger in my Light. It is an enormous pleasure for me to continue to serve the Light, and to work on behalf of all those souls – such as myself – who once became lost. We would like to encourage you every day to remember those souls who still wander through the darkness of ignorance.

I made a visit recently to those lower astral realms - to the lower vibrational levels of darkness. And I must say that I felt great sadness there. I looked about and I said, "So many lost souls". And I prayed for all of them. I am happy to report that I WAS able to bring one kind young lady over to the Light, who was ready to make progress, but there are yet – so very many who remain lost in dark thoughts.

You know when I was alive, the Anglican Church used to do a special prayer during November for all the souls who had died. It was a yearly tradition. Do you remember that day? It was called "All Souls Day", because it was specifically dedicated to helping lost souls.

Tom: Yes, we had something like that in the Catholic Church as well, which was celebrated on November first, I believe.

Rose: You know, I think it is such a good practice. I only wish that I had thought more about this while I was alive. Now I understand – that if I had prayed for more souls that had become lost in darkness – perhaps I should have had greater help during my own life and death. One cannot look back with regrets, but I do now pray for all those souls who are in any kind of mental or emotional darkness, and I seek to bring them the Light, into the Divine Light of God. Just a moment, Fletcher is here.

Fletcher: Hello there. This is Fletcher. We have to tell you that Mr. Cayce won't be joining us tonight. He is working on a special project here, and so he is going to be tied up. So, you are going to have to just put up with Rose and me tonight. We hope you won't mind too much.

Tom: Oh Fletcher, I love talking with you and Rose. And, I treasure all the fascinating information that you are bringing forth. I really do believe that our readers are going to love hearing about what you and Rose and Edgar and Orion have to say.

Fletcher: Oh yes, we are hoping that our message will get out to as many people as possible. You know, when we of the Spirit World - get our minds behind something – things start to happen. And, to tell you the truth, we are simply no longer content to be speaking to only two or three or maybe ten people at a time, as we did before. It is time for the Earth to raise up its vibration, and we are here to help in that process. There are MANY such spirit workers like myself involved in this effort, although you've only encountered us so far.

I am here, Rose is here, but do you know, all around the world, there are many unknown mediums in backrooms, who are never seen by the general public. And yet, they are quietly doing what they can to commit their lives to the work of Spirit. And although their influence may be small, as time passes their impact grows. They are the connectors, those special humans who have become open contact points between our worlds, and they are serving as great teachers, as they witness to our world's existence. Have you even seen an hour glass that shows how time passes?

Tom: Oh yes.

Fletcher: Each little grain of sand has an effect on the passage of Earth time as one reads it. It's like that with each of our mediums around the world. Each of them is like one of those little grains of sand in the hour glass – and together – they add up to a glorious picture. Our worlds ARE in contact. Our worlds ARE communicating with each other. And so, we are kindly appreciating that you are taking the time here to help bring our communications more out in the open, via this book project.

You know, our medium Bob sometimes gets annoyed with us, and he says, "Oh now Fletcher, just go away for awhile. Leave me be. Why don't you go see Tom?" This is the truth. Because, you know, it's a real ongoing relationship we have. And it takes time. So, I understand how he feels. When I was still living upon the Earth, I had people in my life that I didn't always get along with. You know how it is when you are living in the body. Sometimes, you just get tired and you are simply not in the mood for talking with some people, because you feel like they get in the way.

Well, it's the same, when it comes to relationships between our two worlds - because, in our interactions with humans, we know that you sometimes get annoyed with us. There are a lot of people on Earth who actually CAN hear our messages but they tend to push us away. There are people who we talk to every day, and they even recognize us as spirits coming through. But, instead of welcoming us, they say, "We don't want to hear from you. Go away!" And you know, we must always honor their requests. We never press ourselves upon anyone, or force ourselves to be around anybody who doesn't want to share our vibration. Just a moment while we adjust the vibration.

Rose: Hello my dear. I am here. I could not stay silent. Fletcher has allowed me to step forward, because he wishes me to let our medium have a little break from the energies this evening. So, we are going to be very brief with you sir.

I was listening to your conversation with Fletcher. And, I would like to add that there are those who seek spiritual guidance, but even though we are around them, speaking, they are unable to hear us and receive us. They have not yet become consciously accepting of our conversations. And so dear sir, we hope and pray that your work with our medium will allow more and more people to become privy to our whisperings.

Tom: I hope so too. Why IS it that so many humans confuse your whisperings with the other voices that are coming from the media, or from their own thoughts?

Rose: People are SO hypnotized by their TVs and other electronic devices that they don't listen, even when we are speaking quite loudly and persistently. What we find most offensive on the Earth at this time are those humans who not only reject the presence of the Light – but who seek to block the Light from those who wish to receive it. They are spreading a form of atheism. In my day, atheism was already on the rise. It was quite fashionable to say that "God is dead", although I didn't partake of that. And yet, it was considered quite stylish and intelligent to be an atheist and reject God's existence.

You know, it is so ironic for us over here - because we know that to disbelieve in God - is as much an act of faith - as to believe in God. It is a faith in the negation of God's existence; a complete denial of God's Light and love. Unfortunately, many of those who SAY that they do not believe in God are simply those who have decided to reject somebody else's interpretation of the Divine. You know, I suppose that this was part of my problem when I was on the Earth. I would often say, "I don't believe what that vicar is saying. I don't agree with that at all." I used to call much of what the Church said about God, rubbish.

But, you know – I think – what I really rejected back then was not so much the reality of God, but the Anglican Church's interpretation of God. This is why, whenever one speaks of Divinity, one must do so ever so carefully, so as not to turn others against the higher truth of God's reality. That is what happened with SO many millions of people. They left ANY faith in God behind when they left the teachings of the organized religions, which they deemed untrue, and even ridiculous.

Tom: Yes, I've seen that in the gay world in San Francisco. Many people became so angry at organized religion's mean treatment of them - that they just left it ALL behind. They literally threw the baby out with the bathwater.

Rose: Do you remember the Soviet Union?

Tom: Oh yes!

Rose: Do you know, in my day, we had great terror of them. My family - being of the aristocracy - used to say, "My heavens, if the Reds come to England - it will be the end of us all." We had real fear of that happening. It wasn't simply the loss of our material wealth that we feared. It was also the immense brutality and hatred towards anything religious, that the Bolsheviks exhibited.

I heard stories in my lifetime of people in Russia who actually saw the Bolsheviks take people into the fields and forests and shoot them – and then burn their churches to the ground. If the truth were told, I wasn't really a very religious person, but even I couldn't tolerate that kind of brutal behavior towards people who believed in God. I did like the church I went to. And so, I thought that if the Communists came and destroyed our church, it would be a great loss for many people in our community.

I only bring this up because there is still a fear – from our world – that this dangerous attitude of hatred towards sacredness – could arise again upon the Earth. Any society that ignores the sacred dimension and even replaces it with a materialistic way of life is in danger of following in the path of the old Bolsheviks. You in America should not get so comfortable and be SO unseeing - that you unknowingly allow another type of atheistic culture and social order to govern your own country. We don't say this with any sort of fear mongering, or with a wish that you feel terror. We only mention this, in order to help you become more attentive to the moods of the continents - and the thoughts that arise - from their inhabitants. If your economic system, known as capitalism, continues to ignore the sacred truths and spiritual realities, then you need to transform it. Materialism has seen its day – and the time has arrived to move into a broader view of reality, one that honors the sacred in all things.

I would say that in today's world, the Chinese government is still one of the greatest interferences to people becoming aware of the sacred dimension. The Chinese are atheistic Communists. I died – in my last lifetime, before China became a communist nation, but I have watched China from over here. I must say, when I look at the Akashic records, I can see a three-dimensional series of holograms, showing China's entire history. This is how we are able to understand and learn things here - and it is how I saw the history of China and the rise of that Mao Tse-Tung.

You know Mr. Berg, I have great fear still for the people of the Earth. Perhaps it's my prejudice, but I don't believe that the Earth is clear and free yet of the extremely vicious and destructive influences of institutionalized, economic atheism. This new atheism, which has infiltrated the minds of modern man, and which comes clothed in the flashy garb of capitalistic materialism, has already destroyed many people's lives. Even though my own family and I SEEM to have benefited greatly from our wealth and status – on the surface – down deep, we were NOT any happier for it. In fact, I practically lost my soul in the process.

The truth is, God doesn't care what religion you may or not belong it. It's not about the church you attend or the government that dominates your country. It's not about how much money you have, or what your position or picking order is - in the social and cultural hierarchy. What REALLY matters MOST is the condition of your spiritual growth, the condition of your soul! God only cares about the actual state of the soul – and how much you are willing to absorb the Light of Spirit INTO your soul.

In China today, if anyone were to openly say, that they wished to know about God's Light and the Spirit World – they could still be imprisoned or possibly even executed. And so, I DO worry that there is no real freedom in China today. I don't care what the press says - it's not true that the Chinese people are free. There is really no basis for comparing their closed society to the societies of the west. At least in the west, people are STILL free to read about, study about, talk about or participate in just about any kind of spiritual pursuit they wish – and this must be celebrated and acknowledged! Fletcher wants to say something.

Tom: Thank you Rose - that was fascinating.

Fletcher: You know, the other danger on the Earth today is not coming so much from government sponsored, economic atheism – but from extremely fundamentalist religions. I say this because there are religious movements on the rise today - that are so extreme, that they actually put ideas into people's heads that end up turning them against God. We are quite concerned about that! Some extremist religions do things in the name of God that are very destructive, which – from our perspective – looks as dangerous as atheism.

Tom: Do you think that it would be possible to include some kind of teaching in our book, which would help defuse, and possibly even bring an end the to the world war of extremist religions? America is already at war in Iraq and Afghanistan because of the extremist opinions held by many religious and political leaders, and those wars could easily spread to other nations.

I was fantasizing at the beach today that you spirit guides – who live UP THERE in the Spirit World – actually are able to talk to some of the founders of the world's religion. So, do you think we could ask Mohammed and Moses and Buddha and Krishna and Jesus to talk to some of their followers, in order to cool off this dangerous world confrontation? Would it be possible to include some messages – directly from the Spirit World – that might encourage people to give up their most rigidly held religious beliefs systems that promote violence and hatred against other?

Fletcher: Well, that is exactly what we all want over here. It's so true you know. I've met the great Masters and I can tell you - that it hurts their hearts to see what is happening on Earth today.

You know, I have met with Mohamed, who IS over here too - and I can tell you - that this kind of continual warfare is not what he wanted or intended for his people. He never wanted his teachings to lead people to kill each other or cause suffering to women and children. NEVER! What happened was that the ancient scriptures attributed to him have been purposefully mistranslated and misinterpreted. This is similar to what we were talking about last week, when we tried to explain to you, that man projects his fears onto God, especially his fears about himself and each other. If man could only find peace within himself . . .

Let's take a crying baby as an example. The baby is born innocent. Even one that cries a lot - doesn't cry because of an inbred hatred against anybody. And that baby, even in its distress, doesn't look at its mother with hatred, and say, "Well I don't like her because she is the wrong color or the wrong religion." That's totally irrelevant. The baby is innocent, and doesn't automatically blame others for its unhappiness, until it is "programmed" to do so. You see, most forms of hatred must be taught or passed on down from one generation to another – and this is how hatred HAS been continued.

Remember - that whenever a baby is born on Earth, it has just arrived from OUR world. It comes in to the physical plane still innocent and its mind is clean of false beliefs. Its soul is ALSO still connected to the Spirit World. And that is why there is such joy and Light about all babies. They literally radiate the Light of the Spirit World INTO the Earth plane. But what happens, as they grow, is that, once they become acclimated to the material world, they are taught to forget the Light and the teachings from our side. This forgetting is always a great danger - because they get so deeply enmeshed in world of matter – that they forget the presence of Light and love.

After a few years, they forget the existence of their own soul – AND they ignore the souls of other humans, as well. And when they grow up – sometimes they join churches that actually teach hatred, instead of love. They go around saying, "Well, God says those people don't have souls. And, God says that we must get rid of them, even if it means killing them." There is a church on Earth right now - that we are very disturbed about. I believe it is called the Westborough Baptist Church. Have you heard about it?

Tom: No I haven't.

Fletcher: Well, it's a church that we are monitoring closely and may even seek to intervene against. It's an American denomination. This church preaches against people who have died - AT their funerals. They invade the funerals - and claim that it is because gay soldiers are allowed in the military that God let them be struck down. You see, this kind of hateful thinking is not in keeping with God's Light at all. That church is preaching hatred, bigotry and ignorance, which is moving its follower further and further away from the Light. They are in an extremely bad state, because they and are taking their members even further into the darkness than Rose was, when she died. They are teaching hatred instead of love – and that goes against everything we stand for here in the Spirit World!

Tom: How does God feel about this?

Fletcher: God doesn't hate anyone – but His heart grieves when He looks upon those who seek to do harm to ANY of His own children. God never hates any of His children, even the so-called bad ones.

We can look at it this way. A father may have two sons, one who is an angel and has dedicated his life to the highest good – and the other who is bad and has turned to a life of crime and destruction. The father doesn't disown the bad son – His heart only grieves for him. When God sees any of His children using His own name, in order to abuse His other children, He grieves a terrible grief. He can't stand this kind of behavior, which arises from a terrible misuse of free will.

Tom: I can understand this. Even though you told me to feel more happiness last week, as I watched the world's financial crisis get worse, and saw so many people losing their jobs and homes - I felt grief and even fear. The world economic system had a really depressing week. So, how can we feel inner joy and bask happily in God's Love, while we look around the world and see such darkness, upset and grief? How can we handle this paradox?

Fletcher: Well, that's a VERY good question. What you've got to remember, is that deep within you, you have a little spark of God Light that never goes out. That's absolutely true. It's that spark of life that fills your very own soul. The Indian Swamis explained that Divine Spark that exists within you, when they used the ancient terms, "Sat Chit Ananda". Those three words were linguistic definitions they conjured up to describe the three aspects of God consciousness that they had discovered. Ananda meant bliss consciousness. So you see, in your true state, there is always a spark of bliss IN your consciousness. It is forever, because - it is an aspect and attribute of consciousness itself.

What happens is that - when you are living in the body - you start filtering everything through your material senses and especially through your material eyes and brain. And when you do that – and begin to believe that you are ONLY a body - of course, you are going to begin experiencing suffering. Then, when you get to the point when suffering becomes almost overwhelming, you will have to go back within to find that spark of Light inside yourself that is your soul. Once you find your true rest in that Light – IN your soul - you won't be so trapped in the suffering of the world, like were before you knew your true identity. There REALLY is a true rest in the Light, in your inner being. If you rest in the Light, lad, you will no longer feel so much grief.

Tom: So, are you saying that God's bliss, Light and eternal love that make up my soul - are untouched by all the grief of our world? I'm a bit confused here. Since you said that He DOES feel grief about the world's atheism, hatreds and extremist religions – does that also mean then – that He can feel grief - and love – and BLISS – simultaneously?

Fletcher: God is never without His joy and love, because it is his Light, love and joy that create and sustain the entire material universe. He is the Creator of All That Is. And He IS bliss consciousness. He IS love. It is the Fatherly aspect of God, the Fathering face of God, the LOVING aspect of God that grieves for His children, even as He loves them. Even though He knows – and has already told us through, his messengers – that the evil things we are seeing happening upon the Earth right now – will pass. They are temporary dramas – like some kind of illusory spectacle.

This doesn't mean that the darkness doesn't seem real for many many souls – but we must learn to see beyond the "appearances" as Jesus advised – to the end result. "Do not judge by appearances," He said. All suffering souls will eventually return to their rightful place in the Spirit World, and will be given a chance to grow in Light - and find out they have Light within them. Eventually everybody comes back to the

Light – and back into bliss consciousness. We just wish it would be a little quicker sometimes. Just a moment here.

Rose: Hello, this is Rose. Give us just a moment while we adjust the frequency of the medium's vibration. There we are – there we go – now we are coming in. Now let's see.

I do want to say – as one who fell into great darkness – that when one finally crosses over into the Light – the peace that one experiences in that moment - is beyond words. I understand now – that God – as we term it – can't really be known by words – for they are too limited to describe what He really is. The word God is such a limited term for such a Loving Unlimitedness – but we will use it for now.

God IS love – a love far beyond words – an eternal love for us – and not only love FOR us – but a LOVE that IS IN us. God is the Being of Light that knows the true inner self – as well as the outer self of us all. He knows everything about us, because He is IN us. He is IN our soul. His Love IS the life of each and every soul. He knows our courage and our reservations. He knows our goodness and our badness, and always accepts and loves us, no matter what! In spite of it all you have ever done or NOT done – God accepts and loves you.

When our medium was a child he was told all this. Bob had shown an actual visitation from God, when he was about eight years old. Bob was standing in the middle of his home in the middle of the night, when he suddenly heard the Voice of God speak. God questioned him saying, "Bobby, do you believe in Me?" And Bob said to God, "Yes I do, but many people don't believe in me and my experiences." God told him, "Don't worry. You must go and tell the world that I love them, for many have forgotten Me, today."

I tell you that when I hear this story from Bob, I become so inspired. And, I am filled with great joy because it is also because of God's loving purpose - that I am able to come through. It is because of God's Infinite love for all his children that I am able to come here speak to people - and to offer my assistance - in whatever way I can. I wish you to think about that as well, because you TOO are here with a divine purpose.

You aren't living here on Earth at this time, ONLY for your own growth and personal pleasure. You are here also for those who have forgotten who they are and where they come from – and where they are going to. Think of that Mr. Berg. Realize - that you are alive now – on Planet Earth - for others as well as for yourself. You see, that was my fatal mistake in my spiritual life. I thought that I was alive on Earth, only for myself.

When I honestly review my life – I must admit – that every action was ultimately – only for myself. Even when I did charity work, it was only for a tax benefit or for the prestige. I never really cared about those I helped. It was a grave and sorrowful thing for me to come to that realization. Believe me, over here you cannot hide from yourself forever. You will do well - within yourself – to make peace with what I am telling you – for when you accomplish that – you will have a much better time of it.

There are many souls who do their Purgatory while they are still alive on Earth. We all go through that phase. We will do our Purgatory time either over here or over there. It is part of the process. But, those who try to short change their process, find that they are lacking greatly when they arrive in our world. All souls in our world are known by their Light. It cannot be hidden. It can be seen clearly. And I must say, I am most honored to be able to share with you that I have received an increase in my Light. And that I am very pleased to be able to share the Light with you.

Tom: Yes, I can feel your love, and the Light that pours through your vibration.

Rose: We come from our world with a true and all encompassing love. It is not like the love of the world, for in your world - souls usually love conditionally. Even the best of souls on Earth love conditionally. It is a human struggle, I suppose you could say. But, in our world, we wake up and rise above those problems caused by ignorance. Over here we begin – once again - to feel love and purity and goodness in our hearts which reflect the higher reality of our world, and of God, who animates our lives.

There are many people on Earth today who say that our medium and other mediums, are working for the devil. Do you know that Bob has been physically assaulted by church people? Can you believe that church people would do such a thing? They actually cursed him and threw objects at him, calling him evil. I was not working with him at that time – but Fletcher has told me all about it.

And so, we come here with only one purpose – that of bringing the Light of Spirit into your world. We do no harm to our medium or to those who come to him. And yet, the ignorance of many fundamental teachings have permeated the churches upon the Earth, and particularly, if you will forgive me for saying – many churches in the United States. England's greatest challenge now is that it has a greater number of atheists today, than during my time. And even those who do attend church are rather tame, compared to the passionate Americans. Oh, we do have our smaller factions, but – you know – they are much less in my country that in America.

I look across the United States and I say, "My goodness Rose, it could have gone another way for you – had you been born in America and been brought up in one of those churches. Instead of being indifferent towards God, you might have become a fanatic – and used THAT path to damage your soul." I think perhaps, that the fundamentalist path could have, in some ways, been even worse than the one I took. Now however, I am growing with the Light, as I am able, and I hope that as my power increases - I will share all of it with you, and help you to grow in your connection with our world.

Tom: It is a great honor experiencing this process with you, through Bob's work. It's wonderful – thank you.

Rose: Thank you my dear. Fletcher has asked me to step out, for the power is weakening. We have to be careful with our medium.

Fletcher: Oh, hello there, this is Fletcher here. We have to be careful with our medium, so we won't be staying much longer. Do you have any other quick question?

Tom: Yes I do have two quick questions. Is this book we are doing together – the first of many more collaborations – and will it launch us onto the world stage? I honestly believe that the lessons of Light that you are teaching are so worthwhile. How do you see this unfolding in the future?

Fletcher: Well, might we say that over here – that we don't like to think in terms of world fame. But, we do have great interest that our messages being widely disseminated. I won't give you, at this time, details about how this is going to unfold, not because we don't know, but because we want you and Bob to have the adventure and the experience. At this point, we want you to be faithful in doing the work each week. And you have been doing that well.

As you work and develop, more will be given you. What we will say today, a little hint is that you and Bob - and our teachings - will become known far and wide!

Tom: Bob and I are most concerned about getting the message out there. I'm sorry, I don't mean to sound impatient.

Fletcher: We are thankful that you and Bob are so diligent and loyal to our work. You know, there is a saying here – "There are two worlds, and when it's time for the two worlds to unite, nobody can stop it." And that is what we are aiming for here – a uniting of our world and your world. Just keep on doing as you are doing. We promise that many good things are on their way to you. And might we add, there will be more books. This is only the beginning.

Tom: You have already uplifted me and my friends so much with your weekly messages. We are so grateful to Bob for allowing this communication – for we have seen and felt the tremendous value of your teachings. Our lives are so much better for having met you.

Fletcher: it's our pleasure to come here. As for your friends, let them know that they are going to part of it all and we might be enlisting their help in the future. Did you have another question?

Tom: Yes. Last week you told me to be more open and accepting of the Light within me and to not be so stubbornly attached to self criticism - but this week I went through some more bouts of depression –as I watched the world fall ever more deeply into financial chaos. I get angry at myself for resisting the Light – as you said – and I really do want to feel more joy – so what would you advise?

Fletcher: Well, first off. You are trying too hard. Spiritual life isn't always about straining and striving – or extreme effort. This doesn't mean that you don't do the inner work, but it does mean that you go about it in a less stressful way. For example, don't get so down on yourself. We hear you condemning yourself with words like, "I'm not feeling close to God. I'm too into myself." This is how you start the cycle in your mind, by saying things like, "I'll never be any better, because, just look at where I am today."

You are doing what we call, a false comparison here. You are comparing yourself to an ideal image you have of yourself. Only egos compare. You must stop it, along with all words of self-criticism! You see, there will always be people in your world who appear to be greater or lesser than you. There will be times therefore, when you WILL feel greater or lesser than these people, but this only because you are comparing. You know, even in my own life I had this problem. Perfectionism is a curse. But, what I learned over here is that, as you let the scales of fear fall away, the only thing left is the Divine Light. All that comparing you've been doing comes from fearful thinking – that is – thinking that you are not good enough etc.

It's not that you have to go and skin yourself, and strip yourself of everything that hides the Light - all at the same time. Just let the false beliefs that you hold about yourself - that are overly self critical - fall away as they come up. They are no more real than dried out old scales from the back of a fish. Just slough them off. And, don't worry. Stop thinking thoughts like, "I don't feel so good. I must be doing something wrong. I'm a bad person." Banish those kinds of thought because they are of the darkness, NOT of the Light.

Say instead, with gratitude, "You know, I am alive!" And then visualize every thought about not feeling good - as if it was a dried out old fish scale. And then see yourself shedding those old scales. They merely represent adjectives and definitions that you took on, which are no longer appropriate. You don't have to pluck off every one of those definition-scales all in one day, only the ones that are troubling you the most. Know that once you choose to do this consciously, that they will begin to really disappear. Eventually you will begin to feel like a brand new fish – with NO old scales. (He chuckles). Your new definitions of self will be all shiny, smooth and beautiful, made NOT from the ego's judgments of self-contempt, but made out of Divine Light and Love. It's not so much about working hard. It's more about allowing the natural process of this time of cleansing to occur.

Tom: Thank you very much Fletcher. That is really helpful.

Fletcher: You are most welcome. Well, I feel the vibration starting to weaken here. We've got be careful of Bob's nervous system. Once we come through him – late at night like we are doing tonight – he won't sleep well because of his nervous system gets kicked into a higher vibration. Sometimes, we don't really tire him as much – as over stimulate him. It's kind of a funny thing . . .

Tom: I had the same thing happen to me last week. I couldn't sleep all night after our session. I was wide awake until dawn.

Fletcher: Yes, that's because your vibration is increasing in frequency, just like our medium's. But – the more you work together – you will perceive greater and greater benefit, as well. Bob is growing in Light - which is why we are able to come through. But, you are growing in Light as well, the more you are able to receive the messages. So, each of you are being grown at the same time, which is a wonderful exercise for both of you.

We will be stepping out of his body now. We will be sending you AND your friends blessings from our world. And know - that we will be coming again soon.

Bob: (Gasping and breathing deeply as he comes out of trance). Did we get good stuff?

Tom: Wow, we sure did. They hinted that this is only the first of a series of books.

Bob: Oh my God. Well, if that's what they want . . . then I'm all for it. I love Fletcher so much, and I trust him completely.

BOB HICKMAN POSTSCRIPT:

It seems that the more time we spend with the Spirit Guides, the more we learn, not only of the spiritual truths that they impart, but we come to understand these guides as people. To hear of their earthly sojourns is a real blessing for me. I see Fletcher and Rose as 3-dimensional people not just discarnate voices from the Ethers. They have had lives upon the earth as we have. They have felt love, joy, sorrow, and every emotion that is a part of the human experience. I am thankful that I have been given the honor and privilege to work with such fascinating people.

So often we think of those who have passed on to the Spirit World as no longer with us. It is easy to dismiss them as almost having never lived. Fletcher, Rose, Edgar Cayce, they all show us how even in death we retain our humanity. It is nice to know that we will still have care and concern for those on the earth after we depart.

Fletcher's teaching of the true nature of our consciousness, our soul, is refreshing. In a world where atheism is the norm, to see that the reality of our eternal self is one of "bliss" rather than "empty nothingness" gives me much joy and hope. I much value in the teachings of the Spirit People.

As I review the transcripts from this night, I wonder if someday science will find a way to allow the spirits to communicate more directly. If it became possible, I think their teachings would inspire peace upon the earth and those institutions that practice negativity and alienation would find themselves transformed by the power of the Divine Love.

CHAPTER NINE
THE LIGHT SHIP EARTH

October 16th, 2008

BOB HICKMAN PREVIEW:

Tom and I had another late night channeling session. It is interesting to note, that where he was (Hawaii) it was a tropical night, and where I was (Washington DC), the crispness of Autumn was settling in. Despite our different climes and cultures the Spirit Guides united us. As I settled into trance this night, I remember feeling an almost humming energy all around me. I now know that the "humming" was the raising of my vibration in preparation to receive and know the TRUTH that exists in all of us, no matter "who" or "where" we are. Below is the transcript of this most "enlightening" session.

Fletcher: Oh hello there. This is Fletcher. Good evening – can you hear me out there?

Tom: Yes, I can. It's wonderful hearing your voice again.

Fletcher: It's so good to be here. Give us just a moment. We have to get a little more control of the vibration of the body here. Oh there, I think we are OK now. It's such a pleasure to be back here with you. We've had quite a time this week traveling around, looking in on a lot of different people.

Our medium keeps us quite busy, but when we are not working with him, we go and look in on a great many other people. I am a guide to quite a number of people around the world right now, you might say. Oh, it's true that I am Bob's guide predominantly – but occasionally I visit his clients later on - as a kind of follow up. I give them my own personal assistance. I've even been around you this week. Perhaps you've been sensing me.

Tom: I have been feeling you and your vibration is wonderful!

Fletcher: I have to say that I've been peering in on your writing. And, you've been doing quite well with it. You've been hearing our whisperings well, and have been including our little additions, quite nicely. And, I know that Rose is quite pleased with the process, as well. She says that she has never had her words been written up so much. Oh, she used to think that getting quoted in the society paper was exciting, but now she says that she is very happy that you are capturing all her words so nicely. And from our side, there is a lot of blessing here for you. Give us just a moment; I believe that she wants to talk to you.

Rose: Hello Tom, can you hear me?

Tom: Yes I can. It's wonderful hearing from you again.

Rose: I am so pleased to be here with you. It is true, what Fletcher has said, about you capturing all my words so accurately and generously. It is also correct to say, that when I was on the Earth, I used to enjoy having a quote of mine placed in the newspaper or a magazine, in some society column. I used to think that having myself quoted in the paper was the height of success. But, now, I must say, what's left of my human vanity is very much pleased by the fact that my words will be published in a book on Earth - even after my demise, so to speak ... (Laughing happily).

This book project appeals to me greatly, for it gives me great joy to know that finally I will be quoted saying something of value - words that are actually worth hearing. When I was alive, so many of my words were nothing but idle chatter – nothing but gossip – nothing more than a waste of breath. I hope now only to speak words that are filled with God's Light, words that will help all those souls about the Earth - who are wandering in a state of darkness, like I did. I pray every day that no soul will sojourn to that place of Purgatory that I entered for a time after my passing.

Do you now, in these last few months that I've known you, I feel like you are a relative, like you are my dear brother. Therefore, it gives me great joy to come and speak with you this day.

Tom: How sweet of you to say that. I am really touched. And, I must say, that I have been hearing you whispering to me even as I've been transcribing Bob's messages, word for word from the tapes. The more I immerse myself in your words - as they come through Bob – the more I am convinced that your teachings – specifically about your experiences with the Light - are really going to help people. And the more time I spend time on these wonderful transcriptions, the better I am able to hear you speaking to me directly - inside my own mind.

Rose: As you say, I am speaking these words from a place of experience. Many people upon the Earth have simply forgotten that they have come from the Light. When a soul enters the Earth – they are cautioned greatly. They are reminded over and over again NOT to forget the Divine Light that they carry within them. Yet, when many souls return to the Earth, they DO almost totally abandon the truths that we have placed within them. You sir, are one who has never lost that spark of Divine Light, but have safely guarded it, nurtured it and protected it, so that your Light will shine brightly and Light the way for many. I like to speak of the Light, for the Light is the truth. And the Light was my salvation.

Tom: That is a fascinating word – salvation. So many religions promise it, and I myself have studied many teachings that offer it. But, yet – the actual experience of salvation is STILL somewhat of a mystery to me. What exactly do YOU mean when you use the word, salvation?

Rose: When Fletcher and I speak of salvation, we are not speaking about blood dripping on people. We are speaking of something far different than blood dripping off Jesus' crucified body. Many humans today only understand salvation from that old Christian viewpoint. They still believe that salvation comes from Jesus' blood pouring upon them – which they have been told was shed to cleanse them of their guilt and sin. The correct message of Jesus Christ's sacrifice was that one should give oneself for one's fellow man, that one should love enough to die to one's own ego. Jesus demonstrated extreme compassion in his death - and extreme nobility in his resurrection.

You know, I was from a noble family. We were high nobility! And, therefore, we were always discussing the concept of – what it meant to be included in the nobility. Do you know that one of Jesus' titles is "Lord of Lords"? Even my own family agreed that Lord was a good title for Jesus Christ. For me, well I thought, "Since Jesus was the Lord of Lords, the highest nobility, and my family was also of the nobility – well then – that meant we were very close to the Lord. We must be saved." Oh, I suppose that was vanity, misinformation on our part, but we believed it nonetheless. Now I know that our noble rank had nothing to do with our salvation.

I still have many relatives upon the Earth, who are titled – and they think that being of the nobility is equivalent to salvation. But, I must say, that belief system is not helping them find their way back to the Light. The Divine Light is the only real source of salvation. I do try to work with them as I can. But, you know, Jesus said quite clearly, "If they don't listen to you, shake the dust from your feet and move onward." That is great wisdom which was revealed to us – that even Jesus himself did not expect us to be unappreciated martyrs for His cause.

The spiritual life is something that comes to one when one is ready. A spirit guide can only talk, can only point a way - can only do so much - to demonstrate their knowledge and presence. It is up to the individual person, as to whether or not they will accept the show of support as offered by the spirits. It is up to each soul as to how much, and how soon, they will allow in spiritual salvation – and HOW they will utilize that spiritual guidance, to move forward towards the Light.

I recently had the privilege of working with our medium Bob, in a place called Leesburg, Virginia. This is a place that he often travels to. I went with him there, so that he could allow me to speak through him to the crowds. It was a wonderful experience.

I met a lovely young lady in Leesburg who had never heard the truth about the Light, and she said to me, "Rose, will you help me believe in God?" And, I said, "My dear, I am with you at this very moment to show you that my presence here is real. And, as you know, I am a spirit." She answered, "I hear your presence in the room and I know that you are real." So then I said, "If you can believe that MY spirit is here, my dear, just a little aristocrat who died in World War II, can you not ALSO accept, as well, that it is the power of God that has made me present here with you tonight?" She fell on the floor as she was leaving our gathering, sobbing and crying, for she had finally begun to open her heart to the reality of God.

That young woman's experience reminded me of my own self, when I crossed over into the vibration of God's Spirit World and found my faith once again. I cried with joy as I began to grasp the reality of my soul's eternal existence. And I came to understand that all of us, ALL of us, CAN be saved, if that is the word we wish to use. Let's stop thinking of salvation linked up with the idea of martyrdom and bloodshed. I want you, instead, to start thinking of salvation in terms of the Divine Light that is within the self.

Salvation is achieved as the Divine Light grows within your awareness. You will ALWAYS become that which you reflect upon. And, therefore, you would do well, to keep your mind turned up constantly towards the Light. Mr. Berg, if I might be quite honest with you, I must say bluntly that sometimes I see - that you are not remembering to look towards the Light. You forget it temporarily – even today. But, we don't say in this in judgment, only in kind consideration. We wish to encourage you to remember much more vigilantly to keep your focus and attention pointed always towards the Light. Look towards the Light, again and again, and always hold onto its knowledge, for it is of God – it IS God!

All the material things and colorful forms of the world can be very distracting. They are merely perceptions of the senses, and they come and go. They are ever changing. We understand that quite clearly, from our perspective beyond time and space. But also, we encourage you, to not have fear in your material world. Everything in your universe is so temporary and transient. Always remember that, even while you are living this lifetime in and through your body. Turn ALWAYS to the remembrance that God really does exist - and that God loves you!

The Light of the Spirit World IS real! And it is here and now! I want you to keep reminding yourself, every day, that there are many of us spirit friends and guides all about you, who will help you always to access the Light of Spirit. We ARE with you all the time! We are offering our help to everyone – ALL the time! Do you understand the importance of what I am saying, sir?

Tom: Yes, I do. And I appreciate your advice. You are absolutely right about now I spent my past week. I have been watching a lot of fear based shows on YouTube and on the net. And, there is so much anxiety in the air right now - about the monetary system collapsing. So, I have to admit, that I did allow my attention to get caught up in that vibration of "the sky is falling". And you are right as well - that I do sometimes forget ALL about the presence of your Light in my daily life. So, can you describe the Light for us, even more clearly, so we can learn how to hold onto it – even in the midst of this insanity that we are going through as a collective?

Rose: Oh yes, I can. I would be most happy to tell you more about the Light. Let me start by saying that the Light IS God and that God IS the Light. And, that Light, which is God, is also pure Love. (She says this sighing – with a great breath of deep reverence in her voice - which quavers as she speaks.) The Light of God is beyond that which human eyes could stand to look upon directly. Do you know those words from the scriptures which say, "Man cannot look upon God and live." Have you heard this verse from scripture?

Tom: Yes I have.

Rose: This is a true verse. And you know, I am not a strict fundamentalist when it comes to this sort of thing. Yet, it is accurate and true, for that Light of God is beyond physical forms of brilliance. And, should any human in their flesh, should step in front of it, their form would instantly dissolve by its brilliance and power. What a wonderful way to go, if you ask me. (She laughs). None the less, humans cannot stand the totality of the Divine Light in their mortal form, and that is why one must contact the Light through meditation, prayer and other special practices.

There are those who are impatient and say, "I want to see the Light immediately, in this room. Right now." But, this experience is not possible. You can have a glimpse of the Light, however, when you go within yourself via different forms of meditation. God's Light is brighter than ten billion suns. The Bhagavad-Gita talks beautifully about God's Light when it says, "The Light of God is as if ten billion suns arose in the sky at one time." This is merely the beginning of an attempt to describe the effulgence of that Supreme Being. When I was in India, the swami's used to read to me from the Bhagavad-Gita. Are you familiar with the Bhagavad-Gita?

Tom: Yes I am familiar with it, and I've also read the rest of the Upanishads. They are powerful works from the minds of some very liberated Hindus.

Rose: I do believe that the Swamis of India, who were Hindu, read to me from the Upanishads as well, though I must admit that I didn't pay as much attention to their teachings, as I should have. But, I have never forgotten how beautifully they described God, and I thought to myself, "Well, I suppose that if there is a God, this is an apt description – one that I can relate to."

Now that I am in the Spirit World, I am at a great advantage. I have learned that you CAN learn to discern the brilliance of God's Light, though it is more brilliant than ten billion suns. It is through the development of your spiritual sight, that you are able to look upon God's Light, with what we call, your spiritual eyes. Through your spiritual eyes, and through the spiritual vision that looks through your spiritual eyes, you WILL be able to see the Light most glorious, a Light that will never damage your human retina. Do you know how they speak of the moth drawn to the flame?

Tom: Yes.

Rose: Good. Yes, moths are always drawn to the Light of the flame. This story is like the process of your soul's awakening. Think of your soul as the moth and God as the flame. Your entire being yearns for God – like the moth that is drawn towards the Light of the flame. The moth knows that it might die approaching the flame, yet it goes, none the less, doesn't it?

This is how your soul is created. It is made to be drawn to that flame of God, that flame of Divine Light. And this is why, when many pass over, they speak of moving towards a Light, and they describe the feeling as being almost magnetically pulled towards that Light. There are many on the Earth today who are writing accounts about this experience. These true accounts are all about how the soul is drawn like a magnetic force – right into the Light.

Before I left the Purgatory realms, I was in that place of mental darkness, which is the same as ignorance. And yet, I saw above me (give me a moment here) . . .

Fletcher: Oh hello, this is Fletcher. Give us just a moment. We have to get control of the medium's vibration here.

Rose: Hello, this is Rose, can you hear me now?

Tom: Yes I can, you are coming in loud and clear, just like before.

Rose: We are having quite a bit of an electrical disturbance for some reason, which seems to be effecting the vibration. As I was saying, when I was in the place of Purgatory, I saw that Light first, as if it were a pinpoint of Light. And I heard voices calling me, saying, "Rose, come home." And so, I followed those words towards that Light – (speaking very emotionally and reverently).

And just like the moth is drawn to the flame, I too was drawn to the Light, BY the Light. I kept hearing the words, "Rose, come home," until I could no longer hold myself back from that Light. I felt all of my being rushing headlong right into it. The peace I felt was so great that, I would not have cared if merging with the Light meant my utter and complete destruction. This is the nature of how individual souls are being pulled towards God's Allness. God's pull is immensely magnetic, all powerful, and all encompassing. Are you hearing me, Sir?

Tom: Yes. Recently many people around the world became quite excited about the possible arrival of a ship from outer space on October 14th. Many people were seeing this possible appearance -as a metaphor for God's Salvation, coming to help us in the midst of this dark time. Now, many of these same people are sad and angry because nothing happened. So, I was wondering, what can you tell us about God's involvement in human history? Are some extraterrestrials also trying to help us at this time? Does the Light attempt to intervene, but we just don't let it in? Can you and Fletcher help us understand this better?

Rose: I am not as advanced as Fletcher in this area, but I will add my bit on that matter, and he will speak soon as well. God's Light is always beamed upon the Earth. The native inhabitants of Earth may or may NOT become aware of it – but it's here, nevertheless. Help is ALWAYS here! The Light of God is reaching into every part of the Earth, even the farthest jungles of Africa. England had many colonies in Africa. I traveled there once. I visited the swamps and jungles of Nigeria and even there – I could grasp a feeling, an actual sensation of true spirituality.

When one looks upon the native peoples throughout the world – wherever they may be – one can find an inbred awareness of divinity. Even In your own country, the Native Americans sensed the reality of the Great Spirit. They knew the Great Spirit - and sensed the Divine Light of the Creator, in all of nature. The Light of God can be sensed everywhere upon the Earth because God's Brilliant Consciousness is shining always, everywhere, without exceptions. I think therefore, that if humanity would only look for that Divine Light that continually beams upon the Earth, so obviously through all nature, as native people do - it would not be hard to discern.

Tom: I know exactly that you are talking about Rose. I discovered this when I was in the Peace Corps living in the Amazonian highlands of Venezuela. The immense energy radiating all through the rain forest was so vital and alive, and the people were kind and really quite spiritual, in their simple love of life and each other. I could actually feel a vibration of life and love pulsating all around me, in me and all through nature. There were some days when the Invisible Life Force felt so alive and vibrant that it was palpable! And I could see so easily, how it was the creative power of the Light, that was pouring into, and growing all the coffee trees, the vanilla beans, the cacao, the sugar cane and the bananas – and all those main crops of that area. And, here in Hawaii, the merging of Light and matter IN nature is so obvious, especially in our colorful rainbows, flowers, palm trees and gorgeous landscapes. The native people of Hawaii once worshiped the Light Itself, and recognized the presence of God's Light as it played through all of nature. That was before they were taken over by the Christian missionaries.

Rose: Many modern people today, who profess to be Christians, look around them and only see the things of the material, physical world. They miss seeing the Divine Light of the Creator because they only look upon the outer surface layers of the forms in creation. I was such a one when I was alive. I didn't see the Light within the appearances IN creation, even though it is always present for all to see. God's All Creative Light is always available for all who wish to experience it in their everyday world.

The spiritual world, as we have told you, is not some faraway place. It is actually superimposed upon your own world. There is no separation between our worlds except by the apparent distance of our different vibrations. This is what causes people to become confused and believe that we are not present. The imagined distance between our worlds is vibrational and therefore, the so called barriers between our realms are not at all real. The so-called walls between us are nothing more than frequencies or mental energies, emotional, and vibrational states that are based on beliefs.

Each person has the ability, within themselves to absorb or reject the Light frequencies. You see, the Light is always freely given. It is everywhere present and pours in, all the time. It is humanity's free will as to whether to accept the gift, or not.

Here is an example of receiving and rejecting. You may have a neighbor who you perceive as most loving and another neighbor who seems most disagreeable. The holidays arrive and they both give you gifts. You might say to the good neighbor, "Oh you are so kind to give me such a lovely gift." And, you welcome the gift. But, to the disagreeable neighbor you might think, "Oh, I don't want to accept this gift". More than likely however, you will probably accept both the gifts. But, the gift you truly love is the one you will hold close to your heart and remember with affection. The other gift, from the other neighbor, you may place in the closet and try to forget that it even exists. This is how it is with God's Light.

Your own vibration, at different times, causes you to perceive God's Light, as either a loving neighbor or the neighbor you can just barely tolerate. You can always accept the gift of Light and treasure it, and use the gift, as your free will so decides. Or, you can chose reject and ignore the gift of God's Light – although it will continue to always be present for you and with you. When you do NOT accept the gift of the Light, you may then think that the Light has abandoned you, or has gone far away. But this is only because you have not yet become willing to embrace the gift and absorb its Light, and are not willing yet to recognize and appreciate what it offers. This is why humankind thinks and hopes that the Light must still come, although in truth, the Light is always pouring into the Earth plane, and into everyone! Hold on – Fletcher is here.

Tom: That was beautiful Rose. I can understand what you mean too, because sometimes the Light shines into my life really brightly, and shows me a belief, attack thought or anxiety that I need to clean up or forgive, and my first reaction is to reject the message. You and Fletcher are helping me realize that I can be just as stubborn as the most devout atheist, when I am not grateful for the enlightenment that the Light continually offers. I am finally understanding that sometimes the Light comes to illuminate beliefs and thoughts, that I have tried the hardest to push way down in the closets of my subconscious mind, so I don't have to deal with them. This is what you mean by the "unwelcome gift from the disagreeable neighbor" - right?

Rose: Yes. And also, might I add here, that out of what may seem at first glance to be the most disagreeable of appearances, can come the most unexpected and beneficial of gifts. Haven't you ever had the experience of prejudging some event or experience as quite disagreeable, when, in the long run – it could eventually be seen to be the precursor of some great good?

Tom: Yes I have. I wouldn't be living here in Hawaii today if something like that hadn't happened to me just last year. At first, when a big corporation bought my apartment building back in San Francisco, I judged the sale as very disagreeable, as you say, and even frightening. But, in the long run, I learned that the new owners were quite rich and were offering all tenants extremely generous financial settlements to encourage us to leave. They wanted to convert the entire building into luxury condos, which led to my receiving a totally unexpected, but very welcome, financial windfall - that more than paid for my move to Waikiki. Now, I am living in a beautiful condo with a wrap around view of both the ocean and the mountains, and the whole thing started with, what seemed to be, at first glance, a very disagreeable "gift" from a very "disagreeable neighbor".

Rose: Fletcher wants to add something. It has been such a pleasure to speak with you tonight.

Fletcher: Oh hello there, this is Fletcher here. I was doing a chore, so I didn't hear the whole question exactly. Can you repeat it please?

Tom: Yes. We began talking about the hopes of so many people for some kind of a Divine Intervention, like they hoped would happen on October 14th. I asked Rose about the idea of an "intervention" to help the human race through the next few years. I've seen God intervene in my own life, so I know that miracles ARE possible. So, I guess what I am asking is, can the people of the Earth expect MORE examples of divine help, as 2012 approaches? Many people in the New Age community became disappointed and angry when the prediction of the arrival of a Light ship on October 14th didn't come true, and they turned that disappointment into a negative judgment of being abandoned and let down yet once again by God.

Fletcher: Well, it's true that on the Earth, there is a great vibrational shift going on, and so, as the year 2012 approaches, there are many great events coming. And yet, many people are building a vibration of fear about the coming changes, which we don't like. We want you to remember that good, positive energy can be built, just as easily as the bad energy. Good vibrations can actually be built up more easily, once people wake up to the spirit realms, and absorb more of the Light that is pouring onto the Earth at this time.

You've got to understand a great truth, that the mind of man is much more powerful than most people on Earth yet realize. It was by using the power of your own mind that you have developed the ability to dissolve clouds, just as Edgar Cayce told you. Well – just imagine what would result if we multiplied that mind power by five or six billion. What would happen if six billion people were ALL projecting out fear into the skies around your planet, instead of positive energies? Well, that is exactly what is happening!

Haven't you ever wondered why such things as earthquakes occur in highly populated areas? We would like you to notice that whenever and wherever there is a great cataclysm, if you were to study the lives of the people, you would discover that the people were vibrating with great masses of negative energy. We are not saying this to blame them or make them feel guilty for causing the suffering. It is simply that humanity hasn't realized yet, that it has unlimited power to shift vibrations upwards or downwards. Earth changes sometimes occur therefore, as a reaction to the vibrational shifts of the people living in the region.

Right now humanity continues to generate fearful vibrations, especially about the stock markets tumbling. Well, it's only because people believe that the stocks will keep tumbling that creates more of the tumbling. Don't you see that? They are creating the trouble by their own consciousness. If humanity could believe that it had the power to rebuild the markets, then that would be begin happening.

We want you to understand that even those people who say, "I don't have a lot of money in stocks, so it doesn't affect me," are influencing what happens to the markets, as well. Their own minds are equally as powerful as the people who have millions of dollars in the stock market. So, even if you're not heavily invested in the market, your consciousness does affect it.

In terms of humankind's yearning for salvation, which is really a desire for more of the Light, it is true that humanity is evolving. A shift is happening in human consciousness. In the year 2012, you are going to be seeing a huge shift, because at that time, there will be great revelations coming to the Earth about the people from the other worlds. A lot of people will begin vibrating with panic and fear, and will be running in the streets. But, we don't want that to happen AND it doesn't have to happen. We are here to tell you that the changes coming to your planet don't have to unfold in a fearful way.

What we want is for people to be raising their minds and their states of consciousness to consider - there is something more to think about than themselves. Even if they don't believe in God or the Spirit World, we want them to consider that there may be extraterrestrials and other beings involved with Earth's evolution. This is NOT just about a spiritual belief. It is a biological fact. Scientists have already done the mathematics, which show the great potentiality for a certain percentage of life to evolve all throughout the Universe. So why should it be so strange that Earth would be visited, and even influenced, by other life forms?

In regards to the discussion about the ship that was supposed to appear on October 14th – we don't want everybody to be upset with that medium, for she conveyed the message as best she could. But, what happened afterwards was that many people were simply not ready. They were not doing the necessary preparatory work, to vibrate at the place that could receive the predicted visitation. They generated vibrations of fear and doubt, instead of positive expectation and eagerness. So, had the ship fully manifested, well it would have been premature, because the majority of people simply weren't ready - in their states of consciousness.

In time, people from other worlds and other dimensions WILL be making their appearances on Earth. A lot of mediums are running around, giving dates and times about these appearances. Some of them are getting it right and some of them aren't. But, you know, it all comes back to God's timing. Because, God wants the world to wake up and see that it is on the wrong path when it thinks the human race is ALL THERE IS in the Universe. And the truth is, it might take what seems to be an outside force, like an extraterrestrial visitation – to do just that.

You see, a lot of us guides, spirits, and angels have been trying to awaken humanity to the Light, for years, and without much of an impact. So, we just might have to have a full scale alien visitation, which would certainly get everybody thinking. I can tell you, that many of the extraterrestrials know about us – and are fully aware of the Spirit World. And so, when they come and begin to speak about us, the people of the Earth will start to listen. Many races from other worlds are extremely advanced spiritually, but even they will tell you, when they do arrive, that they've got more work to do, as well. Creation is ongoing!

It is true that humankind cannot separate the physical from the spiritual except in their thinking, which is wrong. When they try to separate humanity from the Spirit World and from the Divine Light, they go around destroying the Earth, because, in their own minds, they think it doesn't matter. In many of their belief systems and theologies they believe that the Earth is just going to burn up someday, anyway. This is an old view, which we would like to help bring an end to - NOW.

You know, all of us who lived on Earth, at one time or another, were participants in creating this beautiful place. And those of us, who are here in the spiritual world, still like to look back to see the glory of the Earth. And yet, what we see is that many humans have become vain, conceited and self-serving, which is why they are destroying each other on Earth. They don't understand that they are only hurting themselves. And, therefore, it is our hope, that our extraterrestrial brethren will help us point that out. We want the people of the Earth to become more and more enlightened – and to let more of God's Light into their lives. Give us just a moment here.

Orion: Greetings. My name is Orion. I must bring my wisdom to you today because it is true that upon the Earth, there are many who have forgotten the reality of their souls. They have forgotten that they exist in multiple dimensions. All humans have lived before and will live again. And yet, it is true that there are some souls that are younger souls and some that are far more evolved. Therefore, it is the duty of the older souls to guide the younger souls, because the younger ones have forgotten the spiritual world, and are not yet willing to hear our voices. We now say, "Would that they all could hear our voices."

When Jesus Christ was upon the Earth, he said, "If you cannot believe my words, then believe in the miracles that I do." It is for this cause, the lack of human belief, that miracles will begin to return to the Earth. In the coming years, you will witness a great rise in physical phenomena, such as the world has not seen in many, many years. There will be people, especially some mediums, who will achieve full levitation. There will be séances during which time our voices will manifest on their own. Even our full forms will appear to be seen - teaching.

There is a great necessity, therefore, that this unbelieving generation will gain insight. This is the sole purpose of the miracles of the Christ. More miracles will manifest to awaken people to the Light. Many people have not heard our words, and therefore, must see signs and wonders to open their minds and hearts to the reality of the Light. (At this point a break in the Skype connection ended our conversation).

BOB HICKMAN POSTSCRIPT:

What a wonderful night this was. I was only disappointed that our Skype connection crashed, but then not surprised as my guide, Orion, has the highest vibration of energy I have ever channeled. Fletcher is always careful to only allow Orion to stay in my body for a short while, lest my nervous system become damaged. Channeling too much energy through the human body before it is ready can be extremely taxing to humans and weaken their body's energy field. Fortunately, Fletcher always stands guard and even though this night I was able to channel Orion, the electronic system that we used to communicate with was knocked out for the rest of the night! This is truly life on the edge of the etheric.

The Light that accompanies the higher spirits is an amazing experience. As a medium I can quite literally see and feel the Light that accompanies these exalted beings. I know that Orion and the other guides are quite literally "waiting in the wings" for the revelation of the alien presences. As I write this I look out my window and scan the sky...wondering...wondering if "they" will come tonight to visit me.

Throughout the process of working on this book with Tom, we have both been having intense dreams of being somehow "connected" and "contacted" by our Space Brethren. Could it be that they are teaching us at night while we sleep? It seems that the Spirit Guides continually make reference to this reality. It is a reality I am prepared to accept. I only wonder when they will openly manifest. My strangely vague and veiled memory of standing at my window one night and seeing the massive alien ship outside above my neighborhood still haunts my mind. It is almost as if they tried to block my mind from knowing, from remembering. I am not afraid of the aliens, but hope to directly communicate with them, to learn from them, and to grow into the Light with them. And as the guides have so clearly stated—In the Light is salvation.

CHAPTER TEN
OPEN MINDS OPEN HEARTS
October 22nd, 2008

BOB HICKMAN PREVIEW:

Whenever Tom and I get together, it is always an adventure. Tonight was to be no exception. In the week before there had been prophesied by another medium that a giant starship would appear and make contact with the people of the Earth. When this prediction did not come to pass, many were disillusioned with the spiritual quest and started to abandon hope. Fortunately, my guides shared some insights on that happening and helped us all to see that even though the aliens did not materialize as the medium had predicted, much good came from the rise in public consciousness. I think Fletcher is right when he says that the question of alien life forms bring all people to question who we are and where we are going.

One of the most interesting phenomena that Tom and I always notice, whenever we sit for a channeling, is that as the channeling goes on, the electrical activity around us seems to rapidly increase. As a result, our communications are often severed on the electronic level. This is interesting because the guides always speak of "raising the vibration." This night was super-charged with energy and we had problems keeping the connection. Below is the transcript of this most mystical night.

Fletcher: Oh, hello there. It's so good to be back here with you.

I must say, it has been quite a week over here in our world – so many activities. You know - we don't sleep like humans. Well, even though I am human – or I should say - I am a human spirit. But, we don't think of ourselves – in the body sense – like humans do. There has been an accomplishment . . . (A great deal of electrical static makes the next few sentences difficult to transcribe . . .)

There are a lot of people on Earth raising their vibration at this time. It is very interesting to us – because - we look upon the

Earth - and we can actually see a kind of glow. We often say to each other, "Oh look at the Earth, there is such a beautiful glow. The Light must be increasing in the hearts of mankind." So, I can tell you – from our viewpoint – that the Light is definitely increasing upon your planet.

There was a lot of talk over the last week about extraterrestrials appearing on the Earth and it got a lot of people thinking about what would happen if an alien ship should appear. This is a very good thing. We like that this was all over the Earth, because it got people to question their own thoughts about what they believe about their own reality. Each person on the Earth – is being conformed – to ask, "Well, if there is life on other planets – then - what is the nature of that life? What is the nature of my life?

You know, when I was a young man coming up, we didn't have any such talk about aliens. Oh now, there was the odd person – here and there – who used to say that they saw things in the night sky. But – we would discount their claims by saying - that they were merely seeing meteors - or falling stars, as we used to call them. But, now I have to wonder - if some of those people were not already in contact with other worlds – event then. I say this because - I have been told – since coming over here – that there have been many people who have been working with the aliens for a long, long time, throughout all of human history.

There are beings from many, many star systems who are visiting the Earth. Although, I can't say that this is my specialty – because my work is predominantly with the human side of things. I know that you have been hearing many rumors and reports about alien influence on the Earth. And, so I am here tonight to tell you that – a lot of the things that you have been hearing – they are the truth.

(At this point the Skype connection disconnected us.)

Bob: (Redialing) Hello. What happened? I just got pulled out of my trance with a big jolt.

Tom: Yeah, we got disconnected. There was really a lot of static and then the signal just broke up completely. Want to try again?

Bob: OK, I'll ask Fletcher to pull back on the energy. It seems as if their power is overwhelming the electronics. Let's try one more time and see what happens.

Fletcher: Oh, there we go. I think we are back in the body. You'll have to pardon us. We are having a lot of electrical disturbance tonight. All the electrical activity in the atmosphere is effecting the vibration of our transmission a bit. We will do the best we can. What questions might I answer for you – while you have me here tonight?

Tom: Well, as I transcribe more and more of your messages, and those coming from Rose, Orion and Edgar Cayce – I am beginning to understand that you are developing a sort of curriculum – a whole new world view – that Bob and I will be able to teach. Remember last week – when you told us that we were there - with God – when we co-created Planet Earth? That really blew my mind – so - I was wondering if you could take us through what happened – at the very beginning - stage by stage – step by step. Did we also take part in the creation of the entire physical universe? And - what were we like back then? Were we all part of the one great I AM? I was also wondering about the soul and the mind – and how they are different or alike? I have so many questions.

Fletcher: Sometimes we try to sneak our teachings into our medium's readings for people – but now – it looks like you have done found us out here. Well, it's true – we are trying to teach a history to humanity – based on the truths of the higher worlds.

So, let us begin. In our world - there are many planes of vibration. Humanity must someday come to understand that there are many, many worlds – that we call spheres of vibration. In the beginning of God's creation – we were all there - with God. You were there. I was there. Rose was there. Every person reading this book was there at the very beginning.

So many of you people on Earth tend to forget where you really came from. Even when you die and cross back into the Spirit World – most people don't remember it all – even at that time. It's a process over here - of unfoldment – for as you return to the higher planes of vibration and move closer to the Spirit World – you start to come back to your original self.

What is that original self? That original self is that original soul – that original spark of Divinity that split off from the Godhead. Your own soul is that little spark of Divinity that is within you. But – remember - that spark of Light within you - is still - just as much a part of God - as God Himself is part of Himself. Within each human being - is that very Divinity that was there at the very beginning.

If you look in the scripture – you will see a lot of hidden truths - even though much of what was written in Genesis was mythological. But, if you study the original Hebraic script – you will see that it says, "In the beginning, God created the Heavens and the Earth. Let us make man in our image." The actual meaning of this – is revealing - that we are all part of the Elohim. The Elohim is an ancient Hebrew word that refers to the angelic beings - the divine race - that lived with the Godhead at the very beginning.

Humans are part of that Elohim – although – at a slightly lower level of vibration. But – that doesn't change the fact – that - all of us were there – right from the very beginning. We were there with God and we helped to manifest the Earth through our joy! The Earth was not created out of some wrath or some anger, but was the result of the joyful process of creation. And - humanity's bodily form has evolved and is evolving as part of that process of creation.

The Earth was first started – as the scriptures say – from mass and water and darkness. In the primal beginning we have a predominance of the Yin energy - which was spoken about - in the Eastern teachings. Those teachings described both the Yin and the Yang energies of creation – which were represented by - the polarity of Light and darkness. Even in the western traditions, in the book of Genesis - we hear about the separation of the Light and the dark - as essential - to the very beginnings of creation. Look at those ancient scriptures – and you will see this eternal truth.

In the modern world, so many people are running around proclaiming that the darkness means evil. Darkness only means the beginning. It is essential to creation. Humans have to learn not to be afraid of the dark. The darkness is the very place where one's soul is birthed. This is why people like Rose – when they died – went back into the darkness. This was because her soul had not properly grown – and so – it had to be placed in a place of darkness – where it could grow – until it could learn how to accept, absorb and nurture the Light. The darkness was therefore - the perfect place - where such growth could take place.

When you plant a seed on the Earth, you put it into the dark soil. And so – this is how the soul is evolved. Sometimes it starts in darkness. And – if a soul doesn't grow – it gets replanted. And that is what the place of darkness - called Purgatory - really is. This was never so much about punishment – as some religions taught - but more – about a very necessary time – for allowing soul growth to occur. Each person must eventually do their soul growth – either on the Earth – or in the Spirit World. But, if you do the soul work on Earth – you will get a few more points. It is harder to do the work on Earth - because there are so many distractions. Give us just moment, Rose is here.

Rose: Greetings, my name is Rose. Can you hear me? It is such a pleasure to be here with you this evening.

Tom: Hello Rose. It's wonderful hearing your voice. Welcome back.

Rose: I was listening to Fletcher – with great appreciation - as he was speaking to you – because I learn great amounts from him. And I can tell you that I do understand about the place of darkness, where the soul is grown. It is true – although I have yet to discover it for myself – but I do believe – and have been told – that I too was there in the very beginning – with all the great souls - who manifested the world. Fletcher is correct, when he says that souls do not remember this reality until very much later. Even in the Spirit World – we are still in the process of discovering this reality.

 Death, and the subsequent entrance back into the Spirit World, does not bring one to a place of instant knowledge. It only transitions one to a different vibration. And so - you see - even here - we have much to learn, discover, to uncover - and to have revealed to us - as we are able to grasp it. This is I must be ever so careful when I make pronouncements. For, in all truth, even I don't know all of the truths at this time.

Spirit guides however – do have the advantage of being able to seek out the greater Source – with greater ease. But, that great Source will not and cannot reveal everything to us – because we are not ready for such truths. But, I am here to tell you that – to be in the Light – is a glorious thing. My soul went through a process- where it remembered - little by little – how much I was a part of the Light. And each day, I pray that my soul will grow even brighter.

Over here, we know that each soul reflects that Light. Some are brighter and some are dimmer. My soul is a bit brighter now than it was, even though it has a way to go. I am pleased with my progress, however. For, now I understand - that I was there – as you and our readers were - in the very beginning. And one day – I wish to have full memory of that most magnificent and splendid occasion.

When one starts to fully understand that one is part of that beginning – part of God - it is rather humbling. There is no room for ego, superior mindedness or arrogance. We must never boast and say that we are gods - separate and independent from God – just because - we now realize - that we were there in the beginning. Rather, we must come from a place of great humility - in our simple recognition and appreciation - of our oneness with God's creative intent in generating the universe. Each day, I hope to grow closer to that oneness.

Fletcher: Oh hello there. This is Fletcher. Give us just a moment as we adjust our medium's vibration, just a little bit here. Well, do you have another question?

Tom: I can see that you are developing a world view – which is becoming a major teaching – as our book unfolds. So, I was wondering if you could define some of the components of creation – like consciousness, soul, mind, body, brain and ego. Could you help me understand the difference between Divine Mind, human mind, conscious mind, soul mind – and the attributes of the subconscious and super-conscious minds?

Fletcher: Oh well, you have a lot of confidence in an old army boy – now don't you?

Tom: Yes I do. I find that the teachings that are being presented in these transmissions - are brilliant - and are really helping me wake up. As a teacher, I can see a pattern developing – a logical progression of ideas – that are helping me understand – from a whole new perspective - how creation evolves out of both the dark and the Light.

Fletcher: Well, let me start simply - because truth, as Rose has said – has to unfold slowly. We will take it a little at a time. First of all, it is important to understand that the human mind is made of numerous components. There is the physical brain, which operates the body, and which serves – I suppose you could call it – as a kind of way station for the mind. It's kind of like the brain rests in the brain – although the mind is not contained by the brain. So, when the body dies or the brain is damaged – the mind withdraws from that area.

We want you to understand that when we talk about consciousness, sub consciousness and super consciousness we are dealing with them on two different levels – a physical level and a spiritual level. It is true that the human brain has a subconscious element to it. You might call it - a little bit of a storehouse – which is centered in the head. It holds a part of the spiritual mind as well. Sometimes the human mind leaks out of its physical storage box, you might say, which is why you can sometimes be flooded with memories of past lives.

The spiritual mind is much larger than the space that occupies the physical brain. And so, this is why – many times you'll be having children – who will be saying, "I'm a different person. I can remember being another person before this life." This happens - because sometimes - when the spiritual mind – which has all the memories of all lives in it – has fully settled into the new physical mind – there is still a lot of bleed through. While parts of the physical brain are equipped to hold the spiritual mind - they cannot contain it fully.

When souls are reincarnated - and take on the bodies and brains of new children on the Earth -they have to do a kind of a shrinking down – a bit of a stepping down of vibration. This is so the spiritual mind - that contains all knowledge of all lifetimes - can be housed within the physical brain. The brain accomplishes this with the conscious mind or brain - and the subconscious mind and brain. And so humans, tend to feel a bit segregated within themselves. It's as if one part of the mind seems to hide the contents of other parts. But, this mental segregation is necessary, in order that a soul may function in a body and not be overwhelmed by past-life memories.

Growth is only accomplished when one assumes a new consciousness – and this why one reincarnates – takes on a new body – lives in a place of time – and is willing to experience struggle. The spiritual mind is an integral part of all of this - for it is the spiritual mind that works out the plan - that the soul is charged with living – through the new body.

This is why – as human beings go through their day – that no matter what happens to them – they will often say to themselves, "I kind of know that it's alright – no matter what happens." Someday you will realize – and - this would be good for all of you to look at – that most people who have died – and moved into the Spirit World – would say to you, if they could - that things happened just as they should.

Now, most of you people left on the Earth might answer, "Oh no, that's not right. You can't be saying that. What do you mean?" But, you see – this is why the body is allowed to decay – because – it is at this point in the life plan – that the spiritual mind often comes forward. And that's the mind that says, "It's OK that I am dying of cancer," which allows one to eventually let go of the body.

For those people who are so enmeshed in the body/mind that they think only about the material world – and have so sectioned off the spiritual mind – and buried it under the grey matter of the brain – for them – this time is even harder. They fight – every way they can - to keep the spiritual part of the mind suppressed. They do not want to let it come forward. Many people today are bogged down in materialism. That's because the grey matter – between the ears – tends to take control over everything.

It is important therefore – to learn about- and understand the true connection between the mind and the brain. Advanced souls are those who have learned how to allow the spiritual mind to work in its own proper place and time. Advanced souls have come to understand the difference between the spiritual mind and the brain – and so - they allow them each to work in their own time and way – which leads to the achievement of a perfect balance.

A great example of this is the Dalai Lama. This man walks around the world in a physical form. His mind operates his body and you can clearly see – and he speaks and writes words of wisdom. It's a balance here between the spiritual mind and the physical brain here – that we are seeing. Mind and brain – you must remember – are together – and yet separate. The Dalai Lama – and those who follow him – are wonderful examples of people who understand the true nature of Mind. The Buddha used to say that, "All is Mind". And – well actually it is quite true. For mind is Spirit and - in fact – all is ultimately Spirit.

If you look into the material world – you will see that behind it – exists atoms. What are atoms but molecules and particles vibrating at different rates? If one were to speed up the vibration of objects, it would be possible to dematerialize them or even vibrate them up into pure Light. When the human being dies and leaves the body – what are they really? Are they Light? They certainly are.

The brain exists to support the mind – which is Spirit. The mind is of the Light. This is why each human upon the Earth today - walking around - with a functioning body and a brain – is also a spiritual being. The real power within each person - is the Light. It exists within them – and operates the selves - that appear in the material world through the mind. Light is mind. Mind is Spirit – and therefore – the mind of man is both Spirit and Light. Therefore – when the body dies – it is that self that will eventually go into the spiritual world and into the pure Light. Are you following me lad?

Tom: Yes - which brings me to my next question. When we are told by the great masters that we need to escape the mind in order to come up to the spiritual self – what mind are they talking about? Are they talking about the grey matter mind – or the ego – or the subconscious mind? Would you say that mind is a subset of pure consciousness – or - are they the same thing?

Fletcher: Well, actually, they are all talking about the same thing here. When they advise humans to try and escape the thoughts of the mind – they are referring to the mind of the lower self. They are talking about the fear self – the subconscious part of the brain that has fear – and believes thoughts that are based on fear. The true self within –as the great Indian masters have taught – is Sat Chit Ananda – pure consciousness – the consciousness of bliss.

Once a human rises above the lower self - you can see – that the real mind is the higher spiritual self – and it exists within and through the brain. You don't need to be confusing it any longer. There is the physical brain and the spiritual mind – and they support each other. But – in the end - the physical brain is eventually left behind.

Tom: What is the ego - that gets so guilt ridden and fearful? What would you advise us about the ego?

Fletcher: Well, you see – the ego is actually part of that spiritual self – the part of the self identity - that doesn't want to – or choose to - remember who it really is. There is always the danger, when a soul enters a new body, and takes on a physical brain – that they will become contaminated by the flesh. Oh, we are not saying that you should be hating the body. Far from it!

The body is a blessed vehicle. But, what happens is – when the spiritual mind - that always remembers its connection to God – becomes connected to the lower physical self – it lowers its vibration. The physical body operates at a lower vibration than the spiritual mind. When the higher vibration of the spiritual mind is stepped down and lowered into the physical vibration – it starts to take on some of those elements. The material world – at this point in mankind's evolution – is still filled with a vibration of fear. This is because a lot of people still view the physical life as a struggle for survival.

The issue of survival only persists because human brains still have such greed and fear. This is another example of the lower self coming into play. When the spiritual mind's vibration is stepped down – there is a change. And yet this is necessary. The vibration must be a bit lower to inhabit the material world. If it wasn't stepped down some - you would never be able to even stay in your physical body. But the danger of this is – that with the lower vibration - comes a lower consciousness. And with this – comes the fear.

Remember that - inside the body are many chakras. The lowest chakra – at the bottom of the spine – is made for fight or flight. What that means – is that - this chakra helps us preserve the body in the material realms. You know, humans need a little extra skill because the body's vibration is so dense. So, they charge it up with the energies of that chakra. The problem comes in – however – because that chakra operates from a place of fear. It uses fear in its flight or flight response mechanism.

In the material world – sometimes a little fear is necessary - to move things along – and to assure physical protection. But, many people become trapped in that lower chakra's energy field, which is where the lower self dwells. And so – when you are having a lot of fear, anxiety and guilt – you must look within yourself – and admit that you must be dwelling in that lower self.

Within the body there is a kind of vibrational ladder which goes up to the top of the head – and eventually up – all the way into the Spirit World of Light. The chakras are like the rungs on the ladder. So, when you feel a great deal of negative emotion – you'd best be saying to yourself, "I must be on the bottom rung of my chakra ladder - I'd better start climbing up a few rungs." And, as you climb up that ladder – you will begin to realize – that you do have the power - to leave those lower vibrations and fear based emotions far behind. Sometimes, people get to the top of the ladder and then they get scared. This is primarily because - they tell themselves such fearful things as, "I'm not good enough to be up here with the Light."

The crown chakra is all about Light. Beautiful, pure white Light resides there. But, when you forget that you are from that Light of spiritual mind - it's a little bit uncomfortable – when you start going back into it. The physical brain then says, "Oh, I don't belong here – I'd better go back down to a lower rung." Then you climb backwards down the chakra ladder until you find yourself in that familiar place of fake security. That is where the more old more familiar feelings of fear and anxiety, guilt and self condemnation reside – in those lower chakra levels.

So, it's all about where you decide to climb on that ladder. And, now you understand what is happening within you. When you fall down into those lower vibrational levels, you can now say, "Look at where I am, back down here in fear. But, in the Light of Pure Spirit Mind, there is no such fear. I am part of that higher Spirit Mind – therefore - I have the power to climb up out of these lower level vibrations."

Rose: Hello this is Rose, can you hear me?

Tom: Good to hear from you again Rose.

Rose: You know, I do like Fletcher's analogy of climbing the ladder. When I lived in London, we had a very tall house with a slate roof on it. It was quite a grand roof, I would say. So, we would have to hire repairmen to go up there on the roof – because the slate would need to be repaired from time to time. The workmen would have to climb up long ladders to fix that slate roof.

One time, I decided to go up the ladder to see what was up there. You know, it is true, when one is up there on top of the ladder, the view is quite different. Fletcher's analogy of climbing the ladder within the self – seems therefore - quite appropriate. For it is true that at the higher chakra levels there is Light. I try to dwell consciously in that Light all the time now.

Even we spirit guides still have some challenges in that area. But, our job is to stay in that Light consciously, so we can always be an illumination. There are many beings of Light who surround you and offer illumination. So, even when you are feeling that you have fallen back down into self-condemnation; know that you are never alone – even in the lowest vibrations of dark despair. There are always ALWAYS beings of Light about you – just waiting to bring you the Light, at the mere asking.

Remember however that we cannot force this. In the Spirit World – we cannot force anything. Therefore, we cannot force ourselves or our Light upon you without your willingness – without your asking. But, we are present – always for those who are ready, willing and able to receive the Light we come to offer.

Tom: This ladder analogy is all about raising our vibration up – up – up to the higher levels of love – right?

Rose: Oh yes. It is true – though many people – I do believe – and even I - when I was alive on Earth – would have been lost to this understanding. Fletcher, in speaking of the ladder - is offering something – that one can relate to easily – and therefore - I find great joy in his words.

Tom: I was telling Fletcher that – it seems as if you are developing a kind of curriculum for people who are not very religious or familiar with spirituality. That's why I think this is so valuable. I really got a lot out of your parable last week about the unlikable neighbor and the unlikable gift. I thought that its message was absolutely profound - about how we need to learn to accept the Light - even when it comes in a package that – at first we don't recognize - or even like. Your teachings really seem to be pointing out how to lift up into the Light and accept the gifts of the Light's calling.

Rose: Well, thank you my dear. Since crossing over, I am still learning. And for me to have the privilege to come here is beyond words.

You see, when you leave the body - you will find yourself – as I have said – and Fletcher has told you – vibrating in the reality - that is most in tune with where you have been – in your own thoughts and meditations. This is why humans are always encouraged to be looking within and seeking that inner Light of divinity. The divinity within you will take you back to the divinity that we all shared – at the very beginning.

I myself- am still developing in my understanding - of that mystery - about the beginning of the universe and the creation of the worlds. Remember, there is not only one world. Humans so often only think in terms of the Earth. But, we were there – or so I have been told – since the beginning of the creation of the entire universe – not just the creation of this one planet. It is a great mystery that even I have yet to fully understand. Give us just a moment here.

Fletcher: Oh hello there. This is Fletcher. I want to jump here – although we must be careful with the medium's vibration tonight. I am jumping in here – because it is also important - to be telling you - that each human being has a chance – when they come into the Earth life – to evolve both the mind and the body.

You see, we have been talking a lot tonight about the mind. But, we must add here – that there is still a big movement – in many religions upon the Earth – about destroying the body. They say, "Destroy the body, ignore the body." This is a great error!

Remember – you have been given a body as a vehicle of expression. There is nothing wrong with that body being beautiful. You must also understand – however - that any judgment that compares one body as beautiful – to another - as not beautiful – is a false judgment. In God's eyes, every child of God is beautiful because of the Light of divinity that vibrates deep within.

A really loving parent never looks upon one child and says," Oh, I don't love this kid because of a superficial ugliness of the body". A truly loving parent looks upon a kid – with a heart full of love – even when the physical, surface appearance might not be considered as beautiful as some of the other bodies that are walking the Earth at this time.

So many people on the Earth today - are only looking at the material, physical appearances of human bodies. This is a grave error – for when one judges other beings - only through their bodily appearance – one can be very deceived. Perhaps – even you - in your own time – have seen people who are physically –quite beautiful. But, when you sit with them - you think, "This person isn't very nice. They say cruel things that are hurtful to others." So, the beauty of the body isn't the ultimate criteria for knowing the truth.

Remember that each person you meet is involved in a similar struggle. Every person that you encounter – the so called good people and the so called bad people – are fighting a kind of struggle within themselves. Sometimes this struggle is about the body – and sometimes it's about the heart and soul. But, you must look upon each person with compassion. For those – who are so obsessed by the body – we only bring to them a little more Light – that they may transcend that reality. Eventually – each person will come to a point where they will have to confront the temporary nature of the body.

Take care of the body and preserve it – for it serves one in this plane. You can't have a lot of effect here on Earth - if you are like me – a disembodied spirit – now can you? That is why we so rely on the work of our mediums – to speak through – because – once we step out of our medium's body – people won't hear a thing. It will be silent. And so, we love our medium, who allows us to use his body.

Our medium is a perfect example of someone who is using his body in a good way, because he allows us to take control of his vibration – to mimic the physical vibration. We are not totally – in his body – but we kind of overshadow his body – and - we take control of the nervous system. For all appearances – it does seem as if we are in the body – although – what is really happening - is that we are merely taking control of the electronics of the body. It is because of the energy that we put in – in order to take control – that we must be careful not to overload our medium's nervous system. And so, it is for this cause – that we have great respect and love for our mediums.

Our medium is allowing himself to serve a higher purpose. And - we are most pleased and honored that he gives us this chance. In the early days – he had some fear. But – we were patient – because we never force ourselves on anyone. In time, more and more people will start to give themselves over – to this work – to this higher work. We are most please to be seeing more and more people becoming channels throughout the Earth. They are giving themselves over to higher purposes.

You yourself are already developing in that way. Don't be afraid of our vibration. Continue to receive us and we will give you more. We will be giving you more and more time – and signs – in the coming years. You've got understand – that to be a full-fledged channel takes time. It can be a slow process. It's not that we can just take control – instantly – and start talking through you. It is has to be a slow "getting to know you". We have to become familiar with your vibration – and you have to get know our vibration. And little by little – we become closer to each other.

Actually – sometimes the most subtle of channelings are the most powerful. There were many great artists upon the Earth – that were not aware that they were channeling. And there are many such artists today. Take a painting by Monet, as an example. When you look at such a great painting- but one like Monet – you say, "What beauty! How could someone create something so wonderful?"

Well, it's not hard to create beautiful works of art – if you are working with the spirit people – who see the beauties of life - and who bring over those images - from our world - to yours.

When you visit an art museum or gallery – ask yourself – where does this beauty come from? It comes from a human self – which is spiritual – and - in touch with the spiritual self – and is able therefore - to bring over some memory of beauty- from the Other Side. Many of the great artists - throughout all history - would tell you - that – something took them over.

In our world - there a lot of artists who are just yearning to express themselves. And, so - the greatest artists upon the Earth –are those who are brave enough - to be in collaboration with artists on our side. This again – goes back to the functioning of mind. The mind is the vehicle through which we manifest and create. We do take some control of the brain – so we can control the nervous system. But, really it is the power of the mind - through which we transmit the vibration of our message – and the beauties of our world that inspire the artistic wonders of your world.

Great artists are - in this sense – great channels. Give us just a moment while we adjust the vibration. There we go. I think we are OK. What else may I answer for you tonight?

Tom: I am hearing you all more and more clearly the longer we work on this book. And so, I am quite willing to allow other books to come through me. I really enjoy the process of learning how to be your scribe.

Fletcher: Oh well, we are so honored that you even give us the time of day. So many humans ignore us. Even those who hear us – still chose to ignore us. Sometimes they say, "Oh, it must just be my mind. I must be going crazy." But – we know – that even when people realize that they are receiving input from the Spirit World – many still don't want to any part of it. And – so - they pretend not to care. Even among some Spiritualists, we have many who say they don't want to give over their time and energy to us.

We would like you all to understand – as we reach out to you – that we never take from you more than we give. It's a balancing – for sure. We say – to those who are willing to loan their time and energy to us – we will give back so much more to them. It's never a loss for a human to work with us. It's always a great blessing. Actually - the blessing is all ours. But, we do try to bring a lot of that blessing down to the humans - who will let us work with them - as a kind of compensation. Be assured, that in the coming year we will be tuning more and more into your vibration.

Tom: I so enjoy this. And I must tell you – that I have never felt so blessed. I am so grateful.

Rose: Oh hello, this is Rose here. I am present here with you again. I think I am coming through. You know my dear that the pleasure of working with our medium is surpassing anything that would have imagined. I have told you how he saved my soul from the darkness, during his séance, that night. He told me to cross over. Because of his work, I am able now – to help many others cross.

And now that you have allowed me to come into your vibration – I will even be able to help many more souls cross – as I work with you as well. And – so – I will bring you more and more of my experiences and my messages – directly. You have pleased me greatly by your work with my words. You have captured my words truthfully, and they will go out to many - I pray. And as I continue to grow in the Light - I will share it with you – that you may benefit in the increase of my vibration.

You know – souls may only draw to themselves - guides who they are ready – on some level - to receive. And yet - a great guide may visit whenever he wishes. Some souls on Earth are being benefitted by visitations from great beings like the blessed angels Michael and Rafael. Such blessed angels and higher being are visiting even the lowliest of the Earth – those who are still caught in the lowest and darkest of vibrations.

A human being - to be visited by an angel or an advanced spirit guide must at least be willing – on some level – to be open to that possibility. Even those who think they are in the darkness, and believe they are not ready or worthy for such visits are sometimes far more ready than they are aware of consciously. And so, I have been assured, that - as I am advancing in my own right – I am privileged to share it with those around me – and on Earth and in Spirit. And I will bring to you my announcements as I get my promotions here. This is all I shall say at this time!

Tom: Congratulations. I love having you in my life. Everything about my life is so much richer, happier and more fun since you and Fletcher came to me, through Bob. I am so grateful for your presence with me, and for this great work we are doing together. I love you so much! And thank God for Bob!

Rose: Yes, we do have work to do. And it is such a pleasure. As you are coming to understand and experience – when our worlds unite - many great things are allowed to occur. We only see our partnership with those upon the Earth, as a great joy. For those who are willing to accept our blessings, we get the blessing of seeing you as benefited from our work. And your work – in turn – benefits us. And so, we are in balance and harmony with each other!

BOB HICKMAN POSTSCRIPT:

Tom's words above echo in my mind, "I love having you in my life..." I think his sentiment so perfectly captures how I too feel about the guides. Rose, Fletcher, Orion— they all do so much to help us. Where would I be without them? I also love having Tom in my life as he has challenged me to be more open to my guides. Sometimes it is the "earth people" who lead us to the "spirit people." Tom is one of those earth people in my life.

The more I study the guides teachings, the more I come to learn that only with an open mind can one find the answers one seeks. It takes a lot of courage to admit that you need help from another. I tend to be stubborn at times, and to have to admit that even I need help is a challenge. I think for so long I've felt that I have tackle life on my own. Seeing their words helps me to realize that I too need to be humble and take their help and advice—to simply receive their gifts of guidance.

I am so amazed that the guides come and share so generously of their time and talents with Tom and me. I am always shocked whenever they make reference to me in a session. I don't really think of myself as deserving any praise for this work, yet they always seem so happy to work with me, and continually reassure me that this channeling is "helping many on both sides of the veil." I suppose time will tell if my contribution helps anyone, but right now I am honored to have the friendship of such high-level beings.

I am always amazed at Fletcher's insights on the channeling process and it's manifestation in my life and the lives of others. How it all actually occurs is still a mystery to even me. I wonder about the "great artists" the guides make reference too. Could it literally be that all the great works of art are productions orchestrated from the Spirit World? Reading their words above make me want to go to the local art gallery and study closely the paintings and sculptures. If artists are channels—then that means that the communication between the worlds in on-going for many, and we are not alone. I think about an artist that I am scheduled to do a reading for next month. I need to ask the guides about them. Are they a channel, like me? If artists are channels many times without even being aware—what could an artist do if they were an "active participant" with the spirit guides? I am inspired to research a new area of spiritual reality. The guides are good to us.

If we can have an open mind, we can have an open heart and this will bring us much joy and peace. This is what I have really learned in this session. I only pray I can be wise enough to keep my openness, and learn from these blessed souls who visit us from the Spirit World.

CHAPTER ELEVEN
LEARNING TO LIVE IN THE GREEN LIGHT
November 13th, 2008

BOB HICKMAN PREVIEW:

As with all good friendships, there develops an "awareness" of each other. Sometimes we just "know" when our friends are suffering some problem, and are in need of our help. Tonight was one of those nights for me. All day long, Tom kept appearing in my mind; I just sensed that he was not doing so well. When we sat down to have our channeling, I inquired as to how he was...Tom—being Tom—was full of happiness and joy. Somehow, though beneath his smile and upbeat personality, I felt the inner struggle. I think that Fletcher and Rose were already in the room, and preparing to address this with him. As I went into trance this night, I could fill an overpowering energy surround me. It was the most beautiful feeling of love and Light. It made me feel like I was enveloped in the arms of God. I knew as I went under that my guides had brought a lot of healing power with them.

The wonderful part of being a channel is that whatever gifts they bring to those who come to meet with them; I get to share in some portion of. As they brought Tom so much love and heart healing from the Other Side, I received a portion too. It was a most blessed night. See below this amazing gift the Spirit Guides shared with us.

Fletcher: Hello this is Fletcher. Can you hear me?

Tom: Yes, I can. It's so good to be back in touch with you, after almost two whole weeks.

Fletcher: Oh, we've been around you a lot all this time. We've been watching you clack'n away at that machine of yours. You know, Rose and I are always leaning over your shoulder here, trying to give you a little bit of advice, here and there. And might we say, it's seems like you've been hearing us.

Tom: I have been hearing you Fletcher, and I really love doing the transcripts.

Fletcher: Hold on a second. We have someone else who wants to speak to you.

Rose: Hello Mr. Berg, this is Rose. Can you hear me?

Tom: Oh Rose, I've missed you so much. Welcome back! It's wonderful hearing your voice again!

Rose: We are so pleased to be here with you. Fletcher is so correct when he says that we have been leaning over your shoulder. I'm not one to be particularly nosey, but in this case, I must say that I have been rather nosey. I am so pleased by your attentiveness to our whisperings and to our encouraging words. We are continually trying to refine this process. Do you know, I've never had so many of my words listed publically before and I suppose you might say that I am a bit nervous about it. The publication of this book is most exciting to us, and we are very pleased with you sir, for you have done well.

Those of us from our world are guiding and helping you all along the way. There will be many people in the coming years, whose lives on Earth will be greatly touched by the messages in our book, and you have been SO instrumental in allowing it to unfold as it has. Our medium has great regard for you. And we love both of you immensely. Just a moment, Fletcher wishes to speak. I shall return later, my dear.

Fletcher: Oh well, there we go. Give us just a moment. We are raising the vibration. What might we be answering for you?

Tom: How many more weeks and transmissions do you think we will need before it will be time for me to begin to edit this material for actual publication?

Fletcher: Oh, about four to five more weeks, we would say. We think that we will be able to finish unfolding all that we've got for you at this time, in four to five sessions.

Tom: What you have given us already is an amazing spiritual teaching, which I find to be totally unique and practical. Do you and Rose realize that what you are offering is going to be considered to be very applicable to people's lives, and extremely useful at this point in human history?

Fletcher: Well, that is the aim here. You know, we don't see ourselves as great beings of great knowledge that is SO superior to the Earth. We are merely your guides. To be a spirit guide, one must have had at least one incarnation upon the Earth. Most of us have had more than a few. And so, as we remember our incarnations, we are able to bring our teachings over in ways that people, who are still in their bodies, may easily relate to.

Once you come back over here to our side – then you will remember the reality of Spirit. But- when you are still in your Earthly bodies, you tend to forget it. So, we are here to speak to those who are still in their bodies – and who have forgotten who they are.

Thank you for your words of support and for all that you are doing to capture these transcriptions. We think we will finish off this first book in four to five more sessions, depending how long the medium can allow each session. It depends on our medium's vibration and how long he can sustain us.

Tom: Good, well I am looking forward to preparing this wonderful material for publication. But – I have to tell you – that - this writing thing can be quite a lonely process. Can you help me with that?

Fletcher: It is true - that this kind of work can be a lonely process. But – you know – as you go into 2009 – this will be the time of a new beginning for you.

You have been doing a lot of work over the last three or four months here – work on your spiritual self. You have been learning to let go of much of the fear that's been binding you - for so long.

Inside of each human being – the heart holds within it – love – and it also holds the opposite of love – which is fear. And so - for the last few months- we've been letting you empty out much of the fear that you have been holding in your heart for a very long time. That's why you have had the feeling of it bubbling to the surface. And, this makes you feel a bit overwhelmed.

You have even had to deal with those old religious beliefs about a god who might kill you and throw you into a burning hell. You have been dealing with an old fear - that there might be a god who is punishing you – and it is this feeling – that keeps bubbling up to the surface. Sometimes you feel as if this fear of god – and of god's fiery punishment – is surfacing all around you. But, that's because that old fear has been stuck down in you for so long.

The good news is that - we will be bringing new people into your life – but for now – we want you to be focusing on yourself. Because, as you are purifying yourself – you are also preparing yourself to receive these new relationships. In the meantime – you will be having some companionship – but your true love – the partner relationship you've been waiting for - won't come until later.

Tom: That's exactly what I want to clarify with you guys today. I really need your help in creating some more companionship - to balance out all the alone time - I am spending on this book.

Fletcher: That's what we are doing. Please understand here – that we are trying to socialize you a bit at a time. Think about it this way. When you have a little puppy – you don't throw into the ocean without a bit of preparation. The puppy might drown. So, first you teach the puppy about water by putting it into a sink and let it get used to being in water. And then you might move the puppy out to a little pond – where you can watch it learn about water - in safe surroundings. Eventually – the dog will learn enough about being IN the water – that - it will be ready to swim in the sea with you.

This is the same thing - with your love life. If we were to throw you into intense love – without some more preparation - it would totally overwhelm your present vibration. And, actually, it would not serve its purpose. The overwhelming power of love would not be a benefit to you – if it came too suddenly – and without more preparation. It would - in fact – become a distraction to you. So, therefore – we are acclimatizing your soul – to get back into the concept of having a relationship.

We are going to be introducing you to more people. And – yes it's true – a friendship may be coming to you at the end of the month. But – it's not until next March that the true love will come to you. We don't want you to be so terrified of this idea of loneliness – because – you are NOT going to be alone in your life. Remember that you always have us around. But of course – I know that you'd like to have some friends in the flesh – and you will have that.

You already have some good friends who you talk often. You've got to be listening to them – because they are trying to help you. You've got some shyness in your vibration, you know. We are trying to help you break that down a little bit – by – just slowly –pulling you out into the masses.

Remember this important point however. It's not just anyone that you want to be relating with and making friends with. You've got to be having people in your life who are supporting your spiritual life. We understand that – and - THAT is the kind of relationship we are wanting for you. We don't want you to be just running around with atheists. Oh Lord knows - there are enough of them about. We want you to be with people who have some understanding of your calling – and of the higher realms.

I must say – in all honesty – it is a bit rare in this world - these days – to find people like that – but – you've got be patient and let us work. In the meantime – you must stay focused on your path. You've got to be willing to wait a bit longer – and not be so frustrated. Be watching!

Tom: Yes – I hear you. But even Edgar Cayce mentioned to me - a few weeks ago – that he couldn't have done his spiritual work without his stable home life. So – I'm wondering about that. I love my gorgeous condo – but I would like to have a real home again someday – with real people in it - with me.

Fletcher: We ARE working on this – and you will be having more contacts. What you've got to understand - from the perspective of our world – is that it's very difficult sometimes. We have to do a lot to get humans to listen to us. If you could but know – how much we go through – over here – to put you together with people. You'd be surprised.

We don't ever sleep and we have no time – but – you could say – we are doing a twenty four a day job. We are working on this kind of thing all the time. First of all – we've got to find a human that is truly compatible with your vibration. And then – we have to make contact with that human – so that the situation can be arranged – so that they are enough under our influence to be at the right place at the right time.

And so – this work we do at helping you meet up with just the right people – CAN be quite a challenge to us. Please be patient and - be assured - that we are working on your behalf - and we do not forget your requests for our assistance. We are so pleased with all the work that YOU are doing on our behalf – and so - we are certainly happy – therefore – to try to return the favor.

Tom: That would be so helpful. Sometimes the loneliness feels like a huge weight on my soul.

Fletcher: We are aware of that – but we also know that this loneliness - that you speak about – is not a permanent condition. We see your time line – in a bigger way. And if you could but stretch your auric field – and your awareness - beyond the momentary feeling – you would be seeing that you are growing towards the new life you seek.

Tom: What exactly do I need to learn to grow? What am I supposed to do to complete this monk's phase of my life? What would you advise me to do over the next couple of months – as far as my own personal growth work?

Fletcher: Well – it's important that you be continuing to listen for our voices and for our guidance. Surely you have been hearing us. And the more you practice listening to us, the closer we will come into your vibration.

Tom: I can really feel you and Rose when I am working on these transcripts. You have such a loving, uplifting vibration - a real "feel good" energy! That's why I always look forward to transferring your words into the computer. You lift me up into a really good feeling place - every time – and I love you all very much!

Fletcher: Well, as I was saying – in terms of your own personal growth – you want to be climbing through the chakra system. Because, as you keep your chakras clean - it's kind of like house cleaning – then - you keep the Light flowing. We want you to be using the Light for a continual conscious program of chakra cleansing!

Wherever the white Light goes – it has two qualities to it. It has the ability to send things out from you – for example – you can send out healing energies on the white Light. But - you can also use the other characteristic of the Light - which – is its magnetic power. This is a quality of Light that carries with it the ability to draw in to you whatever you want or prefer.

So, as you keep your chakras clear and strong –you will be drawing more loving experiences to yourself. We would you like to be focusing on the heart chakra. Some people think of the heart chakra bathed in an emerald green glow – while other people visualize it as pink. That's fine as well. Whichever color you see it as is alright, and is the way you should work with it. But, we like to tell you that it is more like a rich green color – like emerald green. This is like the green associated with Ireland.

This rich green color is the color of life and abundance. And so, the more you can consciously surround yourself with the green energy - the stronger the heart chakra will become. Remember – it is true that – what you put out comes back to you. So, if you are sending out a ray of love – well then – you are going to draw back to you the ray of love.

Something else you can be doing here – to enhance that – is to be wearing a green stone – a green crystal around the heart area. You might want to consider wearing an aventurine or an emerald – although an emerald can be a bit pricey. So, maybe something a bit cheaper. An aventurine would work well for you.

Tom: I like the color green. It's all over Hawaii – and therefore – it is the perfect color for me to work with. Green really does represent life, growth and abundance to me. The green of the palm trees, the lush green Pali cliffs – the green ferns and lawns – there is so much green to meditate on here in the islands. And it's all so alive! What else should I do with my meditation?

Fletcher: What you want to do is – focus on the heart chakra first - and then - let the Light in that chakra center expand – so that the color of green surrounds the entire body. Then, you want to charge that with some white Light. As you consciously bring in a little of the white Light – what that does - is that it sets a green tint in your aura.

Filling the heart chakra with green Light allows you go through your day - sending out the energies of love. You will not only be consciously sending out love to others, but you will also be drawing love back in. This practice will help you move forward in your relationships.

Tom: What kind of thinking should go along with such practices?

Fletcher: First of all – what we want you to realize is - that – to be thinking that you HAVE to have love – or get love - actually pushes the experience of love away. That kind of thinking is a form of desperation. You've got to be thinking instead - in terms of, "Well, I'm open to whatever God wants me to have, or what the spirit people what for me." This kind of loving acceptance - makes it easier for us to work with you.

As you set your vibration – and clear your chakras consciously - not only do you help yourself – but – you are also helping us. We can then – take some of that clear auric energy – and move it about. We can stretch your auric energy a bit - kind of like tentacles going out – until it touches people. So, when you consciously set the vibration of your own aura – it helps us help you.

The other thing that you've got to understand here is that you've got to stop looking at yourself with criticism, because self-criticism gets stuck in your aura. When you let yourself think, "Oh poor me, I must be doing something wrong – nobody loves me" - that is not good for you. What we want you to start thinking is, "I am content and whole within myself."

You know - even when you don't have a partner – your spirit can still be completely content within itself. You can be totally content - for this reason and this reason alone - the Light of God exists within you – right now. And - in that God Light - is a vibration of total wholeness.

Now – it is true – that when one is in the body - on Earth – that one sometimes feels a sense of separation from the Divine Light. That is why we are trying to help you to NOT feel that so strongly. We are here to help you bridge the gap between your world of bodies and our world of Spirit.

We DO accept that humans like to have partnership – and we want to say that partnership is a very valuable way to come back to a realization of the Spirit World of love and Light. Humans – by loving each other – lift each other up. And – by being together - they push each other to grow. So – please know – that this companionship you seek – is truly of the Light.

Many times in life – there is a feeling of being a little separate and lonely. Try to understand that – when you were a child - you were often IN the Spirit World. Those visitations with our world made your vibration always a bit different than those around you. And this is also why you always have gone through periods of feeling lonely and separate from the rest of the human race.

But – please don't ever think that you are less lovable than others – it's just that your vibration is higher, lighter and more spiritually attuned. You are carrying around a natural energy from our world – which does not always blend in well with those around you – because they are so enmeshed in the superficialities and surface concerns of the material world.

We will work with you – however - to try and soften your auric energy a bit – so that more people will be drawn to you more easily. We will adjust your energy field – and fine tune your aura - so that people will not feel so intimidated - when they come around you. When you have as much of our Light around you – as you do – sometimes - when people begin to sense the power of that Light – they become afraid and pull away.

It's kind of like - when you try to put two magnets together – at the same pole – there is a natural repellent reaction that occurs. Your thoughts and feelings, which sometimes focus too much on your so-called differences from people, set up a vibration within your aura, which then acts to repel the very love you seek to share and receive. Your energy naturally pushes away the darkness – while many people you meet – are unconsciously pushing against the very Light you bring.

Your feeling vibration – which is a strong, natural need to love - bumps up against others who become afraid of the love you carry – because you ARE an emissary of Light. They pull back – almost in shock - because they are vibrating in darker realms of spiritual ignorance, and can't handle the rapid influx of higher Light energies. They don't even know why they are repelled so forcefully. That is why we will be working to soften your energy – so you can allow in more relationships – where you can share more of your Light.

You haven't done anything to purposefully keep people away or to repel them away. It's not that at all. The main reason for your feelings of isolation - is that the natural energy of Light –

that you have picked up from crossing over into our spiritual vibration and visiting the Spirit World – causes a difficulty in blending in with others on the Earth plane. Even our medium here – has this same problem, as well.

Tom: You are so right. Sometimes, when I walk into public places - I actually feel that people are moving away from me.

Fletcher: Well, you are quite a nice chap. But – the energy that people pick up from you – is not about you being negative - as much as it is - about you being positive. The thing is that – many people on the Earth today are actually afraid of the Light and are repelled by it. They are so enmeshed in the physical world – that - when they are approached by the higher vibrations of the spiritual world – and by the Light of our realms - it shakes up their whole materialistic reality.

Tom: Thank God we are working on this book together - because your presence in my life right now - really helps balance out the loneliness. This project of ours is one of my greatest joys and I am so appreciative that you have come to me.

Fletcher: We are so honored that you have taken the time to listen to us. And, we are so thankful for Bob – as well – for allowing us to use his body to communicate with so many people.

We see the coming weeks and months for you – as being much more joyful and Light. And - your life will continue to expand and be happier – as you place more and more of your attention on your spiritual evolution. This is your real work – at this time - to awaken to the Spirit within. Do you have another question for us?

Tom: You mentioned that I was continuing a work that I began in Atlantis. Can you tell me something about that work?

Fletcher: Well, it was the work of the priesthood. The work of the priesthood is not just about being in a church or temple. The priesthood is about being a teacher in the world. In the olden times – both you and Bob used to wear the robes – and sit on thrones in temples. Oh, you had a lot of fun doing that – but times have changed – and now your temple is the whole world around you. Your robes are the clothes that you wear as you move about your world and interact with the everyday people.

And also, you are continuing the work of the ancient priesthood by coming together with our medium and doing this book. By listening to our voices and sharing our messages – with others – you are doing the teaching work of the priesthood. This work that you are now doing with Mr. Hickman is an important part of your ongoing life's journey. You are both journeying together – still IN the priesthood.

When you were a school teacher – you were very much a minister to your students. You didn't just teach them about arithmetic. You also taught them about the reality of the spiritual "self" within. You were acting as a priest incognito – might we say. That's the way we wanted it to be.

In this day and age – because of the rise of atheism and disbelief – the priesthood is a little bit more hidden. You and Bob are part of that hidden – mystical priesthood. We want you to be talking more about your book – and especially – your teaching about the spiritual Super Self within all children – not only on the internet – but also on YouTube.

In the material plane – people minds have short attention spans. When I give a message to someone through our medium – I often have to offer it many times before people listen. When people are not spiritually inclined – we have to talk even twice as much to them.

So, you will have to repeat and repeat and repeat your message –over and over again - until people begin paying attention. And – as you practice this - we will certainly be doing all we can to bring the consciousness towards you. As you work on opening your heart chakra more and more to the vibration of unconditional love – not only will you draw in more companionships and partnership – but you will also be drawing to yourself - those whose hearts are open to the spiritual truth you teach.

In the heart chakra – exists both spiritual love and sensual love. The two can actually be accomplished as one. Isn't that efficient? Higher relationships always start at the heart chakra. Once the heart is truly ensconced – as primary in your relationships – then all the other chakras are connected to it.

Focus on the heart chakra – from now on. Practice the green Light meditation. This is a different way of being in relationships - for you – and will take some practice, but, you will be doing fine with it!

Tom: So, why has it been so hard to get people to listen to me and my message? The biggest break I've had so far was when Shirley MacLaine interviewed me. What's happening? What can I do?

Fletcher: The thing is – that many people are not listening to their guides right now. People are having a great fear about the economy – which makes them operate more from their lower chakras. We are not saying that in a critical way –because we all have to work on our chakras. Even spirit guides have chakras and must work on keeping them clean and clear, as well. We are beings of Light – and our chakras are made of that Light. We never lose our chakras – because they are part of the eternal self.

Many people are crossing through intense emotions of fear – rather than working on their chakras. So, they must be approached over and over again. Don't be afraid to ask for help, for endorsements and for assistance - from those who have offered it – or from those - who are in positions of influence.

The problem that we are running into – is that there are a lot of clashing energies here. So, we must work to help stabilize people's vibrations – because - their worldliness is getting in the way of helping - in our spiritual work. The material world feels like such a struggle to so many people – at this time – that their fears are blinding them to the work of Spirit.

You must keep promoting your ideas and your teachings. Soon you will have two books to promote – and you will be finding your agent. We see New York as fertile ground for your work - although we don't see you moving there – at least not for the next four years. We actually see you staying in Hawaii for about a year, and after that, we think that you will be returning to San Francisco.

Tom: Wow. I hadn't even thought of that. Are you sure?

Fletcher: You will be returning to that place in about a year. Opportunities will open that will draw you there sometime next year. We don't want to give too much away, but we do see you attracting some new options - and we see San Francisco as being - an area of great opportunity for you. We think that you would do better in a more liberal area – like San Francisco – where there is not as much negativity as there is on the east coast. If you only knew of all the difficulties we have to face – working with our medium in the Washington D.C. area! You would not like it or feel comfortable here!

So, what you've got to be understanding – is that your work – could be coming - in the form of giving seminars. And – we must say – also – that the possibility of new partnership will be having an impact on your upcoming move – and will be an influencing factor!

Tom: OK. My prayer to God has been – to just show me where to go and what to do – and I will follow the guidance. I just want to be of service – and go to wherever I am led. So – although I am shocked about this idea of returning to San Francisco – I WILL leave Hawaii and go back to the Bay Area, if that's where Spirit leads. I will follow!

Fletcher: Opportunities will open all in the right time. The way will become clear. Give us just a moment. Rose wants to say something.

Rose; Hello, this is Rose, can you hear me, my dear?

Tom: Yes, I can. And I love you so much. You and Fletcher are such help to me!

Rose: Oh, we love you too, my dear. Fletcher is a blessed soul – and we are working together - for you - on many different levels and many different planes. You have much good ahead of you in the coming year. You will have a new relationship – and two wonderful books that will be highly publicized. You will be making preparations for a move. There is much for you to undertake.

We do not give you all the answers – or all the details at this time – because – even we – in our world – are still evolving your future. The truth is – on a deep soul level – YOU are evolving your future. We only assist in what you have already charted for yourself. At this time – please understand that we have great plans for both you - and our medium. You have taken on much – and are slowly building a new foundation - that will support you for many, many years to come. You have before you – great opportunities coming - for teaching, enlightening and loving, as well.

Tom: Well, I am totally willing to go where the opportunities guide. You know how much I want to teach again – and how much love I have in my heart to share. And, I am REALLY going to love teaching what you and Fletcher have taught me in the past few months.

Rose: We would be most honored if you would share our teachings, and we do hope that you continue to do so. As we have told you – this is only the first of a series of books. Fletcher has assured me of this. Wonderful opportunities ARE coming!

You must be patient with us however – and understand – that we are also still evolving. Sometimes I speak and act too rashly as well – and Fletcher has had to take me to task. There are timelines to be considered. He has said to me, "Rose, you cannot say things will happen – until they are better prepared."

Just remember – that any delays that seem to keep our predictions from coming true – on time - are always for your soul's betterment. We must always honor the guidance WE GET - from the guides like Orion - who are even higher that we are. They tell us that – if we rushed things – they would not come to fruition or maturity in the best way for all involved!

There are many guides even higher than Fletcher and I – who we must always answer to. Even though we sometimes think OUR timing - is the right timing – advanced spirits like Orion can – and often DO - override our plans. Orion understands the karmic connectedness of souls – and the interworking of all of these things. And it is to such guides that even we must answer.

When you put your whole self into your spiritual work – you will feel much more alive and much less lonely. And – I promise - that we will help raise your vibration – so that you will no longer feel the feeling of loneliness bearing down so heavily upon you. Remember my dear - you have many loving guides around you always!

When I was alive on the Earth I also sometimes dealt with feelings of loneliness. I was in a loveless marriage, you know. I married – oh yes – and I had a husband – who I had a friendly kind of general affection for - but that was all. I did not have love with my husband – for I married only for prestige and money. And so, there were times – when I also felt a kind of lonely emptiness. But – do you know what happened to me, my dear? In those empty times I did not even stop to reflect upon it. I simply brushed it aside. As a result of that – I had limited growth in my spirit.

The suffering that you are enduring is a sign of the great love and Light you have within you. One cannot miss love unless one is filled with love. I had very little love – and therefore I could hardly miss love. Oh – I suppose you could say – that I did miss love rarely and occasionally –but not in the depths – like I can see in your vibration. You feel very much for those you love. You feel deep love for those you left behind in San Francisco – and for those you have yet to meet physically – but already feel touching your vibration. From our world – your feelings of love look quite noble. We see your wishing for the higher things of life – life-loving relationships - with great joy.

Fletcher's work and the higher guides work are leading you into higher realms of vibration – so that by the springtime of next year – you will be so thankful that events are unfolding just as they are. We guides help many souls – and we are helping you always! I would stay right at your side always – except sometimes - I am called to what you might call – emergencies. And of course, Bob keeps me very busy as well. I love him so very much – and I am very dedicated to his work – for – without him – I would not be where I am today.

Tom: Where do you go when you are not talking with us in this way? Can you tell me something about your typical day up there in higher realms?

Rose: I help many souls – and I have many friends that I visit often. Over here - we visit with each other – very much like you do on Earth. People here have houses and homes. Here in the Spirit World – we can have exactly the kind of home we desire. So – I have a home very similar to my old house in Mayfair. It's a grand affair with five floors and it's quite lovely indeed.

When my time is not being spent in visiting people – I am attending meetings and councils - where I am learning how to be a better guide. Higher beings are teaching me by example. I am often shown scenarios of events occurring on the Earth – when I can see – first hand - how the higher guides are intervening. I am often taken out with other guides, like Fletcher and Orion – and shown situations – at close hand – to observe – so I can understand the complexities of our work.

It is true – that I am a junior guide and still learning. So - I sometimes err – and when that happens – the higher guides always intervene to help set things right. That is their job – and they are a gift to God and the universe – and especially - to the humans whom they serve.

You know – I must tell you – I still love my cocktails (she laughs). And so – I do go to cocktail gatherings up here - where I still enjoy drinking martinis. They are made not out of alcohol – however - but of pure Light. I remember my time back on Earth when I used to wonder if there would be cocktails in Heaven. I mentioned it casually to my vicar at my church – who told me that I was too worldly-minded – and should give up such silly thoughts. But he was wrong! We DO have cocktails in Heaven.

The amazing truth is – that we CAN and DO have these pleasures here in Heaven – pleasures that are similar to those special pleasures - that we were so fond of one Earth. The difference between the cocktails of Earth and the cocktails of Heaven is that – here - you can never become intoxicated. We DO have drinks here – but they only mildly stimulate us – and give us pleasure- without ever making us feel out of control – which sometimes happens to people who drink too much on Earth.

Tom: That is wonderful news. So – would you say – that what you are feeling - is a kind of divine intoxication?

Rose: Yes. It is really the Light of the drink that we imbibe. This is what we are really enjoying. Finding joy in life is of great importance!

I wish to tell you – that I do want you to have more fun. Everyone should have fun in life – you know. So I will be bringing out my stick again – to stir up the nest – when you are out cocktailing at the pubs – to bring you more companionship.

I had grand times on Earth – and I want you to enjoy grand times on Earth, as well. You deserve more joy and much more fun – for you have done – and are continuing to do - great work for the spirits – and - on our behalf. So, we WILL be giving you assistance in this regard – for your work is important – and you deserve grand joy.

Tom: I so appreciate that Rose. Any help you can offer would be welcomed.

Rose: You know – we are trying to get our medium out and about much more as well. We are hoping that he will take more breaks – and have more fun – as well. He works so hard – and we do monitor him.

Tom: Can you tell me a bit more – about - what my main work is at this time? What is my number one task?

Rose: Your task – my dear – is already before you. You are already doing it. Your task is - to do all you can – through your life, your writing, your teaching and your daily interactions – to help those around you - to open up to God.

So many people have forgotten God – or – have great fear of God. There is still – in your world today – a myth that God hates everybody and wants to burn them in fire. I used to believe that – even when I was alive. But – the truth – my dear – is that God loves everybody and wishes to bring them into His Presence - and into the Light of His Salvation.

Do you know – there is much writing about salvation in the Bible. But – it is so misunderstood. Mr. Cayce taught me – that to be saved – actually means - being saved from the fires of one's own fearful consciousness. People say, "I want to be saved from the fires of hell", without understanding what this actually entails. What I want you to understand today - is that – "being saved from the fires of hell" – means being saved from the fires of one's own consciousness of fear. It is from the fires of one's own making – that people need saving. Those fires we speak of - are made out of the negative thought forms that people focus on – those lower vibrations - that pull them down into the darkness of ignorance and feelings of separation from God's Light and love.

Yes, there are tales of people who have died and have said that they have seen a fire – but - there are no real fires of hell upon death. Those so called - hot fires - are only the fires of false thinking and negative feeling. If one were to cross over with a consciousness infused with Light, then it would be the Light of God's Love that would welcome them and embrace them. The Light never rejects anyone who reaches towards it!

Those who have reported that they saw the fires of hell – after death – are misinterpreting what they saw. Those fires were really the fear and rage within their own consciousness reflected back at them. What they encountered when they passed over – therefore - was only their own consciousness of fear, self loathing, anger, doubt and self-hatred mirrored right back at them.

If one could let but a little glimmer of God's Light into one's self – one's mind would quickly feel those self inflicted fires of hell – completely quelled. The fires of hell would be easily replaced by the cool, calm, quiet serenity of God's Light. Do you understand what I am saying?

Tom: Yes, I do. And - I have really enjoyed your account of what you experienced after you crossed over. Can you expand on what you went through personally?

Rose: Souls who are advanced – when they die – are instantly absorbed and welcomed into the higher realms of God's Light and unconditional love. But – souls like mine – who were absent of love – and wallowing in spiritual ignorance – often DO find themselves in a kind of void. But, even there – in that void - if they would only cry out this prayer, "God help me", their time in the void would be greatly shortened. In fact, they would be instantly received into the Light.

Even when I was there – in that void - I used to see little glimmers of Light – and hands above me – reaching out for me. Little did I realize that the spirit guides were reaching out for me – even then. I had fear of them and I thought, "Who are these people above me?" and I turned away from them. My own spiritual ignorance and blinded me to the very people who were trying to save me.

You know – when a soul falls into that pit of darkness – it is not that God is punishing them for anything. What is happening –

quite simply – is that they are being allowed a place for a time out. They are set apart – temporarily - in order to recollect upon the reality of how and what they have lived – and the nature of the soul. If there were absorbed instantly into the Light with no love within – it would be too much. They would be neither happy nor content.

And since, we know that the highest realm of God in a place of pure joy and love – it only makes sense – that to attain it – you must have some joy and love in your own soul. Don't you see this? Remember the Hermetic axiom - "as above so below – as below so above". This is a reminder that – it is the very love and Light which you allow into your soul - while upon the Earth – that will take you to that which is above. And that which is above will come down to your soul.

And – so that is why I was able to be lifted out of the pit – out of the darkness, because – in my soul – I began to allow the Light to come in. There was a point when I began to listen - and I came upon this thought, "I DO believe that I need help from something higher than myself." Remember, by dear, I walked in that darkness for so long. I did not even know that I was dead.

And so, after I crossed over – I eventually entered into our medium's circle – that night – because they were praying to help souls such as mine. It was then that I realized the improbability of walking down a street in London one moment – and then find myself – standing – the very next moment – in a living room – being told that sixty odd years had passed. For me – it had seemed only minutes – for in the spiritual world we have no real time. But – when I found myself standing in the living room of this medium, looking about I finally began to realize that I was not in my home – and that something mystical had occurred.

It seemed to be – in that moment – that I had literally teleported (that's what you would call it) – I had teleported from a street in London - into a totally unfamiliar living room. I then listened – as members of the circle told me, "Rose, you have died. You are a spirit". I didn't want to believe them at first- to be honest. But – then - I said to myself – "Perhaps I should listen to these people." All it took was that one brief moment of letting go of my arrogance – of giving up my old thinking – for this realization to occur. In that moment – I was transformed. I merely let go of all my old conceptions of the realities of life and death.

I heard the members of that group telling me to pray to God – to go over to the Light. There are souls waiting for you. And then Fletcher came and said, "I am prepared to take you over, my dear". And I thought, "Who is this man?" You know –it was very interesting – because – when Fletcher appeared – he was all in a glow – full of a glowing Light – and looked to me like an angel. And then he pointed upwards to a kind of portal, in the middle of this home – where I saw hands reaching down.

I was amazed as I thought to myself, "Here I am standing in this strange home. I was in a dark void and now I am here. I have come through some kind of portal of Light – in order - to find myself in this living room." And, as I thought this – I began noticing the existence of a second portal of Light right above me. It was kind of like a beam of Light – coming down towards me – with hands reaching down.

Then I heard Fletcher say, "Hold my hand, we are going up to them. Raise your hand up." And so, I held onto Fletcher with one hand and reached up with my other hand to the hands above me. I was instantly lifted up – and felt as if I was floating. I cannot really describe it. Words simply do not suffice to explain such an experience. All I can say is that – I crossed through another doorway - and OH my dear – it was magnificent – beyond anything you can imagine. The Light of God is beyond any experience that human words or human senses could ever hope to describe or grasp.

Do you remember that account in the Bible – that tells the story of when Moses went up to the top of his holy mountain? And when he returned it was said that his countenance shown like fire – for the presence of the Lord was upon him. Do you remember this?

Tom: Yes I do. I have identified with the Moses archetype for many years, because I see myself as a kind of modern day Moses. My dream is to liberate the world's children from many the modern day pharaohs - like the atheistic and materialistic thought systems - that seek to make them into slaves or "Uncle Tom's". The huge belief systems of our materialistic – the many "isms" - age are like dictators that teach kids to ignore the sacred, and to live their lives in spiritual darkness.

Rose: You ARE bringing that Light to them – so well – that very same divine Light that - I experienced when I finally let it reach into my life and pull me out of my own darkness of ignorant thinking. It is a shame still for me to think that I went through my entire life – forty odd years – and did not ever once – realize the truth of the Light. So many people upon the Earth today – SO many - my dear – are living in that spiritual darkness. They simply ignore the presence of the Light altogether – and they live out their whole lives - as if the Light of God did not even exist!

It is true. You have brought - and ARE still bringing - the liberating Light or truth to many people – and THAT is truly salvation. This is why we are so pleased to be in communication with people like you and our medium – for our work is being accomplished through you.

Fletcher has told me that I will be anchored lovingly - to our medium - for many years to come. You know – I am still in training - and there are many wonderful things yet to unfold! I am continually learning from great beings - many of them much higher and wiser than myself. There is freedom of Spirit here - but there is also this hierarchy - and an order that we must honor. It has a place – and is for the good of all. We love our medium and hope to keep him with us for many more projects such as this.

Tom: What would you suggest that I do – in the immediate future – to not be so impatient with how slowly things sometimes seem to be unfolding? I would say that my greatest source of upset is my impatience! What you suggest for me to do - to feel the joy of the moment – instead of always being so obsessed with what's just around the corner? I have always been so future-oriented and I can see that this is NOT serving me well, any more.

Rose: It is still important that one look at time in terms of segments, you see. Many times, humans will look at the entire day stretching before them – and say, "Oh, this grand day before me – all these responsibilities I must do – I should be doing this and I should be doing that . . ." And what happens is that they get themselves all bogged down and burdened before they've even begun.

So, we would suggest that you think of your day in terms of minutes and segments of no more than five minutes each. Just think, "What would I most like to accomplish in the next five minutes?" This is not such a difficult task. You can meditate for five minutes – and then go on to something else. One CAN learn to be fully present in the moment – if one learns how to allot oneself only five-minute segments. Then - the task is simply to live out – each of those five-minute segments – one at a time.

We don't want you to worry about the rest of the day or think thoughts like, "If I don't control things – my whole day may fall apart". What we would suggest is let that anxiety go – because there really IS no way to know – for sure - what will happen on down the line. But – we DO have some semblance of control over our thoughts and our feelings and even our actions in the present moment – in each of our five minute segments. When you break your day up into these smaller segments you will have a greater sense of being present in the now moment. You will have a greater awareness of presence in each and every moment – which will automatically alleviate much unneeded anxiety.

The fear and emptiness that you sometimes feel as loneliness come from looking ahead too far. You are thinking thoughts like, "How am I going to get through this day?" And you are focusing on too many thoughts that are fearful about your tomorrows. This kind of obsessive worrying causes your day to pass you by – while you wallow in fear and anxiety about a time that has not yet arrived. That is not good for you – now is it? And, where does that leave your faith?

Tom: Impatience and a lack of faith go together, don't they?

Rose: Very much so. Very much so. We want you to know however – that your impatience is actually of a more noble type. The things that you are impatient for - are - not so much the materialistic things of the world – but are the things of the Spirit. And that is a much more noble type of impatience. Though, even that should be curbed occasionally.

Relax all your anxieties about your upcoming return to active teaching. You will not be returning to the old form of teaching in the school system, but will instead – be giving your own seminars. You will be a free agent. We see you teaching at universities as a guest speaker, as a lecturer. Although - you are not quite ready yet for this to unfold. Your development is still ongoing.

We've been working with our medium to do more on his YouTube channel, and his audiences are growing. Just look at the numbers of viewers. We would suggest that you do more talks on YouTube, as well. It has been a great help to him – and we think it would also help you. We see you supporting each other this way. You've helped him very much and he wishes to help you. We would like to encourage to you to collaborate on some of your videos. It's a wonderful format - where each of you can share your ideas with the other publically. We think that this kind of collaborative work would be most enlightening for all parties.

You could actually begin this collaboration by offering a kind of a teaser on YouTube – where you talk specifically about this upcoming book. That would create interest. You might wish to begin to introduce the idea of our book to the public – to hint around - that something wonderful is coming soon. It wouldn't take much effort at all. The YouTube spots could even be as short as two or three minutes each. We will be doing more to encourage people to be attracted to your messages. We will do our best to draw more and more to you – to encourage, enlighten and direct.

Tom: Thank you Rose – I really appreciate tonight's more personal conversation.

Rose: Oh, it is our pleasure my dear. You know, from our side – we know that all of our messages are important – whether we are speaking directly to you – about your specific questions– or to a large group of a million. Every soul is valuable in the Light – and it is necessary that everyone have an opportunity to receive spiritual nourishment – sometimes on a personal level - as well as in large groups. We believe that talking about some of your more personal concerns CAN offer us the opportunity to offer guidance - to help many other people going through similar struggles, as well. Do you have any other questions before we say goodnight?

Tom: Yes I do. I'd like to ask about that home you live in – in Heaven. How exactly did you create that gorgeous home in Heaven? That would be fascinating for our readers to learn about.

Rose: Yes, you see – in our world – the power of the mind creates everything. It is true that you have an etheric body – but it is really the mind that does ALL the creating. The etheric body is only an encasement for the mind – for the spiritual mind. This is why you are encouraged – while on Earth – to develop higher and higher thoughts. For – by the mental training that one accomplishes upon the Earth – it makes one's transitional time into the Spirit World much easier. The higher and better your thoughts are - while on Earth – the easier time of it - you will have when you cross over to our world.

Over here – one's glory is determined by one's accomplishments upon the Earth – specifically in relation to how you have used your time to develop your awareness of Spirit. Now remember – you have incarnated many times - and your soul is continually going through stages – in an ongoing evolution of spirit. So, every soul is at its own stage of evolution of spirit – I should say. When you come back to our spirit realms – you will reveal your growth in glory. Everybody who has ever gone to the Earth – comes back with some new degree of glory. And that degree of glory is brightened each time one has a successful incarnation.

As one's soul becomes brighter – one's abilities begin to increase and expand. For example – when I first crossed over – all I could manufacture was clothing for myself. I could not make a house materialize. Such things were completely beyond me. And so, when you are a new soul over here – the higher souls do step in - to prepare things for you – in order to welcome you.

So, when I arrived in the Spirit World – I had a house prepared for me – by others. It was a beautiful home – might I say – and it was most welcoming!

Tom: That's just like here – isn't it? I remember Fletcher and Edgar Cayce saying that you all helped me get this wonderful new condo here in Waikiki! The glorious place came to me so easily - that it isn't much of a stretch – for me to believe - that you spirits were helping. I am still amazed every morning when I wake up – and see the panoramic view of the mountains and ocean right outside my lanai.

Rose: Yes, we did arrange things for you – for - you are reaping the rewards of many years of devoted service - teaching many souls about the Light.

Tom: Thank you so much. When this place so unexpectedly place fell into my lap - like it did –with absolutely no effort on my part - I suspected that I was getting help from "on high" – even before I met you all through Bob. And when I look back over my whole life – I've always sensed instances of "divine interventions".

Rose: Yes – you are right. We DO help and we often can intervene – when asked - even in those most practical of matters – like housing.

As I was saying – after I finally rose up into the realms of Light – and began to realize I was in the Spirit World – I began to notice what I was wearing. When I had the thought, "I'd prefer to be wearing something else", I heard a guide answer me with, "If you don't like what you are wearing, you can change it."

And then I said, "But where is the store to buy clothes?" I believed that stores were still necessary because I was so new to the Other Side and hadn't learned yet – about the power of creative thought. I had much to learn about the power of mental creation, at that point in my soul growth.

So, my guides began to teach me about creation - by saying, "Everything created here is accomplished by the power of your mind. You must learn to visualize that which you want to wear. So, close your eyes and begin to think about your ideal clothing. What would an ideal outfit look like and feel like to you?"

So, I began to think about what an ideal outfit would be like and I said, "I would prefer a long pale blue and silver cocktail dress to wear." Once I decided that my most preferred, ideal outfit would be a beautiful blue dress – like the one I used to wear as a young woman in London - I was then told to focus on it with my whole mind, and with all my attention.

They said, "What does it feel like to wear the dress? Can you actually feel yourself wearing it?" I told them that I could feel it and I could sense it quite clearly - with my imagination. "It's a very nice dress. It's quite soft and I can feel it flowing." This was easy for me to do since I had worn one just like it many years before.

"Then look down Rose," I was told, "and open your eyes." And, when I opened my eyes, I was wearing the very creation I had visualized. But, that was only the beginning for me, for I was then told, "In time you will learn to make palaces with your mind – if that would be your choice." And I said, "Oh well, I don't know about that," for the idea of creating with my mind was still so new to me.

Then they said to me, "We want you to make a house now. Visualize a house that you would enjoy living in." And so - I tried and tried - with all my might – to visualize my house –exactly as it was in Mayfair – back in London. But - all I saw appear – was the doorstep. You know – when you walk towards a grand home – you can see a little transom – like a step of marble. Well, that is all I could see – just the marble. So I said, "Oh my goodness – all I can see is marble. What IS that?"

And they said, "That is your doorstep."

"I created that?" I asked.

"Yes Rose, you created that with your mind and the power of your imagination."

"But I visualized my whole house, "I said, "So, why do I only see the doorstep?"

"Because your mental powers are not yet developed sufficiently," they answered. And so, they sent some guides to help me build my house. Really – I must say – that my house here - was created by others - for which I am most grateful.

I eventually learned that – as one realizes the freedom AND the power of the mind to materialize whatever is preferred – through imagining – one's creative power increases. This is how one prepares oneself for further evolution in the spiritual world.

You remember I told you about my visits with the swamis in India? Well - for swamis like that- who have spent their whole lives meditating and materializing – the transition to the Spirit World is no problem at all. It is easy for them. For me – it was quite a challenge, might I say.

Tom: Is that materialization process what we are supposed to be learning here on Earth as well. Are we here to learn how to manifest our own realities through thinking, feeling and visualizing?

Rose: Oh, very much so. Although - in the Earth plane – manifesting is even harder than in our world. This is because you are fighting against a material nature that is – in many ways – the exact opposite of who and what you really are. So, you must bring your material nature under the subjective power of your spiritual nature - and that can be most difficult. For humans who can accomplish that alignment – however - life becomes a miracle in the process.

Tom: How DO we accomplish that?

Rose: It is accomplished in the same way that it is done in our world. It is done through intense visualization. But, it is not just seeing the object of your desire that is needed. It is a KNOWING of the object – having a full emotional knowledge of the object of your desire - that is needed, as well.

For example – when I thought of my dress – I had to feel the dress on my body. I sensed the weight of the dress – the color – the texture – and the pleasure the dress gave me. So, the more time that humans give to the actual details of their visualizations – the easier will be for the manifestation to occur. As you think, so you are! Just a moment, Fletcher is here.

Fletcher: The medium's body is winding down here. We've got to be careful with him – and - so we will be stepping out of the body now. It has been our pleasure to be with you – and we send you our blessings and our greetings. We are looking forward to coming again.

Tom: Thank you so much. It is always such a gift to me – to receive your wonderful messages – and I am looking forward to completing our first book. See you next week!

BOB HICKMAN POSTSCRIPT

The power of Love runs through this whole transcript. I can hardly believe that I have been a vehicle for such a message to pass through. I see here true wisdom, true compassion, true Divine love in every word my guides have brought through. I really do think they know us better than we know ourselves. I feel they are united to our hearts and minds in such a deep and profound way. So many times I know that I get "weighted down" with the world—and forget how to love and how to live in that love. I pray every day that I can be a channel of this Light and Love. Now if only I could pay attention and really live their message.

Whenever I read the teachings of these mystic souls who come to us in our sittings, I feel so uplifted, so inspired. It really is hard to live in the "NOW" – but I like that they have shown us all a way to try.

According to Fletcher, Tom and I were members of a mystic priesthood in former lives. I wonder if we did channeling then? Could it have been in Atlantis or ancient Egypt? I've always sensed I lived in both places. Is this former existence why he and I met so easily and became friends? What did we talk about then as we sat on our ancient thrones? I wonder if Shirley MacLaine was there with us. She was the connecting thread (on the earth plane) for us. What about her? Maybe she was with us then too.

So many thoughts pass through my mind. It seems that every word the guides impart leads me to a million more questions. I don't know that I will ever have all the answers—at least in this life—but it is fun to wonder, to speculate, to dream of all the possibilities that are out there for us. The more I reflect on the words regarding living in the NOW—the more I think that maybe there is really no such thing as past, present, or future. Maybe all time and existence are literally NOW. If that is true—then we also inhabit all of our incarnations simultaneously—so maybe incarnation is really just about focusing on a particular goal—and whatever goal your Higher Self is working on is where you are in your current consciousness.

I read Rose's description of coming into my séance chamber the night she was "set free"—and again I sit stunned into silence. I remember this night so well...It was the very first night of meeting her. I am thankful she is in my life. Tom seems to benefit also from his friendship with her. I wonder if she was part of the past that Tom and I shared. The more I study the transcripts the more I know one thing—we are never really alone for we are continually monitored by the blessed souls on the Other Side. They sustain us with their Light.

I wonder of the power of the mind. If Rose is able to materialize clothing and homes on the Other Side— can we do it here? Are these powers available to us BEFORE we go to the Spirit World? I think about the psychic research at places such as Duke University. The doctors say we only use a small portion of our active brain. What about the rest? Do the secrets to Eternal Life rest in there? At some point in our evolution will we be able to access those hidden parts?

What if we could materialize things on the earth? Would that end crime? Would people be challenged to expand their minds to create wonderful things? Would humanity (on Earth) use this power to create destruction? I have heard the guides say that the Atlanteans destroyed themselves by abusing the power of the mind. Would we do it all over again? What about our Space Brethren? Have they learned of these powers? Do they use their minds in such ways as Rose speaks of?

My heart and mind tonight are filled with wonder and joy. Wonder at the potentials that await us all, and joy that I get to share in at least of a small part of it now by my association with the guides. I look at the stars in the sky and think—"Yes. We really are children of the Light."

CHAPTER TWELVE
GIVING IT OVER TO THE HIGHER POWER

December 3rd, 2008

BOB HICKMAN PREVIEW

Having returned from my Thanksgiving holiday, I was excited to sit with Tom again. I think for many of us, the Thanksgiving holiday is anything but a time for thanksgiving. For many, this holiday symbolizes stress. Stress of the past, stress of the moment, stress of the future all combine at holiday time. Many people feel they have to just "get through" the experience. Not everyone is better for it. Earlier in the evening, Tom and I talked about how over the years, family gatherings for each of us had their stressful moments.

Fortunately for me, the stresses of the holidays are relieved by knowing that I have the best friends in the world. Those who know me, know that my spirit guides always seem to give me the right words to handle those who might be less tolerant while in the presence of a medium. I think knowing that there really is a "Higher Power" – call it, God, Divine Source, Higher Self, helps me find my way. The guides time and time again remind me that I am so fortunate to have the opportunity to follow a spiritual path.

It is commonly said that good friends bring out the best in us, and I think it true. When Tom and I get together, we always feel inspired to explore the mysteries put before us by our guides. Whenever I go into trance, I never know who will come through, or what will transpire, but I know one thing—I always learn something fascinating. This night was no exception. Below is a most inspirational transcript.

Fletcher: Oh hello there, this is Fletcher. Can you hear me out there?

Tom: Welcome back Fletcher. I've been looking forward to talking to you!

Fletcher: It's so good be back here with you. You know, over here in our world, things are moving along quite rapidly. There are so many good changes coming upon the Earth – and yet – we see much fear still, among the humans. So, we are trying to help bring a little more of a peaceful vibration to the Earth's environment. We've been around humans a lot more.

There are great leagues of – well I suppose you could call them – guides and angels – who are coming down to the Earth plane now – to try and alleviate some of the fear. If the negativity were to continue – without some monitoring from OUR side – you would see greater cataclysms upon the Earth.

The human mind is so strong. It has such power within it – that left untrained – and with enough negative energy – it can actually create earthquakes. As you know, all about the world, there's been a lot of large energy shifts over the last few years, like tsunami's, floods, earthquakes and volcanoes. Some of those events were generated by human minds.

If you might be recalling – remember - how we told you about the importance of using your mind – more consciously – to produce more positive effects? Edgar Cayce talked to you as well - about the necessity for training the mind in this way - which is why he encouraged you to practice dissolving clouds with your focused thinking. You must realize that your own mind can create matter or destroy matter. So you see – this mental energy – this vast power - that is IN your mind – right here and now – MUST be guarded, trained and consciously focused.

Over here in our world, we can actually feel the vibrations - that are coming from minds - of those living on the Earth plane. Have you ever been walking on the Earth near a large electrical source? Sometimes the hair on the back of your neck will stand up on end. It's the electrical static in the air that causes your hair to respond. Well, that is similar to the kind of vibration – that - we can feel over here in our world. I must tell you – that - what we are feeling is a lot fear coming up from the Earth right now. And so, we are coming in to the Earth plane – more strongly - to alleviate some of that fear.

It's kind of funny – but - if you were to ask your friends – and the people who live around you – if they had noticed a bit more calm coming in over them – they would probably say "yes".

Your neighbors would tell you, "it's the strangest thing, but in spite of all my worries about the economy - and my relationships – and my house payments - and my car expenses – I am feeling much more peace and calm, than usual."

What's happening is - that they are receiving confirmation on the soul level – an inner knowingness – communicated to them – by us – an assurance that it's all going to be OK in the end. That is the energy that we are helping to bring down to the Earth right now, in the hopes that humanity will move forward on its evolution. The human race can't grow when people have all that fear clogging up the mind! Do you understand what I am saying?

Tom: Yes, I do. And I thank you. I felt such a strong influx of peace all last week, during Thanksgiving and my birthday. I so appreciate your sending me that energy of calmness. It was really palpable, although I didn't realize that it was coming from you. But, it makes sense to me – because the feeling of peace was so much stronger and joyful, than anything I've felt like that - in a long time.

Fletcher: Over here, we never think much about birthdays because nobody is born and nobody dies. We do have celebrations though– when people cross over here – and come back home. Souls keep going and coming - back and forth between worlds. So, we don't use numbers to delineate any of the specific dates for those comings and goings. Remember - we don't have time over here.

We are not fixated on dates of birthdays on calendars, but we did send you our greetings in the form of the peace wave. And we are most pleased that you were tuned in enough to be able to perceive our peaceful presence all around you on your special day. We sent you the energies of peace and calm as our special birthday greeting.

Tom: It was the perfect gift Fletcher – and it felt great Fletcher, thank you.

Fletcher: Just a moment, there is someone else here who wants to speak with you.

Rose: Oh, hello – this is Rose – can you hear me?

Tom: Yes I can, and it's wonderful hearing your voice again Rose. Welcome!

Rose: I am so very pleased to be here with you again. I also wish to bring to you my personal sentiments for your birthday anniversary.

You know, when I was on the Earth, my family used to have great celebrations for our birthdays. One year, my father even gave me a pet monkey for my birthday. You know those sweet little monkeys that come from India? Well – that was what I got for one of my birthdays. It was the cutest little animal, and I named him, Mr. Jack. I don't know why we came up with that name. It may have been one of my staff. But – I remember we called him Mr. Jack - my pet monkey.

You see – over here - (she chuckles heartily) – Fletcher says that he forgot all about the Earth custom for celebrating birthdays – and is making fun of it all. But, I want to tell you - when we DO see that one of our charges is having a birthday like you did – a day of deep self reflection and celebration – we are reminded of our own humanity, and our own time upon the Earth. And so, I wish you many blessings for your journey in this life, my dear friend.

Tom: I felt so peaceful and happy. And I guess – that I really did sense that you and Fletcher were with me. So, thank you so much for doing that!

Rose: We are always here to serve you and guide you. I once had a good friend - who was a devout Catholic. He told me that the Catholics have a wonderful prayer about guardian angels. Perhaps you've heard of it. If I remember it correctly - it goes something like this, "Angel of God, Guardian Dear, to whom His love commits thee here, even this day, be at my side, to Light, to rule, to guard and to guide." Isn't that a beautiful prayer?

Tom: Yes, it is beautiful. I will use it. Thank you so much.

Rose: This prayer was really made for the higher beings, for the angels. But you know, I like to think that even I can participate in some small measure, in expanding my ability to guide. Here, there is a hierarchy, which means, there are beings much higher and greater than Fletcher and myself. Always remember, Mr.

Berg, that you are all in contact with great beings and they are helping you always.

Michael the Archangel has been making many visits to the Earth, I have been told. For, he has been leading the effort – very much – to bring a greater sense of stability to the Earth – in order that it will continue along its progression. It is so important that you remember and understand that you are never NEVER abandoned. About you - at all times – there are many of those from our world.

There are millions of humans upon the Earth today – particularly – the souls I see in your nursing homes. D o you know what I am talking – nursing homes- those places where invalids go?

Tom: Yes I do. Both my parents died in nursing homes, I am sorry to say.

Rose: You see, many souls who are sent there become very trapped in their own fear. We don't like them – I must tell you – because, as spirit guides - we can feel the vibration of those places – and it's one of great fear. We seek always to bring Light. But – one finds a kind of "culture of death" - in such environments – in many nursing homes. Not all nursing homes are fearful, but many are – and people dread them and fear being sent to them. Even in my time – people dreaded being abandoned by their families – and being placed in such places.

When I look in on nursing homes – I sometimes say, "Look at those poor people, feeling so abandoned by their families". That is why we spirit guides visit them. There are many souls in those homes – that we specifically go and visit. We pay special attention to them, because they are getting ready to cross over, and yet, they have great fear of crossing. This is simply because there is no nobody there reminding them of who they really are – and where they are really going. And so we do much work and are ever so present in those unhappy environments. We work always to bring those people the healing Light – that will ultimately bring the home.

It is a lovely thing to work with those who are preparing to cross over. And yet – in some of those nursing homes – we find souls who have become very Earth bound. These "Earth Bounds" sometimes become so locked into the bodily conception of life – that - they do not allow themselves to rise higher than the body. There is so much of this going on these days – that we have much work to do upon the Earth.

People such as yourself – and also our medium here – help give glimpses into our world - to those souls who have become too bound to your world. And we thank both of you ever so much. If we can help the humans – as Fletcher was saying- to let go of the fear – we shall see great progress upon the Earth. Can you imagine sir, a world in which people are not afraid of life or death – but understand instead that it is all transition?

Tom: Yes, I have felt a kind of new world being born in the last couple weeks – with the election of Barack Obama. It really does feels as if there is less fear and more hope down now. Things seem to actually be getting better down here. So, please tell Michael the Archangel, thank you for his help!

Rose: We are working, you see. In your country – I have heard Americans say to me, "We believe that God is blessing the new president of the United States of America," and I agree that it is true. In England, we always said that our monarch was blessed by God, and we used to sing, "God Save the King". Yes, we used to say, "God bless good old King George the Sixth", for he was our monarch back during World War II. The present Queen is also blessed.

The world leaders - make no mistake – are all known by name – by Michael the Archangel - and he watches them. Yes, we are most pleased to see the joy that is increasing - and is slowly – little by little - breaking down the fear upon the Earth.

Tom: Did you spirit guides and Michael make the victory happen? I haven't seen this much joy in the world – over the selection of a leader – in a long, long time - or perhaps - ever.

Rose: Well, you know my dear. We cannot take credit. We cannot say that we influenced your election. For, that is of the human realm and we always must allow humans their free will. So, the choices that Americans made were all done through their own free volition. If I were to be honest - I would say that I would have liked to have had some influence to assure such a victory – but – in our world – we know that the course of events that are MEANT to happen - DO occur.

We are not so privy as to take part in politics except for merely guiding those who are in those places of power. From our world – we were able to see both outcomes. And, had there been a different outcome in your elections – and the other man had won – we would have guided and blessed even that one. Michael the Archangel would have given him his angelic blessing, as well.

From your limited Earth perspective, you often see things in terms of – "it is the beginning or the ending of the world". But, we do not see things like that at all over here. In our world, we say that life is continuing and ongoing – and if we see that a world leader is heading towards a decision that would create destruction on a great scale - we would do our best to intervene to stop that. I have been told that – often – the higher angels have intervened often – in many world events – to prevent total destruction of the planet. It is in those times- that we do take part and intervene.

Tom: I know how much you love India. So, could you please tell Michael the Archangel that India and Pakistan are threatening war with each other – and need some help down here – to keep the tensions from escalating into all out war.

Rose: Do you know – I was in that place of darkness – when India separated from our empire. And in some ways, I must say – that I am glad that I was not upon the Earth - or in a place where I could have witnessed that – or where I could have observed it. So much suffering has come to that region through those unnecessary hostilities between religions. The real God of love and Light does not EVER discriminate against certain religions. He does not care whether one calls himself Muslim, or Hindu or Christian or in my case – Anglican – which was against the Catholics in my day. The Protestants and Catholics have been against each other for many years in Europe. These religious rivalries are so often based on false doctrines and concepts that still hold sway over the minds and hearts of men, and lead them onwards towards false visions of reality.

Tom: What would you like to say in our book – to try and end religious hatreds and religious wars? What could we say to the world – that could convince them to end those hatreds?

Rose: Well, you know – from my perspective – I have to say – I speak from a position of having been someone who was part of a colonial empire. So, I think that the greatest mistake that humans make – and I put myself squarely in the guilty seat with this – is that the human mind believes in the concept of superiority and inferiority. It is a racial concept – that says – one race or group of people is better than another. The false concept of superiority – once accepted for one's groups - is then translated into governmental superiority – and ultimately into religious superiority.

Here is my answer for the book. There is a way to end the religious, economic and political hatreds which are based on bigoted concepts that believe in the insane idea - that some people and groups are superior and others are inferior. If humankind would only stop and say, "We are all living in vehicles of clay", this hatred would end quickly. You know where the word human comes from? It comes from the root word "humus". You know this – right?

Tom: Yes, I do. I think I heard you whisper this into my ear many years ago when I was writing my book – because I did point out in UTC, that the term "human race" is a much too limiting concept. The word human totally misses the broader metaphysical truth - that we are Divine Cosmic Super Beings - who are housed in these vehicles of flesh, only temporarily.

Rose: It is true. So - what this means - is that the human part of us - is the man of the Earth, the part of us that is made of clay and humus. All of us - really - are living in bodies made of carbon, with elements of soil, earth and of course water. So, no-one can ever claim superiority. Our bodies are all made out of the exact same elements. This is where people like Hitler make their mistake. They think that they are the best – or superior – because they haven't yet come to realize that all people are made of the very same substance and the same materials.

Tom: Yes. That reminds me of Carl Sagan's famous quote in his series "Cosmos", where he said so pointedly, "We are made of star stuff." I loved that!

Rose: Ultimately, even beyond the bodily conception of life - there is another reality – the spiritual truth - that - within each soul – without exception – there is spiritual Light. Light is within each and every soul. If I were to say to you, Mr. Berg, what is the difference to you – between the Light in your bedroom and the Light in your living room - what would you tell me?

Tom: I'd have to say that there is no difference.

Rose: Yes, absolutely. Light is the same everywhere. It is Light – wherever it shines. When analyzed- Light is always what it is – pure Light. It doesn't matter the form in which it appears. Light is universally consistent – and is therefore – always Light. Wherever you go in the universe, Light has the same spectrum. And when you break it down - you can see that it always has the very same colors of the rainbow. Light has all the same wavelengths no matter where it appears universally. And that's just the material Light.

The spiritual Light is even more pure than the material Light. It is that spiritual Light that is within you. And so, ultimately, whether you wish to believe in the spiritual reality, or in the bodily concept of reality, one cannot differentiate between humans, either in matters of flesh, or in matters of spirit. For those who read this – even for those who call themselves atheists – even they must acknowledge that the body has the same elemental structure, ultimately, whether one is Muslim or Jewish or Christian or Hindu. The race and the culture are unimportant – and do not make us different - for they can never alter the basic atomic structure of the body.

So either way you chose look upon the human body – whether you accept only the material physical concept of the body's reality - or also believe in the spiritual concept of the body's reality – there is ultimately no real difference between any of us. We are all ultimately made of Light – whether you see that Light as physical Light – or see it also as spiritual Light. Do you understand, Sir?

Tom: That is absolutely brilliant. Yes, I do understand.

Rose: That is what I wish you could convey to our readers. Fletcher is here and wishes to say something. Just a moment while Fletcher steps in here.

Fletcher: Oh hello there. Here we go. I think we're in the body. Can you hear us out there?

Tom: Yes, I can – loud and clear. Welcome back.

Fletcher: It's so good to be back here with you again. I am holding steady around the vibration of our medium quite well tonight.

So, anyways, I wanted to address what Rose was speaking about. When I was a young man on the Earth, I became an atheist because of all the religious wars. You now, I've spoken to you about my auntie who was a Spiritualist. I also had a mom and pop who were Catholic to the core you might say. And so, I would look from side to side, back and forth between my mom and dad and my auntie. My mom and dad didn't like my auntie very much and they used to say, "You shouldn't mix with those Spiritualists."

So, I would ask myself, "What's so bad about my auntie?" But, then I would go my auntie's house and she would be talking all about life after death. And, I found that i just didn't believe that stuff. So, I felt myself stuck between both extremes. One extreme was all about following the rules of the Catholics, and the other extreme didn't have so many rules- but was pushing me to believe things -that for me seemed a little scary.

And so I said to myself, "Between all these extremes, I can't find no peace." And so then, I thought, "Enough of it." That was when I gave up all religion and became an atheist. But, atheism, you know, leads to a place of inner emptiness in the spirit. And, so I ended up having I an experience like Rose did – when I died. I found myself also in that place of darkness. But, because of the prayers of my auntie and all the people in her Spiritualist church, I was pulled up into the Light.

And so, if I were to say something to try and end all the religious wars around the world – I would say, "Everybody's got to look at their own beliefs." People have to find that – well – as the Buddha would say - the middle road between extremes. Each extreme is a stressor to the people who have to encounter it – whether it is extreme conservatism or extreme liberalism.

You know, if you could travel the middle road – where you find the truth for yourself – but don't be forcing it on anybody by saying, "This truth of mine applies to every single person on Earth and everyone has to follow it just like I say" – then you would allow people to search for their own truth.

And they would begin to seek out their own truth - because they wouldn't feel so threatened by your truth or by some religion's truth. That was my problem. Everyone else's truth seemed threatening to me. That's the way it felt to me. And so I said to myself, "Well, I don't like either of these extremes." And that was why I left all religion. I had enough of that stuff.

For example, now on Earth – we are seeing a lot of extremism. The Christians have it – and the Muslims have it – and even the atheists are a bit extreme in some ways, by pushing atheism as the only acceptable truth. As you know Mr. Berg, when you were teaching in the classroom, you were under the pressure of a religion – actually – which was a religion – not of Spirit – but of atheism and materialism.

Tom: Boy, you can say that again. I write about that in my book. I saw clearly how the religion of materialism was in control of the school system - and that's why I brought free speech back into my classroom. I wanted to give my students a chance – during each day – to discuss a wide variety of belief systems – and not just the religion of competitive capitalism. That is why I called my book, "Uncle Tom's Classroom" because I wanted to point out that the government was unknowingly enslaving kids into only one particular belief system – an economic belief system - based on hyper competition, unbridled consumerism and the constant acquisition of money. The school system was teaching kids to only look at life through a materialistic lens – which is not only unfair and dangerous – but also cuts them off from understanding "who-they-really-are" in the grand cosmic scheme of things.

Fletcher: You are right. Materialism is just as much a religion or a philosophy as any other belief system. This belief system of materialism is actually destroying the Earth. For, it is another form of extremism. So, you see - when people get themselves disconnected from their true Light within – as Rose was telling you – they get disconnected from the truth – because the Light within IS where the truth is found.

You've got it right, Mr. Berg. More people need to be listening to you and finding the truth of the Higher Self - because when they do that – the outer "isms" and divisions start to disappear. And, when they disappear – then the fighting stops. Without all the false divisions and "isms" there is no reason to fight - and nobody will fight. This is because people will finally understand that their neighbor is the same as they are – in fact – they will see that the neighbor IS the self that they are here to learn to love.

Tom: Yes, just like the bible quote, "Love thy neighbor as thyself".

Fletcher: Yes, that's what the Good Book says. You know, the Lord Jesus told it like it was - but few people got the simple message. We should not mistake simplicity for lack of depth or spiritual truth. Sometimes, the most profound messages are the simplest ones. I think, that if you asked each person who is part of a religion - to go back – way back - to the beginning of that religion – and sum up their religion in one or two sentences – we would find them to be alike. That is what we want people to understand.

Write down your religion in one or two sentences. Now, we know that all the rules and regulations of the religions would take a lot more time and effort than that – but – we still want you put down your understanding of each religion - in only one or two sentences. Then, compare them. You could fill many pages with all the rules and regulations from all the different religions – but ultimately – if you were to describe the religions in ONLY one or two sentences, the sentences would look alike. If humans would do this exercise, they would begin to ask, "Why are we killing our neighbor?

You know, my family has Irish roots. And, we see that in the Earth today there has been a lot of fighting in Northern Ireland. The Catholics and the Protestants are fighting one another. That kind of behavior is hardly of God – now is it? They are splitting hairs over what the Pope said and what the Archbishop of Canterbury said – but for what? Well, why don't people just stay quiet and – just stay home - and live in peace with their neighbor? Why can't they just love each other?

The reason - you see - is the falseness of religious doctrine. There is so much pride and arrogance among many of the religious AND political leaders of the world. You've got to look at these leaders around the world and question the validity of their belief systems – when they say that - it is right and honorable to kill people. Where do you find that in any of the holy books? I challenge you. You can't find that it's right and just and honorable to kill - in any of the books – not even in the Koran.

Tom: I agree completely.

Fletcher: So, you see. People must go back to the simple reality behind their religions. Religion - in the purest sense – is really about a relationship with the Divine. Oh, it's not about following the rules. All those rules that religions have put upon the people of the Earth have been like a noose around people's necks.

And so, what are people going to do when they realize that the religions have a noose put around their neck? They fight it. So many people have been noosed around the neck by religions today. We hope – as spirit guides - to be able to relieve some of that pressure they feel around their necks – by bringing them back to an awareness of our world.

Tom: This book is really going to help. You mentioned on July 30th, that you want Bob and me to use this book to teach the truths of the Spirit World – truths which you and Rose are sharing with us – in these sessions. Would you like to talk about those truths in a bit more, as we near the completion of this first book? Can you clarify those basic truths for our readers?

Fletcher: Oh well - the truth is – you have uncovered one of the basic truths in your own book - and that is – the truth about the soul within. The first thing you need to teach people – is the truth about the Super Self that is the Spirit within them. It is in that Super Self - where it all starts. So, make sure that you keep teaching that – because the truth of the Super Self is part of your calling. You know, your book came from our world - combined with the experiences you went through your own journey. It really was a project between the worlds, as is this book.

Tom: I know. It's amazing and true. You and Rose are now verbalizing things that I wrote about in the book four years ago. You are putting into words today – what I heard in my head years ago.

Fletcher: There you go. You see a truth. That is the first truth that you've got be sharing with our readers. We spirit guides are constantly talking to you - and teaching you - and guiding you

– even when you haven't yet realized that we exist – as real participants - in your life's story.

The next truth that we want you to be teaching about is the reality of life after death and what that means. As you know – Rose has shared with you - her story of what happened to her – after death. And – I myself - have told you how I too passed through that place of darkness. Now, I don't say this to scare people, but to educate them.

We don't want to encourage humans to think that they are going to hell. No, not at all. But, we also don't want people to die – or I should say – cross over – without realizing that there IS a karmic balance to deal with. Remember, "As you sow, so shall you reap." You see, each soul who is born upon the Earth, is here - to raise their vibration. They are here – on Earth – specifically to learn now to do move up their vibration. Life on Earth is a chance to do this. This is a great truth.

The Beings of our world are closer to you than ever, because the veil has been thinned over the past few years. We have accomplished this thinning – because we have seen the turmoil upon the Earth and wish to offer our help. And yet - even WITH our help at hand – a lot of people are still wanting to turn away from our help - and so - they ignore and reject the spiritual Light we bring. And so, we want you to share with them – about - the reality of our world – so that they will know that they are building their souls in one direction or the other.

But remember - even those – who you may think – or judge – are the darkest of souls - are also loved by God. God never hates people or burns them, even though some religions have taught that nonsense. Teach always - that the God who loves us all - will never force a soul to be in the Light - if that soul – through an exercise of free will - doesn't want to be in the Light. God will wait patiently – for all eternity - for every soul to eventually come home.

The other truth that you want to be drawing out in this book – to help all those who will be reading the book – and who will coming to see you – try'n to understand what you are teach – is that they are loved. There is a lot of belief in the world today – that people are alone and not loved by each other or by God. Nobody on the Earth is actually ever alone – because our world is overlapping your world. No person on the Earth need ever be thinking that they have been left alone or are unloved. You know, I thought – for a long time in my own life – that same thing. One day – when I was a young chap – after I became an atheist – I walked into a chapel – where I saw a statue of the Sacred Heart of Jesus. I felt a small tear rise up from deep within my mind – because I remembered how much comfort I'd once derived from my belief in the kindness of Jesus and in his Sacred Heart. But, once I thought of myself as an atheist – I decided that Jesus was no longer true, and I could no longer take solace in the love of His Sacred Heart.

All that happened - however - was that my perception or my reality had changed – not the truth. The truth of God's love was still there. It was real and still with me. The truth was - that I was loved and supported by beings from the Spirit World. I just did not know it or understand it at the time. A lot of people upon the Earth are like I was – for they feel like, "Oh well, I can't go back now – because I gave up believing in God a long time ago and I can't be goin' back now. It's too late."

The truth is that – no matter how strongly you once decided against the existence of a world of Spirit - you can always go back to believing in a loving God Source - the original Spirit - who gives all life –and who IS all life. It's never too late to wake up to the existence of the Spirit World and this God of life – this Great Spirit who gives life and Light to everything and everyone in this universe and beyond. God IS life and life IS God! God IS Light and Light IS God!

Not even those souls - who might feel tempted to give up their lives – and reject the gift of life - by committing suicide – or dying prematurely - are EVER forgotten or abandoned by eternal Love – or by Life. These are the very people who we are trying to reach the most - to let them know - that there is no despair so great - that you can't be helped. Life is always a gift from God. And, miracles upon the Earth DO still occur. We know this is the truth - because we are doing our best to help facilitate miracles, whenever we are allowed to do so.

Humans need never feel alone - because they are not alone. Nobody is ever really alone - because our world is not some far-away place. It's right here with you – only vibrating in a far different frequency. Our world of Spirit is vibrating right where your Planet Earth is – just on a higher and different frequency. This is all people need to understand. Give us just a moment to adjust the medium's vibration here.

I suppose - one of the other great truths - for inclusion in our book – is the wonderful news that - not only is our world of Spirit and Light - real AND true – but - there IS open communication between our different dimensions of existence. There is a direct access – a real communication link up - between our Spirit World and your human world. We very much want our human readers to understand this astonishing and comforting truth about our overlapping existences. Communication between our worlds is always available to all those who want to have it.

A lot of people on the Earth say, "Oh, I can't talk to God. I have to go to the priest." Or they think, "God won't forgive my sins unless I go to confession." They think such incorrect thoughts, such as, "I can't talk to my auntie who died, because I'm not holy enough. I have to let the church people do it for me."

Well, those thoughts are simply NOT true. We spirit guides want to talk to you humans every single day. We love the communication. And – if you talk to us – we WILL be talking back. We will help you to hear us because - we want humans to know that our world is real – AND we are actively participating every day in our communication with all of you. Do you understand?

Tom: Yes, I am understanding that – AND - feeling the truth of it more every day.

Fletcher: Humans have become so enmeshed in the material plane – and - have been so disconnected by the Earth culture of this time – that - it makes our work so much harder. They have become so disconnected from their spiritual selves. But, we want you all to know that you ARE very brave souls to come into the Earth plane at this time.

Do you know, there are quite a few humans on Earth right now who are having a feeling of homesickness for our world? They miss the Other Side – they miss living in our world. So, we would like all our readers to know that – in our terms – your Earth lives go past as fast as a day. Don't give up hope. Don't give in to despair and complain about "how hard it is". You might say,

"Oh, I've got another fifty years down here on Earth, before I get to go home" - but – from our perspective - it's a very short stay, and the time will go by quickly. We don't worry about you – when you sometimes feel this homesickness – because it's only natural that you would miss your true home. So, don't worry about it - when you feel this strange feeling homesickness – because you will come home soon enough.

Humans weren't made to live on the Earth forever. They were only made to come to the Earth realm for short periods of time. That is why humans who can't let go – when their time comes to return home – are those – that Rose was talking about – who are so attached to the Earth – and afraid of crossing over – that they end up in nursing homes. If only they would remember who they were – they would go back home without so much struggling and fear. Hold on there – we are going to adjust the vibration.

Rose: Hello, this is Rose, can you hear me? I can never stay silent when Fletcher is talking about something that is dear to my heart.

I want to speak directly to those who are listening to our messages - and reading our words – which you are so faithfully transcribing for us. I wish to say here – as clearly as I can – that you all have access to our Spirit World – and to our assistance - twenty four hours a day – not just on Sunday.

You know – I held that belief about Sunday - when I was on the Earth. I used to say, "Well, I'll sort it out on Sunday when I see the vicar". I did realize that I had to ask for help – occasionally – from a Higher Power. I was not totally daft, nor did I think that I was totally without access to some kind of spiritual help. But – I did believe– as so many still do today - that I had to go through the vicar for my spiritual help – which is what I would do on Sunday. I never knew that I could seek and receive help from God, without the vicar's interceding for me.

So, I would go to church on Sunday and pour out all my troubles onto the vicar – placing all my concerns in his hands. God bless that poor vicar for always listening to me so compassionately. I unburdened so much of my soul to him. And yet, all my worries were vanity issues. I am actually embarrassed and ashamed to say it – but I used to go to the vicar and say such things as, "Oh, vicar – will you pray for me. I am so worried that my cocktail party will not make the standard that I'm used to." The vicar never judged me for that. He was ever so kind and he would say, "Oh, there, there Rose, whatever you do – do it with joy in your heart – and God will bless it."

You know – that was a true message he was giving me, but instead of taking that message and understanding what he said, do you know what I used to do? I used to slough it off. I used to go home and say, "Oh, it's all good and well for him – but he doesn't have the ambassador from Spain coming." And you know – in rejecting his message – I missed the simple truth that I could have let God be part of my parties. Just think how splendid my gatherings would have been - if I had allowed them to have a spiritual air about them. They would have been filled with Light – you see. And I could have influenced world events on a greater scale. But – I did not follow my vicar's advice and did not allow that to be. So, I lost many opportunities to bring Light to other souls.

This is the main thing I want our readers to remember, if you remember nothing else from this book. Remember that - you don't have to wait until Sunday to "let the vicar look into it", as I did. You already have that power to access God - and us - at any time. And it would do us great joy – to hear from those of you on Earth – who would call upon us. Each soul has about them innumerable friendly spirits – so - if they would only ask for a manifestation or a word from your spirit guides – the words and answers would be readily and promptly given.

Tom: I really like the revolutionary teaching that you are sharing with us today – that you are free - and even can even invite God to help you give a cocktail party. In Jesus' new book, "The Course in Miracles" - he says over and over that "God's will for us happiness." And yet, we live in a world culture that says that God is fearful, angry and even emotionally disinterested. Can you tell me about the aspects of God known as the "Lamb of God" – or the "Sacred Heart of Jesus" – the more joyful, caring, loving side of God – so we can begin to feel that God DOES desire for us to enjoy life and be happy?

Rose: Oh yes. This is something that I immediately learned upon my ascension into the Light. You see, humans have been given such misdirection. They have been taught about a God of wrath. That is a mistake, my dear. You see, one must look at the Spirit of God as either absolute love or absolute hatred. God cannot be both, now can He?

Tom: Right.

Rose: This is because you cannot have two absolutes in the same God Being, or you would have contradictory realities. We want you to see that God IS joy, complete all encompassing joy. Joy – which IS God – actually permeates the human being. But, you will never know the divine joy that is within you - as long as you hate yourself, the world, God or your neighbor.

As you know, the great swamis of India used to tell me that I was "Sat Chit Ananda", which meant that my Inner Being was made of eternal life, eternal joy and eternal consciousness – and that I will always exist. Well, I didn't understand their teaching - back then – but I can tell you from my experience of crossing into the Light – that I felt the IMMENSE joy the swamis talked about – instantly and profoundly!

What was so profound and joyful to me was actually –that – there was a kind of recognition. For I realized, that I HAD encountered the Light in those quiet moments of my life on Earth. And yet – I did not absorb it while on Earth. Those same quiet moments of joy are the kinds of moments that you experienced this last week. You simply felt peace and joy come over you. That was the Light that you felt. Do you realize that it was the Light you were feeling?

Tom: All I knew at that time –w as that I was immersed in a very good feeling.

Rose: The peace and joy you felt came from the Divine Light and Divine Love. They were gifts of Spirit - you might say. What you must do now - is reflect on those feelings - and try to recreate them in your mind. Eventually, they will become a secondary habit to you. And it will become most natural for you to instantly elevate your consciousness to that vibration of Light. Every human on Earth has been given a little glimpse and a taste of the Light – at some time or other.

Just look at a baby when it smiles. There is such a Light all about them. That Light and joy that you see in a baby's eyes and hear in its laughter – gives us a glimpse of divinity. Each human must look back upon their life and find a moment when they felt absolute freedom, absolute peace, absolute sense of oneness with the universe – it is that peace that you carry over in our world. This past week you've had a small glimpse – but if you were to magnify the feeling you had a million million times you would perhaps – begin to get a sense – of what the Light feels like over here in our world.

Humans must begin on an inner journey – of feeling for the love of God they have within them. And they must come to an understanding - that divinity is NOT something to be feared – but instead – is an all powerful loving Light – that can be and should be - embraced. You can do this by reflecting on those moments in life – when the reality of God touched you. This is the reality that is called God. Do you understand?

Tom: Yes, I do. So are you saying that when we feel inner joy that we are feeling God?

Rose: Oh yes. But, do not mistake the feeling of inner joy as the totality of God. For, joy is only one aspect of God - that will lead you on a road towards God.

Tom: How can we come to really believe that God wants us to be happy and joyful – in a religious culture that has taught us that God is a being who wants us to have lives of suffering and struggle? When you mentioned how you and the vicar talked about inviting God's joy into your cocktail parties – I thought, "That's not what the Catholics would have said. Their serious God would NEVER have helped out at - or even condoned - a cocktail party." So, I'm wondering - how can we bring God into our regular every day experiences, like our parties and our sex lives- when we've been taught that God judges those things as worldly and hedonistic?

Rose: As I recall – dear sir – the Lord Jesus DID help with a cocktail party- when he turned water into wine for the wedding feast in Cana. So, you see - at the end of the day – it all comes down to a choice that each human must make. They must dare to risk the belief that there is a God that loves them as they are – in their totality – or they will choose that there is NO such God. It ultimately comes down to one making a leap of faith. I used to say, when I first heard about the leap of faith from my vicar,

"I'm not leaping into anything. It could be a public hazard I'd fall into. What is it – some kind of cloud – or something?" The idea of a "leap of faith" simply made no sense to me at the time I first heard it.

But – the truth is – each human must ultimately decided whether or not to make such a leap. You see, if I had done it – while still living upon the Earth – I would not have found myself in that place of darkness, when I died. There are different kinds of leaps, of course. Sometimes one can only take a little baby leap. And at other times – one finds the courage to take a full leap - into the mysterious chasm of the reality called God.

If you were to ask me, "Where will I find myself, if I DO take that leap of faith?" I would answer, "You will find yourself surrounded and enmeshed completely in God's Love. You will not fall – but will find yourself supported – and held up - by God."

There is a scripture in the Holy Bible that says, "Do not believe in the spirits – but test each spirit to see if it is from God." This is a wise saying. And, as a spirit – I don't mind being tested at all, now and then. The reality that you must understand – is that - for a human soul to find real freedom – one must learn to meditate and look within.

Everybody is searching in the outer world. Even the religious people are searching in the outer world. I had a very good friend who would travel all throughout the world – to Italy, to France, to Germany, to Rome and even to Russia in search of religious relics supposedly having a mystical connection with some holy person, or other. When I would ask her what she was doing during those travels, she would tell me, "I must go see the saints' relics – I must get closer to God."

Now you know my dear, there is nothing wrong with venerating sacred things. For I do believe that – yes – they do touch one with the divine. But, the thing is – if she would have just looked within – even at the very first shrine she visited – she would have found that joy already. She would not have needed to travel to find that joy, because it is already IN the Light of consciousness - that is within us.

I used to tease her by saying, "What do you get out of seeing a bag of bones?" I was not a believer - at all - in that kind of thing. Our church didn't teach us about holy items or relics as being important to our worship. I used to tell my friend that her bags of saint bones were morbid – rubbish. But, she explained to me, "The relics have a touch of grace in them."

And I asked her, "What do you mean – "grace" is in your relics? I don't understand such rubbish. How can grace be in an object?" But – it was her belief – and she stood by it - that she could actually feel a bit of God in her sacred objects. In all reality, I must say – that there is some truth in what she says. There is a special sanctified power that is found in holy items and holy places – because they have been consecrated to divine work. But, you see, the relic or holy site offers only a brief glimpse of a greater reality and should be used primarily to drive one inward. If my friend had been willing to meditate, and look inward, she would have found grace without the need to travel so far so far and wide. Why go all around the world looking for yet another piece of grace, when grace already exists within one? Of, Fletcher is here – hang on just a moment.

Fletcher: There we go. We're back in the body. We are not going to be staying too much longer, because it's taking a toll on our medium's vibration. But – what else might we answer for you tonight?

Tom: I would like to follow up on the amazing idea – that we can bring the joy of God into our cocktail parties – and into other such worldly experiences. What is the BEST method for bringing God's joy into our everyday, so-called mundane experiences?

Fletcher: Well, you know – it is a truth that my auntie used to tell me. She used to say, "Fletcher, find joy in the simple things. When you put on your army uniform and your polish up those shiny brass buttons –you feel joy – now don't you?" And I would admit that I did feel joy polishing those buttons. I liked to look of polished metals – especially polished brass. It always gave me joy to experience the smell and the look of shiny polished brass. It kind of always made me happy!

And so - she told me- that it was good a good thing - for me to find the joy in that. Then, one day she gave me a little copper penny. And she said to me, "I polished this penny up just for you because I know how much you enjoy looking at shiny metal." And do you know, I carried that little penny around with me in my uniform forever – and it was with me even when I died. You could say it was a kind of a talisman. This was a good thing for me – for that penny taught me - that it is often the littlest of things that bring us the greatest joy – especially when they are touched with love.

My auntie didn't have much money – and so - that little penny could have bought her a slice of bread. But, she gave it to me – out of her love - just so I could feel joy while carrying it about. That little penny meant more to me than all my other possessions put together.

Tom: So, it was like a talisman or relic of grace – because you felt love in that penny – right?

Fletcher: Yes, because the penny helped me feel closer to love – which always elevates the spirit. And, I think - that was one of the things that saved me from having to spend much time in the darkness - after I was killed. Even though I DID go into the place of darkness, I only stayed there for a few moments. My soul was closer to the Light than Rose's when I died, because I'd allowed love and joy to be with me – in the form of that penny. The penny represented all my auntie's prayers for me - which I felt during the time I was in the war. Even though I wasn't a big believer in my auntie's spirituality – I didn't fight against it – or block it. I knew her prayers and that penny were coming out of her love. And so, I simply allowed it to be – and on some level – the love my auntie put into that penny uplifted me, and even gave me Light.

So, nowadays – when you see people who are depressed, try to find a little something to lift up their spirit. You don't have to preach to them about God. That's hardly going to help them. Most of the people on the Earth today don't want to hear about God. And you know what? God is not such an egomaniac that He wants people to be talking about Him all the time, anyway? But, what God DOES want from you, is to reach out to those people who are depressed - in a spirit of love – and if you DO reach out in love – you will raise up their vibration – and you will help move them up into the Light. This is how people can find joy – just in the simple things. Invite a neighbor over for a cup of tea. Look around your neighborhood and see who is feeling lonely this time of year. I bet you – that right near you - there are people who are feeling a lot lonelier than you. I bet there is an elderly person nearby – who could use a visit. Why don't you seek them out and find them? Giving such a visit could bring the Light of God to them - and in turn – move your soul up into the Light as well.

Well, we are going to have to step out of the body, so as not to tax our medium further. It was such a great pleasure sitting with you tonight – and we hope that we have brought you some good information – that blesses you. And we thank you for taking the time to be with us. Just a moment, Rose wants to say a quick goodbye to you.

Rose: Hello my dear. I have just a moment here – but I just want to bring you our blessing as well – from our world. And I want to let you know that I will be continuing to guide you. Fletcher has told me that there will not be many more sessions – until our book project is completed. But – do not fear – I will be with you in the coming weeks. And even though the book shall be done – we will not be finished with you. We want you to know that. We have been so pleased to have been with you. I'm going to go now – for Fletcher is calling me. I must step out of the body . . . . (Her voice trails off into silence). . .

Tom: Thank you Rose!

BOB HICKMAN POSTSCRIPT

AMAZING is the word that comes to mind when I study the guides' teaching from this night. It seems that they are teaching us how to keep that connection. It couldn't have come at a better time. As I said in the Preview above, the holidays can be stressful.

I find it fascinating that Rose, now in death, is beginning to really grasp the teachings of the swamis she met in India. Her words make me wonder if I should travel to India. What would I find there? Would I learn at the feet of the masters as she had done? I notice that Rose seems to later on say that her friend travelled all over the world seeking to see relics to "connect" to God. Interestingly, Rose tells us that her friend need not have travelled so far, for the "connection" to God was within her own heart all along.

As I review Roses experiences, I think about my conversation with a spiritual healer that occurred a few days after this trance session. The healer claimed to do "Reconnective Healing." The healer told me that I need not so much seek healing as recognize that the healing is already within—I am totally perfectly aligned and whole inside. I wasn't sure I believed him until I myself experienced a session of Reconnective Healing. Amazingly during the session, I really did discover and experience that I really am connected to the Divine Light. I know that the guides have taught me this, but there really is a difference between "head knowledge" and "heart knowledge."

I am also so inspired by how Rose shares about how one can even include the Divine in something as mundane as cocktail parties. I laugh when I read about her going to her vicar asking for prayers to get through her parties. I think her vicar is a saint to be so kind and patient with her worldly concerns. But her vicar was right—God could and would be present if she would simply "invite" Him. I think about the coming Christmas holidays and know that I will once again have to join with family in situations that are always perfect. I realize that I only need to "invite" God to be present with me and that can quite literally transform any situation. I think back to the previous years and realize that I had never really "invited" God to join my gatherings. I like Rose's Vicar's advice and decide that this is going to be a new part of my spiritual practice. My consciousness shifts gears—instead of "begging" for God to help me "get through" a stressful time, I am going to "invite" the Divine to be present at all times.

Fletcher's words about his precious little penny that his aunt gave him warm my heart. I think of all the chances I have to give little presents to those I hold dear and resolve that this too shall become part of my spiritual life.

CHAPTER THIRTEEN
PARTING WORDS

December 18th, 2008

BOB HICKMAN PREVIEW:

I remember this night, almost with a sense of melancholy. Tom and I had been meeting weekly since the summer, and I couldn't but feel a bit sad as we had decided this would be our last session together for this book. I suppose it is the feeling that is common amongst people who have worked together on a project intently to feel sad and somewhat empty at the conclusion of a project. Fortunately, I knew that Tom and I would still be friends even after this book project, but I felt I was going to miss our regularity in meeting. It was true that Tom and I both had growing careers and I hoped that this would not really be "the end" though on this night, it did feel that way a bit. I knew Tom was starting to get public attention from his film work, and his book seemed to be getting into more hands. I was happy for him but I guess worried that sudden fame would sweep him away. My client base had grown considerably and I felt myself being pulled more and more into my work. Even the best of friendships need work, and I hoped Tom and I would continue to stay in touch. Amazingly—it seems that our Spirit Friends have future plans for us to do more work. Below are their wonderful messages.

Fletcher: Oh hello there, this is Fletcher. We've got to be especially careful tonight, because – when we come in a bit too strong, we can blow out Bob's computer. (My first attempt to talk with Fletcher tonight, via Skype, caused such a strong energy surge, that Bob's computer crashed.)

Fortunately - our medium's body is better able to handle our energy than the electronics he uses. It's only the equipment that has problems. So, we will turn down our energy a bit tonight, so as not to cause another interruption in our connection.

Tom: Good, I can hear you loud and clear Fletcher.

Fletcher: It's so good to be back here with you. And, might we be saying, that you've been really attuning to our vibration all week long. We've been around you, sensing you, watching your energy field as you transcribe our words. The energy of Spirit has been swirling around the top of your head, almost as if you're wearing a big tall hat. It's actually the energy of your auric field that is whirling and swirling around your head. That is what is allowing you to be much more sensitive to our higher realm and our higher frequencies. It's kind of like you've got your spiritual antenna up, you know what I mean?

Tom: Yes I do. I can hear you so clearly when I am working on the transcripts. I am conscious that you are actively helping me edit the sentences as they flow into the computer.

Fletcher: We see you from up here. It's wonderful that you are becoming more and more receptive to our whisperings. It takes a heightened awareness to do what you are doing for us. More and more people upon the Earth today ARE trying to bring themselves into this heightened state of awareness. In fact, this is why we are writing our book – to help humans become better listeners to the guidance that is constantly being offered by our world to yours!

Back in the old days my auntie, the one who was the Spiritualist, used to invite mediums to her house. And the mediums would say, "Fletcher, you've got to become aware of the spiritual vibrations that are all around you." But, I just thought it was a bunch of craziness, and said, "Vibrations – what are you talking about?"

Well, you know – back in those days – we didn't have television yet and we didn't know much about the early inventions that involved electrical vibrations. So, the idea of tuning into vibrations was a bit strange and unfamiliar to us. But now we are trying to bring your world into a greater state of awareness - which humanity has WITHIN its own bodies ALL the receptors needed to communicate clearly and easily with our world. These receptors were put into humans from the beginning of time as I understand it.

Humanity never had to lose its conscious connection to the Other Side - with the Spirit World, because all humans were made with this built in radio receiver. Many humans on the Earth today are activating their receivers and are starting to pick up the waves again, those frequency vibrations from our realm, the higher energies that are coming in and swirling all around. Our medium, and others like him, are wonderful examples of humans who have opened up enough to let our messages flow to Earth!

But, you know, the problem is – that there are a lot of people who are scared of the antenna inside of them that connects them our world. They reject the whole idea. And, if you point out to them that they've got a spiritual antenna right there IN their head - and that antenna can be tuned to receive incoming messages from the Spirit World, they will have none of it. In fact, there are still some places on your planet, where people will even call you a heretic and want you killed for saying such things. It's strange how so much of humanity wants to forget its own gifts, the very gifts that were given to it by the Creator, the gifts that link up our worlds!

Tom: Yes, I know. I used to teach my students that we all have, within us, an inner cell phone that can connect us to the higher dimensions. We can use our inner cell phones to call up the Cosmic Super Self and get guidance whenever we need it. Some of my kids "got it" easily and did learn to tune into their Higher Selves, while there were always a few who refused to believe that this kind of communication was possible and stayed glued to their video games and other outside stimuli.

Kids are so brainwashed these days, to think that the ONLY reality is the outer, physical world – while the inner world of spiritual power is totally ignored. Public schools certainly to everything they can to deny kids access to their inner antennas!

Fletcher: Well, you know, I was guilty of denying the existence of the inner receptors, as well. Because, when I was a young man on Earth, I was a complete disbeliever in all spiritual knowledge. Time has passed however, and I've been shown that it is all true. And I am here talking to you today because of that very ability. It's very fortunate for us that our medium, not only can raise his antenna, but can keep the antenna up long enough, so that we can establish a strong connection through his body. It is only because he uses his inner antenna to receive us that we are able to manifest as we do.

He brings us in on a specific wave length and then we occupy his body for a short while. It's only because he keeps his antenna up, that we are able to be with you here tonight, in this audible way. Sometimes though, the antenna goes up and then it goes down. Electrical energy disturbances in the atmosphere of the planet can create a lot of problems. Perhaps you yourself too have felt such electrical disturbances in your own life.

Just a moment here. Well, we know that you have some questions for us today, and we are most eager to answer them for you. We want to know what else we might be doing for you while we're here tonight?

Tom: Mainly, I would like to make sure that we include everything that you and Rose and Edgar and Orion want to tell the world, in this first book of ours. Speaking about vibration, you probably know that right now the idea of the Law of Attraction is very popular in our cultural conversation. So, I was wondering if you all would like to comment on the Law of Attraction for our book?

Fletcher: Oh, very much so. Well, let me tell you, first of all, that the Law of Attraction works on the same principal as does the antenna we were talking about. Think about it. Inside your human mind, you have this invisible antenna that goes up and down. Now, your antenna can be used as both a receiver AND as a transmitter of vibration. Your antenna can be used in different ways and with different purposes!

Sometimes you use it to send out thoughts to people, which is what you call mental telepathy. And sometimes you receive thoughts back, and that's another type of telepathy. Those who become even a little proficient in this can learn how to send out vibrations, in the form of positive ideas TO others, and then draw BACK information and assistance, in a most tangible way. In fact, people are constantly sending and receiving thoughts, back and forth, without even realizing they are using their inner antennas to tune into each other.

So, you see, if a person wants to bring financial stability into their lives, what they've got to do is send out a specific signal or request, that says, "I want some financial stability." That energy is then combined with the energy of many others of similar thought. You are tapping into – I suppose you could call it – a sort of energy pool, a pool of potentiality. In our world, everything you ask for ALREADY exists in a vibrational frequency, in a pool of spiritual potential. The energy that you send out from your mind to the spiritual realm – eventually taps into - and accesses this great vibrational pool, which is IN and OF the Divine Mind.

Tom: Your pool analogy reminds me of Snow White's wishing well or Disney's wishing star. All you had to do was wish – or ask - and the miracle would come from the magical realms.

Fletcher: Yes, asking is THE most important first step. Whenever an energy vibration comes back to the Earth - from the pool of potential, it is activated by your requests. The spiritual energy is then manifested in tangible ways and appears on Earth, in material forms. A lot of humans walk around talking about all the amazing things that have apparently come to them from out of thin air, and they call these manifestations miracles. And I suppose, from their perspective – when their prayers are answered - it does seem like a miracle has happened. But, from our perspective, it is simply the working out of the Law of Attraction, which IS the law of the Universe.

In the past, we have talked to you about the various levels of the Universe. We have told you that there are spirits that exist on vastly different planes of vibration. The higher spirits can always go down and visit the lower spirits in the lower worlds, but those of the lower worlds cannot ascend up to the higher realms until their vibrations are prepared – and they get into alignment with the higher frequencies. It is the same thing with the Law of Attraction you see.

The very frequency vibration that is sent out from your mind in the form of a request has to be compatible with ideas in the Divine Mind, in order for the manifestation to occur. A lot of people say they want to use Law of Attraction for positive change but they don't understand that, in the material world, physical action does sometimes have to accompany the positive spiritual vibration. The two work hand in hand.

For example, you might say, "I want to draw to myself, the perfect job". Well, that's all good and well, but then you have to send out that vibration, and work on seeing it going out into the ethers. Use your antenna to ask for and receive help from our world. Then you must imagine that your answer is being drawn back TO you, in a form that feels complete. You may suddenly feel guided to do something purely physical as well, like making a phone call, or sending out a resume. This is because sometimes - when your answer comes to you, it may need some physical thing to attach itself onto.

It goes something like this. First, you ask for guidance. You beam out a request for help, on a beam, to the Spirit World. You are using your antenna to beam up your request to the Spirit World, while asking for help in manifesting the perfect job in your world. Then, when your prayer request gets to our realm, your asking affects the pool of energy that contains all prosperity and success in jobs. In our world, there is an answer for EVERY one of your so-called problems!

So, after you ask, the energy with the answer pulsates out of the pool of Spirit potential, and is beamed back at you. Answers and opportunities pour into your life. But for that to happen, we may need your tangible cooperation, like writing a resume, or going to a specific place, in order to create the perfect avenue for our response. You may feel guided to go somewhere, or do something – totally spontaneously. This is because your spirit guides often need tangible objects and avenues to use to manifest your goals.

Ponder this! How could we write this book of ours, if you and our medium refused to perform the necessary actions on the physical plane? "When Worlds Unite" could never be born without the combined actions and energies from BOTH our worlds. This act of creation is a cooperative effort. So, please don't be thinking that it's only energy that makes things happen. It's actually a combination of both energy and physical action that allows the Spirit World to work together with you, to cause positive manifestations. Have I lost you yet, my young friend?

Tom: Your comments make me wonder about my actions in the past two years trying to get publicity for my book, "Uncle Tom's

Classroom". I sent out press releases, made lots of YouTube videos and spent quite a bit of money. I've taken a lot of action without many concrete results, except of course, for the interview with Shirley MacLaine and attracting Bob and you all into my life. And - I am MOST grateful for those manifestations.

But, is there something ELSE that I am not yet understanding – when it comes to manifesting my dream of "getting the message out there"? I really DO believe we need to save our kids from the brainwashing of the material systems of control – and I KNOW that my book would help a lot of people! So, please tell me – what do I need to understand yet about manifesting success for my writings.

Fletcher: Well, it's simply a sign to you that you've got to work more powerfully on becoming a MUCH BETTER TRANSMITTER of your intentions! Now, we are not saying this to criticize, because you have already come so far from where you were back when you began THIS book project. But we want you to know that helping us write "When World's Unite" IS actually part of the plan for helping you grow into your destiny.

We feel that you ARE developing your transmitter power greater and greater now, and you have come into a much better position vibrationally, than when you first published "Uncle Tom's Classroom". And so now, the efforts and the actions that you will expend will be seen as having much greater results. Don't forget that we are sending you power and guidance all the time. Keep your antenna up, so you can hear our messages, follow our leads, strengthen your thoughts, and you WILL find your success.

Tom: Thank you Fletcher. This idea of making thoughts strong reminds of me of how the ancient Hawaiian Kahunas used to accrue mana through deep breathing. They had special breathing techniques in order to fill their ideas with power. The Kahunas believed that ideas were real things and that they could fill them with mana and will power in order to make them grow into reality. Can you explain this strange practice in terms of the Law of Attraction? Are you saying that I need to fill my ideas with this kind of vital power – so they can become strong enough to break into the cultural conversation?

Fletcher: Well, the Hawaiian Kahunas you speak about were very advanced souls, and in many cases, were priests of the ancient ways. Make no mistake about it. The ancient teachings of the Hawaiian Kahunas are actually reflections of the Lemurian and Atlantean cultures. Those ancient teachings from Atlantis and Lemuria are indeed found within the Hawaiian's utilization of vital breathing, mind control and will power.

The important thing we want our readers to understand is that the Hawaiian Kahunas were correct. They understood that thoughts can and DO take form. They knew that thoughts can and DO become things, in and of themselves. The ancients knew that thoughts have tremendous power for good or for evil. This is why modern day humans must learn about mind training. People must be much more careful in guarding the mind. They must be must more conscious of what they put into their minds – and how and where they point their minds. There are some people upon the Earth today who are particularly strong in this kind of mind power, and they use their thoughts to control people, both in good ways and in bad ways.

Think about this in terms of developing the mind. The mind has to become strong to be able to manifest. You must remember that you have an inner antenna that is broadcasting and receiving. You've got to become strong in your mind, to send out a powerful vibration, just like a thought beam. And, you have to be equally strong to receive the answers to your prayers, to receive the attachments, so to speak.

Tom: What do you mean by "attachments"?

Fletcher: You know how you receive those attachments in your electronic emailing system? You know how emails sometimes come to you with attachments? Well, you see, those attachments are something like the miracles you receive on Earth, the answers that come from the Spirit World, in response to your requests. Your thoughts and intentions, those ideas created in your mind, must be made really strong, so that they are equal to the task of calling back the answer from OUR plane to YOUR plane. Your thoughts must be powerful enough in vibration and high enough in frequency, to carry back and manifest material objects or physical experiences.

So, if you have a weak thought, it might get to the source of the pool in the Spirit World, but the problem is, the thought doesn't have enough strength to carry back to the Earth the attachments which are the actual answers to be manifested. There is not enough strength in the request, not enough belief and passion in the thought, to successfully bring back to the Earth all that you think you want or need.

Tom: I'm sorry, I don't quite get it. Can you explain this a bit more clearly?

Fletcher: Think of how our medium accomplishes his work. If he wasn't really passionate about the importance of his work, and fulfilling his calling, then we could not work with him and THROUGH him, as we do. Our adventure with Bob is a cooperative effort between our worlds, which he had to really think about, believe in and WANT, before it could occur. This passionate wanting may or may not have been totally conscious, but it was absolutely necessary. We can say the same thing about you as well. If you hadn't sent out a powerful and passionate call for help and guidance about YOUR calling, we wouldn't be here with you, working on this book right now!

Tom: I know what you are saying is true. And I so appreciate that you heard me and came into my life. And, thanks so much for urging Bob to contact me when he did, for it has been a total joy to work with you all. My life has been transformed, as my understanding of the Spirit World has exploded into awareness.

So, ARE the Hawaiians correct when they say that we can put more strength into our thoughts and intentions by using deep breathing techniques? Those Kahunas were able to heal bodies, win battles, walk on fire and do all kinds of amazing feats – using deep breathing to accrue mana.

Fletcher: Well, I don't wish to change their teaching one bit because they told it exactly right. You see, within the human body, there is pranic energy as the Hindus call it. And, it is true that that energy is manifested and increased through the breath. There IS life and consciousness in the breath. The root meaning of the word "spirit" actually refers to the "breath of life". When God created the first man, as it says in the Good Book, He breathed Divine life into him. In some senses, that is metaphorical. But, in another sense, it is quite literal. God's breath is STILL in you, breathing through you - which means God's Spirit and God's Power are with you, even now!

Tom: I have found out while living here in Hawaii that the syllable HA, in the word HAwaii, actually means the Breath of Life. So, I believe that, Hawaii has become a symbolic place for me, and for many people, to come and breathe in the God Breath that permeates all the natural beauty here. The ancient Kahunas taught that the place of power WAS the deep within the inner space of absolute silence, and that the best way to get to that place was through deep breathing. Hawaii is really a code word, from ancient times, that means we are living IN and BY and THROUGH the Breath of God.

Fletcher: The important thing is, when you hear the ancient stories and read the ancient scriptures, such as those of your Bible, you must understand the stories as both literal and metaphorical. That may sound like a contradiction, but in our world we see the truth that inspired all of the ancient teachings. There is a spiritual reality beyond that which appears upon the Earth. The ancients taught the truth of the spiritual reality, and of our Spirit World. And their practice of deep breathing can assist in connecting with the Spirit World – and manifesting spiritual power on Earth. Manifestation can be met through the practice of deep breathing, because breathing, practiced consciously, opens up the energy centers of the body to the creative power, and to the "Breath of Life".

Remember, there are seven energy centers within the human body, the chakras - that connect you to the spiritual self. Breathing, therefore, IS a powerful way to strengthen and open those vortex centers – AND it increases your transmitting and receiving abilities. It's not so much the numbers of breaths you take that strengthens your energy centers. It's more about the quality of the breaths. Three good deep breaths, well done, generate more power than a hundred half hearted breaths. And so it is important that each person, when they are breathing, draw in the "Breath of God" carefully, slowly and thoughtfully.

Consciousness has an overall effect on every level of reality. So, if you use your breathing, to consciously breathe in the spiritual vibration that activates the prana in your energy centers, you become increasingly powerful. Combining prana, or the breath, with consciousness equals great power for manifesting thoughts into matter. You don't want to be always rushing the process of your breathing. Take in three deep breaths. Just practice holding each breath a bit, after you breathe in for a few counts. This will stabilize your pranic energy – and will greatly help you manifest your mental ideas into physical reality. This is why the ancient Hawaiians, Indians and even the much older Egyptian and Atlantean cultures taught these same breathing techniques as steps towards manifesting desires.

Tom: Yes, I remember how you told us last week that we create matter with our minds. So, I was wondering about the extent of this power. Could I walk along the beach and create a diamond in the sand, just with my mind - if I focused my intention on the idea, with enough faith and expectation?

Fletcher: Oh yes. Such things ARE quite possible. In fact, they happen every day! We were ALL given, at the very beginning, the power to create forms in the physical plane – BY our Creator. Don't forget – all of us were there with the Creator, at the beginning. We are ALL aspects of the Original Creative Consciousness that made this entire Universe extend out of the Mind of God. Your minds don't remember it now, because you have lived countless lives in the physical plane. But, in the very beginning, you were all there with our Creator, and you ALL participated in the spiritual energy of creation that became this Universe where you now live. And so, that creative power has never been taken from you. It only lies buried deeply within us all, in both humans AND in spirit guides.

We can tap into that creative power with such practices as deep breathing, for deep breathing can and does take our vibration to a higher place. It helps us raise our vibration and therefore, increases our energy, which makes our thoughts more filled with power. Remember that everything in the material world, that appears solid, is only a form of thought energy that has slowed down enough to materialize.

Tom: Wow, that sounds like Einstein's famous equation, $E=mc^2$.

Fletcher: Yes, your physicists ARE also teaching you the truth that ALL material forms are made out of energy, information and Light. And so yes, in terms of creating a diamond in the sand, the answer is that you most definitely can do so. Although, it WILL take a lot of work on your part!

Tom: I know many people here on Earth these days - who are really trying to learn the secrets of "creating reality". In fact, the words "you create your own reality" have become the most famous buzz words of the New Age movement. How would YOU teach our readers to create their own versions of reality? What might you add to our understanding of how we "create our own reality"? Could you please explain it as clearly as possible – so even beginners could "get it"?

Fletcher: The most important thing that you've got to do is develop your focus and attention. You see – the problem for many people is that - they have never learned how to still the mind. The fact that they cannot still the mind stands in the way of their creative power. Once the mind reaches a still point – however - it is like an engine whose power is building. When the mind is not racing about – thinking about all those old worn out beliefs and concepts of limitation – then the energy for creation is not dissipated. And so, if you want to begin to manifest your desires deliberately – and on purpose - you must first find yourself in a place of deep mental stillness. Give us just a moment, please. We are having a problem . . . with the frequency here.

Tom: Thank you so much Fletcher. This information matches up perfectly with the latest New Age/quantum physics teaching about how important it is to find that "zero point" place of absolute stillness within, from which – we are told - all creative inspiration and power springs. It is theorized that THIS absolutely still place within – this zero point – is the Kingdom of Heaven that Jesus was talking about. It's the source point of miracles, where we interface with our own Cosmic Super Self, which is connected with God's Selfhood as well.

Fletcher: Yes. Here we go. Stillness of mind is of absolute importance. Once the mind is stilled, and the churning of thought stops, then the creative and inspiring power of the inner spirit is more accessible. This is how our medium is able to tune into us – by becoming still within. When I was a young man, my auntie, the one who gave the séances, used to always tell me that I should learn to sit still. Sometimes I would go to her séances and she would say to, "Fletcher, just be quiet and sit still – you're disturbing the vibrations." And I used to look around the room – and I would say to her, "What are you talking about, Auntie? All I see are a bunch of crazy women here. What ARE these vibrations that you're talk'n about?"

Well, the truth is, although I don't think my auntie understood it back then, but - they were tapping into the power point that comes with the stillness of the mind. Now it all makes sense to me. I remember being at her séances, and watching spirit lights form. I didn't understand what I was seeing at all. The lights would fly around the room and the tables would begin to rock off the ground. But now I understand that those manifestations were created because the minds of my auntie and her friends were completely and totally stilled of human concerns. They had stopped their human doubts and fears, which allowed the spiritual energies to come through without resistance.

And so, if a powerful mind is trained and practiced - to be stilled – such miraculous manifestations can be learned. Think what humanity as a whole could do – if it were unified in this understanding. Once the mind of man is stilled – and the limiting, negative thoughts were stilled - you see – then the process of positive co-creation could truly begin. That process of deliberate creation can ONLY begin within the inner stillness of mind.

There was a great writer – perhaps you know of her – Helena Blavatsky. She used to speak about going to that place of inner silence. And this is a great truth. If you were to look at all the ancient scriptures, you would see that they all talk about what started creation. Do you know what that was?

Tom: Tell me!

Fletcher: It was the Word. If you look in your own Bible, in the Book of John, you will see that it says, "In the beginning was the Word". And it says that - it was the Word - that manifested the whole universe.

There is also – in the Hindu religion - you see - a sacred word called Aum. The Hindus say that it was that vibration – of Aum – that manifested - or caused the entire universe to come into existence. In order to chant Aum properly – the Hindu priests would tell you – you must still your mind. So again we have – in a different place and in a different culture – a teaching that says - it was a vibration – a Word - that arose out of absolute stillness - that began all of creation.

The fact that the original vibration or Word that created the universe – arose out of a pure stillness - is a truth that humanity can draw from and learn from. For those who are reading this book – if they were to chant Aum each day for only five minutes – they would find that their minds were becoming more single pointed. And they would find – that as they do the deep breathing – and practice calming the mind with Aum – that they would start manifesting their desires at a more accelerated rate.

I encourage you to do this as well, sir! Hold on just a moment – Rose is here!

Rose: Greetings, my name is Rose. Can you hear me?

Tom: It is wonderful to hear your voice again Rose. Welcome back.

Rose: We are so pleased to be here. I could not stay silent. I overheard Fletcher's teaching and I said to myself, "I must come and speak about one of my favorite subjects".

I traveled a great deal while on the Earth, and I went to India several times, as you know. When I was there, the great swamis taught me all about the word Aum. I used to say Aum to myself, even though I didn't really believe in it – mind you. Aum carries with it a powerful vibration - and it doesn't matter at all - if one believes in its power or not. Aum IS powerful in and of itself! Therefore, even though one may NOT believe in it, one can still receive great benefit from repeating it. I didn't believe the swamis when they said that Aum could generate realities. They said that the universe came from Aum, but I just didn't believe that – not even one bit.

But, you know, I cannot deny that something beneficial always happened within me while I was chanting Aum. I remember sitting in my room in India, saying Aum over and over. It was lovely – and I always felt better after that. I would think, "Those swamis may be a bunch of crazy liars, but at least they've got THAT right." And so, I will echo support for Fletcher's words. Since coming to the Spirit World, I have had the great privilege of uncovering many of the great mysteries and realities of humanity, and I have come to understand how everything connects. This has been a great area of fascination for me!

Tom: Me too! I am so curious about the secrets of the Universe and how it was created – and WHY. What ARE the laws of the Universe, as YOU see them? What ARE the major principles of creation that we humans need to learn? What would YOU tell our readers about these laws and principles, Rose?

Rose: Well you see, following Fletcher, I must begin by saying, "Yes, the stilling of the mind is of utmost importance". That is the first principle that I learned in India, how to use Aum to calm down the thoughts in my mind. So, we could call the first principle of creation, "Calm the Mind with Aum".

The second principle that we must share with our readers, is that there is no manifestation on any level unless the vibration of love is present. It is the love frequency that generates all reality. This is why the material and the spiritual worlds are able to exist at all. It is because of God's love that encases and encompasses our worlds, that our existence is made possible. Were God to withdraw His very Love, all things should fall into dissolution and decay. The entire universe is held and embraced by God's Grace and by His Love.

If you see a baby or a small child in the hospital, they always say, "When a child is born, it must be held. Did you know that the infant mortality rate is much greater if a baby does not feel the love of being hugged?" This is a great truth, for love is the only real power that sustains life. Where there is love – there is nurturance and existence and growth. You must learn to love and hold your ideas and your dreams close to your heart, as if they were beloved, innocent babies.

And, for those who wish to generate, for example – prosperity or abundance – or for those who want to draw to themselves some sort of manifestation, they must have a heart and mind that is vibrating with love! For, if love is NOT present as a real energy, then all the attempted transmissions in the world are for nothing. So, we would call the second principle of manifestation - "Love Your Dream like a Baby." Your dreams will never manifest if you don't love them and nurture them, with all your heart and mind and soul – just as you would love and nurture your most beloved new born baby.

Tom: That's really powerful Rose, thank you. I never thought of imagining my dreams and wishes as babies that need my love, in order to grow. Are there any other principles or laws of the universe that we need to include in the book?

Rose: Well, I might say, these first two are giving humanity quite enough of a challenge as it is. I think that if they were to master the first two principles - about calming the mind and loving the dream - then they should have done well. Even I myself have not mastered these first two principles completely. Remember these words well, my dear. Physical death does not suddenly make someone an all-powerful saint. It only brings one into the Spirit World. And so, even though I now live in the Spirit World - I still have much work to do, to learn how to apply the principles of creation, in my own experience.

I suppose that another principle that I have been uncovering over here – a principle that we might share in our book is the reality of our own connection with Divinity. Each and every person, here or on Earth has an eternal connection with God, which must eventually be recognized and lived. It's not merely enough to just have a still mind. We must go beyond that stillness - to having a loving heart. And then, we must open our heart to loving God WHILE we love our dreams! Without loving God first – and finding Him within - and without recognizing that Divinity as the very Source of all our creations, our highest and best dreams could die, limp on the vine.

People must learn about God AS Love. God is unlimited, unconditional love. The problem with humans on Earth is that they don't feel connected with God's Love. They feel totally separate and cut off, rather than at one with Divine Love. We could call this principle, "Loving the Kingdom of God Within". For Jesus himself spoke of this principle first when he said, "Seek ye first the Kingdom of God within you – and THEN - all the other things shall be added unto you."

Tom: Why are people still so outer-directed, anyway? Why do we humans ignore that inner kingdom? Why are people feeling so cut off from God?

Rose: It is because people on the Earth are so very judgmental and critical - of themselves, God and each other - especially when it comes to HOW they love. Their judgmentalism literally cuts them off from having a calm mind, remembering to love their dreams – and it also makes them forget that God lives within. Human love is so often limited and conditional, while Divine love, which we must eventually learn how to vibrate with, is always unlimited and unconditional.

So, the next important principle, that we need to understand in order to manifest anything - is to remember we have a place inside us where God's Spiritual Kingdom reigns. Then we must learn how to love the truth of that Spirit Realm that lives within – both within ourselves and within each other. Then we must remember the truth that we are ALL of the Light – and that we ALL carry God's Spirit in our hearts and minds. We must come to understand that we are all God Beings, and that we all carry the power of God's Love deep within us.

Tom: Yes, I see. It's like the nucleus inside the atom – right? The inner nucleus is God! Everyone has a similar nucleus within them - that is the powerful God Presence, the I AM, right?

Rose: Yes, you are correct, my dear. You yourself DO carry Divinity within you! You ARE the Light of God shining upon the Earth! You are love! You must accept this and learn to love yourself! It is only when humans think so little of themselves that they forget their own nucleus is made out of God's Spirit. They can't or won't love themselves, or each other, because they refuse to love the God who lives within. That is a great problem and challenge upon the Earth at this time!

Please remember, as Fletcher said earlier, that we were ALL there at the very beginning when God created all of creation. We were all part of the original vibration, the Word of God that created all the many universes. Therefore, the vibration of God's Word is within us still, at this very moment, always and forever! God's Word is vibrating within us, and through the power of absolute Divine Love, is creating us by filling us with the breath of life!

And so, another principle that you must come to know is that – you have the mind of God in you as well. The mind of God is the mind of Light. Having this awareness means that you understand and feel IN your vibration, that your Light IS the Light of God. What is Light? It is the conscious awareness of Spirit, the mind of you that feels "I AM Spirit". Your Light of consciousness and God's Light of consciousness really ARE one! Your life and God's life are one! You are connected!

Tom: Yes, that is what I teach in "Uncle Tom's Classroom" – that the individual "self" is the extension of the one vast Cosmic Super Self! We are all branching out from one great cosmic Tree of Life. We are all sparks arising from one great cosmic fire! We are all wavelets on one great ocean of consciousness and bliss! If only we could share that truth with kids, early on in their education, they wouldn't have to fall so deeply into the world's unhappy programming that disconnects them from "who they really are".

I am so grateful that Bob and other channels like him are demonstrating how connected we humans really are to the Spirit World. They are courageously doing the connecting for us - through their conscious contact with the Spirit World. You and Fletcher and Edgar and Orion have proven to me – beyond the shadow of any doubt – that we are ALL at connected with spirit realm.

Rose: Exactly. Our medium does great work by being such an extraordinary antenna. His work and the work of many others like him are proving to the world that our realms are connected. In fact – I must tell you that our worlds actually overlap. You can feel this reality right now even as you write and read these words. Some very real vibrations of the Spirit World can be felt in our words tonight - in these very words that you are transcribing for our readers. Can you feel the energies vibrating?

Tom: Yes I can, most definitely. That's why I love doing these transcripts – because I love riding the vibrations of your words. They make me feel like I'm surfing waves of happiness, love and oneness.

Rose: Jesus himself taught the very same idea of oneness, didn't He? He was the most extraordinary representation of oneness with God that has ever incarnated upon the Earth. I remember in my old church, the vicar used to read the scriptures, in which Jesus spoke clearly about this connection with the Father. The Good Book itself quotes Jesus as saying, "I and the Father are One. The Kingdom of Heaven is within. You can do greater things than I have done because God is within you. The Kingdom of God is within you all. Ye are Gods."

I used to think, "Oh well, that's easy for him to say you know – because He's God, right?" I was so filled with doubt and resistance to the things of Spirit. But, the truth is - my dear - that we DO share in the Christ Light and in God's One Spirit. The Christ Light and God's Spirit are present within each and every soul, even if the soul denies that presence. For, if it were not for the presence of Spirit, there would be no life in any of us, no matter which world we inhabit. Remember, you already have the Light of Spirit within your soul and within your body. If you can tap into that Light, it will lead you to the higher realms. And, your manifestations will be made more complete.

You know, when we speak of all of these issues, there are many more principles. The universe is very complex and even I don't claim to have all knowledge. I am uncovering the truth bit by bit, however, and I think part of humanity's growth is to uncover such truth. The ancient cultures, such as the Indians and the Egyptians were much more profound in their understanding and application of the great spiritual truths. Their technologies and wisdoms have long been forgotten, which brought on what have been called the Ages of Darkness. You know, we speak of the Dark Age as being a thousand years ago, but humanity is in the Dark Age on the Earth – in many ways right now today – because humanity has forgotten the Light of Spirit that lives within.

When we speak of an age of darkness, what are we talking about really? Did the lights go out in the castle? Not really. What we are referring to is the darkness that has come over the minds and hearts of mankind. The mind of modern man has – in part - lost its illumination. It has lost its awareness of the Light within, the Divine Light of Spirit that illuminates all wisdom and knowledge and truth. But, when the Light of Spirit is allowed to return to the human mind - there is an illumination within the soul – and then there is access to true love and to the higher vibrations. Humanity must remember that, and open up to the reality of the Spirit World, to the Great Spirit called God, and to us!

You see, there are so many truths, yet to discover. I suppose you could say that I am taking a journey with our readers, as I too continue to uncover answers. We are on a grand journey together – a kind of spiritual treasure hunt and I hope to continue taking this journey with you Mr. Berg, and with all those who are reading our book. Please know that I am learning and unfolding just like you.

Life is always a series of learnings and unfoldings. It does not stop when any one body dies. In fact, in many ways, it truly begins in that moment of transition from one world to the next. One need not wait until a physical death, however, to begin to understand the mysteries of the Universe. One can begin to search for the spiritual treasure house, right in one's own home, within one's own family, and especially, within one's own self. Discovering one's one spiritual self – is to find the greatest treasure of all! It is what the English writers called - seeking and finding the Holy Grail!

The spiritual Light must no longer be hidden within the human sense of self. Jesus himself said, "What value is there to put one's Light under a bushel?" The human personality is that bushel which must now be lifted, so we can find the treasured Grail underneath. The Light and love of Spirit must be discovered, seen and shared within each and every soul. Spiritual truth, goodness and Light are the very vibrations that raise both the mind and body into higher realms of knowledge and love.

You know, when I look in upon your planet today, I have mixed feelings. And I say to myself, "The people of the Earth are in the darkness". Sometimes, I really do feel that way. And then, there are other times when I look down into your world and I can actually see Light shining up from the Earth and I say, "The people of the Earth are shining with a great and wonderful Light." So, I guess what I am coming to understand is that, we are all a mixture of both Light and darkness. The truth is, we are all a bit of both – now aren't we?

Tom: I totally agree. Some days I feel so connected and filled with the Light – while on other days I feel totally confused and cut off from God.

Rose: Don't' worry my dear – your Light and your glory will NOT fade. They will only continue to increase and grow, as you unite your human world with our Spirit World. Even I myself find that I am growing in degrees of glory, over here. It is true that if you were to see me with your physical eyes, I would appear very bright and glowing, for that is the form I have. But, the Light of my spirit is actually dim compared to many others over here, who glow with a much brighter degree of glory. They glow with a powerful luminescence. There is not a degree of Light on the Earth plane, with which I can compare it – in order to adequately describe the how brilliantly some spirits glow in our world.

Do you know those halogen lanterns you have on Earth? You know how bright they can shine? Well, they would be seen as very dim, if they were to be carried over here. Does that give you some understanding of the difference I am talking about? The halogen lanterns on your planet, bright as they appear to your physical eyes, would seem extremely dim here in our world. The way to increase the Light upon the earth is to look into the scriptures, and study the many spiritual truths in books like your Bible. Those scriptures have opened up a new level of understanding to me, and greatly increased my experience of the Light, since coming to the Spirit World.

Just think about the way the Bible describes Jesus on the mountain of transfiguration. Do you remember that story when he goes up to the mountaintop with the disciples?

Tom: Yes, I do. That was in the Book of Luke, Chapter 9, when Jesus took Peter, James and John with him up into the hills and Moses and Elijah appeared to them – right?

Rose: Yes. Edgar Cayce and I have often spoken about that extraordinary event. He told me all about it many times. He loves the stories of Jesus that are covered in the scriptures so very much. I remember Edgar's words. He said, "Rose, when Jesus was on that mountain he began to glow with heavenly Light, and his garments shone white as snow. The scriptures say so."

I also remember hearing the vicar preach on this subject, as well. But, I was in such darkness at the time – I used to think, "What kind of distraction is this, anyway? I don't see why it's so important." My dismissal of that wonderful account of Jesus lighting up was because I didn't understand the point the vicar was trying to make. Now I see that he was actually using the story of Jesus' transfiguration as a way of teaching us an important principle. He was trying to show us that all humanity has that same Divine Light within us, as well. There is a Divine Light of Spirit that is shining in and through us, just as it shown through Jesus!

Moses and Elijah also appeared on the mountain that day, and spoke directly with Jesus and the apostles? You see, they were demonstrating the reality of the Spirit World – and showing how OUR world CAN and DOES merge with yours. They were communicating a teaching about the Principle of the Light Within. The reason that Jesus was able to shine and glow as he did on that day –was because he was vibrating with a higher vibration, a spiritual vibration – made of pure Light.

Jesus was living in and AS that superior vibration! His energy level was so superior that he was able to raise his vibration high enough to manifest his true form as a Divine Being of Light - to his disciples. At the same time, he was able to open the door between the worlds, so as to bring down Moses and Elijah to the Earth. They too were glowing with Light as they came down from the Spirit World to stand with Jesus on the mountain, that day.

This manifestation of the spiritual Light within was not to be limited only to Jesus. The transfiguration of Jesus, and the appearance of Moses and Elijah, were meant to inspire us and teach us, to remind us that we too have this Divine Light within us. Jesus has said already in scripture - that we will do greater things even than he did. The Light of Spirit IS the power of God within us all. He predicted that others, coming after him, will not only learn to do the kind of works that he did but will eventually learn how to do even much greater things.

Tom: Like what? Can you give us some practical examples from your own perspective?

Rose: Yes, my dear. In regards to your previous discussion with Fletcher about manifesting the diamond, I liked that one! You know how much I have always adored diamonds - so I very much enjoyed your conversation about finding a diamond miraculously on the beach. And I must say that I was quite impressed by your request. It was bold and brash and it showed how well you've been listening to us, and how much you have been taking our message to heart!

It is quite true, Mr. Berg - that IF you could find the Spiritual Light within, well then, a diamond would certainly be quite easy to manifest. But, you must follow our principles. Your vibration must reach a higher frequency level first. You must raise your vibration to a level in consciousness where you merge with the Spirit within, that same Spirit that was with God when the universe was being created. Humans do have the potential to materialize physical things, using their spiritual powers, although I would say that not many on the Earth today have developed their creative potential. Most of you have totally forgotten that fertile time before the beginning of creation, when we were "at-one" with God's Spirit, cooperatively creating our physical universe - literally out of nothing but thought and loving intent.

When I was visiting India I saw a swami who knew and practiced the principles of manifestation. He actually materialized a sapphire for me – literally out of nothing. He held out his hand before me and showed me that it was empty. Then, he said, "Look at the palm of my hand." He didn't move. He just stood there. Then, he merely opened his hand, and out of nowhere, there appeared a most beautiful sapphire, which he gave to me. I eventually had it set in a broach which I took back to England.

These so-called miracles are much more accepted in India than in the western world. And certainly in my day, when I went back to England with my sapphire, I didn't tell anyone where I got it. I simply said that the sapphire was a gift and left it at that, because I didn't want people to think I'd gone mad. Manifesting jewels out of thin air was considered impossible my most people of my day. I never will forget that reality however, the level of consciousness that the swami demonstrated so clearly to me, when he created my sapphire out of nothingness. I know understand that he materialized that jewel out of the vast stillness and deep power of his own Spirit mind.

Humanity must think in terms of looking much more to the east, because many of the swami's of India are still maintaining and living those truths. If you look at the history of the Earth, much spiritual wisdom has come from the enlightened masters of the east. Even Jesus was from the Middle East. Many of the great masters like Yogananda and Vivekananda were great spiritual beings from the east. The present culture's of the western world are really quite young, as I understand it, for the cradle of civilization began in the east and migrated to the rest of the world. The ancient knowledge is present therefore, IN the east - because their civilizations have had more time there to evolve.

Give us just a moment. Fletcher wishes to speak with you.

Fletcher: Yes, well, it is obvious that Rose is learning a lot over here. And, I have had to learn a lot as well, because the Universe is still continuing to unfold and evolve. There are always new worlds being created and new manifestations going on. Don't be thinking that the Earth is the only place where the issue of manifestation is being discussed and practiced. The idea of co-creating with God is going on everywhere. There are countless planets, all over the universe and other life forms . . . . and people on . . . (the transmission abruptly broke here.)

Bob: (Calling back . . .) What a shock THAT was to my system. When the connection breaks off like that – I sometimes come out of trance too fast. I really feel Light headed – dizzy. Do you want to continue?

Tom: Yes, but only if you are up to it.

Bob: Let me see if I can go back under and hold onto the vibration a little longer. There is a great deal of power in here, tonight. I can feel it, and a lot more information. Give me just a moment.

Fletcher: (Deep breathing . . .) Oh, there we go. We're back in. You will have to pardon us. We've raised the vibration so high that we have disturbed the electrical apparatus again. It's good to be back here with you.

As I was discussing with you before, many people on the Earth have completely forgotten who they are. And, because of that forgetfulness - they forget what creative spiritual abilities that they were born with when they became human. If human beings could come back to remembering these main points of: (1) cultivating a stillness of the mind, (2) following the processes of deep breathing, (3) allowing Divine Love to vibrate in their hearts, and (4) understanding that Divine Love IS a tangible reality that exists on many planes – and (5) knowing if they could raise their vibration up into the Divine Light and merge with Spirit, then they would find that the things they wish for, manifesting easily.

Remember, one of the other most important principals of all – there has to be some love behind every aspect of creation. The principle for humans - is that you have to feel worthy of the vibration that you want to live. This means that you have to love yourself while you're attempting to create anything on the physical plane. So, this is accomplished through living love, which means, by truly loving your neighbor, loving your world, giving up your habitual judgmentalism and following the kind and compassionate attitudes that Jesus explained so clearly during his "Sermon on the Mount". Jesus made the principles of good living really quite simple. He taught humanity, "Love your neighbor as yourself, and love God – ALSO as yourself." That is how you create the good life while on Earth. It is really THAT simple, because, it's only by love that power is given to our thoughts, to our will, and to the ideas that grow in the mind.

If you look at someone who seems to be successful on Earth – but doesn't seem to have or express love, ask yourself – "where do they get all THEIR creative power from, if love is what is always needed to manifest anything?" Well, I'll tell you where they get their energy from. They draw it from those around them, from grabbing their attention in negative ways. If you look at the great and most terrible leaders of the world – like the Stalins and the Hitlers – they didn't operate, or create things, from a principle of love. The power they used to make things happen was drawn from manipulating and tapping into the love energy that was in others. And they used the love, or blind hero worship that people had for them, to make terrible things happen. And so they took all that love and adulation that was given to them so freely and lovingly – and they twisted it – so as to use it for evil (or destructive) purposes. They literally pulled in the love of their followers, and used it like fuel, because they did not have the ability to love within themselves in order to manifest their reality.

What they DID have was the awareness however – that they needed power to manifest their own particular versions of reality. So they grabbed the power from the confused love and loyalty of millions of fanatical followers. They literally stole their creative energy, when they took away their focus, and then they funneled that energy into their own manifestations. Today, this practice of stealing energy and love can be seen in your schools and workplaces. Unawake teachers and employers, often – without even realizing it – grab the consciousness of their students or employees – in order to manifest whatever the kind of reality THEY most prefer, regardless of what the students OR the employees may want or need in their own personal lives. And of course, powerful governments, big religions and large media organizations often do this as well, when they pull in unsuspecting young people to fight foreign wars, police the masses, work in mind numbing jobs, or just ignore the important issues that need cleaning up on your planet. Do you understand what we are saying?

Tom: Yes, I understand completely. In fact, I wrote "Uncle Tom's Classroom" out of a huge love for all the students I'd ever served, because I actually saw that they were having their God awareness squished out of them by the demands of the systems. My intention with UTC was based on my love for the idea that ALL kids have a right to be free to be who they REALLY are, not some kind of cultural carbon copy of "normalcy"—whatever that is!

I saw so clearly – in my three decades of teaching all grades from K through 8th - how the huge worldwide thought systems were literally sucking the love and life right out of our young people. The state and media were stealing their attention, grabbing their focus, imprisoning their minds, and squelching their natural love for life, by forcing them to focus on (and believe in) "the program". Every large system has a specific "way of life" that it's selling, and our beloved kids are left with no way to "stay awake" to WHO THEY REALLY ARE.

They are lied to from the "gitgo", forced to read out-dated texts about the Earth's hyper-violent history. They are convinced to believe many false beliefs about the meaning of life, rather than discover and trust their Spirit Source within AND enjoy their fun-loving affection for life and each other! I saw how the dominant economic paradigm of our time, capitalism, was brainwashing our youth, and gathering in THEIR energy, by ONLY teaching them one way to fit into the needs of the system. The formula was clear. Hard work and subservience to the system = success. Serve the system or die out on the street as a homeless person!

The public school system and media do NOT help our kids wake up and become free thinkers, nor do they assist them in celebrating their diversity, or in discovering their inner Cosmic Super Selves. The military industrial complex that President Eisenhower warned up about, has now accomplished exactly what he said that he feared. It HAS almost completely taken over the minds of the American people, sucked in all the people's energy (like in "The Matrix"), and twisted the high ideals of the "American Dream" into serving its own profit based, power hungry purposes.

So Fletcher, how can I get UTC's message – that our kids deserve to be liberated from this matrix of control – out and into the world's conversation? How can I build up more love for this idea myself, so as not to become so discouraged and frustrated in the interim that I quit before I succeed? Where and how can I accrue enough power to really and truly begin dehypnotizing and liberating our youth from the brainwashing of the military industrial complex, on a much larger scale? I know children CAN wake up to WHO THEY REALLY ARE, because I saw it happen in my classroom in San Francisco. So, how CAN I move forward most efficiently and effectively, in order to help the younger generations wake up and discover their Divine Cosmic Super Powers, while there is still time?

Fletcher: Well, first of all, we want you to see that you are NOW much more conscious of your inner God spirit AND your mighty connection with the energies of our Spirit World than at any time since you were a young man. This expanded consciousness, higher vibration AND re-alignment with the Creator, have increased your powers on Earth far beyond where they were when you first published "Uncle Tom's Classroom"! Please realize, my dear friend - that you have already accomplished so many of your original goals. Don't be so self-critical and impatient with yourself and the timing of this unfoldment.

Remember, there is ALWAYS anOther Side of the coin that must be considered. The people you want to participate in your new reality must also be vibrating at the same, or nearly the same frequency that you and your teachings are vibrating in. That's why WE have come into your life and into your world, at this time. We are working to adjust and even raise the vibration of many people with whom you will one day interact. We are working with their spirit guides, as well – so as prepare them to become more open and ready vibrationally - to receive and be a better match to you and your message.

There are great many souls on the Earth who will be receiving the teachings that you are being prepared to offer – who haven't been vibrationally ready, up to until now. So we want you to understand the reason for the so-called delay. The delay has actually been allowed to exist, so that you could become stronger and more tuned in, within yourself. This is because you are going to have to be very VERY strong Mr. Berg, to handle the amount of people that you will be coming into contact with in the coming years. In the next year, to two years, you are going to be seeing yourself moving up quite a bit - into a much higher profile. Your first book, and OUR new book, will be seen and read by many MANY people.

Therefore - please know, the future evolution of your writing and teaching, the very success that you want to be manifesting, is already growing stronger. Your success is being created, even as we speak. Your patience during the last few years has served you well. Your success is like a seed that is growing in the soil of the Divine. Please know that it is now beginning to sprout. We see this project with Bob as an important stepping stone for both your careers.

Tom: Thank you so much for your encouraging words. I so appreciate your support - and I know that you are right about this needed time of preparation. I WILL have to be strong to stand up to the many voices of darkness and obstructionism that still seek to brainwash our kids into total servitude. Bob is really an inspiration to me, the way he stands up as a medium, and acts as a human telephone to your world, no matter what people say about him. From what he has told me, his journey hasn't been easy.

And, I HAVE felt the power surges and amazing insights that you are offering, which brings me to my next question about OUR book's completion? What else could we add to make it even more insightful and "cutting edge"? Our book is such an incredibly practical teaching which can and will help awaken many people from the present dark age of hyper-materialism and disconnectedness, don't you agree?

Fletcher: That is absolutely right. Many dark ages have come and gone on the Earth throughout all of recorded history. But, remember, those of us who are the Light bearers have always been at work upon the Earth, as well. That Light of Spirit cannot EVER be extinguished completely. Like we said before, the sun never stops shining – even when the planet turns on its axis and brings on night. The Light of Spirit never goes out either, no matter how many people may temporarily turn away, go into denial or try to ignore its influence in their lives.

In terms of this book being closed – well – we must tell you that it will never be closed. Our present sessions will only be stopped temporarily so we can publish. There will be more future editions of our conversations. Though this first offering may seem to end rather abruptly, that's because we aren't really done. The truth is that we will NEVER really be done, because there are so many more transmissions coming. Just as we keep on transmitting through our medium – we will also keep on with additions to this book.

There is no way to conclude this book because there is SO much more to say. There is no ending to the many ways we can transmit the Light of knowledge to those who still wander in the lower realms of mental darkness. There is no way of making this kind of offering all nice and tidy, but if we were to attempt to tidy up this first volume just a bit, we would like to say this. We will now speak directly to our readers - to each person who is on the Earth and who is reading this book at this very moment in time.

"You are not reading this book out of some mere chance occurrence. You have been drawn to this book by our vibration. It is our vibration that has called you here today. It is our vibration that is pulsating now throughout your mind and soul, as you read these words that are coming to you DIRECTLY from the Spirit World. Whenever this book is read, either aloud or silently, our vibration and the energies of our spiritual world WILL be present. And please know that we bring – on the wings of our vibration – the love and Light of the Spirit World into your world. In you exists a great untapped potential that is yet to be uncovered, discovered, explored and expressed. It is the potential that comes from re-aligning with your spiritual nature and with the vibrations pouring into you from the Spirit World. "

Tom: I called this untapped potential, the powers of the Cosmic Super Self in "Uncle Tom's Classroom". My kids were amazingly receptive to this knowledge, because they were still young enough to feel their inner power AND their connection to the heavenly realms.

Fletcher: That is why Jesus said we must become like the little children. Unfortunately, after people are educated and grow up, they lost their inner connectedness and begin looking around and saying to themselves, "Oh, I don't feel powerful. I've got a lot of fear inside of me, not power. I'm not such a high being that I could converse with spirits, or learn how to use spiritual powers." But, right now, dear reader – let me tell you this as strongly and clearly as possible. As you are reading these words, and hearing these messages, we spirits ARE present with you. YOU CAN FEEL US IF YOU TRY! The human world and the Spirit World are merging. In fact – they HAVE merged already. We challenge you, therefore, to look closely at our message and to feel our vibrations coursing through you right now. We guarantee that you will begin to sense a new level of power flowing through you, a power that comes from Spirit.

Please know that the words in this book are POWERFUL because they are quite literally made out of the Light and love of the Spirit World. Light and love are the invisible God powers that sustain the entire universe. They are not as far away from you as you may think. They are not some abstract notion. Light and love are right in your very own hands – right now. They are the powers that sustain you and fill you. This very book that is being created – and that you hold in your hands - is a manifestation in tangle form - of that same Divine Love and Light.

For many years, we have looked upon the Earth for channels who would be willing to bring forth our messages – and we are deeply grateful that the two of you are assisting us in getting this book – from our world to yours. Please know that you are spiritual channels as well. For, as you open up contact with your own spirit guides, and with your Higher Self, not only do you merge with your spiritual identity, but you also connect for all the inner spirits of all those around you.

Our medium here has devoted his life to serving – to being a messenger, a medium and a channeler. He has dedicated countless years to helping our world reach into your world, and we are so very honored and pleased to be working with him. But, we are honored and pleased also - when anybody upon the Earth gives any kind of thought or attention to contacting our world. As Rose would say, when you remember to call us, we are AUTOMATICALLY drawn to you. It's a very reciprocal relationship. We are never really so far apart from your world, so you don't have to get all perfect and holy to be able to communicate with us. All you have to do is talk in our direction, and we will surely answer back.

In time, we will get a good rapport going between us. We hope in the coming years – to be bringing more volumes to you, so that together, we will continue on this amazing journey. Please know that there are many in the Spirit World who are journeying with you. There are many who are traveling with you right now, right where you are. As Bob has so wonderfully exemplified through his mediumship, none of you are ever really alone. There is not a single one of you who is alone. We are here, right now, WITH those of you who are reading our words. We are looking over your shoulders at this very moment!

Remember, by the very presence of our words on this paper here, our vibration and our power are present with you. If you don't feel so connected, then we would suggest that you read the chapters out loud - read our words aloud. And then you will hear our words in your very own ears. Ask a friend to read our messages to you out loud and then – you WILL be able to hear us, as well as feel our vibration coming to you through the vibration of their voice. You WILL be able to hear us and actually FEEL us in the vibration that is coming through the reading and speaking of our words out loud.

Each of you must remember the Light of Spirit within you, and to realize that you are loved. You ARE love! There is not a single human being upon the Earth that is beyond God's love. There is nobody who is so far distant from God that they can't, at a moment's notice, be back in His loving arms. Can you believe that you're loved?

Tom: Yes I can. I have much evidence of this love in my life, not the least of which is this time in Hawaii, basking in the sunlit glories of this Garden of Eden. The South Pacific is turquoise, the Pali cliffs are verdant green and the sky is a soft baby blue today – so Divine Love is TOTALLY in evidence, as it pours through this natural masterpiece. I guess this is why people refer to Hawaii as "paradise".

Fletcher: Yes, the glory of the Spirit World merges with the beauty of the physical world quite obviously in your Hawaiian Islands. We have come to you here and now, to give you further evidence of this spiritual merging, and also to remind you that your life will continue after physical death. We are speaking to you today, to give you evidence of the reality of the Spirit World, right here and right now, and to assure you it is your spirit that makes you immortal. The life of Spirit is here with you, and IN you, at this very moment. I myself, as I've told you many times, was not a believer in the spiritual world. And, yet, I find myself here, still existing and very much alive in this spiritual dimension, and speaking to you now, through our medium's body.

Many people come over here totally unprepared for entering into this reality. We are speaking to our readers this day, so you won't be one of those who are unprepared. On the Earth, if you are planning a trip, you think to yourself, "Well, I am going to travel to this far away country. I am planning on visiting this foreign place - so I'd better be reading up on it – and find out about its culture and its customs. What type of economy do they have? What is the environment like? What is their language?" This is a natural preparation.

Well, someday all of you will be coming to the Spirit World. So, you would be doing well to prepare yourself by considering this knowledge about us and our spiritual dimension. We don't ask you to grasp it all in only one day. But, just take it a little bit at a time, here and there, as you are able. It'll do your soul well. As you read these words, you will be feeling our presence more and more, and then – you won't feel so very lonely.

Many of you, who are reading this, really do still believe that you ARE alone in the world and you feel that nobody cares about you. And yet, all around you right now, we are present, and you will feel us - if you ask. You have around you at this very moment, countless guides, angels and friends from our Spirit World. Ask us to reveal ourselves to you and we will! Look for evidence of our presence everywhere and let us know you are open to our friendship. We ARE your friends and companions! Do you want our friendship? We are so very eager to help you. Give us just a moment, Rose wishes to speak.

Tom: Thank you Fletcher, that was beautiful. I DO feel your presence and your friendship.

Rose: I cannot help but echo Fletcher's words. I think so often of those who are on the journey towards the Light. Each of us is – on a daily basis – either moving closer to the Light or farther away from it. I pray that everybody reading these words will remember - that those in darkness, like I was when I first crossed over – really DO need you to pray for them. Will you pray for them? Will you ask for them to receive all the help they need to achieve the Light.

I promise all of you – that if you will but pray for others – and especially for those who are crossing over into our world, you will have many friends waiting for you when you arrive. There will be countless souls liberated by your prayers, and helped by the rays of Light and love that you send to them. Each single prayer is like a beacon of Light that will guide souls all the way home safely to the Light. And someday, when you are in need, those you prayed for will all come and gather back together, to help you rise into the Light as well.

Do not be deceived into believing that your material, physical world is permanent. Many humans have made that mistake. I myself was one who thought that the material world was the ONLY world worth thinking about. And yet I had many opportunities to learn about Spirit even then. I sat with many great teachers during my life on Earth and each of them brought me a truth about the spiritual reality. But you see, I was haughty and vain and I didn't want to heed their words of wisdom. Please don't be like me. Please use all your challenges as opportunities for growth. Please let us teach you while you are still on the Earth, and things will go better for you.

Understand that you are loved UNCONDITIONALLY by the Creator. Our Creator is not a God of judgment and damnation, as you have been told by some religions. That is a lie. The Divine only seeks to embrace you in a vibration of total love, kindness and support. You humans have created this myth of an angry, distant and unforgiving God - out of your own fear. And, it is simply not true! The truth is that God is embracing you EVEN NOW, nourishing your life, although your mind may not be able to understand or accept it. Who do you think is beating your heart and pumping your blood and making the air flow in and out of your lungs, right now? It that is not God at work within you, then who or what is it?

Remember my dear that our Spirit World is not far away from yours. And so, we are able to come to any of you who call upon us – at a moment's notice. And, I echo Fletcher's words by saying that it is our great pleasure and honor to serve you. Around each of you are many friendly spirits. Some of you have loved ones who you've been wondering about . . . Pray for your loved ones who have passed over already. Pray for them and ask them for a message. They will give it to you. If they cannot speak to you directly – others will come in their place, and bring you're their messages in ways that you can understand. Even animals and birds are messengers. So, if you are open to our reception – you will receive much.

And so I wish to conclude my message today by reiterating Fletcher's words. In the very pages of this spiritual memoir, are our vibrational presences. Speak our words out loud if you will – and we will feel that we right there with you. We love you and we send you our Light. We are ever present in guiding, for that is our task and our great pleasure. For this reason, we send you these "memoirs from the Spirit World". My name is Rose.

Fletcher: Oh there we go. We are back in the body again. We've got to be sensitive to our medium's vibration. The power is growing weak here. So, we will conclude by asking - if there is anything else we can do for you tonight?

Tom: I was just wondering, are you going to bring in Edgar Cayce or Orion again, to add their comments to this "spiritual memoir", as Rose put it so eloquently?

Fletcher: Well, give us just a moment. We have to check here, to see if our medium's vibration can sustain them. (Sighs). Well, it looks like there IS a little bit of reserve power left – in his system – so I think that we can do that. We are going to bring over Dr. Cayce first.

Edgar Cayce: Well good evening. It is certainly a great pleasure to be back here amongst you. I have been listening with rapt attention to all that has been brought over to our readers tonight – and it is my great joy to come here – once again - to speak to each of you.

When I was alive and on the Earth, many people would come to me and ask, "Mr. Cayce, can you please help me?" I used to always say, "I cannot help a soul – for - only God CAN help you." I tried to turn every soul I could towards the Divine Light. And I would tell them, "Seek God and you will find the truth. Please know that even my own guides counsel people to always go directly to God." I understood - through my channelings – during my last lifetime on the Earth – that the Universe wants to support us. It wants to heal us and to nurture us. The problem is - that many humans to not believe that they are worthy of being nurtured, healed and loved – but they are! Ask yourself what you believe about this?

Remember what Jesus used to say, "What child would come to the Father, asking for help - and not receive it?" Those of us over here in Heaven – or the Spirit World as some now call it – are always with you and we continually offering our guidance. I like to call the Spirit World Heaven because I grew up calling it Heaven. I prefer using the word Heaven because - it truly IS Heaven over here. The spirit people really do love each other and support each other over here. This world in which we now abide really IS quite Heavenly; therefore the name Heaven is quite appropriate.

But, what I would like you to see today, is that you don't have to wait until you die to reach a heavenly state of consciousness. Heaven can begin on Earth for you today. That's what a lot of people in the churches are forgetting these days. The churches task isn't to convert the world to certain dogmatic beliefs. Churches should exist ONLY to teach people that God loves the world - to teach the world about love – not about fear! Churches should NEVER teach people to fear God or life, or each other! But, alas, this is not yet the case upon the Earth – not at all!

If the people of the world would feel loved by those who lead the churches, and if the churches would REALLY treat people with love, a spiritual love that comes from the depths of the heart, we could see a great transformation. I'm afraid, I must say, even as a Christian, I fell short many times in that area. But, I don't hold too much regret and sorrow, for I know that I did the best that I could on my journey. And I must say, Mr. Berg, that there are many good people, doing VERY good works – even in the most repressive churches within organized religion. Even though some of the great religious institutions still seek domination and control of the world, there are large numbers of very spiritual people within those organizations, who are working for us, and WITH us to bring God's message of love and kindness to everyone.

It is very important therefore, that each person simply remember to follow his or her own life journey as it unfolds. Don't judge yourselves so harshly, because – you know – as you judge, so will you feel judged. Love yourselves a little more each day and do your best to stop judging. Understand that, with God's grace, anything is possible. Look within for the healing answers. They are already in you, just waiting for you to turn in the right direction – to find them. They are in your real spirit self.

Life is such a grand mystery. I now understand that I was a channel for various healing forces in the Universe that chose to use me to do God's work. But remember, those various forces can still be channeled by you today. There is much more knowledge accessible, now that you have learned about hypnosis, suggestion and vibration. There are so many new discoveries about the workings of the brain and the mind that are being made available to you. People are learning about the different elements and activities of the human mind. We didn't have advanced brain surgery in my day. But, now, because of such breakthroughs, science has come to understand that the mind has much more do with electrical vibrations, than we ever knew about in the past. And it is THAT very electrical activity that allows us to be present and to manifest OUR vibration IN YOU – as we are doing now. It is through vibration that we communicate with our medium.

But, what I would like to say to our readers today, is that you don't have to be a famous medium to have a real ongoing connection with our world. All you need is the desire to have it. If you want it – you will have it! In truth, everybody has this connection within the Higher Self already – although for many, it just goes unrecognized. So remember this. Once you remember how to channel your own Higher Self, you will be channeling the truth of God. And so, it is so important that each person reading this look to his or her own Higher Self. Let that Higher Spirit Self guide you.

Some of you who are reading this may say, "I'm not sure that I even believe in God or a Higher Spirit Self." That's alright. I don't think that you are so much an atheist or even an agnostic – you are simply somebody who has not grasped the true reality of God as an all encompassing Spirit. You are not really rejecting God, you are rejecting somebody's interpretation of God - and that's alright. In fact, that can be a very important and necessary step in your own spiritual awakening. There are a lot of interpretations of God in your world that should be rejected. So, if you don't find an interpretation of God, in your lifetime, that makes sense – that's alright too. Just remember that within you is your Higher Self – and I suggest that - you could at least begin to acknowledge that. It is there within you , with or without your interpretation!

So, you CAN learn how to channel that Higher Self even if you don't feel comfortable with the idea that you can channel God - or any other heavenly spirits. The Higher Self within you is already connected to God and Heaven, which means that you WILL receive a message directly – just as if it came over from myself or Rose, or Fletcher or Orion, or any of the great and good spirits that inhabit our world.

I would ALSO like to remind all you that your life – as Rose has said – and Fletcher has told you as well – your life experience on Earth will go by very quickly. And so, don't be foolhardy by thinking, "Oh, I'll get around to my spiritual work someday, but

NOT today." Because, you know what? THIS is the time to go within yourself and discover your Spirit Self! I used to think I had much more time on Earth, too. And yet – my sojourn on Earth ended rather abruptly and I left my body quite young.

It was only then, when I crossed, that I fully realized just how many opportunities I had given up on the Earth by not listening to and following the advice of those Spiritualists who were trying to advise me. I dare say, I could have done much more, had I taken care of myself better and lived longer. But, I'm trying to continue my work from this side now, and I am hoping to do some good still. This is why I have come to you today!

Please remember that life is a journey which never ends. Your real life is of the Spirit and it is - therefore, immortal and eternal. You know, for those who think that the grave is the end – well – they've got quite a surprise coming. That's all I'll say for now, and I don't say that with any criticism or judgment. I am just telling you the truth as I know it. There is a whole other world of Spirit, where life goes on and on and never stops. And I think that humanity is starting to see this other reality more and more.

You know, on the Earth right now, you are seeing great advances in scientific exploration and knowledge. I used to say to myself, "Edgar, there are so many people in the world who say they don't believe in God, especially some of those scientists. It is amazing to me that there are still some very intelligent people who look at the mysteries of science and the marvels of creation and still do NOT see the hand of the Creator at work." Well, that's not for me to judge. Some quantum physicists are actually waking up now – and realizing that there IS a creative intelligence at work in the Universe. I am simply pointing out that I DID see the hand of the Creator while I was alive.

Think on this. Whether you believe in an intelligent and loving Creator or not, most of you DO realize that you have an "invisible other self" within you. You think, you reason, you hope and dream, you feel, you get excited and you love. That's your "invisible self". The part of you - that IS the life force and is able to love – IS the "invisible self" that is "at one" with your Higher Self. It lives through your physical self while you are on Earth, but it is not dependent on that physical self for life. It is an expression of life, of the Source, and of God.

Think about a time in your life when you felt pure love and connection. Everybody has had at least one experience in their lives when they felt that - "all's right with the world" – when they felt that they were connected to everybody and everything. That's the Higher Spirit Self, which you can feel when you are MOST awake within your physical life experience. Can you connect to that invisible part of you again? I know that you CAN – if you just settle down and get quiet – and begin to look deep within yourself. Look inside yourself and still your mind. Feel that the Higher Self is not far away. It's right within you. It's as close as your very own breathing. It is that which is CONSCIOUS and ALIVE within you! And it is connected to the Higher Self within everyone else In fact – in a very mysterious way – your Spirit Self is at ONE with the Spirit of everyone else, and with God!

I'd like to conclude my time here by telling everybody who reads this, "Look within and discover the existence of that Higher Self. Find it and let it be your guide. It guided me for many years. And, I think that the readings in my office at Virginia Beach are testimony of the fact of this spiritual reality. Go and search out my files. I tell you, I am still as amazed by those readings, and all the extraordinary healings that came through the work, as you might be. But, then again, that's the mystery of the God Spirit that lives within, the mystery of the Higher Spiritual Self at work. If you let it come through you – you can do such things as well.

I never claimed that I was anybody great, or that I was some kind of prophet. I've been called "the sleeping prophet", but I wish they would stop referring to me in that way. I was just a man who gave his best trying to serve God and love his neighbor. If you do that you'll achieve greater things than I did – far greater things. It has been a pleasure to talk to you . . .

Tom: Mr. Cayce, can I ask you one last question? What shall we tell the people from your association – and ALL the other people who will undoubtedly question whether or not you really ARE really Edgar Cayce - and that you really ARE speaking in this way, in this book. What shall we tell our readers about you and your participation in this book?

Edgar Cayce: All I would care to say - is that, those who have studied my teachings and my writings know my vibration and my voice. And that is all they need to know to distinguish the validity of these messages. My vibration IS recognizable! The truth of my involvement is manifest in my words and in my teachings. If you were to study the scriptures and read what I've written before - and you were to study what I've channeled before - my presence here would become obviously manifest. And it can be seen through this documentation.

I'd also like to say Mr. Berg that I am a spirit who has incarnated many times AS a human. I am therefore - not a finite object to be owned by anyone or by any organization. Anybody who would claim that they own me or my spirit, well . . . they simply can't claim that now. I am an eternal spirit and no human can own a spirit. No immortal spirit can EVER be owned, regardless of what the body may experience temporarily, while on Earth. Humans can claim that they own the readings that are owned by the foundation in Virginia Beach, I suppose, but even that is a bit questionable, since the readings are a gift of Spirit. The fact is that, nobody can claim to own me – for I am a spirit who is eternally free. And, I will continue to live and to work from here in the Spirit World, so as to guide those on Earth wherever there is an open door.

Tom: Thank you. I will keep the door open!

Edgar Cayce: You are most welcome. I must step out of the body now, for Fletcher is calling. My name is Cayce. (Deep sighing . . . clearing of throat . . . coughing.)

Orion: Greetings, my name is Orion. We are present here with you today in order that we may add our time and our teaching to this publication. We wish for each person – who is reading our words – to know that you are beings of immense Light. We come to you today to remind you - that you are great spirit beings who remain eternal and immortal, even while passing through your Earth experience.

You are not some mere passing conglomeration of material reality. That is only your cloak of flesh for your current human incarnation. Your real self has existed in lifetime after lifetime –

in countless lifetimes. More times than you can count, you have existed. And you will continue to exist far beyond this present body.

Many of you who are reading this have felt that – perhaps – you are at the end of your Earthly incarnations. For those of you who are receiving these words – we want you know that many of you ARE – indeed - completing your incarnational patterns on Earth. Many of you have grasped so many great truths. You have learned the valuable lessons that the Earth plane offers. And remember, when we speak to you of your soul's journey, we are not limiting that to just this present lifetime, but many.

Some of you who are reading this may say, "I feel so uneducated and so limited." But, we want you to understand now, that you have already lived many MANY lives. The sense of limitation that you feel only comes from your extremely narrow minded human perspective. But, we see you on a greater scale and are aware of a far greater reality. When you let us lift the veil of forgetfulness, you will be as all knowing as we are. And you will see who you truly are. For many of you – this awakening will lead you to an awareness of all that you have already accomplished throughout all your past incarnations.

Those of you who are reading this book have been led here, as Fletcher has said. You have been drawn here to our words. It is not a coincidence. It is our power that has drawn you to this publication. It means that you have felt the Spirit World. We have given you the spirit for reading this book. You have heard our call, which means that you already have within you the vibrational frequency which allows you to be able to receive truth.

 We do bless you and send you our greetings. And we wish you to know – that whenever you feel that you have lost your way – you must simply call upon us – and we will set you back upon your course. Many humans upon the Earth forget that they are even ON a journey. It is very easy for humans upon the Earth to get mired in the material world and to forget their TRUE reality, to forget the true essence of their real spiritual being. That is why the spirit guides come, in order to assure you – to inspire you – to liberate you. That is why we are called spirit guides, because we help you traverse the challenges of the human dimension, from our higher dimensions, from our world of pure Spirit.

Tom: Sometimes this process of awakening feels so familiar – like we've done it all before. Why is that?

Orion: This is because many of you have past-life connections with Atlantis. You AND our medium were both temple priests in that ancient civilization. And so, this feeling of having gone through this kind of spiritual quest before will be very common – for many people on the Earth today are reincarnated from that time period. What you are doing today IS in fact, very similar to what you did back then. You may also find yourself feeling drawn towards working with crystals and studying paranormal truths. You may even find yourself seeking out mediums or channels to receive further messages. All of this is a sign of your soul's ongoing journey – and shows that you have crossed through many lifetimes. You are hungry for a conscious connection with our world once again, just as you were while you were living in Atlantis.

But also remember, in your world, throughout all history, there are always those who mock this reality, those who say that the Spirit World is only rubbish - those are the younger souls, when it comes to living upon Planet Earth. Many are only just now beginning their journey through the Earth plane, through this place the Bible called the "far country". You must have unconditional compassion on them. Even the "prodigal son" benefitted from his sojourn in the "far country", for it forced him to contemplate a return to the Father. So, do not judge these new souls who have just begun their lessons on Earth and say, "Why must people shun me and my spiritual interests? Why must they ignore the great spiritual truths?" But, look at these people with love – and think, "I am very fortunate that I have ALREADY crossed through so many lifetimes – that I do NOT feel a need to fight truth when it is presented. I can gratefully accept the free gift of truth however and whenever it is given."

You were once just like those who balk at the spiritual life. There were times when many of you laughed in the faces of divine beings just like Rose did. She has told you her story about her trips to India – and of how she mocked great priests and swamis and teachers around the world. Her mocking only served to push her further away from the vibration of truth and Light. It was her resistance to the Light that caused her – after her death during the Blitz - to spend sixty Earth years in a place of darkness that she describes as Purgatory. It was her own free choice denial of the Light that kept her FROM believing in – and entering the Light.

Remember therefore, that if you should ever find yourself in a temporary time or place of darkness – it is quite simple to escape from that condition. All you must do is remember to pray – and ask to be guided home. Call out for help and we will answer! All those souls that were wandering with Rose in the darkness could have been liberated at a moment's notice if they had only said – in all sincerity, "I want to go home. Please help me." You know, many of those in darkness actually received visitations from angels and yet, through stubbornness and pride, they turned those great beings away. They just couldn't believe they were worthy of assistance, or that there was another world made of pure Spirit, towards which they might ascend. A soul is never forced into the Light. A soul in only invited with love.

So invite with love all those you encounter, and allow them to BE. Allow them to come and be part of your reality. Some will come and agree with your reality and some will not. But in time, the seeds you have planted will manifest and all souls will return to the Light of spiritual beingness. Those of you who are reading this scripture are simply those who are the leaders in this awakening process. You are those who have already heard the call of Spirit from within your depths, and are leading the journey back to the Light. My name is Orion.

Tom: Thank you so much Orion.

Fletcher: There we go. The medium's vibration is growing a bit weak. Is there anything else that you'd like to ask?

Tom: Are we going to do more books? Will there be more transcriptions?

Fletcher: Our main interest is that our initial words and ideas be printed. If you are reviewing this scripture with Bob and you come across something that seems lacking - and you think our words haven't fully captured our message, we will come and clarify that for you. We will help you edit the final version of this, our very first book.

Tom: Since I won't be talking to you every week I was wondering - who IS my number one spirit guide? Which spirit will be my primary teacher from now on?

Fletcher: Actually, Mr. Berg I have moved into the position of being your primary spirit guide. For, if you are to accomplish all that you have set out to do, I am going to have to be closer to you and work with you. But, you also have around you the powerful vibration of the great Angel Raphael. He is working with you and helping you achieve your goals, which are OUR goals, as well. You need to recognize and remember him and the other high beings, who are with you, as you progress forward on this adventure you call your life on Earth. The Archangels also seek to help you awaken the young people of your planet, by liberating them from the old thought systems that are - even now - collapsing all around you. Therefore you and Bob will all be receiving much help from many MANY high beings as the Light becomes stronger and more powerful on the Earth by the day.

Tom: Thank you so much Fletcher. That is exciting. I will definitely be looking forward to working on more books with you in the future. I'm ready any time you are. Just let Bob know . . .

Fletcher: We will definitely be doing that. Know – that we are not done yet. Rose is back here and acting all excited too. She just won't settle down. She says, "I am ready to start our second book tonight". But, we are going to have to tell her that we will have to hold on a little bit.

You haven't heard the last of us – you can be sure of that. We will be looking over your shoulder while you're working on the last part – here. We will be with you, helping you edit - just as we are always helping our beloved medium, Bob. But, I DO think that's enough for now. Humans need time to digest what we've already given, and we don't wish to overwhelm anybody. We will be so glad to come and help you whenever we can! Just ask! This is Fletcher. (His voice fades away).

BOB HICKMAN POSTSCRIPT

What an amazing night this was. The guides all came out to visit. I remember awaking from my trance at the end of the evening – so amazed that a few hours of time had passed.

As I look over the words tonight, I am struck again at the amazing compassion of the guides. They are trying to impart to all of us words of wisdom. I think of how lucky I am to have Fletcher working with me. I wonder if he will always be my guide, or will eventually move on. I think of Arthur Ford and remember how Fletcher stayed with him until the end, and hope this is a pattern that will repeat.

Tom's questions of "attraction" and "manifestation" give me pause, and make me think about how I too need to participate in being part of the manifestation of success. I wonder if the law of attraction is what has drawn the star people here? Are they picking up humanity's vibration—and does that vibration sing out fear of being alone?

For me this night revolved around issues of being alone. Even though the guides are quite literally with me, I suppose I was feeling alone. It really is true that one can be in a crowd, and yet be all alone. I thought about the closure of this project, and as I said before, wondered if Tom and I would really meet up again. In hindsight—I now see that there is no way we could not be friends and keep up with one another, as the guides are the ones who brought us together in the first place! And according to the guides—we have more books coming! I am happy when I read this.

Fletcher, Rose, Orion, Edgar Cayce...They have all become such an important part of my life. I study their words and cannot yet believe that all this amazing information they impart comes through me. If only I were more aware...but I suppose that that is why they are able to bring the information—I step out of the way to let them through. Being a trance channel is certainly a fascinating life. I am drawn to think back over the last 10 years and how much channeled information I have been privileged to be a vehicle for. I wonder about my early clients...Where are they now? Are they still hearing Fletcher's voice within? I wonder about all the channelings I've done that were never recorded, and for which I never received validation. What came through in those sessions? Is someone, somewhere, still remembering the channeled teachings? How is their life different? Better? Worse? The same?

I suppose time will show the value of the guides' teachings. I know one thing, however, Tom and I both feel renewed, inspired, and uplifted by the words of guidance we have received from the Other Side. As I write these words I look to the night sky, watching the stars twinkle outside my window. The sparkle of the stars brings me back to contemplate Rose, and her experience of the materialized sapphire in India. I wonder if I will someday be able to do such a feat. If objects can be materialized—can they also be de-materialized? According to the Spiritualist history—there exist records of the spirits doing such things. I think about the great Yogis of India and wonder if they are still doing such feats today. What if I could de-materialize my own body? Where would I go? Could I travel to the Pleiades star system? Do the Pleiadians use this form of travel?

I re-read Orion's words – still trying to grasp just "who" this spirit is. His energy is so powerful that my body's nervous system strains to contain his energy. Yet—after a session where he comes through, I feel inspired, refreshed, invigorated. I wonder what Orion looks like. He is the only guide of mine who I have never directly seen. I have perceived him as brilliant Light, yet never directly encountered him in a bodily form. Perhaps at the higher levels we are pure consciousness—and maybe it takes the form of pure Light. It makes sense to me that it could be just like that. I wonder how a being is capable of overseeing the evolution of entire worlds. I question how this is done—yet cannot deny that Orion seems capable of such a feat. Fletcher has told us that we were all there "in the beginning," at the creation of the world. It makes sense to me now that if we have forgotten our "super-self" then of course we are capable of destroying the very world we've helped to create. We have lost our link to all that brought us here in the first place. I think about concepts of evolution and wonder if in the future, science will discover the spiritual component that is part of all life.

I look over and see a copy of "Uncle Tom's Classroom" sitting on my desk. As I pick it up I see Tom's picture on the cover and think about how amazing it is that we have met, become friends, and now co-workers of Light. I re-read the inspirational testimonies at the beginning of Tom's book and feel honored and fortunate to have found such a friend. A few years ago I read a quote somewhere that said basically that one should be careful when choosing a book to read—it said that reading a book was like taking your very life into your hands—for you never know how a book might just change your entire life. As I look at "Uncle Tom's Classroom"—I think this is one book that has truly changed so many lives, including mine.

The guides revealed in this chapter that their very essence, their vibration is contained in the words of this book. I am inspired to now re-read the entire book in one sitting – just for the pleasure of experiencing this high vibration. Of course, I realize that such a feat is a bit much for so late in the evening, but none the less—the very thought inspires me.

It's late now and I think it time to head off to bed, just before I turn off my computer, a call comes in from Tom.

"Hi, Bob—I was wondering if we might be able to have another session next week with the guides...I think there has been so much that has occurred in the last few weeks that we should maybe get their perspective. I feel that the alien issue is going to become more important in the New Year as Barrack Obama takes office, and I would like to hear some input from our friends in Spirit."

A smile crosses my face—"Yes"—I say to Tom, "It would be my pleasure." As I hang up the phone I am still smiling—I know our work is not done, nor will it ever be done. I head off to bed wondering "What is next?"—and knowing that our friends in the Spirit World will soon be taking us on new and fascinating adventures.

CHAPTER FOURTEEN
GOING FORWARD
February 11th, 2009

BOB HICKMAN PREVIEW:

Over the last few months of 2008, so many changes started to unfold, Barrack Obama became President of the United States, and Tom and I became curious as to what this might mean for the future of individuals and the country moving forward. It seems that in America a new administration always means change. Sometimes that change can be good and sometimes it is not so good. In reviewing the previous channelings, Tom and I noticed that the Spirit Guides were revealing more and more about the connection between humans and the 'Star People'. We wondered if there was coming further advancement on this front with the openings of a new administration in Washington. Ironically—at this time, I had also started to receive many letters from the public about UFO phenomena. Many people wrote and told me that they felt as if they were "somehow connected" to alien beings. It seemed a fascinating combination of subject matter and timing. Tom called me and said that he had felt that the Spirit Guides were not done yet, and sensed that he needed more clarification on some areas of concern about the coming changes that kept popping up for him. We agreed that we felt that some guidance was necessary. As I sat down in my chair and dimmed the lights, I could already feel the presence of the Spirit People. What was revealed points to even greater truths to come. Below is a transcript of this session.

Bob: Hi Tom, I'm ready for our last session. How are you?

Tom: I'm great - and really excited. Thanks so much for agreeing to this last follow up session. There are so many questions now about Barack Obama's presidency and the economy and the possibility of more openness in Washington that I thought it would be a good idea to give the spirits a chance to comment on these events for our book, "When Worlds Unite".

Bob: I agree. But, I never know what they'll say about any given subject. I'll go under now and – let them speak for themselves. I have to turn the lights down, because I can't go into trance when my living room is so bright.

Tom: OK. I can't wait to hear what comes through. Let's go.

Bob: Give me just a second. (Breathing deeply as he enters into a deep trance).

Fletcher: Oh well – good evening. It's Fletcher here and it looks like we have a good night here to be chatting.

Tom: Hello Fletcher, welcome back. It's great to hear your voice again.

Fletcher: It is so good to be here. Just give us a moment while we stabilize the vibration around our medium. Alright, his vibration is stabilized.

I wanted to come in tonight to touch on some important issues for you. Oh, it's very very true – what you be saying here. You know, we've been watching the Earth. And, there are a lot a changes going on here. But, we are quite pleased, we might say, from our side, to be observing Mr. Barack Obama as president of your country. He's been a good leader so far. But, he is a bit young and a little wet behind the ears. We don't have too much fear for him however, because we see him as leading the country into greater and greater Light.

As you know, we look at world leaders from the sense of the vibration that they carry. Some leaders bring in vibrations such as darkness. Oh, we've seen a lot of them on the world scene. Remember how Rose told you about Hitler and all the darkness that he brought. There was Stalin as well, and now, that crazy man over in North Korea. So, the Earth has had a history of lots of leaders that brought in darkness.

But, we are watching Mr. Obama closely and we think that this president is going to be moving the country closer to the Light. It's not coincidental that he has become president at this time in your nation's history. For, the Earth is going through huge changes as you move closer and closer to the year 2012. I must be reminding you here, that – even though many people are yelling that it is the "end of the world" – we know that 2012 is

NOT the "end of the world". What is going to be happening is a massive rising in consciousness.

You know, there is going to be – at that time – an even more open display of – what you call "the aliens". We prefer that you call them your "Space Brethren". There seems to be a lot of concern right now – about "what IS the truth about the aliens"? Many people are already trying to get through to the president. And they want to say, "Oh Mr. President, we KNOW that we have been seeing the flying ships all over America and you must tell the country about it now."

And, we agree, the presence of the Space Brethren upon the Earth IS a great truth. There are many crafts from other worlds, and other dimensions flying around Earth every day and each night. In fact, there was a flying ship that appeared over Washington during the inaugural, and perhaps if you research this a bit, you might be seeing mention of it. There is evidence here -there is cause for us on OUR side to believe - that there will be advancement in this area of what you call - "full disclosure" - in due time. But we must add here, that your president has not yet been fully informed of all that has gone on before he took office. He has not yet had the full story revealed to him at the time of this transmission.

When one becomes a leader, like Mr. Obama – they have to deal with those manipulators behind the scenes who have the greater knowledge. And – we must say – that those people behind the scenes – are very slow to reveal their secrets to the one on Earth who holds the office of President of the United States. But, don't be doubting – or I should be saying, you can be assured that there are those at the highest levels who now want to release the information. And of course, there also those who have great fear of a world-wide panic that they believe could occur upon the Earth, should such information be released too quickly.

Right now, we see a bit of a delay, because there is much concern about the economic impact of such a release. With the economy in such a place of instability – well, there's going to be even more fear in those people who say, "This is NOT the time to put that kind of news out. The economic instability we've got and the problems with the stock market could even get even worse if we disclose too much, too soon."

Mr. Obama is slowly coming to the awareness of the greater truths. But, he has not yet met with all of those in the Pentagon who have all the knowledge. He has not yet been fully briefed by those people who know about the flying ships and the beings from other worlds who have already contacted us. But, be assured that he will slowly be opened to this reality, and he will soon come to understand it in all its fullness and implications. Just a moment while we adjust the vibration here.

Well – we believe that Mr. Obama will not be beginning his real knowledge about the beings from other worlds, until later in the spring. It'll be around the time of May when he will actually come into a much full knowledge and awareness of the reality of the American government's contact with those who have come from other worlds. There is no doubt that there are those in the American government who have direct contact with beings from many worlds, in fact they have had direct interaction with them, for many decades.

There are those on the Earth, who have been called "the reptilians". They have been in direct contact with the United States government for many years. There are also those from Zeta Reticuli. You know, they are the little Grey people who have been running around, conducting experiments on animals and humans. They too have been in contact with the American government for quite some time. And of course, there are also the Nordics, from the Pleiades.

At this time, there is an agreement in place that allows these Grey beings to conduct their experiments as long as they do not publically or openly display themselves. But, of course, as you know, there is an openness that has been starting to come to the Light. There has been a breach of contract that has started already on the part of the Greys. You see, the time IS coming when all humanity will need to share in the knowledge that they have – so that the Earth will not have to go into a cataclysmic state.

As 2012 approaches, there is going to be a great arising of a new wave of spiritual consciousness. But, you know, that means there is ALSO going to be, what we can call - the rising of an "anti-consciousness". This "anti-consciousness" will be projected out by those materialists upon the Earth who don't want to progress – those who want to continue to follow only selfish agendas – those who want to stop this growth of spiritual truth upon the Earth. They are the manipulators who have an agenda to control the human race and want to keep you locked into the old materialistic paradigm. And so, we must tell you - there WILL be a continuation of an age old war between the Light and the darkness. This war between "consciousness" and "anti-consciousness" will go on - as it has gone on in the past, is now going on - and will continue to go on for some time to come. This war between the Light and the dark is going on within each and every one of you, even as we speak.

Mr. Obama will find himself at the center of all this – and he will soon be asking himself the big questions and scratching his head. There will be many late nights, while sitting alone in the Oval Office, when he will soon be saying, "Why is it that we can't let the human race know about the presence of begins from other worlds and dimensions, when in fact - they are already very active upon Earth? Many people of the world already know this is happening." And yet, he will be pushed by two opposing sides. On one side, there will be generals with more open minds saying, "Mr. President, we believe that the American people are now ready for disclosure." While on anOther Side, there will be other generals, the ones who are more materialistic and of a lower consciousness, saying, "No, Mr. President, we cannot disclose this now. We just don't know if it will create a mass panic, or what it would do to the stock market. It cannot be allowed to happen."

Well, the truth is that many of the world governments – which have been in collision on this matter in the past – will soon be working together. If you've been watching the news, you may have noticed that the Pope has already issued a statement from the Vatican, saying, "It is not a sin, nor does it go against Catholic doctrine, to believe that God has created life on many other planets in many star systems." I wish I had heard that from my own Catholic priest, when I was a young man. Because, it might have kept me from going down the road I did. But, none-the-less, we must now look forward to the changes that are coming.

For, the Vatican to make such a statement public at this time is proof that there is a great deal of secret knowledge available about contact with beings from beyond the Earth. In fact, there are many governments like Iceland and some of the governments in South America which already have declared to their people, that they are openly pursuing a policy of openness and research in regards to the question of an alien presence on Earth.

The United States government will begin to join this cause, more openly in the coming year. It will NOT occur though, in the time frame that some proponents of "full disclosure" are requesting, because there are those forces yet – that are raising great fears about it possibly causing greater economic instability. Actually, the economy of the United States IS going to start to stabilize a little later in the year. And at that time, you will begin to notice a greater sense of positive energy going into this area. So, we encourage you to be patient with your President. We want you to know that the call for "full disclosure" in the spring is too soon. The timing is not right – not quite yet.

Rest assured, however – that the "powers that be" are allowing more and more evidence of the alien presence, to come to Light. And, this process will only increase. The United States government – you know – is kind of looking the other way now - as more alien craft are allowing themselves to be seen by greater and greater multitudes of people all around the planet. And there will be even greater displays coming later this year and beyond. As we get closer and closer to the latter half of 2009, we will start to see a vastly increased level of alien activity in the skies. This will cause many people – who never believed in alien UFO's before – to begin asking themselves about the meaning of what they are seeing in the sky. They will begin to say, "Could these unidentified objects be identified after all? Could they be of extraterrestrial origins? Perhaps the alien presence IS real, after all."

When they try to contact the Pentagon and ask the generals in the government, they will shake their heads and say, "Well, all we can admit publically, at this point, is that some of these crafts are classified as unidentified." And that IS the truth for many people in the government still – isn't it? For, they haven't yet fully identified where ALL the craft are coming from – and so

– they are not really lying when they define them as unidentified. This is how they rationalize, that they can openly talk about the subject – without creating any kind of security breach or scandal.

But, soon, you will see that even those who are most entrenched in secrecy will begin to narrow down what the word "UFO" really means. They will slowly begin speaking more specifically – and eventually their language will shift totally. Watch for this! For, as those in the White House read more and more of the top secret reports – and they begin to understand what is going on - they will start to say things such as, "The unidentified craft that are being reported to be flying in the air space above many countries in the world, are definitely NOT of American origin." Once you hear them say that the unidentified crafts are definitely NOT of American origin, you will know that the American government's "full disclosure" process - the openness that you seek - has finally begun.

When we speak about "full disclosure: – we must be telling you not to expect it for at least another year. There are many preparations that yet must be made. It will take a year for the new people in Washington to learn the full history of what has been happening, to read all the reports, to analyze what the information means, and then – to figure out how to best release the secret information to the media, so as to NOT send the economy into another tail spin. There is a great fear that this could have a negative impact on religious life and socio-economic life. That is the crux of the fear.

And yet, there ARE already those in the government of the United States who are well aware – that the aliens pose no threat to us anymore. They know this because they have come to understand - that if the aliens really wanted to take over the Earth, they could have done so already. They are that powerful! Any takeover by the aliens would be immediate and without any delay. Any war between them and us would be instantly lost by the human race. This fact is known already by many in the government, which adds to their fears of "full disclosure". To reveal the relative impotence that the world governments actually have – when compared to the great powers of the many species of beings who are here from other worlds – could cause shock and dismay around the world.

Do not doubt Sir, there have already been extensive negotiations between the alien races and the governments of Planet Earth. Those of our world have known about this for some time, because we have been monitoring these negotiations. We spirit guides take great interest in the evolution of our charges on Planet Earth. Give us just a moment. Somebody else is here.

Rose: Greetings, my name is Rose. It is so good to be here with you once again. Do you know – when I was upon the Earth, I saw one of those flying ships. One of my friends saw it with me, as well. We already suspected there was something beyond the Earth, even back in our day. But, since those were the war years, many people attributed the flying ships to Hitler, thinking they were drone ships coming from Germany. But, you know, if you saw them, as we did, with the bright glowing lights that radiated out from them, you would have no doubt – my dear – that those ships were NOT from our world. I have not yet been made privy to many things, but I HAVE been told by Fletcher and Orion that there are many exciting events about to unfold, regarding these ships. We will definitely see many dramatic changes over the next two to three years. It will all begin to speed up in the coming year.

You know, we used to always say, when I was upon the Earth, that our leaders come to us from God. We used to pray, "God save King George", and now we pray for the Queen. We would also pray for the Prime Minister and all those in authority, whoever they might be. And so, I join with all of you in praying for your new leader, Mr. Barack Obama, that he may find the answers he seeks. The people of the Earth are ready for more openness now, although there are still some who resist the vibrations of Light.

The consciousness of those individuals, who want an end to government secrecy, is being raised. I do not see the result of disclosure as causing people to run wild and screaming through the streets in panic. Humanity is at a point now – that were the truth to suddenly be revealed - some people would simply refuse believe it – while the majority would say, "We knew it all along, so why all the hullabaloo?"

Really, it's all about evolution. The Space Brethren - I like that term, for it really is the truth – our Space Brethren are simply US. It is true that humanity and the Space Brethren are all interconnected, one to the other. They are us – from another time and another place. And we are them. And it is time for our world's to come together. It is time, as we say, for the worlds to unite. And so you do have my support and my prayers, and I watch with you, as we await the great changes that are coming. I pray that I eventually will be admitted into the higher councils of Spirit and then I will learn much more about the evolutionary processes that are occurring upon the Earth at this time. I do what I can.

One must earn the right to the higher levels of Spirit, you see. There is no automatic entitlement. In the Spirit World there is no automatic granting of honors and titles. All positions here must be earned. We must work diligently and continually to earn higher and higher positions in the world of Spirit. In time, I pray that I too shall be admitted into the council. And then I shall have greater knowledge of those who guide Earth's evolution. My name is Rose….(voice fades away).

Tom: Thank you Rose. That was absolutely fascinating.

Fletcher: Give us just a moment. We are stabilizing our medium's vibration here. (Deep breathing.)

Orion: Greetings, my name is Orion. I have come to bring you great understanding of that which is about to come upon the Earth. There are many now upon the Earth who are waiting for a revelation of those who come from the other worlds. Rose has spoken truly when she said that "they are you and you are them". From our position in the world of Spirit, we understand the evolution of humanity, and it is true that it is interlinked with those of the other worlds.

The Pleiadians, the Essessani, those from Zeta Reticuli – all of them are interconnected, one with the other and also with the Earth. It will be those from Zeta Reticuli who will make the first appearance publically upon the Earth. This is beginning already. If you would just notice how often now their images are appearing on book covers and even in fun items for children. The faces of the Greys are appearing everywhere now, on lunch boxes and t-shirts and clothing items. And, it is really a release of knowledge about their presence upon the Earth that is being given to humanity. This is to slowly soften the panic that might ensue, if the image were not made familiar through this gradual process.

These entities from Zeta Reticuli, or as you call them "the Greys", are from a most advanced species. They come here though, for they have – in many senses – struggled with their genetic makeup. Over many years, they have evolved their heads and their minds, and this is why they appear to have such large skulls. For, within the forms of those large skulls is vast intelligence. But, they are limited in their choices, for their own worlds are experiencing climactic conditions that have endangered them. They have experimented with genetics to such an extent that they have even endangered themselves. One could say that the Greys are an example of a science that has been taken too far, in its quest for growth and intelligence and expansion.

Although they do have knowledge of Spirit, they have limited their bodies in order to grow their minds. This is not as we would wish it from our perspective in the world of Spirit. Their genetic engineering has caused an imbalance. It is this very imbalance that has drawn the Greys to the Earth. For, on the Earth they find renewed hope – in the DNA of the human species. The human genetic pool, which they are tapping into - can and IS revitalizing their race, which was on the verge of dying out.

When you see the small Greys, as they are termed, you need not fear, for they mean no harm. Because of their extreme intellect, they have been falsely characterized as unfeeling. Yet, they DO have a great, gentle wisdom and compassion. This is evident to many of those who have encountered the Greys face to face – and haven't fallen into abject fear. They could tell you that the Greys impart a message to each of them, and to humanity – that could be interpreted as a message of salvation.

The Earth as we know it – is in great upheaval, and so - the Greys could be seen AND WELCOMED as the saviors of the planet. This is because they are bringing the human race the very wisdom that will help your race to NOT follow the same path that they went down – and thus – you will be given the knowledge to save yourselves from their mistakes, at the exact time you need it most. It is through this cooperation between worlds, between the Greys and the humans of Planet Earth, that each planet will be saved. Your book's title "When Worlds Unite" is most appropriate, in this context.

Those who come from the Pleiades also bring the message of salvation. They are truly your brethren and many upon the Earth actually resemble them physically. They are the Nordic beings in appearance. They will appear publically - in time - as well - and they will be well received. But, it is with the Greys that many of you will first have open and public contact. After that step, waves of others shall come. We are guiding your leaders upon the Earth, to assure greater communication. People from the government of the United States, are at this time, meeting with leaders in Europe, to discuss these truths about contact. Mr. Obama will soon be shown more of these discussions – for he has not yet been made aware of all that has gone before, and IS going on already, in secret.

The fortunate thing at this time is that Mr. Obama's mind is open and his heart is FOR the people, as well. He truly wants to serve the people who have called him to this position of such great power. We do not meddle in the day to day politics of the Earth, but we do attempt to guide the higher truths into the minds of those who work in the world's governments. In one sense, you could say that we ARE governing your leaders, even though we do not infringe upon their free will. We only remind them of the higher truths - which they are free to either choose or reject.

We feel that in Mr. Obama, we have one who is most aligned to the Light. Fletcher has spoken the truth, when he told you that Mr. Obama will come to an openness and will eventually wish to reveal the truths about contact between worlds, to the American people. His struggles against those of the military command though – those who wish to hold back the truths are just now beginning and will continue. But, be assured that there ARE many in your government who are prepared to release the truth, so that they no longer have to bear the terrible burden of holding these secrets away from the public.

The world today is very different than it was at the time of the end of the last great world war. For, the Light of the human species has evolved. Many of those souls from that era have now reincarnated in order to see the completion of that which was started in their time. It is true that there are those who worked for your government who knew about the contact made with a saucer that was downed in Roswell, New Mexico, in 1947. Many people of that generation have returned to the Earth, in the hopes of seeing and helping the truth come to Light – the very truth that they saw themselves, when they were alive. And it these high-spirited, high-minded souls who will guide the opening of the records for all to see.

The timelines that the proponents of "full disclosure" seek are still a bit premature. As you move towards the latter part of the summer, the opening will begin within Obama's White House. "Full disclosure" will not unfold for at least another year, although it IS in the making. This time line is necessary, because there are still some forces that need to come into agreement on this matter. "Full disclosure" will not be an isolated act by the Americans. The action on the part of the American government will come in combination with participation of many other governments. In togetherness, they shall find the answer for HOW to proceed with this world-wide awakening. You must realize that this event WILL be a world-wide awakening, although America may seem to lead the way.

Solidarity must be established FIRST among the leaders of the world, because "full disclosure" will have a profound impact on global economic markets everywhere. In the material world, truth and Light often are at times - at odds with the forces of materialism. And it is the material balance that is slowing the process. Humanity is ready for the truth, and will receive it at the proper time. But, again, we must say, it is the fear of the materialists that holds back the process. There is no longer any need for the truth of contact to be concealed any longer, and we do agree that it needs to be released soon. It shall be released in the coming year! (Deep breathing.)

Fletcher: Oh hello there, this is Fletcher. We must stabilize the medium's vibration after a visit such as this from Orion. It takes a toll on his nervous system. What would you like to discuss tonight?

Tom: First of all, thank you so much for your guidance about moving back to San Francisco.

Fletcher: We are most interested in your evolution. And we feel that moving back to San Francisco is the next step in your journey of awakening. You are going to be having a lot of revelations in the coming year.

Tom: One thing I just realized today was that Orion was just reading my mind. I didn't even have to speak my questions and he would hear them anyway – and answer each one, almost as fast as it would pop into my mind.

Fletcher: Oh, you have to understand that Orion is an advanced guide, much greater than me – although I am a great guide myself. I have been moving up the ranks here, but Orion comes from a place that is outside of your time/space continuum. He has never incarnated on the Earth, although he IS a high master who is guiding humans from his very high vibration on the Other Side. He IS connected with humanity AND with the other worlds.

Tom: I have a question about you, Fletcher. Some of our first readers have asked me to ask you about your relationship with Arthur Ford and especially Reverend Moone and his "Moonies". Would you like to clarify what really happened, and possibly correct what is already circulating about you, on the internet? We would like to hear your version of what happened back then, first hand.

Fletcher: Well, first of all. There are a lot of half truths, out there. What happened, at that time, with my old medium Arthur Ford was that Mr. Ford was indeed in contact with Reverend Moone. If I might say, and be honest – I tried to warn Mr. Ford away from Reverend Moone - but he was most adamant that this man was supposed to guiding the world. Mr. Ford has attributed to me words - that in truth – were never mine and were never from me. I don't mind saying that I am much more pleased to be working with this medium, because he doesn't make my work so difficult to accomplish. He doesn't fight me like Mr. Ford did and he doesn't over drink.

Mr. Ford drank a great deal and would sometimes claim that I made statements that weren't necessarily what I was trying to put across. You see, when a medium is not fully compliant, he can actually block the channeling and get himself in the way. I tried to warn him. I used to say, "Mr. Ford, you've got to stop drinking so much. It's interfering with our vibration."

We are not able to take control of the medium's consciousness, when someone is drinking as much as Mr. Ford did. What happened was that there was more of him and his own thinking – in some of those readings – even though he said that it was me. He was actually hearing himself – not me - when he made some of those more outrageous comments. His hard drinking did not allow me to come through as clearly as I wanted.

You've got to understand where I'm coming from. I certainly loved Mr. Ford and he tried his best to serve the world. But, he was a human with many flaws. And I have to tell you – I think I earned my wings working with him all those years.

Tom: That is really interesting. Have you seen Mr. Ford in the Spirit World? Do you converse now?

Fletcher: Well, we have an occasional meeting, but I've got to be honest with you. We don't have too much communication at this point, because of Mr. Ford's limited spiritual growth. He was still drinking heavily – up to when he crossed over – which greatly influenced WHERE he ended up vibrationally – IN the Spirit World. What I am trying to say is that we are not at the same level.

Tom: I'm also interested in your relationship – if any – with Houdini. Or, have people on the internet just made that up about you, as well?

Fletcher: We did make the contact for Mr. Houdini, but there was a problem. Arthur Ford wasn't in the clearest state of mind when we did the channeling – and so the information I brought over became a bit muddled when it was repeated. Mr. Ford didn't fully listen to what I was bringing over – for if he had – there would have been greater truths revealed that could not have been disputed. There are many who like to say that Arthur Ford was a fraudulent medium – but it's not true. He had his weaknesses as a human – but he DID receive messages from our world – which he attempted to share.

As for Mr. Houdini, well, we admire his quest for truth – for he was always trying to find the "truth" about Spiritualists and Spiritualism. Unfortunately for some people, he went about his quest in a negative way. He used to attack some mediums who were actually quite legitimate. Some of them were frauds and deserved exposure – but there were many authentic mediums that he injured in his quest for knowledge and truth. He should have allowed the spirits to work a little closer with him – instead of putting up a block to them. He was so sure - and so eager - to prove that the mediums' contacts with the spiritual world were NOT real – that he tried very much to destroy the truth – even when it was in front of him. Houdini discredited a well known medium at that time, named Miss Marjorie. But – we want to tell you that Mr. Marjorie did channel, and she WAS a valid medium. She truly did channel.

Tom: Fascinating. What about Sir Arthur Conan Doyle, the author of Sherlock Holmes? I've read that he did a great deal of research on this subject – in order to help spirituality and metaphysics come to the fore. What can you tell our readers about Sir Arthur Conan Doyle?

Fletcher: Oh well, I don't think you could find a person with a bigger heart and a greater openness to our world than Sir Arthur. He and his beloved wife were truly blessings. Unfortunately, the problem with Sir Arthur – was that sometimes – he was TOO open and – he allowed himself to be taken advantage of by unscrupulous people. He was much TOO trusting of some people who were actually lying to him and were giving him fraudulent information about so-called spiritual matters. We think he would have done better if he had been a little more discerning and a little more testing of the information that he was being given. It was his own unquestioning trust in some of that false information he received that got him into trouble at times. It even led him to be labeled as – well you know – as a bit of kook in his day – because he believed things – and talked about things - that were later to be easily disproven. Having been a little more discerning – he would have learned how to better discern actual spiritual reality – and therefore would have had much more credibility. Oh, but we say, "God bless him for all the work he did."

Tom: Thank you so much Fletcher. This has been extremely helpful.

So, let me get this straight. You are now at a level in Heaven, in the Spirit World, where you do not necessarily rub elbows with other souls who are NOT at the same level as you. Is that what you are saying?

Fletcher: Yes, that is true. Over here there are layers upon layers upon layers of what you would call reality. They are like spheres or worlds, in fact. That's how we see them, like spheres or layers of reality. The higher you are – the more you can be available to other levels that are lower than yours. But, the lower level souls can't go higher than their own level of awakening and spiritual evolution. The higher spirits can go lower, but the lower spirits can't go higher.

Here is an example. Orion is vibrating at a higher sphere than me. He comes down to talk to me, but I can't easily pass up there – where he is – to be with him and talk to him up there. He has to come down to my level for us to converse together. There is a kind of barrier between our levels, a barrier made out of vibration. Think of the middle C on your piano. That middle C can't go up to be with a higher C because its vibration is different, it is lower. They CAN harmonize, and communicate - but they can't ever be in the same vibration. That is because the lower C vibrates at a lower vibration, and the higher C vibrates at a higher vibration.

As Rose was telling you, people have to earn their way up to the higher levels – even over here. We each have to try our best. Evolution of the soul doesn't stop when one leaves the Earth. Oh no. It continues over here in the Spirit World. Some people choose to stay here and grow – and some choose to go back to the Earth. It takes a higher and more advanced soul to make a new incarnation on Earth, because reincarnation is a big task to accomplish. The Earth is a place of negativity still, and so all souls are cautioned before re-entering the Earth's vibratory level. They are told quite clearly, "If you go down to that level of Earth's vibration, you might lose your way. Be prepared for that, because if you DO lose your way, you may find yourself in a place of darkness." This is always a concern.

But, in terms of your question, sir, there ARE souls that I don't like to mix with even here. I don't particularly like to go down to the darker regions, which are the lower vibratory levels, in the astral plane, which Rose has described as a kind of Purgatory. Think about it like this. Would you like to go hang out in the Panhandle District of San Francisco? You know - that part of the City where many of the people on heroine are living. It's not a comfortable environment for you – now is it? That's because it doesn't resonate with YOUR vibration, and can even feel abrasive and harsh.

Oh, of course, you may choose to go into the parts of your City where people are vibrating at lower levels of consciousness, but it's usually just to do acts of mercy, not to spend long periods of time. Sometimes you may want to offer help to the homeless and those who are lost temporarily in the dark, negative thought vibrations of self-hatred and suffering, but you wouldn't want to live there full time, if you could help it. The strong but false belief that life and God are cruel is what traps so many of those people, and that vibration of self-inflicted suffering is just too unpleasant for you to bear for very long.

Tom: I agree. I can feel it out there sometimes, and it goes against my own life experience. I have learned that God is always ready to help us and awaken us, as soon as we ask for help. The night that the flood waters froze one inch from coming into our house, proved to me – beyond a shadow of any doubt – that God is loving and caring and benevolent. But, many of those street people have simply given up on life and therefore – on God. They see themselves as abandoned and cut off from the God Force completely.

Fletcher: It's the same over here, you see. There are those who cannot believe that the Spirit World is real – so they sleep and sleep in a kind of darkness, even after they have crossed over from their Earthly lives. And, we've got some souls over here who don't know they've died. They still believe they are heroin addicts and alcoholics, and they keep trying to satisfy their addictions. It is a fruitless and miserable pursuit however, which they eventually DO realize. This is why we advise people to try and conquer their addictions while still on the Earth. If you die while still believing you are addicted to some material substance, and you cross over believing that you still NEED that particular material substance, you will find yourself in a difficult situation, because we have no material substances over that can satisfy that craving.

That is where the spiritual world comes in. Our work is to try and help wean people off their addictive attachments to any kind of material forms. People sometimes get so lost in their identification with material forms, structures and patterns of behavior while on Earth - that they actually think that they ARE their bodies and the roles they play in the dramas of daily life. They become completely lost in their material world. Our work – therefore - is to slowly but surely help people to stop identifying so strongly with a sense of "self" that is ONLY material and physical, and to assist them in waking up to the spiritual realms as well. We are working to help people realize that their true identity is Spirit, not form.

So, in terms of "where do I live?" I live in the vibratory rooms where I feel the most comfortable. Arthur Ford hasn't reached the spiritual spheres or vibratory levels where I live. He still has some growth to do because he didn't quite kick his habit before crossing over. I tried to warn him. He DID make it a bit challenging for me while I worked with him.

Tom: Do you have relationships up there in your world with the aliens and extraterrestrials who have crossed over from THEIR worlds into yours? Do souls all look the same over there or do they look different than human souls?

Fletcher: Every soul that comes to the Spirit World inhabits its own plane of vibration. The so-called aliens have their own plane of vibration over here – where they can feel most at home. I have seen entities that have come from other dimensions completely. But I have to say that I don't really know them that well, because I work mostly with the human realm. I do have access to them however, and can visit them if there is a reason. But even in their realm there are different levels, for they too have their own evolutionary paths.

Tom: Are you saying that there are "countries" in the Spirit World, separate areas where different species and different races "hang out" mostly with their own kind – where they can be together.

Fletcher: Yes, that's right but - it's not "hard and fast" like segregation, mind you. It's just that souls that are alike tend to be drawn together. Do you have any more questions, Sir?

Tom: Let's talk about the future of these two books - "When World's Unite" and my first, "Uncle Tom's Classroom" (UTC). Elizabeth, a good friend of Shirley MacLaine's, just returned from Obama's Inaugural and has urged me to send UTC to people in government, ASAP. She said they are looking for new ideas for educational reform - and that she sees me - as the voice of the children. She wrote me an email in which she said, "Nobody tells the story better than you," which really inspired me to follow up on her suggestions. She wants me to mail my book to influential people in Washington, soon. What is your guidance on this subject?

Fletcher: Completing this new book, "When Worlds Unite", with Mr. Hickman, will be most helpful at this time. Working with him is the very best thing you could do right now. As for "Uncle Tom's Classroom", I would think about sending it only to the Democrats. We put you into this time and place – not by chance – but for a reason. Focus on the people in the Democratic Party because they will be the most receptive to your ideas. The Republicans – oh I'm sure they will be alright – but they don't quite understand how stuck they are in their old mindset. Some of them are still bitter about the election. But, the Democratic Party is feeling more jubilant now – so if you target your mailings to those in that party, you will have success.

I would also seek help from your friends, particularly Ms. Elizabeth and Ms. MacLaine for specific names to contact, because they know people who are influential and powerful. They are closer to people with influence, and can see better who may be more receptive to your ideas. I would also be including Hillary Clinton. Oh, I know that she is now the Secretary of State, but she has always had a great interest in educational reform – and I believe that UTC would be well received by her. You talk highly of the Clinton years in your book, and show clearly how education thrived under her husband's presidency. She would show it to others. And you also want to be reaching out to Nancy Pelosi, for she is a good soul who is most interested in the average common man. And she has a great interest in the local effects of what government is doing. Your plans for education would be well received by her.

Tom: So, why has it taken me so long to get UTC off the ground?

Fletcher: There has been a shift in the Earth's vibration. What you've got to understand is - there are many things that are occurring around you - that have shifted the focus of the energy there. Had you achieved great success too early – and began to focus too much on book sales in local markets – you might not have been open to these suggestions about focusing on the federal level. So we kind of held things off here, for you – so the energy could prepare a way. We have been arranging to have people in place, who WILL move your book into higher levels. Remember Mr. Berg, we are not so much interested in your personal economy - as we are that your message reach the highest level that it can, in the right way, and at the right time!

You are here primarily for spiritual work. Not that there's anything wrong with making good money. But, it might have caused you to get sidetracked, to be thinking, "Oh look at how many books I'm selling here and there." You might not have been so open and ready for this new guidance about focusing on Washington, and the positive political impact UTC will have at this time. We are keeping you completely open now, so that you have total flexibility to take your book anywhere that you are guided. We see it as MOST important that you do not fall under the control of any manager or agent who might try to take your freedom away from you. You would not have liked having someone manage you or tell you what to do with your time.

Tom: So, this whole adventure with my book just keeps evolving and changing by the day? Is that what you are saying?

Fletcher: Oh, yes. It does. But, understand that the evolution is for a higher good. Both UTC and "When Worlds Unite" are for the higher good of humanity. It is not so much about your personal benefit any more. This unfolding, ever changing process is so that the world may receive the truth that you capture so well in your writing. And we WILL do whatever is necessary to ensure that occurs.

Tom: Do you and your other spirit companions, who work as guides, actually have the ability to whisper (for example) in Nancy Pelosi's ear and Hillary Clinton's ear – so when I try to contact them about my book – they will be MORE receptive? Do you have some real influence in opening them up?

Fletcher: Oh yes. This is how we work, you see. We speak to THEIR guides and sometimes we speak to them directly. There is a chain over here that we have to follow. But, the fact is – that I HAVE been assured by Orion and other higher sources that this IS a direction for you now to go. You are doing right and the timing is right. If you had tied yourself up with another publisher or agent, they would have taken control of your expression – which would have limited your access.

We ALSO think it would be a very good avenue for you and Bob to publish the new book, "When World's Unite" on your own, because it's important that you get the message out there. In time, it will be picked up by another publisher. We had hoped that we had found the publisher – a man who Bob was working with, and who showed interest – but he is not following the higher path at this time. The man's a bit distracted and more worldly than we had expected him to be. So, we don't see an opening there and we ARE disappointed. We have been telling Bob this but he didn't want to hear it. But, now he's coming to understand it, you see. If you were to publish "When World's Unite" on your own, you would have it out there for many people to see. And it would become known.

You know, Bob's name is getting quite well known in high circles all over the world. We are trying to make him more and more visible. As we have said before, his name will help carry the book. We'd like him so stay free, as well – and not get locked into publisher's schedules - which is why we suggest self-publishing at this time. This path will give you both the freedom that you need to get the book out there in a way that will allow you of each to continue to do as you want. In time, you will be received by other publishers.

We'd like to add here also - that Ms. MacLaine will be coming back into your life once again. You are not gone completely from her circle of influence. You must continue delivering these messages to her. When she hears us through these transcripts, she will recognize our voices, because we have been speaking to her directly, already.

Tom: Absolutely. Thank you. This has been very very helpful. So, do you have any more advice for us tonight?

Fletcher: Oh yes. We'd like to give you encouragement and to let you know that we are so pleased for all the work that you have been doing. We predict that this new book is going to be seen by a lot of people. Don't worry – that you may not instantly see it being carried about in a public arena by famous people. Just know that it's at home on their coffee table and being read at night. The outward appearance doesn't always manifest the truth. And so, know that our words will be read at high levels, and that there will be many people who will gain important knowledge. You can be assured that this has NOT been a waste of time for either of you. And we dare to say, that you've gotten a lot out of it yourself with the relationship that has developed between us. Please know how much Rose loves talking with you as well.

Tom: This experience really HAS changed my life for the better. And I feel a lot more self-confidence than I had before I met you all.

Fletcher: Well, you see – that's our work. We come into the Earth's vibration to bring up the consciousness. Oh, you have it within you all the time, but we had to open the little door that was blocked. That was our goal and IS our goal, still. Now, you see how good you feel - because you have been able to work with us. And, might we say – not ONLY have we been helping you - but you have been helping us, as well. If we can get more humans to do the same, then the world will become a little brighter each day. And THAT is our goal. When you help us by putting out your books, you are opening minds to our voices. And many people's spiritual journeys will get started once again.

Do you know, Ms. MacLaine – when she wrote that book named "Out on a Limb" – she took a big chance – now didn't she? But, I think that if you were to ask her, she would tell you that she was directed from OUR world to release that book. It wasn't just some marketing thing – oh no - it was part of her calling and her journey. And, as she found her way, through daring to go out on that limb – she had great joy in return. She helped many lives find spiritual truths. Many of those who were trapped in the darkness of atheism, no longer find themselves there. It was because of her book that they now find their minds open to the Light of our world.

Your book, "Uncle Tom's Classroom" and this new one, "When Worlds Unite" will do the same kind of valuable work as Ms. MacLaine did with "Out on a Limb". You and Bob should be pleased with yourselves for you have both answered the call. We - in our world - aren't so interested in controlling you or taking you over, or making you be slaves. Oh no – that's NOT what this is about. We only bring you our Light, in the hope that you might be receiving a little bit – and in turn – pass it on.

It's like in a church. You know, when I was a young lad, we used to have these candlelight prayer vigils in our church. The priest would begin the ceremony by lighting one candle – the first candle. And then he would pass his candle on to a person in the congregation who would Light their own candle, and who would then pass it on to the next person. One by one, each participant would Light their own candle, until the whole church was ablaze with candlelight. It was quite beautiful as the entire church became illuminated – all from a single flame. And I used to always say, who would have thought that one little lone Light could have so much power and influence. And yet, it's there for all to see.

We want you to know that each of your books is like that candle that was passed around my church. As they are published and sent out into the world - and passed around from one person to another – the flame and the Light are being expanded. You are doing the same work that Ms. MacLaine does - and therefore, the Light of Spirit just keeps growing on Planet Earth.

Tom: Thank you Fletcher. Now, I have a question that fascinates many people like Shirley MacLaine that about 2012 and the changes that are coming. What can you tell us about the role our galaxy is playing in what is going here on Earth? Is the Milky Way galaxy an actual living being like the Mayans believed? And - is the sun also a living being?

Fletcher: Yes, they are living beings – but not in the way that you understand living beings. They are consciousness – they are the very same consciousness that exists in every material item. The sun has a consciousness. The Earth has a consciousness. The stars have a consciousness, and yes – even the galaxy has a consciousness. But remember, even the floor upon which your chair rests at this very moment has a consciousness. The chair that you sit on has a consciousness. The books that you hold have a consciousness.

So, it is true – as you have been told - that the vibration of this consciousness is rising. And because the vibration of this consciousness is increasing, humanity's vibration gets to increase as well. The difference for humanity however - is that it has a lot of low level ignorance to overcome – ignorance that is a lower vibration than what is coming in. So, much of humanity chooses to fight the higher vibration, rather than let it in. This causes hard times on this planet – as people actually resist the raising of consciousness. The Earth is one of the places in the universe that is still somewhat dark. We are not talking about darkness, in terms of sunlight. We are talking about spiritual, mental and emotional darkness. There are still many people upon the Earth who are resisting the Light that is coming in with the new, higher vibration of consciousness. This is why many of the alien beings are so concerned about Earth at this time, because they see that the holding onto darkness could lead to great destruction. Were the people of the Earth to refuse to allow consciousness to be raised, this could cause worldwide destruction, which would have an adverse great effect upon the entire galaxy.

A world cannot be destroyed without other worlds being affected. And so, the extraterrestrials and spirit beings come to help raise the consciousness of the people of the Earth while there is still time. We know that the Light of Spirit will win and that the universe – as it gets closer to 2012 – will grow in Spiritual Light and higher consciousness. This period of growth may seem a bit cataclysmic at times – as we've said before – with some earthquakes and imbalances on the Earth – but these are only the growing pains that are pushing your planet towards an awakening. And it is this awakening of a higher consciousness, which the human race will participate in. 2012 is not the end. It's only the beginning.

Tom: That makes me wonder about your earlier predictions for our economy. How can capitalism improve by the end of this year – as you have said it would – if it holds onto its dark vibration of greed, its hyper materialism and the totally unfair way that workers are now being paid? There is still so much inequality between the very rich and the very poor. It doesn't seem at all fair that a CEO of a large bank could make a hundred times more than a teacher educating inner city kids. How can this be resolved?

Fletcher: Well, you see, that's a very good question. There are changes already happening within the power structures all over the globe. As a greater amount of liberalism takes control there will be a greater awareness upon the Earth – an awareness of humanity's changing needs. The new President of the United States is already starting to restore some balance, as he works to bring health care to the poor of the Earth. And this will succeed. If people's basic needs are met, there won't be such concern about greed, now will there?

Greed and capitalism feed off of each other because they create a false illusion – that there are not enough resources on the Earth to supply everyone. But, the truth is – there is enough food and enough money and enough supply for every person to be fed and clothed and housed. It is an illusion of capitalism that says that some people get supplied and some don't get supplied. But, with the changes coming to your nation, there WILL be a greater distribution of the wealth and you will see an awareness grow that will open up more and more to the idea of sharing. Be watching at the local level. There will a greater kindness, neighbor to neighbor. The idea of sharing will grow and grow - first on the local level and then it will expand.

Capitalism – in and of itself – is only a system of exchange. We don't see the system disappearing from the Earth at this time – but we do see it being sensitized – which will begin at the local level and grow upwards. And, the idea of sharing will also be starting at the top and moving downwards, as well. Then, we think – these two waves of change will meet somewhere in the middle. The problem was that – for the last several years – there was little or no activity at the top – to try and help those at the bottom. But, that's changing. And the bottom people will start to thrive again and live!

Tom: My concern is that people like teachers are paid so much less than the big corporate executives. How are we ever going to get our system to pay people fairly for what they are really worth? What could be more valuable than a teacher's contribution to our society - and yet, teachers make so much less than the top CEO's of the major companies? It doesn't seem right that some CEO's receive million dollar golden parachute when they retire - and teachers receive so much less, when they retire.

Fletcher: Well, sir – your question is actually based on fear. There is a focus on fear that you are going to lose what you've got – at the hands of those you see as having more power and money than you. But, we assure you, that the changes that are coming upon the Earth ARE going to lead to a greater equality. The system has been in place since the beginning of your recorded history. And, we don't see it changing too rapidly. But, what IS changing already is the consciousness of those who are in positions of great power. The ruthlessness that you have seen is going to start to disappear – as a greater awakening comes upon the Earth.

The world that is coming will be very different than what you have known. And dare we say, once the alien presence is more openly known there will be greater unity. People will not feel the need to fight so much anymore. The world will become more united in the coming years. And so, you must set aside your fear and trust the process that is unfolding. And seek and trust our guidance always.

Tom: I really hear you. I have to admit that we teachers did often have a lot of fear - which was why we so often gave our power away to those in authority over us. That's one of the reasons I wrote, "Uncle Tom's Classroom". So, what would you say – representing the Voices of Heaven – about making people's pay equal to their real value? Do you know what I'm saying?

Fletcher: Yes, we do, but you've got to understand that the human population will not do this until they fully evolve. And this equality will not occur overnight. Remember what I told you – that 2012 is only the beginning. As humanity evolves, changes will come. But, evolution is a slow process. If people want to see the equality you talk about - coming into their lives - they must each become agents of change. And that means that the executives have to be willing to share the wealth. There WILL be those put in power who will come to this awareness. And teachers will eventually receive the benefit of that shared wealth.

We don't wish to see wealth destroyed upon the Earth, for it is a function that serves many. It is part of the growth of the soul. If there was no quest for wealth on any level – there would be no ambition. And ambition is of the soul which teaches balance. Remember - if we were to eliminate ALL negativity there would be no point in coming to the Earth. The Earth is a place of growth that has negativity inbuilt, in order that you might have a place to test your spirit. It exists so that you can come to understand that you have incarnated here to test your spirit. Do not lose faith, or your love of life - for when you return to the Spirit World, you WILL find the peace that you may have missed while on the Earth.

Tom: I hear you. Orion said that the Greys are here because we DO represent hope for them. What would you say is Orion's meaning when he says that we represent hope?

Fletcher: Well, I believe that what the Earthlings represent is the will of the Spirit. It is only in the human race that you see the concept or idea of always being able to start over again. And this is something that the Greys don't really have – and therefore want. Their emotions are kind of flat. And so – to grow their own spirits, they have to take on passion. Humanity has that passion.

Do you remember when there was that tragedy down in New Orleans – and we saw all the flooding? People suddenly came together to save one another. People who might not have even liked each other before the flood suddenly came together to help each other. And then they all vowed to rebuild their lives. That's real passion. Other people, of other worlds other than the Earth - might have been tempted to just lie down and die – and go back to the Spirit World. But, not humans - for humans fight on even when there is little hope and they seem to be fighting against all odds. They never give up. This is a lesson about soul growth. And in that area – the people of the Earth have made great progress and are very advanced. In other worlds the beings there seek to learn from the many human examples of spiritual strength.

Tom: Can you tell me a bit more about what you mean by ambition?

Fletcher: Oh yes. Ambition is necessary. It was your own ambition that brought you here to the Earth. For you knew, while still in the Spirit World – that you were lacking in some areas. And you were ambitious to grow. All of you have this innate ambition or quest for the growth of the soul. And then, there is the more worldly ambition – which is the quest for the growth and comfort of the body. The word ambition can be applied in many different ways.

People actually incarnated upon the Earth to advance their souls, but once they got here, many forget that they came with this strong healthy ambition for growth of the soul. And then – having forgotten their real ambition - they end up seeking only comfort of the body. You see, if the ambition for comfort of the body becomes the ONLY ambition – it often leads to terrible things like theft and robbery – and the destruction of other lives. Ambition is not bad in and of itself – provided it is primarily focused upon the spirit rather than on the body.

Tom: I hear you. I decided to move here to Hawaii because I wanted to be in a climate that was more comfortable to the body than the cooler Bay Area. But – the comfort hasn't made me happier than when I lived in San Francisco.

Fletcher: But you see – the thing is – the soul must also be nurtured. One can provide the body with all the comforts of the world, and yet – the soul can still feel totally empty. We see this happening a lot these days. Many people on the Earth today – who are the most powerful and most wealthy - have everything that the Earth can offer – and yet their souls feel desolate. They have no Light in them. Rose was one who had such an experience. Perhaps she can address this a bit. Give us just a moment.

Rose: Greetings, my name is Rose. I could not help but poke Fletcher on the shoulder, so I could have my say in this matter. I would agree with his definition of ambition as the power that motivates the soul to seek more and more avenues for growth. I was one – as he said – who had everything. I had all the material comforts. I was born into a titled family. We lived in grand mansions and country estates. I traveled the world. I had clothes worth millions of dollars and diamonds worth even more. I had beautiful automobiles, Rolls Royces, and a staff to wait on my every need. But yet, I had nothing within me. The emptiness in my soul was a terrible reality that I had to deal with.

I would go to church and talk to the vicar. But I felt no consolation there because I refused to open my mind and spirit – and become humble enough – to allow God's Light to penetrate my soul. Because I did not do that – I was left desperate. So, remember – when ambition only focuses on the physical comforts and competitive triumphs of the body – this narrow mindedness leads to most of the troubles on the Earth. If those very people - who obsessed ONLY about physical appearances and conditions - would turn their ambition back towards their original intent for soul growth – they would see the great gifts of the Spirit. And they would experience the great joy that come with those spiritual gifts, even while living their human lives.

Tom: Can you remind me again – what ARE the gifts of the Spirit?

Rose: The bible speaks of these spiritual gifts as love, patience, kindness, tolerance, self-control and above all – charity. These are the gifts of the Spirit - and experiencing these gifts while on Earth in physical form – was what humankind was originally created for. That is why you came to the Earth and became human - to test the resolve of your souls to live in and access the principles of Light and love. Yet, sadly - many people have forgotten and abandoned the purpose of their original quest. This is why you see so much sorrow upon the Earth today.

Tom: Did you choose to be born into nobility and great wealth in order to learn this lesson?

Rose: Yes I did. I was warned you see. My council warned me. They said, "Rose, you are setting yourself up for a great danger of losing your soul and any awareness of Spirit. You have chosen one of the most difficult of paths in this incarnation – for the world of the wealthy upper class can be a great challenge to the spirit."

I suppose you could say that I was kind of a young soul and still am in many ways. You see, I would not heed the advice of the council. Our spirit guides would never interfere with our free will, unless we were about to cause a grave error that would result in total destruction for the Earth. Our spirit guides will not stop our incarnational choices. They will never force us to do anything. But they will warn us – and I WAS warned. I did not heed their warning. So, it is true that when I came to the world – I got lost during my stay.

Tom: But, you WERE found and you DID receive help when you needed it, and you WERE saved by the Light - so it seems to me that your story turned out for the best. And now you are helping us. By the way - is Queen Elizabeth experiencing the same kind of challenges that you experienced when you were part of the nobility?

Rose: Oh yes, but I must say - Queen Elizabeth is much closer to God and much more spiritually inclined than I was in my last incarnation. Do you know – she prays every day. She is very spiritual. She is an example of one who has overcome the challenges of high position and great wealth for she truly has a real relationship with God. She has a powerful faith that illuminates her soul. She does have the challenge however – of being surrounded by many who are quite immersed in the material world. And she HAS had her own spiritual challenges – which I cannot talk about. But, unlike me – she has never EVER forgotten God.

Tom: My friends and I have figured out that you must have been part of the royal family and that the reason you are calling yourself Rose is to protect them – is that right?

Rose: Rose is a name that I have given you – a name that you can know me by as we interact. But, it is true – I had a different name but I cannot reveal it at this time. You must understand that many people who alive on the Earth right now would be affected were that name to be revealed.

Tom: Do you have any more advice for me?

Rose: As one who has traveled greatly and been in very high-profile positions, I feel most qualified to advise you. Always be polite – you see. Even when people are rude – you must not react rudely to them in return. I am not saying that you are rude, my dear. I am just warning you because there will be people who will treat you rudely - in a condescending way. But, I want you to keep smiling, nonetheless. We don't want you to be fearful or paranoid, but be mindful of your public image. For you will be in a much more high profile position. You must keep promoting you book, as well. You are most talented, having helped write, produce and direct two films. And now you are helping us author this new book, "When Worlds Unite". So, remember, you are multi-talented. All of your skills are most impressive and must be shown to their fullest potential. You must shine like the star that you are!

In the next year you can also look forward to a relationship that will be stable, committed and loving. We don't wish to give you any more information about your future at this time, my dear. Just let it unfold and remember that we will be with you – helping you all along the way. We will be showing you great things as your future unfolds.

Tom: I so appreciate our friendship Rose.

Rose: I too am so very grateful because I so enjoy working with you. I am so thankful that you dare to hear my voice and allow me to come to you like this. Our medium is most gracious to allow us to use his organism in this way. We are so thankful for him. And every day - I am continually looking out for him and for you.

And please give your dear friend Barbara a message from Edgar Cayce. I have a received a message from him about the work they did on her body. He says that he is most joyful about her healing and he wants her to know that he will be with her in the coming years. He will come to her and bring her more help as she needs it in the coming years. Fletcher says I must step out now – because our medium's vibration is becoming weak.

Tom: I know. It's getting late.

Rose: Let us step from his body. Yes Fletcher – I am moving out. My dear, I send you my blessing. I will be in touch with you and we will speak again, soon. Oh, if I may say one parting word before I go. Fletcher has told me quite clearly that there WILL be more books for you and our medium to work on together. So be assured – you have not heard the last of me! My blessing to you, my dear . . . (her voice fades off.)

Tom: That's wonderful news. Thank you Rose – I love you!

Fletcher: There we go. We're in the body. OK here. Well, our medium's vibration is getting a bit weak now and we don't want to tax his system. So we will be stepping out of the body now. We have so enjoyed visiting with you here tonight and we hope that we have been answering all your questions.

Tom: Would you like to add a special good-bye to our readers? This session is going to be the last chapter of our book.

Fletcher: Well, we just want to say to all of those who are reading this book, "All about you are many guides and angels. We are not far away. We are only a whisper away. When you think of Heaven, don't think of it as far away, beyond the stars. We are as close as the very air around you. We surely are. If you want to be in Heaven, you've got to start by making your mind heavenly. That means raising your mind to higher thoughts. Don't give in to despair, even in the darkness."

"Always remember to reach out – for there are many helping hands – reaching towards you as well - from our world. We love all of you and we would never leave you. Remember what Jesus said – 'I will never leave you nor forsake you'. He really meant those words. If you were to call on your Higher Power – whether you call it Jesus or Buddha or Allah – please know that God's Vibration and Light are with you at every moment. You are truly a child of God. And God – in His infinite mercy – has surrounded you with angels and guides and friends to help you on your journey."

"Many of you who are reading this may be thinking that there are no spirit guides around you. And you say to yourself, 'I am not good enough for a spirit guide to help me.' Let me tell you as clearly as I can - stop thinking that you are not worthy of our help. You ARE good enough. Just remember Rose's story. Look at what happened to her. She was practically an atheist and even she got taken in by the guides. How much more will you – who even half way want to have our help – be able to receive it? You WILL be helped. It's not hard to receive our help. Just remember that we are as close as the air you speak with and breathe. We are right with you at this very moment – and every moment. We are in these very words that you are reading! You CAN feel us if you try? Our worlds are not far apart. They are superimposed - one upon the other."

"We will ALWAYS guide you if you ask for our help. It is our great pleasure to come to you and to help you - for it is our calling as spirit guides. And this is a calling that we will NOT abandon. We really DO love all of you and we only await your invitation for us to work with you. We are here – with you - right now – so that you may know that our assistance is real and available. The time is coming – indeed it is here – when our worlds will be seen as united once again. The world of Spirit is not far away from you. It is right here, right now - with you always - just as Jesus promised. May God bless you all. My name is Fletcher."

BOB HICKMAN POSTSCRIPT:

I am so glad that Tom and I joined together on this project. The more I see from the Spirit Guides, the more I am aware of how the future is already now starting to unfold. The idea of our government participating with other governments in the release of information regarding the UFO phenomena is thrilling to say the least. I only hope that the Lightworkers on this planet will come out in force to support this release and all work together to help others who may still operate from the lower-self paradigm of fear. Our country's highest ideals of freedom and tolerance must come to the forefront if the Guides' work is to come to pass.

As I review these transcripts I am also more and more inspired by the very goodness that my guides exhibit towards all who come in contact with them. It seems that they are eager to reach out to all who seek the spiritual path and assist them in growing in the Light. I can't help but wonder who Rose really is. Perhaps someday she will tell us the truth of her real name. It is evident that she wasted her earth life in vain pursuits, but I find great comfort in the fact that she reminds us even the most hardened souls will eventually be "won over" to the healing presence of the Divine. I wonder about Fletcher, and what all he is really up to when not doing readings with me. I can see that he takes on many "other" projects besides just helping me with readings. I think back to the night when he first came to me at that séance and I shake my head in disbelief of how much he has helped me over the last 10 years. I wonder about the people of Earth, so many secure in their comfortable worlds—how will they respond to the coming revelation that we are not alone in the Universe? I also think of the third world and developing nations. Will alien technology improve their lives and free them from disease and useless poverty? How will our contact with the Space Brethren change our spiritual views? Will we see finally a unity amongst the peoples of the world? Will the world's religions finally start to agree that we are ALL children of the Divine?

So many questions I have yet to know. But I trust in my guides and know that it will all be revealed in time. I think of the magnificence of Edgar Cayce, and am humbled that he came to speak through me. I think of Tom and feel joy at having the privilege of working with him and getting to personally know him. I know that Rose and Fletcher are working to help him find the peace and joy he has been seeking. I am humbled by Tom's devotion to a spiritual quest and challenged to renew my commitment to the journey.

As I write these final words I look out my window into the night sky. I try to find the star systems I have heard contain life; I look for the Pleiades and wonder just when I will again meet with them. I silently send a message to the Star People and Fletcher, Rose, Orion, Edgar Cayce and invite them to work with me. I know they will help and I know – that the truth of who we really are will come as our worlds unite.

About Bob Hickman

Born in Alexandria, Virginia, Bob Hickman is a life-long Washingtonian. He was trained in the Spiritualist Church, where he found and outlet for his natural inclinations of clairvoyance, clairaudience and prophetic vision. A gifted psychic-medium, Bob has helped thousands find peace and consolation on their earthly sojourns through contact with the Spirit World over the last 25 years. His readings are, as he likes to say, "Never scary, but fun and enlightening."

Bob's channeling has opened entire new worlds to him as well as his clients. Clients range from your next door neighbor, to Hollywood celebrities, to heads of state. He is a regular guest on radio talk shows all over the country, and has even received awards from YouTube for his psychic-themed videos which draw thousands of viewers.

An accomplished author, he also will be releasing the biography of his life as a psychic-medium, entitled, "A Message from the Spirit World" in Fall 2009.

Bob, who enjoys working with people, is still available for private readings and group sessions. He can be contacted through his website at www.robert-hickman.com.

LET THOMAS ALAN BERG HELP YOU!

Thomas Alan Berg has enjoyed over thirty years of teaching, writing, counseling and offering spiritual/metaphysical/educational support to thousands of students, parents and educators, who sought alternative learning strategies to the present public school system's hyper materialistic paradigm. He believes strongly that his classroom tested "Cosmic Curriculum of the Super Self" is the next logical step for how we can truly educate (and free) our children's minds and hearts - by waking them up to the vast parameters and powers of the multidimensional selfhood that pulsates within them.

He has become convinced through experience - that when students are offered free speech and open debate IN the classroom - and are not only allowed - but encouraged to ask the "big questions" of life - they soon remember and rediscover "who they really are" in the "grand cosmic scheme of things". When children are permitted to have a free say in what they learn, what they focus on, what they talk about, what they think, what they read, what they explore - and what they eventually do with their lives and their talents - they soar beyond all previous limits.

With all our old institutions tottering on the brink of implosion, the time has arrived to bring back free speech and polemics into the educational paradigm - so children can explore, discuss and debate the "meaning of life" - beyond the old "ologies" and "isms" that no longer serve our highest good. Our beloved young people deserve better from us - than the worn out brainwashing of "economic competition" that they've been receiving in the name of public education. And they really are eager to break free of what they see as the system's "mental matrix" of control and domination!

Thomas Alan Berg resides in San Francisco, California and can be reached by visiting either of his websites - www.thomasalanberg.com or www.uncletomsclassroom.com. He can be contacted directly at his personal email address - bergland@sonic.net or by calling 415-244-2572. After two years of deep introspection and spiritual R&R in Hawaii, Tom has been guided by the good spirits who speak in "When World's Unite" - to once again make himself available for public appearances, talks, consultations, conferences and private counseling.

Tom is looking forward to an ongoing collaboration with Bob and his "good spirits" - and will be transcribing Volume Two of this series about the spirit world and humanity's future - when the spirits signal they are ready for the next important phase of instruction. Tom and Bob are convinced that the more mankind allows the human world and the spirit world to unite, converse and actively collaborate - the better the human race will do - as we pass through the epochal doorway of 2012 - and move beyond - into a New Age of expanded God Awareness and spiritual enlightenment!

VISIT TOM ON THE WEB TODAY!

www.thomasalanberg.com

Available by phone at:
415-244-2572

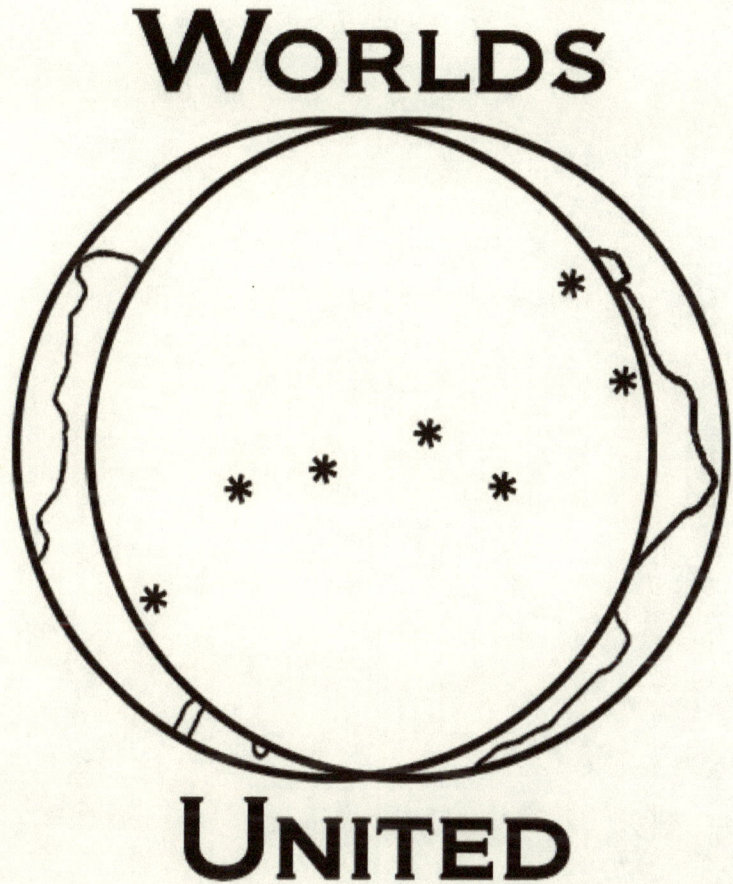

www.ingramcontent.com/pod-product-compliance
Lightning Source LLC
Chambersburg PA
CBHW021759220426
43662CB00006B/124